Deterrence and Security in the 21st Century

China, Britain, France, and the Enduring Legacy of the Nuclear Revolution

Avery Goldstein

D1468354

STANFORD UNIVERSITY PRESS
STANFORD, CALIFORNIA

Stanford University Press
Stanford, California
© 2000 by the Board of Trustees of the
Leland Stanford Junior University
Printed in the United States of America

Library of Congress Cataloging-in-Publication Data

Goldstein, Avery
    Deterrence and security in the 21st century : China, Britain, France,
and the enduring legacy of the nuclear revolution / Avery Goldstein.
        p.   cm.
    Includes bibliographical references and index.
    ISBN 0-8047-3736-3 (alk. paper)   :   ISBN 0-8047-4686-9 (pbk. alk. paper)
        1. Nuclear weapons—China.   2. Nuclear weapons—Great Britain.
3. Nuclear weapons—France.   4. Deterrence (Strategy).   5. China—
Military policy.   6. Great Britain—Military policy.   7. France—
Military policy.   I. Title.

UA835.G65   2000
355.02'17—dc21   00-27395

This book is printed on acid-free, archival quality paper.

Original printing 2000
Last figure below indicates year of this printing:
09   08   07

Typeset in 9.5/12.5 Trump Medieval

For My Students

Acknowledgments

For comments, criticisms, and advice at various stages in this project's development, I thank Jean-Marc Blanchard, Bill Burr, Tom Christensen, Lowell Dittmer, Joanne Gowa, Devin Hagerty, Ed Mansfield, Jack Nagel, Robert Powell, Norrin Ripsman, Song Jiuguang, and Kenneth Waltz. A University of Pennsylvania Research Foundation grant supported my research and travel. For their hospitality during my visits, I thank the staff of the Center for Chinese Studies at the University of California, Berkeley, the Institute of American Studies at the Chinese Academy of Social Sciences, the Foundation for International and Strategic Studies, China's National Defense University, China's Academy of Military Sciences, the Beijing Institute for International Strategic Studies, the China Institute of International Studies, China Institute of Contemporary International Relations, and the China World Watch Institute. I thank my colleagues (faculty and staff) in the Political Science Department at the University of Pennsylvania for their intellectual companionship and assistance. And for their much-appreciated help and advice during the publication process, I thank Muriel Bell, John Feneron, and Sharron Wood of Stanford University Press.

Earlier versions of some of the material in this book appeared in articles published in the journals *International Organization*, *Security Studies*, and *The Journal of Strategic Studies*, and are included here with their permission.

As indicated in the dedication, I am deeply indebted to my students at Penn. Over the years, their challenging questions have frequently forced me to rethink ideas that I had come to take for granted. Their enthusiasm and interest have made research a much less lonely experience. Finally, I am grateful for the encouragement and support of my wife, Karen Tulis, our children, Julia and Loren, and our four-legged companion, Dreyfus. They, along with all the members of our extended family, give life the meaning without which work would be cold comfort.

Contents

Figures

Deterrence and Security in the 21st Century

1

Introduction

Much recent writing about international politics properly highlights the changes that have followed from the collapse of the Soviet Union and the end of the Cold War. In contrast, this book identifies an important continuity that will characterize political-strategic affairs into the twenty-first century. It explains why, although its role has receded in public consciousness, nuclear deterrence will remain at the core of the security policies of the world's great powers and will remain an attractive option for many other less powerful states worried about adversaries whose capabilities they cannot match. The importance of this strategy for ensuring vital interests will endure as long as (1) the international system remains an anarchic realm, (2) states place their national interests above supranational interests, and (3) no fully effective counter to the destructiveness of nuclear weapons is devised. This continuity is to be expected despite, indeed as will be explained below partly because of, the emergence of a new international system in which serious military threats to vital interests are unclear, the use of force is judged irrelevant to resolving most international disputes, and states' interests are increasingly defined in economic, rather than military, terms. After elaborating on the reasons for this general expectation, I illustrate the argument by examining Chinese, British, and French security policies during the decades of the Cold War. I suggest that their experience, rather than that of the Cold War superpowers, better reflects the confluence of strategic and economic constraints likely to remain relevant in the post–Cold War world. Understanding the incentives that shaped their military strategies will help clarify why the attractiveness of nuclear deterrence will endure in a changing world.

The preceding assertions about the continuing importance of nuclear deterrence and the relevance of lessons about it drawn from the bygone era of the Cold War may seem odd. With the end of the Cold War, it has more commonly been argued that the key role of nuclear weapons in the security policies of states is, or should be, ending as well.[1] A broad consensus seems to prevail that the problem of nuclear security is now primarily a matter of managing the potentially serious risks of proliferation—regional nuclear conflicts, nuclear terrorism, and fanatic state leaders with nuclear weapons at their disposal. If so, these are challenges for which the strategic lessons of the first four decades of the nuclear era may be of marginal relevance. But if this belief is mistaken, then a narrow policy-driven focus on these newly prominent nuclear concerns may be at least insufficient.

How, then, can one assess the broader question of the likely role nuclear weapons may play in the international system of the early twenty-first century? One approach is to draw on the insights of existing theories of international politics and strategy. What does theory lead one to expect about state behavior in the sort of circumstances emerging in the post–Cold War world? Another approach is to examine the historical record to see whether and in what ways the logic of such abstract theories has been borne out in practice and to seek parallels between the influences shaping behavior in the past and those likely to operate in the future. The analysis in this book combines these two approaches, drawing in particular on the insights of neorealist balance-of-power theory and strategic studies and considering them in the light of China's, Britain's, and France's experience in the four decades after World War II.

The Cold War security policies of China, Britain, and France reflected a common strategic logic. Each ultimately embraced a policy that had as its top priority the deployment of national nuclear forces sufficient to dissuade threats against vital interests, a priority that led all three to rely on a distinctive strategy of deterrence of the strong by the weak. While each also supplemented this policy by forming alliances with others and by procuring nonnuclear forces, each viewed its national nuclear deterrent as the indispensable core. Why? To answer this key question, I focus on the interaction of three features of the Cold War world—the international system's structural constraints of bipolarity and anarchy and the availability of nuclear weapons technology. I explain why bipolarity and anarchy established conflicting imperatives for these security-conscious second-ranking powers—the former indicating the necessity of depend-

---

[1]Some of the strongest calls for denuclearization have come from individuals who played a prominent role in nuclear policy formulation and implementation during the Cold War. Especially noteworthy is the effort by General George Lee Butler, who gathered the signatures of 60 prominent military officers from around the world in support of his call for working toward denuclearization. See James Brooke, "Former Cold Warrior Has a New Mission," p. A12; R. Jeffrey Smith, "An Ex-Warrior's About-Face on U.S. Nuclear Policy"; also Paul H. Nitze, "Is It Time to Junk Our Nuclear Weapons?," p. C1.

ing on one of the two superpowers as a security guarantor and the latter underscoring the potentially grave dangers of doing so. I then explain how the revolutionary change wrought by military applications of nuclear technology shaped the way they decided to cope with these conflicting structural imperatives. Why, and in what sense, were national nuclear weapons viewed as an appropriate answer to the security problems China, Britain, and France faced? Why were these three countries not only reluctant to settle for an economically more sensible and ostensibly more credible alternative of relying on the security provided by a superpower ally, but also willing to risk the benefits of such alliances in order to realize their nuclear ambitions?

In addition to examining past policies, this book also looks ahead. What does the logic behind the Chinese, British, and French decisions to develop, deploy, and maintain nuclear forces suggest about international security in the no longer bipolar post–Cold War world? As will be detailed in Chapter 2, bipolarity created a distinctive set of circumstances within which all three operated. The military and political challenges of survival in a bipolar world partly explain the attractiveness of nuclear deterrent forces to states facing a daunting military threat from a superpower adversary. Yet these cases also suggest that the rationale for pursuing an independent nuclear deterrent, while shaped by the historically distinctive conditions of bipolarity, more importantly reflected the strategic choices of self-regarding states facing more powerful adversaries and constrained to operate in an anarchic international system in which nuclear weapons are available. As such, the experience of China, Britain, and France illuminates a security dynamic that is restricted neither to the era of bipolarity nor to its second-ranking powers. Indeed, the concerns that motivated their decisions to field independent nuclear capabilities also motivated the nuclear ambitions of other states during the Cold War and are likely to continue to do so in the coming century.

In exploring the security challenge China, Britain, and France encountered, I draw on neorealist balance-of-power theory. Neorealist theory highlights the situational constraints on states in the international system, in these cases the constraints of anarchy and bipolarity. The arguments it provides, however, identify only some of the influences shaping a state's security policies. To understand why these three states embraced independent nuclear deterrent strategies requires combining the examination of international constraints with consideration of their national attributes, especially the resources they were able to muster in the post–World War II era. It also requires a careful clarification of the logic of the deterrent policies these three states adopted, especially because many asserted the strategic marginality of their small nuclear forces during the Cold War and viewed them mainly as status symbols or (potentially dangerous) nuisances for a delicate superpower balance of terror. By contrast, I will argue that the Chinese, British, and French determination to deploy the nuclear forces they could muster is better understood as a sensible response to their international circumstances in light of available resources, and that it constituted the basis of a prudent security policy regardless of debatable nonsecurity benefits (such as prestige). To substantiate this argument, I draw on the theoretical literature in security studies to compare the logic of a nuclear deterrent strategy with its alternatives, and, more importantly, to assess its viability for states whose resources only enable them to deploy modest arsenals that pale in comparison with those their principal adversary fields. In such cases, nuclear deterrence must be practiced not only with forces that will be greatly outnumbered, but also under the unusually trying circumstances where retaliatory forces are *relatively vulnerable* to attack and where, in virtually every conceivable scenario, it would be *irrational* for the state practicing deterrence ever to choose to launch whatever nuclear forces it might still have on hand. Thus it will be necessary to demonstrate that formulations of the logic of nuclear deterrence that require invulnerable retaliatory forces and threats that can rationally be executed are misleading. This standard view of what is often termed rational deterrence theory may well be rooted in the experience, or at least aspirations, of the Cold War superpowers more than the requirements of strategy. Part of the payoff from studying these three cases is a reconsideration of the theoretical warrant for such claims and the policy implications that follow for existing and emerging nuclear states.

Chapter 2 outlines the theoretical argument and provides the conceptual basis for the historical case studies that follow, as well as the foundation for some of the implications about the post–Cold War world highlighted in the book's concluding chapters. Chapters 3 through 6 assess the experiences of China, Britain, and France. The description and analysis reveal that despite sharp differences in their domestic politics and history that contributed to the distinctiveness of each country's experience, all three ultimately embraced remarkably similar, though certainly not identical, nuclear deterrent policies and for remarkably similar reasons. Such similarities are easily overshadowed in descriptive work that highlights each case's undeniable distinctiveness. Although my purpose is to draw out the underlying similarities, the distinctiveness of the Chinese case in several respects makes it the most revealing of the three and it is treated in greatest detail. China faced more pressing threats, had more limited resources, and had to surmount higher hurdles to deploy its nuclear deterrent than either Britain or France. Beijing's decision to make an independent nuclear deterrent its top strategic priority not only brings into unusually sharp relief the logic that drove all three states' thinking during the Cold War. It also underscores the broader relevance of this logic for states other than the world's advanced industrial powers that believe they face similarly challenging security situations.

Before proceeding, however, it may be helpful to address three questions about the cases on which I focus. In what sense can one lump China, Britain, and France together as "second-ranking powers" during the Cold War? Can much be learned by focusing on the experience of states that operated in the shadow of the leading superpower actors on the international stage? And, specific cases aside, why devote more attention to a well-studied, bygone era so unlike the world we face today?

THE COLD WAR SECOND-RANKING POWERS

The label "second-ranking power" is difficult to define in the abstract, but as a practical matter, at least in the context of the Cold War, it is easily understood. The problem one faces in trying to come up with a general scheme for classifying states according to their capabilities has been evident, too, in debates among international relations scholars about how to define the term "great power."[2] Most definitions have emphasized a resource-based index that combines features such as military assets (weapons and troops), the economic foundations of military power, and the political-organizational ability to exploit these capabilities effectively. Typically, however, resource-based definitions have trouble accounting for qualitative variations in the quantities measured, amorphous subjective or "human" influences, and the fact that resources useful in one domain may prove ineffective in others.[3] Frustrated, many fall back on the pragmatic notion that one knows a great power when one sees it. Indeed, though debates over defining the abstract concept of a great power are inconclusive, rough consensus usually prevails when one turns to lists of the great powers in particular historical periods.[4]

[2]For a useful summary of some of the attempts at defining great powers, see Jack S. Levy, *War in the Great Power System, 1495–1975*, pp. 13–18. See also Ted Hopf, "Polarity, the Offense-Defense Balance, and War," pp. 478–79.

[3]On the difficulty of relying on quantitative indicators, see Levy, *War in the Great Power System*, pp. 14–15. On the problem of scope and domain, see David A. Baldwin, "Power Analysis and World Politics."

[4]Kenneth N. Waltz, *Theory of International Politics*, p. 162; Levy, *War in the Great Power System*, ch. 2.

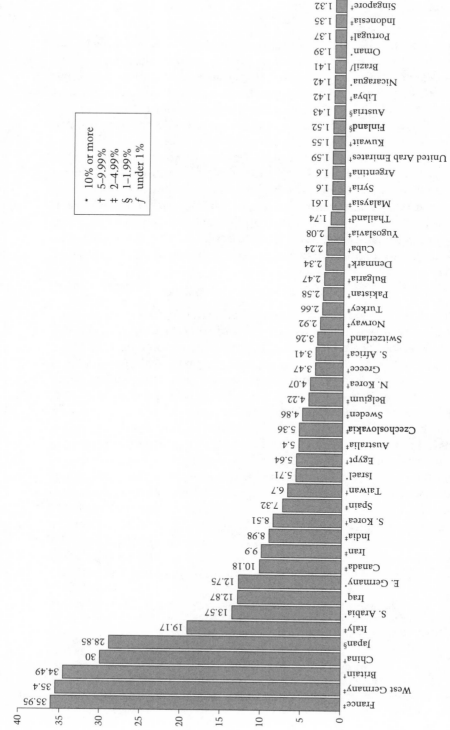

Fig. 1. Military Spending, 1988. (Billions of 1988 U.S. dollars. Based on *The Military Balance*, 1989–90, except estimate for China)

Legend:
* 10% or more
† 5–9.99%
‡ 2–4.99%
§ 1–1.99%
ƒ under 1%

France‡	35.95
West Germany†	35.4
Britain†	34.49
China*	30
Japan§	28.85
Italy‡	19.17
S. Arabia*	13.57
Iraq*	12.87
E. Germany†	12.75
Canada‡	10.18
Iran‡	9.9
India‡	8.98
S. Korea‡	8.51
Spain‡	7.32
Taiwan†	6.7
Israel*	5.71
Egypt†	5.64
Australia†	5.4
Czechoslovakia‡	5.36
Sweden†	4.86
Belgium‡	4.22
N. Korea*	4.07
Greece†	3.47
S. Africa†	3.41
Switzerland‡	3.26
Norway†	2.92
Turkey‡	2.66
Pakistan†	2.58
Bulgaria†	2.47
Denmark‡	2.34
Cuba†	2.24
Yugoslavia‡	2.08
Thailand‡	1.74
Malaysia‡	1.61
Syria*	1.6
Argentina‡	1.6
United Arab Emirates*	1.59
Kuwait†	1.55
Finland§	1.52
Austria§	1.43
Libya*	1.42
Nicaragua*	1.42
Brazilƒ	1.41
Oman*	1.39
Portugal‡	1.37
Indonesia‡	1.35
Singapore†	1.32
Poland‡	1.27

Similarly, in this book I adopt a methodologically unsatisfying but practically useful approach given my focus on security affairs. Looking at one of the most important indices of national power, military spending, it seems sensible to group together five states as the Cold War's second-ranking powers—Britain, China, France, Germany, and Japan. In terms of military spending, once they recovered from the ravages of World War II, this cohort was rather clearly set apart from the superpowers on the one hand and from the much larger group of less powerful states on the other. Unlike most other states, during the Cold War these five were able to fund military establishments that seem modest only when compared to those the superpowers fielded.

The upper boundary separating these five from the United States and Soviet Union is easiest to draw. The second-ranking powers funded military establishments that were impressive in absolute terms and by historical standards, but were decisively overshadowed by the resources the superpowers were able to devote to this purpose in the half century after World War II. By the last decades of the Cold War, each superpower was spending upwards of $250 billion (1988 dollars) annually on its military. Great Britain, France, China (for whom budget figures are disputed), Germany, and Japan were each spending roughly one tenth as much—$25–35 billion.[5] The boundary between these five and the world's other less powerful states is somewhat less clear because the magnitude of the difference is not as large. Even here, however, the gap in military spending between these states and the next major grouping was impressive (see Figure 1). With some temporary aberrations, only four other states spent more than $10 billion annually on defense.[6]

[5]Most uncertain are the estimates of defense spending by the People's Republic of China. Official Chinese figures almost certainly understated the total, putting it at much less than $10 billion. See, for example, "Jin Shinian Wo Jun Junfei Chengdijian Qushi," p. 45. The ranges of foreign estimates seem to converge in the area of approximately $30–40 billion (1988 U.S. dollars) and 6–7 percent of GNP through the 1970s, followed by a decline in the 1980s. See *Chinese Defense Spending 1965–1979*; Dwight Perkins, "The International Consequences of China's Economic Development," pp. 132–33; Ronald G. Mitchell, "Chinese Defense Spending in Transition," pp. 606–8; SIPRI Yearbook, p. 231; Robert S. Wang, "China's Evolving Strategic Doctrine," p. 1053; J. David Singer and Melvin Small, "National Material Capabilities Data"; *The Military Balance 1987–1988*, p. 145; *World Military Expenditures and Arms Transfers*, p. 54. For purposes of this book I assume a rough total of $30 billion. On the difficulties of accurately estimating defense spending by socialist states, due to complications such as hard-to-compare currency values and inputs with nonmarket prices, see Franklyn Holzman, "Are the Russians Really Outspending the U.S. on Defense?"; "Soviet Military Spending"; "Politics and Guesswork"; *The Military Balance 1995–1996*, pp. 270–75.

[6]Of the four, three (Iraq, Saudi Arabia, and before 1989 East Germany) devoted a

Defined in this fashion, the five states I label second-ranking powers comprised a distinct group of actors on the international scene. They were states with resources sufficient to generate the full variety of weapons that modern technology made possible, but in a setting where there were two actors whose more massive military efforts they could not hope to match. This book, however, focuses on just three of the five—Britain, France, and China. Discussion of the German and Japanese cases is left to the conclusion because of the special historical circumstances in which they operated during the period under review. The victors of World War II imposed restrictions that the foreign policy elite and general public in Germany and Japan embraced. These restrictions, though sometimes questioned in private, effectively constrained the debate about security policy, most importantly precluding serious consideration of the entire range of strategic alternatives and force deployments, especially nuclear, that could have been sustained given the resources at their disposal.

WHY FOCUS ON LESSER POWERS?

Definitional matters aside, if "the story . . . of international politics is written in terms of the great powers of an era," why study the security policies of lesser powers during the Cold War?[7] Two reasons stand out. First, examining their situation and how they responded to it brings into relief key issues in the field of security studies—the distinctions among alternative strategies (such as the often confused and conflated notions of deterrence and defense), the constraints shaping the choice of security policies, and the consequences of these choices for relations with allies and adversaries. Although scholars did not ignore these topics during the Cold War, the overwhelming focus on the policies of the two superpow-

---

rather large share of GNP to this purpose and would, therefore, have been hard pressed to "catch up and stay with" the capabilities of the other five. Saudi Arabia and Iraq each devoted more than 10 percent and East Germany (of no interest after 1990) devoted more than 6 percent of GNP to defense spending. The fourth, Italy, devoted 3 percent to defense and could conceivably have made the effort (World Military Expenditures and Arms Transfers, 1987; The Military Balance, 1987–1988). See also Figure 1. Although the distinctiveness of military spending by the second-ranking powers on which I focus was apparent for most of the postwar era, it is true that the barriers to entry were lower for the second-ranking power club than the superpower club. Judging by the size of GNP and the modest share they allocated to military spending, Canada, Brazil, India, Spain, and Australia probably could also have become second-ranking powers.

[7]Waltz, Theory of International Politics, p. 72.

ers, especially the United States, and perhaps also the predominance of American scholars in security studies, may have biased our understanding of such issues.[8] To the extent this focus distorted contemporary debates about strategic affairs, the result reflected not so much ideological or cultural bias as a tendency to forget, or at least pay little attention to, just how atypical the Cold War superpowers' situation and experience were. After World War II, the distinctiveness of the massive capabilities the United States and Soviet Union could muster compounded the long-standing distinctiveness of their geographic circumstances as vast continental states relatively distant from the central theaters of international military conflict.

Advances in airpower and especially rocket technology had, of course, somewhat eroded the natural security buffer enjoyed by the United States in the Western Hemisphere and, to a lesser extent, the Soviet Union at the easternmost edge of Europe. Nevertheless, it remained conceivable, indeed some believed it likely, that a third world war could erupt in Europe or Asia and be brought to a conclusion before its devastation touched the American and Soviet heartlands. Direct use of military force, even the localized use of nuclear weapons in the most plausible theaters of initial engagement, would not necessarily have produced catastrophic damage to the United States. For the Soviets it was also possible, though more difficult, to imagine that the buffer of its Eastern European empire and the vast distances from the Far East might insulate the nation's heartland from the worst effects of a variety of limited, perhaps even nuclear, warfighting options in the Central European and Pa-

[8]Exceptions to the focus on the superpowers in security studies during the Cold War include the histories of British, French, and Chinese nuclear weapons programs introduced below, as well as Geoffrey Kemp, "Nuclear Forces for Medium Powers, Part I"; "Nuclear Forces for Medium Powers, Parts II and III"; Graeme P. Auton, "Nuclear Deterrence and the Medium Power"; Douglas J. Murray and Paul R. Viotti, eds., *The Defense Policies of Nations*; Catherine M. Kelleher and Gale A. Mattox, eds., *Evolving European Defense Policies*; Shai Feldman, *Israeli Nuclear Deterrence*; and Jonathan Shimshoni, *Israel and Conventional Deterrence*. Reflecting perceptions of strategic importance during the Cold War, but undoubtedly also availability of information, The Nuclear Weapons Databook series first published its authoritative volumes on the United States (vols. I in 1984, II and III in 1987) then the Soviet Union (vol. IV in 1989), and only in 1994 its volume on Britain, France, and China. See Thomas B. Cochran, William M. Arkin, and Milton M. Hoenig, *U.S. Nuclear Forces and Capabilities*; Thomas B. Cochran et al., *U.S. Nuclear Warhead Facility Profiles*; Cochran et al., *U.S. Nuclear Warhead Production*; Cochran et al., *Soviet Nuclear Weapons*; Robert S. Norris, Andrew S. Burrows, and Richard W. Fieldhouse, *British, French, and Chinese Nuclear Weapons*.

cific theaters. Geography did not afford most other states, certainly not the three under examination here, the same slack during the opening rounds of a major war, especially one where the collateral damage from nuclear exchanges could easily spread beyond the theater of direct engagement.[9]

For the United States and Soviet Union, the enduring, though eroding, advantage of their geographic circumstances increased the range of potentially acceptable options for the use of military force during the Cold War. In addition, the massive human and material resources on which their political leaders could draw enabled them to behave as though they could afford to avoid the necessity of choosing among purportedly plausible scenarios for which military forces might be required. These two superpowers, like all states, of course did pay attention to the opportunity costs of military spending. But with a few exceptions, until the late 1980s they acted as though this was a weak constraint.[10] The absolute size of the American economy made possible historically unprecedented peacetime military budgets by drawing on only 5–7 percent of GNP.[11] For forty years the American voters supported political leaders

[9]Even London would have been at best 300 to 500 miles from a theater of nuclear exchange limited to Germany, whereas Moscow would have had a 1,000-mile buffer.

[10]The United States and the Soviet Union varied the attention they paid to the guns/butter tradeoff. The American record is well documented in John Gaddis's discussion of the alternative versions of containment (Strategies of Containment). Khrushchev's attempt to substitute more bang for the buck in the late 1950s and Gorbachev's arms control initiatives of the late 1980s mark the obvious Soviet attempts to reallocate national wealth from defense to nondefense spending. The extent to which high levels of military spending reflected the reasonable pursuit of virtuous redundancy rather than the wasteful results of bureaucratic and political self-interest is debatable. Massive military budgets supporting the panoply of strategic options the superpowers pursued could be seen as an effort to build sufficient redundancy into their security organization. Adding redundancy is a rational engineering response to a situation where the stakes of failure are inordinately high and there is great uncertainty about the appropriateness of any one approach. On the virtues of redundancy in organizational design, see Martin Landau and Russell Stout, Jr., "To Manage Is Not to Control"; Martin Landau, "Redundancy, Rationality, and the Problem of Duplication and Overlap"; James D. Thompson and Arthur Tuden, "Strategies, Structures, and Processes of Organizational Decision."

[11]Even as the relative strength of the U.S. economy internationally diminished, defense budgets increased. Despite warnings of an American economic decline that many attributed, at least partly, to excessive military spending and the attendant federal budget deficits, a buildup initiated in 1980 continued throughout the last decade of the Cold War. For representative views in this debate, see Paul Kennedy, The Rise and Fall of the Great Powers; Samuel P. Huntington, "The U.S.—Decline or Renewal?"; Joseph S. Nye, Bound to Lead. Only in the early 1990s did the United States begin to seriously consider major reductions in defense spending. See William W. Kaufmann, Assessing the Base Force; Kaufmann, Glasnost, Perestroika, and U.S.

who accepted the opportunity costs of significant national wealth devoted to investment in the military, as opposed to civilian, sector. And
although there were disagreements about the costs and benefits of this
allocation of resources, throughout the Cold War military competition
the U.S. economy demonstrated a capacity to maintain satisfactory levels of performance. Such was apparently not the case for its superpower
rival. By the mid-1980s, the Soviet leaders decided that the grinding
military burden of its competition with the United States had to be
eased, prompting the foreign and domestic policy changes that brought
the Cold War to a close. But for the four decades of the Cold War, the Soviet Union had maintained its superpower position by relying on an
authoritarian political system to tap a much larger fraction of its smaller
and less technologically advanced economy.[12]

In short, sensibly or not, during the Cold War both superpowers be-
haved as though the economic constraints on military spending were
loose. This practice allowed budget makers and strategists to plan for a
breathtakingly comprehensive array of options for the use of force. In the
terms employed below, the superpowers' massive military funding supported an ability to employ force directly and indirectly, serving deterrent, defensive, compellent, and offensive strategies relying on a wide
variety of nuclear and conventional weapons.[13] By contrast, most states,
including those studied here, are more tightly constrained to focus on
the economic and strategic sensibility of their military budgets.[14] Their

---

Defense Spending; William W. Kaufmann and John D. Steinbruner, *Decisions for Defense;* Michael E. O'Hanlon, *Defense Planning for the Late 1990s.*

[12]Estimates for the Soviet Union's Cold War military burden now greatly exceed
the contemporary belief that the figure was 10–15 percent of GDP. Some suggest figures well in excess of 25 percent. The link between the heavy burden of military
spending and the demise of the Soviet Union is a matter that falls outside the scope
of this book.

[13]In the more transparent U.S. case, the emphasis after the late 1950s was to
increase the strategic choices available to the president, including the use of irregular conventional forces for counterinsurgency operations, air, sea, and land forces
for limited or general conventional war, and a large and varied array of sophisticated nuclear weapons to serve an increasingly complex set of nuclear options. On
the relation between economic constraints and the coherence of U.S. strategy, see
John Gaddis, *Strategies of Containment.* For a survey of the growing list of nuclear
options funded by U.S. military spending, see Fred Kaplan, *The Wizards of Armageddon;* Scott D. Sagan, "SIOP-62"; Desmond Ball and Robert C. Toth, "Revising
the SIOP."

[14]On the tension between preferred policy and what was possible in light of economic constraints in the British and French cases, see David S. Yost, "French Defense Budgeting," pp. 579–80. For an argument that the Cold War second-ranking
powers could have afforded to follow in the footsteps of the superpowers by increas-

sensitivity to such constraints usually reflects a combination of geographic proximity to perceived threats and more severely limited resources for dealing with them than was the case for the Cold War superpowers. Thus the sorts of clarifying pressures that only intermittently forced the United States and the Soviet Union to carefully consider the coherence and efficiency of their security policies (usually in the context of an unnerving crisis or a sharp economic downturn), typically loom larger in the calculations of states. The experience of China, Britain, and France arguably better reflects the tough choices most face.

The preceding suggests another reason for directing greater attention to these second-ranking powers. As will be suggested in the book's concluding chapters, in the post–Cold War era economic constraints on even the great powers in the emerging international system of the twenty-first century are more likely to be tight than loose. The sorts of pressures these three states faced during the Cold War—to choose from among alternatives, or at least establish clear priorities, rather than fund a large array of options—are the sorts of pressures the leaders of most states, great and small, are likely to face in the early twenty-first century. Thus the lessons about strategic policies one draws from their experience may be of more enduring value than those that heavily rely on the atypical experience of the Soviet and American superpowers.

WHY MORE ON THE COLD WAR?

Although it shifts the focus from the dominant superpowers to three of the second-ranking powers, this book argues for the continuing usefulness of lessons from the Cold War. This may seem odd given the dramatic changes that swept the globe in the last decade of the twentieth century. Although scholars, opinion leaders, and policy-makers continue to look to history for guidance, as a resource for assessing the validity and reliability of their insights, much commentary on the emerging "new world order" of the coming century gives relatively short shrift to the recent history of the Cold War. Instead, when crises arise or contingency plans are drafted, the historical analogies trotted out are the well-worn classics of July 1914 (for renewed turmoil in the Balkans) or Munich 1938 (for recurrent confrontations with Iraq or North Korea). There are sound reasons for recalling such distant events, even if they are now more than half a century and several technological generations removed. But it would be surprising if some important lessons about the contem-

---

ing their strategic options, see Graeme P. Auton, "Nuclear Deterrence and the Medium Power."

porary era were not to be found in the recent history of the four decades after World War II.[15]

Nevertheless, one may be skeptical about the usefulness of the relatively recent history of the Cold War. First, the existing evidence is thin and uneven when compared with more historically distant eras. Despite waves of declassification, many documents remain unavailable, especially on nuclear matters, and key archives have only been selectively opened. Moreover, because the events are so recent, a lack of detachment may cloud scholarly judgment and exacerbate the ever present concern about distortions in the first-hand accounts the numerous living history-makers have supplied.[16] Second, the character of international competition has changed dramatically with the end of the Cold War. The demise of the Soviet Union marked the end of a distinctive historical era during which the usual competition among great powers was sharpened by a Manichaean ideological antipathy and reinforced by the apparent zero-sumness of a bipolar world. As the new century dawns, the titanic ideological struggle is over, and rivalries in what many see as an emerging multipolar world are likely to be more diffuse.

Given questions about the quality of available evidence from the Cold War and concerns about its relevance now that the nature of competition among the world's great powers has been transformed, what is to be gained from further studying this recent period in history? This book suggests that some of the Cold War's most important lessons may be hard to identify if one looks only to the experience of that era's superpowers. If one instead looks to its second-ranking powers, one more clearly discerns the influence of constraints likely to shape international security affairs into the twenty-first century. Despite the collapse of the Soviet empire, three key features of international life remain unchanged—the anarchic structure of the international political system, states that place national before supranational interests, and the nuclear revolution in military technology. In order to explore the consequences

---

[15]As archives open, much historical research and reinterpretation of the Cold War is taking place. But research based on these documents seeks mainly to clarify and correct the details of the historical record rather than to identify general lessons about international relations. Two especially rich and convenient resources for following such document-based reinterpretation are the *Cold War International History Project Bulletin*, available online at http://cwihp.si.edu/default.htm, and the documents collected by the National Security Archive available online at http://www.seas.gwu.edu/nsarchive/.

[16]The sometimes important discrepancies between evidence contained in declassified documents and the memoirs of two giants of U.S. Cold War foreign policy, Robert McNamara and Henry Kissinger, provide ample reason for skepticism.

of these three enduring characteristics of world politics after the Cold War, I examine their influence on the policies of China, Britain, and France, states whose choices were profoundly shaped by their constraining effect during the Cold War.

One final caveat should be added given the book's emphasis on the role of military force. This selective focus does not result from a naïve belief that military concerns are the only influences shaping states' security policies. Indeed, in analyzing the military-strategic choices of China, Britain, and France I highlight the importance of other concerns, especially economic and political ones. I do not, however, attempt to comprehensively incorporate every influence on state strategy in my explanation. I devote relatively little attention, for example, to the roles of personalities and internal bureaucratic struggle, both of which would be essential to a full description of the formulation and implementation of national security policy. Such influences (some of which are introduced in the historical discussion) help account for variations in the security policies of different states facing similar constraints and opportunities, as these cases reveal. This, however, is a book mainly about the reasons for important similarities in a strategic theme, not the undeniable variations on that theme.

2

Theoretical Foundation

This chapter draws on neorealist balance-of-power theory and conceptual work in strategic studies to identify important constraints and opportunities that mold the security policies of states in circumstances like those that China, Britain, and France faced during the Cold War—an anarchic international system in which they might have to rely on themselves to deal with threats from an adversary whose capabilities they could not match. The case studies that follow then examine the ways each of the three actually responded to their circumstances.

During the Cold War, China, Britain, and France defined their national interests principally in terms of preserving the status quo against potentially serious threats to their territorial and political integrity.[1] For

[1]This definition is consistent with one of the central simplifying assumptions upon which neorealists have relied for developing elegant theory—that all states are motivated to ensure their survival as autonomous political units. In reality, of course, most states have additional interests beyond this assumed minimum. Some states have sought to champion their own highly prized values (religious, economic, or political), recommending or imposing their way of life beyond their borders, while others have sought control over foreign territory, not just because they deemed it essential to the survival of the homeland but in order to increase their international power. These second-ranking powers also had interests beyond merely preserving the status quo that influenced their international relations and sometimes their force requirements. Britain and France had to cope with the challenges of dismantling their empires. China had irredentist claims over territory in its immediate vicinity, most prominently its assertion of sovereignty over Taiwan, that called for revision in the status quo. Nevertheless, for each of these states such interests were clearly subordinate to the priority task of dealing with the potentially catastrophic threat to the homeland represented by a superpower adversary. The priority was most evident when these states modified their international behavior (e.g., the Taiwan Straits Crises and Suez Crisis discussed in subsequent chapters) in order to avoid triggering superpower actions that might risk core interests.

Although the neorealist theory employed here relies on the simplifying assumption of a survival motive, other contemporary realist statements do not. Among modern realists, two alternative perspectives stand out. John Mearsheimer assumes that states are motivated to maximize power (an assumption that also informed

them, as for all states, national interests establish the goals for which they may need to deploy military capabilities. Though military forces alone will not always be sufficient for the realization of such goals, they are often a necessary ingredient for their pursuit in the international arena.[2] The anarchic structure of the system within which states operate establishes this necessity. Neorealist theory depicts the international political system as an anarchic realm, defined by the absence of a superordinate agency that can reliably resolve disputes among states.[3] Over the centuries, changes in technology and people's beliefs about the ethics or efficacy of the use of force have modified the consequences of coexistence in such an anarchic international realm, but one central implication of this structural feature of world politics endures: states decide for themselves if, when, and how they will use force to pursue their interests—a matter national leaders ignore at their peril.[4] And, as

Hans Morgenthau's classic version of balance-of-power theory). Randall Schweller also questions the usefulness of the minimal assumption of neorealism but instead argues for the theoretical and empirical importance of distinguishing between revisionist states (which may give rise to bandwagoning) and status quo–oriented states (more likely to behave as balance-of-power theory suggests). See John J. Mearsheimer, "The False Promise of International Institutions"; Hans Morgenthau, *Politics Among Nations*; Randall L. Schweller, "Bandwagoning for Profit."

[2]For an early but still illuminating discussion of the enduring role of military force that responds to claims about its growing irrelevance in an economically more interdependent world, see Robert J. Art, "To What Ends Military Power?"

[3]Among international relations scholars a lively debate about the meaning and application of the concept of "anarchy" continues. Careful examination of the merits of the arguments offered by both critics and defenders of the usefulness of the concept falls outside the scope of this book. Instead, I begin with the premise that modifications of the anarchy assumption do not fundamentally change the consequences for state behavior discussed in this and subsequent chapters. For a sampling of the debate about anarchy among international relations theorists, see Helen V. Milner, "The Assumption of Anarchy in International Relations Theory."

[4]Others have made this point and it requires little elaboration here. Disagreement arises, however, over the scope and domain for the use of military force. Some claim its relevance in international politics has greatly diminished in the late twentieth century, either because of the costs of modern warfare, or because of an expanding zone of peace among liberal democracies. On the alleged obsolescence of war in the modern era, see John E. Mueller, *Retreat From Doomsday*; James Lee Ray, "The Abolition of Slavery and the End of International War." On the debate about the democratic peace, see Michael W. Doyle, "Kant, Liberal Legacies, and Foreign Affairs"; Doyle, "Liberalism and World Politics"; Bruce Russett, *Grasping the Democratic Peace*; John M. Owens, "How Liberalism Produces Democratic Peace"; David E. Spiro, "The Insignificance of the Liberal Peace"; Christopher Layne, "Kant or Cant: The Myth of the Democratic Peace"; Henry S. Farber and Joanne Gowa, "Polities and Peace."

will be made clear in the course of this book, state leaders worry not simply about the physical or cartographic implications of the use of force, but also its political implications: sovereign states aim to enhance their political autonomy as well as to ensure physical protection.

In examining China's, Britain's, and France's response to the rigors of life under anarchy after World War II, I focus on the ways in which they dealt with the possibility that military force might be needed to ensure their national interests. I seek to explain their choice of a strategy for dealing with what was their principal, though not sole, Cold War security problem—coping with the threat a superpower adversary posed to their autonomy. The theoretical framework for understanding their choices is presented in two parts. First, I draw on neorealist balance-of-power theory to identify the situational constraints they faced as states operating in a system dominated by two actors with vastly superior capabilities. Second, I draw on strategic theory to identify the alternative policies from among which these states could choose in order to cope with the security problems their circumstances posed. Neorealist balance-of-power theory highlights the bipolar, anarchic structure of the Cold War world that confronted China, Britain, and France with strong but conflicting imperatives. On the one hand, bipolarity established the necessity for them to depend on one of the superpowers to guarantee their security when it was threatened by the other superpower, an adversary whose capabilities they could not hope to match on their own. On the other hand, the international condition of anarchy encouraged a preference for self-reliance. Unable to escape this predicament, lesser powers could respond to its conflicting imperatives more or less wisely. Strategic theory highlights the reasons why leaders in China, Britain, and France decided that a security policy emphasizing deterrence was the most prudent response. Deterrence became especially attractive because the nuclear revolution in military technology altered the relative effectiveness, affordability, and robustness of the available alternatives.

CONFLICTING IMPERATIVES IN THE POST–WORLD WAR II INTERNATIONAL SYSTEM

Bipolarity

World War II marked a structural transformation of the anarchic arena within which states operate. Before World War II the international system was multipolar; from 1945 until the end of the Cold War it was bipolar.[5] Despite variations in their ability to manage alliance partners and impose solutions on regional actors, in the postwar world the United States and the Soviet Union were set apart by their capacity to influence, though not control, events around the globe. Bipolarity dramatically altered the ways in which states attempted to ensure their security through the practices explained by balance-of-power theory.[6] As ever, states could counterbalance perceived threats by internal means (i.e., increasing their own capabilities) or by external means (i.e., forming alliances). But bipolarity changed the relative importance of these two techniques, and in different ways for states of different capability.

Because the superpowers' aggregate capabilities dwarfed those of other states, alliances with less powerful actors, unlike alliances among great powers in previous multipolar eras, could not decisively affect the balance of power between these duopolists.[7] Each superpower's security ultimately depended on the awesome resources it could generate inter-

[5]Polarity here refers to the number of great powers in a given international system. For some purposes, this simple notion is insufficient and analysts will be interested in polarization, the degree to which the world's states are organized into competing blocs, or the concentration of capabilities, the relative power shares maintained by the system's greater and lesser powers. See Edward D. Mansfield, *Power, Trade, and War*.

[6]Morgenthau, *Politics Among Nations*, chs. 11–14; Kenneth Waltz, *Theory of International Politics*, ch. 6.

[7]The gap between the superpowers and all others reflected more than just disparities in the nuclear stockpiles. Absent nuclear weapons, the distinction would have remained. For reasons set forth below, the security dividends from nuclear weapons derive mainly from the dissuasive effect that accompanies the possession of a fairly small retaliatory force. The greater international influence of the superpowers during the Cold War derived not from the possession of superfluous nuclear warheads, but from the distinctive range of capabilities (economic and organizational resources, ideological appeal, and nonnuclear military assets) each could bring to bear. Indeed, the logic of the argument offered in this book suggests that absent the punitive power nuclear weapons offered second-ranking powers, the advantages of the superpowers during the Cold War would have been magnified. Cf. François Heisbourg, "The British and French Nuclear Forces," pp. 313–14. Because the clout of the superpowers was multidimensional, at the end of the Cold War one Chinese writer argued that although the future would see a shift to multipolarity, the transition would be a "long process"; the distinctiveness of the United States and USSR (Russia) "particularly in the area of military strength" would endure for the immediate future despite their relative economic and political decline (Peng Di, "Prospects for World Peace as Viewed From the Present International Strategic Posture," p. A5). At least in the case of the United States, the advantages endure and suggest that any shift to multipolarity will be a slow one. But the collapse of the Soviet Union and Russia's inability to address its internal problems led to an unexpectedly rapid shift to what some termed a unipolar world in the 1990s, rather than a smooth transition from bipolarity to multipolarity. I return to this issue in the concluding chapter.

nally. For the system's other states, however, the implications of bipolarity were quite different. Some, such as those examined in this book, might wield capabilities that were impressive in absolute terms and indeed relative to many others. But none could deploy forces comparable to those of the United States or the Soviet Union. Consequently, when even the most powerful of the system's remaining states confronted salient threats from one of the two superpowers, bipolarity constrained it to turn to the other superpower as the only viable counterbalance. Meeting their most daunting security challenge seemed to require resources they could only gather externally (i.e., by tapping a vastly more powerful ally). Bipolarity, then, considered apart from other international and national influences, implied dependence on a superpower ally as the ultimate guarantor of security for states that believed a superpower adversary might jeopardize their vital interests.[8]

This implication of bipolarity drawn from balance-of-power theory is consistent with the implication drawn from another major strand of international relations theorizing—the collective goods theory of alliances first suggested by Mancur Olson and Richard Zeckhauser in 1966.[9] Although Olson and Zeckhauser had acknowledged that there would inevitably be both collective (or public) and national (or private) benefits from member states' military spending, they asserted that the infeasibility of excluding partners from enjoying the security supplied by an alliance justified treating that benefit as a collective good (i.e., a good whose consumption cannot easily be made exclusive and for which consumption by some does not diminish its availability to others).[10] Their theory predicted and explained free-riding by smaller allies,

[8]Michael Ng-Quinn emphasized the constraint of bipolarity as the key to understanding the foreign policy of one second-ranking power, China. See Michael Ng-Quinn, "Effects of Bipolarity on Chinese Foreign Policy"; Ng-Quinn, "The Analytical Study of Chinese Foreign Policy"; Ng-Quinn, "International Systemic Constraints on Chinese Foreign Policy." Cf. Carol L. Hamrin, "China Reassesses the Superpowers." Though agreeing with Ng-Quinn on the significance of this structural influence, for reasons stated below I believe a better explanation of the PRC's strategic policy requires also considering the other features of the postwar world on which I focus.

[9]Mancur Olson and Richard Zeckhauser, "An Economic Theory of Alliances."

[10]Ibid., pp. 272–73. The theory of collective action itself, on which Olson and Zeckhauser's collective goods theory of alliances is based, acknowledges that few goods meet the strictest definition of a public good. Referring to Paul Samuelson's classic work and Richard Musgrave's and John G. Head's discussions of it, Olson noted that the twin defining characteristics of a public good, nonexcludability and jointness of supply (nonrival consumption), are rarely exhibited in the real world. See Mancur Olson, The Logic of Collective Action, pp. 14n21, 28n44, 40n61; also James M. Buchanan, "An Economic Theory of Clubs," pp. 51–63. Olson emphasizes infea-

especially in an organization (like NATO) where one state's capabilities far exceeded those of its partners.[11] Because a superpower's self-interest and capabilities gave it sufficient incentives to counter the common enemy of the alliance (i.e., supply the collective good of security) regardless of its partners' behavior, it would be neither rational nor necessary for the latter to shoulder the full military burden of which they were capable. Others building on the insights of Olson and Zeckhauser highlighted the ways in which the nuclear forces of the superpowers made it particularly easy for allies to ride free on their extended deterrent effect, as long as the superpowers had forces ample enough to alleviate concerns about opportunity costs in carrying out retaliatory threats (satisfying the condition of nonrival consumption) and were committed to stand by their partners (satisfying the condition of nonexcludability).[12] According to the collective goods theory of alliance, then, the *economic*

---

sibility of exclusion as the key defining feature of collective goods, though many also exhibit "a large measure of jointness." See Olson, *The Logic of Collective Action*, pp. 14–15n21. Indeed, with regard to the cases under examination here, in which the collective good of alliance security is supplied by nuclear deterrent forces, the requirement of jointness of supply or nonrival consumption poses few problems as noted below.

[11]For critical commentary questioning whether the joint security benefits from an alliance satisfied the definition of a public good, see Mark A. Boyer, *International Cooperation and Public Goods*; William R. Gates and Katsuaki L. Terasawa, "Commitment, Threat Perceptions, and Expenditures in a Defense Alliance"; Gregory G. Hildebrandt, "Measuring the Burden of Alliance Activities"; James C. Murdoch and Todd Sandler, "A Theoretical and Empirical Analysis of NATO"; John R. Oneal, "The Theory of Collective Action and Burden Sharing in NATO"; John R. Oneal and Mark A. Elrod, "NATO Burden Sharing and the Forces of Change"; Bruce M. Russett, *What Price Vigilance?*; Todd Sandler, "Impurity of Defense"; Todd Sandler and Jon Cauley, "On the Economic Theory of Alliances"; Todd Sandler and John F. Forbes, "Burden Sharing, Strategy, and the Design of NATO"; Wallace J. Thies, "Alliances and Collective Goods"; Jacques van Ypserle de Strihou, "Sharing the Defense Burden Among Western Allies"; van Ypserle de Strihou, "Comment."

[12]For further discussion, see Avery Goldstein, "Discounting the Free Ride." A few participants in this scholarly debate briefly noted the problematic assumption of nonexclusiveness even with regard to deterrence-based alliance strategies, but did not fully explore the implications of this observation for the usefulness of the public goods theory of alliances. See especially van Ypserle de Strihou, "Comment," pp. 60–62; but also Sandler and Cauley, "On the Economic Theory of Alliances," p. 335n6; Russett, *What Price Vigilance?*, p. 95; Sandler and Forbes, "Burden Sharing, Strategy, and the Design of NATO," p. 427; Oneal and Elrod, "NATO Burden Sharing and the Forces of Change," p. 440; Oneal, "The Theory of Collective Action and Burden Sharing in NATO," p. 384. For an argument linking the purity of the public good to the substitutability of allies' forces rather than the distinction between deterrent and defensive strategies, see Thies, "Alliances and Collective Goods," pp. 328–29.

rationality of letting the alliance leader carry a disproportionate burden should be expected to reinforce the *strategic necessity* in a bipolar world of depending on a superpower patron to counterbalance a superpower adversary.

Anarchy

Yet China, Britain, and France did not comfortably embrace dependence on superpower security guarantees in the bipolar world, power-balancing logic and economic advantages notwithstanding. In part, as will be noted below, their dissatisfaction stemmed from compromises of foreign policy autonomy that were necessary to retain their patron's support. More importantly, dissatisfaction reflected an unavoidable concern that their superpower protector might not fulfill its pledge to support smaller allies' interests when they were actually threatened by the common superpower adversary. This fear of abandonment, as Glenn Snyder labeled it, limited confidence in the military adequacy of alliance-based security and diminished the economic attractiveness of simply riding free on the superpower patron's protection. The fear itself was nothing new. It was a consequence of the most enduring characteristic of international politics—the anarchic ordering principle of the arena within which states coexist. In the absence of a reliable mechanism for enforcing international agreements, abandonment by a diffident ally is a risk with which states have always had to live.[13] Although treaties may enshrine common concerns, prudence dictates that they be viewed as binding only as long as self-interests are congruent. The connection between anarchy and the fear of abandonment, then, predated the Cold War era. But the intensity of the Chinese, British, and French fears reflected two features of the anarchic international system after World War II that most clearly distinguished it from its predecessor—bipolarity and the presence of nuclear weapons.

In a world that is not only anarchic but also bipolar, the fear of abandonment is exacerbated because junior partners can make only a marginal military contribution to a superpower ally's security. Though alliances have never been coalitions of equally capable actors, in the multipolar world that existed before World War II alliances were comprised of great power members each of whom could make at least a significant contribution to dealing with the collective concerns that held them together. Doubts about the usefulness and reliability of allies rooted in the

---

[13]See Glenn H. Snyder, "The Security Dilemma in Alliance Politics"; also, Thomas J. Christensen and Jack Snyder, "Chain Gangs and Passed Bucks."

condition of anarchy certainly existed. In particular, under multipolarity states worried about the possibility that their allies might, if geography and military-strategic conditions permitted, try to pass the buck in crisis or war, hoping that others would shoulder the burden of resistance.[14] But such risks notwithstanding, under multipolarity self-interest also constrained partners to look out for each other's needs inasmuch as alliances were genuine mutual security pacts. The buckpassing fear of abandonment was present, but limited by the military value of all partners that motivated alliance formation in the first place. When territory and the relative size of weapons inventories were important, if varying, determinants of victory and defeat, as they were in the pre-nuclear multipolar world, allies had strategic and not just ethical reasons for standing by their partners. Indeed, the strategic value of allies in the pre-nuclear multipolar world could, as Thomas Christensen and Jack Snyder explain, give rise to the opposite of the buckpassing pathology, chain-ganging or entrapment. When geography, military technology, and strategic beliefs led states to believe that the integrity of an alliance was indispensable for their security, a single ally could drag the rest into war because none was willing to see the alliance fray.

After World War II, however, the gap in capabilities between the strongest actor and all others in each of the two principal alliance networks weakened the strategic glue binding allies in ways that distinguished the bipolar era from its predecessor. Under bipolarity, the duopolists' allies, lacking the military value of great powers in the multipolar era, understandably worried that in the event the superpower adversary threatened their national interests, a self-regarding superpower patron dreading the risks of involvement might not fulfill its prior pledge of support. Such abandonment might be ethically reprehensible, but the military capabilities forfeited would not be decisive. This calculus would seem to suggest the strategic irrelevance of alliances for the superpowers.[15] Yet bipolarity actually established conflicting imperatives for them (as it did for their less powerful allies) that limited the logic of abandonment.

Although bipolarity meant that the intrinsic military value of a superpower's allies was small and irrelevant to the balance of superpower capabilities, bipolarity also encouraged a belief in the zero-sumness of an intensive and extensive global rivalry between the system's duopo-

[14]See Barry Posen, *The Sources of Military Doctrine*; Christensen and Snyder, "Chain Gangs and Passed Bucks."

[15]See Waltz, *Theory of International Politics*, pp. 170–72.

lists. This belief increased the reputational value of allies.[16] Even if a superpower did not care much about the actual military or economic clout an ally could bring to its side of the ledger, it was constrained to worry that its principal rival might interpret abandonment of a partner as a sign of weakness, possibly inviting a challenge on more important matters. This superpower self-interest in preserving an international reputation for resolve reduced their allies' vulnerability to threats from the common adversary and suggests that the allies' understandable fears of abandonment were actually overdrawn. In a bipolar world, neither superpower could act against smaller states with impunity. Instead, each had to wonder whether the other would feel its reputation required it to respond.[17] One practical and important result detailed below is that this effect of bipolarity may have helped discourage first the United States and then the Soviet Union from carrying out plans for preventive attacks on China's nascent nuclear arsenal. Both had devised such plans, and both were hesitant to execute them without assurances that the other would acquiesce.

Bipolarity, then, yields an unavoidable tension between the temptation to abandon allies because of their small intrinsic value and the self-interest in backing allies because of broader concerns about reputation. How can one make sense of this apparent indeterminacy when thinking about the effects of bipolarity? One plausible conclusion is that a superpower will be hypervigilant and support its allies as long as the costs and risks of reputation-enhancing solidarity are acceptable. If the costs and risks are high, the superpower will instead focus its attention on the intrinsic value of the commitment, increasing the likelihood of abandonment. Thus, if support for an ally results in the gradual accumulation of costs that become unacceptably burdensome, this might produce a shift from a focus on reputation to intrinsic value. The American commitment to and disengagement from South Vietnam may be a good illustration of this effect. But the test of experience over time is not the only possible influence determining the inclination to abandon an ally, reputational costs notwithstanding. Available military technology and strategic beliefs may also play important roles.[18] The advent of nuclear weapons and the vulnerability to thermonuclear devastation that emerged as the Cold War unfolded made it difficult for the superpowers

[16]On the distinction between intrinsic military value and reputation value, see Glenn H. Snyder, *Deterrence and Defense*, pp. 30–40.

[17]I thank Tom Christensen for reminding me of this distinctive feature of the bipolar world.

[18]See Christensen and Snyder, "Chain Gangs and Passed Bucks."

to indulge reputational concerns in confrontations that carried much risk of what could be quickly catastrophic escalation. Self-interest could motivate great powers in the pre-nuclear multipolar world either to pass the buck or chain themselves to their gang of allies. In a bipolar world with nuclear weapons, self-interest tips the scales in the direction of abandonment for the alliance leader if solidarity entails much risk of military conflict with the other nuclear armed superpower. As will be explained below and illustrated in the case studies, however, while such nuclear risks increase the probability of abandonment and cause allies to worry about the real value of a superpower's security promises, those same risks inhibit aggression by the other superpower, who must hedge against even a small probability that the promise might actually be fulfilled. Still, states like China, Britain, and France prudently worried that in a world of mutual thermonuclear vulnerability the logic of self-preservation would lead their superpower ally to forsake them if the alternative was entrapment in a dangerous showdown. In particular, they reasonably feared that the temptation of abandonment would be strong if such a showdown arose over interests that they, but not their patron, defined as vital. Under those circumstances the benefits of alliance, though desperately needed, would be uncertain.

What then could the superpowers' allies do about the dangers inherent in the apparent necessity of depending on a strong but self-interested patron? Though unable to *eliminate* the risk of abandonment and, thus, exclusion from the security benefit an alliance promised, less powerful states could nevertheless attempt to reduce the risk in two ways. One is an attempt to raise the price the superpower patron would pay for abandonment. Through deferential behavior that established the junior partner as one of the superpower's most obviously loyal allies, it might increase the reputational, though not the intrinsic military, cost to the superpower of failing to fulfill its international commitments. This approach exploits the incentives bipolarity provides for the duopolists to view international politics as a zero-sum game. Moreover, the advent of nuclear weapons may have increased the opportunities to do this. Deterrence theorists have highlighted the importance of reputation in a nuclear age where the credibility of threats may well turn on the questionable willingness to run risks more than the unquestionable capability to inflict the contingent punishment. Under such circumstances, one's willingness to stand by allies confronting a common adversary might be interpreted as a general index of one's resolve relevant to the credibility of untested nuclear threats. Allies might, in other words, try to exploit the interdependence of a superpower's extended and primary deterrent policies.[19] Their hope is that the patron will worry that the common adversary might view hesitation in living up to commitments on behalf of so loyal an ally as casting doubt on the superpower's resolve to take risky actions even if its own interests were at stake.

The other approach for less powerful allies to attempt to reduce the risk of abandonment in a bipolar world is to emphasize the severity of the threat the superpower adversary poses. With heightened concern about the danger confronted, the junior partner hopes that its powerful patron may be less inclined to tolerate losses to the common enemy, even small losses that might not be vital to the superpower balance of capabilities, but could affect the perceived balance of resolve.[20] To the extent it succeeds in encouraging "hard-line" sentiment and concerns about intense superpower rivalry in debates among the superpower ally's foreign policy elite, this tack complements the first.

Such efforts aimed at reducing the likelihood of abandonment and increasing the chance the superpower would continue to supply alliance security as a collective good were evident most prominently in the early postwar policies of the People's Republic of China (PRC), discussed in Chapters 3 and 4. Until it could overcome the daunting technological hurdles to deploying a national nuclear deterrent, strategic and economic rationality constrained the PRC, preferences notwithstanding, to settle for a large measure of dependence on the security provided by a superpower ally. China's dissatisfaction with this situation, however, suggests why states are reluctant to accept the dependence inherent in fully embracing the economically attractive free-rider alternative and why instead those able to become more self-reliant often make the costly effort. States can act to reduce, but cannot eliminate, the grave uncertainties of life in an anarchic realm where the fear of abandonment reflects the fact that alliance security is a benefit that actually fails the key public goods test of nonexcludability. Although the probability of abandonment might be small, the consequences, especially in the nuclear age, could be disastrous. Additionally, the first approach to minimizing the risks inherent in depending on others calls for a degree of

[19]See Snyder, *Deterrence and Defense*, pp. 30–40. On the interdependence of commitments, see Thomas C. Schelling, *Arms and Influence*, pp. 55–59, 116–25. On the complexity of manipulating perceptions of a state's reputation, see Barry Nalebuff's discussion of Jervis's reputational paradox in "Rational Deterrence in an Imperfect World." For a powerful challenge to the belief in the overriding importance and manipulability of reputations for resolve, see Jonathan Mercer, *Reputation and International Politics*.

[20]On the importance of balances of interest and resolve as well as capabilities, see Richard K. Betts, *Nuclear Blackmail and Nuclear Balance*, esp. ch. 4.

to a security patron that is likely to be politically unattractive
aders of sovereign states. Domestic political imperatives, espe-
the modern era when nationalism is a central component of re-
.gitimacy, reinforce the international political constraints that
rage a quest for greater self-reliance.[21]

ne political unpalatability and strategic uncertainties associated
with free-riding offset the economic attractiveness of depending on a
superpower patron. Instead, during the Cold War China, Britain, and
France faced strong incentives to develop the means to provide for their
own security, a daunting challenge given their severe disadvantage in
resources compared with a prospective superpower adversary. How
could they hedge their bets and become more self-reliant under circumstances where it was not possible to match forces with the enemy they
feared most? To answer this question it will be helpful to specify the alternative strategies on which states can rely to ensure their security,
and in so doing to more carefully consider the implications of a third
feature of the post–World War II world—the availability of nuclear
weapons technology—that shaped the policies these three states
adopted.

STRATEGIC ALTERNATIVES: THE USES OF FORCE

Carefully distinguishing among key strategic concepts is especially important in order to clarify my use of some familiar terms. Figure 2, and
the descriptions provided below, offer a highly stylized typology that attempts to depict the chief distinctions among (1) the ways force may be
used, (2) the goals for which force is employed, (3) the strategies developed for achieving those goals, and (4) the military means for carrying
out such strategies.

The broadest distinctions are those between the indirect and direct
use of force (the upper and lower portions of the figure)[22] and between
the interest in preserving or altering the status quo (the left and right
portions of the figure). When a state seeks to achieve its objectives by
actually employing the military means at its disposal, it is engaged in
the direct use of force as part of either an offensive strategy (to alter the

---

[21]As one Chinese analyst put it, "Nuclear force is an important material condition that helps medium-sized nuclear powers free themselves from manipulation
and control by superpowers and to play their part in world affairs" (Zhang Jianzhi,
"Views on Medium-Sized Nuclear Powers' Nuclear Strategy," p. K29).

[22]This is similar to Robert Art's distinction between the "physical" and "peaceful" use of force, though my subsidiary categories diverge from his (Art, "To What
Ends Military Power?"). Cf. Alastair Iain Johnston, *Cultural Realism*, pp. 109–17.

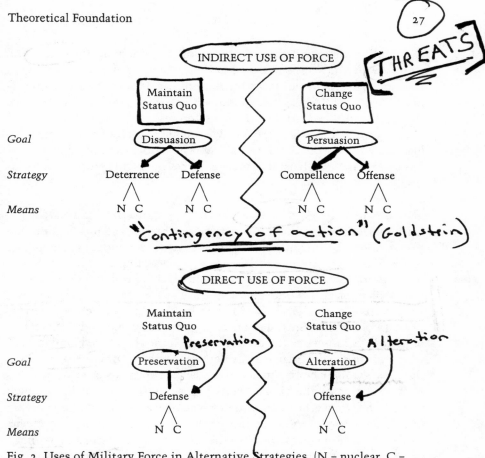

Fig. 2. Uses of Military Force in Alternative Strategies. (N = nuclear, C = conventional)

status quo) or a defensive strategy (to preserve the status quo). When a state instead seeks to achieve its objectives by influencing the adversary through *threats* to employ the military means at its disposal, it is engaged in the indirect use of force as part of either a persuasive strategy to alter, or a dissuasive strategy to maintain, the status quo. Such indirect use of force aims to affect the behavior of an adversary by indicating the "contingency of action," while the actual use of military force supporting the policy is held in reserve. In the strategic studies literature, this sort of indirect use of force has normally been discussed in debates about the requirements for practicing deterrence and compellence.[23] Here I sug-

---

[23]In discussing the indirect use of force, Thomas Schelling's uses various terms including "latent violence" and "the diplomacy of violence" (Schelling, *Arms and Influence*).

gest a fuller typology of the indirect use of force, including defensive and offensive alternatives, one that is attentive to a broader set of combinations of goals, strategies for realizing those goals, and means for implementing the strategies from among which states may choose. Because the principal international security interest of China, Britain, and France during the Cold War era was maintenance of the status quo (dealing with threats to their vital interests), I focus mainly on the various deterrent and defensive approaches relevant to this purpose.

Maintaining the Status Quo

Dissuasion by Deterrence. Strategies provide the link between political objectives and the military means to pursue them. When dissuasion is the goal, states attempt to discourage others from challenging the status quo by threatening to employ force according to one of two strategic alternatives, deterrence or defense.[24] Dissuasion by deterrence threatens to punish the adversary in ways so terrifying he dares not initiate a challenge, regardless of his ability to actually achieve narrow military objectives. Such dissuasion by deterrence may rely on nuclear or nonnuclear forces as the means by which the threatened punishment would be inflicted. Dissuasion by deterrence relying on nuclear forces is the most familiar, with threats to devastate the prospective aggressor's society serving as the classic scenario for punishment. Although such nuclear deterrence has had pride of place because of the indisputably horrifying nature of the punishment that could be inflicted, the means of punishment is not essential to the strategy. Conventional, chemical, or biological weapons may not be judged as effective as nuclear forces for deterrence, but there is no in-principle reason why they cannot be the chosen means for fulfilling this dissuasive strategy's requirements.[25]

There is also no reason why the threatened action need take the form of retaliatory blows delivered against the prospective aggressor's homeland. What matters is that the adversary's decision is swayed by the belief that the costs of military action, *even technically successful military action,* are unacceptable. The recognition that only a pyrrhic victory is possible may be sufficiently discouraging even if one's na-

[24]This depiction of defense and deterrence as alternative dissuasive strategies follows Kenneth Waltz's usage. See, for examples, Waltz, "A Strategy for the Rapid Deployment Force"; "Toward Nuclear Peace."

[25]Thus deterrence is not a strategy whose relevance is limited to the nuclear era. See George H. Quester, *Deterrence Before Hiroshima.* For a discussion of some of the differing effects of nonnuclear as opposed to nuclear punitive weapons, see Steve Fetter, "Ballistic Missiles and Weapons of Mass Destruction."

tional territory is left unscathed. A prospective aggressor certain he can accomplish his military objectives, that he will win the war in a technical military sense, may yet refrain from initiating action if the anticipated losses (in terms of blood, treasure, or political power) are deemed unacceptably steep.[26] Deterrent threats by the prospective victim to lose in a grisly fashion, fighting to the last man or employing crude nuclear, chemical, or biological devices on his own territory once it is occupied may have this effect. Or, as the Chinese attempted, one may threaten an adversary whose military victory cannot be prevented, with the prospect of a protracted popular resistance movement that will make occupation an unacceptably painful experience. Differences in the military forces that would be used notwithstanding, all of these approaches are examples of dissuasion by deterrence because they rely on threats of punishment to achieve the goal of discouraging an adversary from initiating action inimical to one's interests. As ever with the indirect use of force, if the policy is successful, the major military action supporting the policy remains unused. A nontrivial implication is, then, that successful instances of dissuasion are difficult to document. Neither the effect (inaction) nor cause (force not used) are easy to establish with confidence. This methodological problem has bedeviled empirical tests of deterrence theory.[27]

Dissuasion by Defense. States may also use force indirectly to achieve the goal of dissuasion by relying on a defensive strategy. A strategy of dissuasion by defense discourages the adversary from challenging the status quo by threatening to confront him with insurmountable obstacles to achieving his military objectives. It seeks to convince him he will be unable to achieve his goal, regardless of his willingness to absorb punishment. As with deterrence, either nuclear or nonnuclear capabilities may serve as the means for fulfilling the requirements of a strategy of dissuasion by defense. Whether one relies on troops armed with anti-tank weapons, battlefield nuclear devices, counterforce-capable strategic nuclear arms, active or passive ballistic missile defenses, digs moats,

[26]Aside from the loss of human life and material assets, a country's leaders may worry that prosecuting the war will destabilize the political foundations of their rule. Though hard to quantify, the loss of moral authority may result in the withdrawal of popular support for a democratic regime or military and elite support for an authoritarian regime.

[27]See Christopher H. Achen and Duncan Snidal, "Rational Deterrence Theory and Comparative Case Studies." The debate is complicated not only by the need to consider counterfactuals, but also by the dispute about the comparability of cases from the nuclear and pre-nuclear eras. See James G. Blight, "*Psychology and Deterrence* Book Review."

or builds walls—if the deployment is designed to convince the adversary that he should not attack because he will be denied military success, then force is being used indirectly to serve a strategy of dissuasion by defense.

When dissuasion of challenges to the status quo is a priority, which strategic alternative will states embrace? Variations in their ability to muster the capabilities and resolve that make threats of punishment or denial credible partly determine the choice between the deterrent and defensive alternatives. But, it should be added, even when a principal strategic emphasis in a state's dissuasive security policy is relatively easy to identify, the state will typically combine deterrent and defensive threats in order to accomplish its goal.[28] As was the case for China, Britain, and France during the Cold War, although dissuasion by deterrence may be a logical choice when the costs of establishing credible threats to mount an effective defense are prohibitively high, there is usually an incentive to mix in defensive capabilities if at all possible. This incentive is provided by the fear that even well-devised dissuasive strategies may fail, and the hope that if they do, vital interests can still be protected. If dissuasion fails and a shift from the indirect to the direct use of force becomes necessary, defensive capabilities are more likely to prove useful than those tailored to the punitive purposes of deterrence.

Preservation by Defense. Why might states lack confidence in well-devised dissuasive strategies? Prudent leaders may worry that uncertainties about relative capabilities or resolve could lead an adversary rationally to calculate (or perhaps miscalculate) either that the punishment he will absorb is acceptable or that he can overcome one's defenses. Or leaders may worry that an adversary will not even calculate as a rational actor. Such concerns encourage states to hedge their bets by preparing for the direct use of force in an attempt to secure those vital interests against which they may be unable to discourage attack. In the event such operations are necessary, forces originally deployed to fulfill the requirements of dissuasion by defense, capabilities specifically designed to convince the adversary he would be denied military success, will be easily converted to the effort to actively protect vital interests. By contrast, forces originally deployed to fulfill the requirements of dissuasion by deterrence may be of little use if dissuasion fails. Capabilities

---

[28]On the distinction between deterrence and defense, as well as their combination, see Art, "To What Ends Military Power?"; Waltz, "A Strategy for the Rapid Deployment Force"; Waltz, "Toward Nuclear Peace." Cf. Snyder, *Deterrence and Defense*; Robert Powell, *Nuclear Deterrence Theory*, pp. 7–12.

designed to inflict punishment may yet prove valuable (especially if one shifts from a strategy of deterrence to compellence described below), but their military effectiveness as part of an effort to fend off the adversary's assault is less certain since that is not the purpose for which they were deployed.

Changing the Status Quo

Because the chief concern of the three states on which I focus was to maintain their interests in the face of superpower threats, at this point I include only a few brief comments on the uses of force to change the status quo that are depicted in Figure 2. The book's concluding chapter reconsiders this topic as it has become part of the debate about the strategies some prospective nuclear states in the post–Cold War world may envision.

A state seeking to modify the status quo can pursue this goal through the indirect use of force by employing either of two strategies of persuasion. Or it may attempt to effect the desired changes through the direct use of force married to an offensive strategy.[29] The alternative strategies for persuading an adversary to comply with one's demand for change are compellence and offense. The logic behind these indirect uses of force mirrors that embodied in the dissuasive alternatives of deterrence and defense. Persuasion through compellence seeks to convince the adversary to accede to changes in the status quo by relying on threats to inflict unacceptable punishment if compliance is not forthcoming.[30] Persuasion through offense seeks the adversary's compliance by threatening to take action that will produce the desired changes regardless of the adversary's efforts to resist. As with the dissuasive strategies of deterrence and defense, the military means fulfilling the requirements of compellent or offensive strategies may vary. And as with the strategies for maintaining the status quo, should it be necessary to shift to the direct use of force, the military effectiveness of means procured for threatening punishment (compellence) may well be negligible compared with those specifically procured for their usefulness on the battlefield (offense). But here the neat parallel between dissuasive and

[29]The desire to alter the status quo is not equated with aggressive impulses, since it may reflect an interest in redressing the consequences of prior aggression and restoring the status quo ante.

[30]Thomas Schelling coined the term "compellence." See Schelling, *Arms and Influence; The Strategy of Conflict.* See also Art, "To What Ends Military Power?" For an illuminating study of the complications in trying to practice compellence against the Vietnamese communist leaders during the U.S. involvement in Southeast Asia, see Wallace Thies, *When Governments Collide.*

persuasive strategies ends. Devising workable persuasive strategies for
the indirect use of force, especially those relying on threats to use nuclear weapons as a way to change rather than maintain the status quo, is
generally more difficult and complex than devising workable dissuasive
strategies. The nature and important implications of these differences
for the role of nuclear weapons in the post–Cold War world will be addressed in the book's conclusion.

Comparing Strategies to Preserve the Status Quo

States, like the three examined here, whose chief concern is preserving
the status quo can select from among an array of alternative defensive or
deterrent strategies. On what do they base their choice? Part of the answer to this question follows from the recognition that strategies and
the forces that fulfill their requirements are not formulated in an economic vacuum. States obviously differ in the resources they can muster
to pursue their interests, however defined. Yet even wealthy states face
opportunity costs; national resources devoted to dealing with military
security concerns are resources not devoted to raising the people's standard of living or maintaining a state's international economic competitiveness. To the extent states confront such tradeoffs, they have reason
to be sensitive to the return on their security investment. One way to
hold down these expenditures is to seek security on the cheap by free-
riding on the military efforts of an ally. For reasons already highlighted,
however, in an anarchic world such free-riding will be limited by the
need to purchase private insurance (a national military capability) as a
hedge against the possibility of abandonment, especially in the nuclear
age. The amount of insurance needed will, of course, be determined by
the risks confronted. For some, a modest and inexpensive conventional
military capability may suffice. For those facing powerful or threatening
rivals, however, greater expenses must be incurred. If a state is unable to
offset the military capabilities of its adversary as required by a strategy
of dissuasion by defense, and is unwilling to fully entrust its fate to
more capable but potentially diffident partners (allies or international
organizations), dissuasion by deterrence may be the most practical alternative.

More costly than dependence but less costly than the defensive option, deterrence can provide a self-reliant hedge against the risk that one
might have to go it alone against a much more powerful adversary. Not
all deterrent strategies will be equally attractive, however. As will be
suggested below, both logic and China's experience during the Cold War
indicate that the conventional (i.e., non-nuclear) deterrent alternative is

likely to be judged unsatisfactory by states facing powerful, technologically sophisticated adversaries. The consequences of the nuclear revolution in military technology when combined with the strategic logic of deterrence indicate why China, Britain, and France embraced dissuasion by nuclear deterrence as the central pillar of their national security policy. Although it was more expensive than dependence on a superpower patron, nuclear deterrence not only satisfied the need for a measure of self-reliance, but also was a strategy that was affordable (unlike the independent defensive alternatives) and robust with respect to plausible threats (unlike the alternative of conventional deterrence). As perceived threats dictate selecting from among expensive alternatives, the incentives to spend scarce national wealth on nuclear, rather than conventional, forces to serve a strategy of dissuasion by deterrence become stronger.[31] The shortcomings for China, Britain, and France of the defensive and conventional deterrent alternatives help account for their emphasis on the nuclear option.

Shortcomings of Defensive Alternatives

Procuring the forces sufficient to support a self-reliant defensive, rather than deterrent, approach to dissuading aggression by a superpower adversary with vast military superiority would have placed enormous strains on the economies of the Cold War's second-ranking powers. Credible defenses against nuclear attack were beyond the capabilities of any state during this era, including the superpowers.[32] For China, Brit-

[31]This assumes military budgets exceeding the minimum needed to develop and deploy a modest nuclear arsenal. Through the late 1980s, this probably limited the candidate states to those with annual military spending in excess of two or three billion dollars. Of the known nuclear powers in 1988, Israel's budget of $5.71 billion was the smallest. Threshold state Pakistan was spending $2.58 billion. See Avery Goldstein, "Robust and Affordable Security," Appendix A. On the costs of developing a viable retaliatory force, see Gene I. Rochlin, "The Economic Burden of a Nuclear Force." For an interesting forecast of the declining costs of fielding a modest nuclear arsenal from the perspective of 1963, see "Memorandum for the President, Subject: The Diffusion of Nuclear Weapons with and without a Test Ban Agreement," Feb. 12, 1963.

[32]The complex set of issues involved in the debate over the viability of dissuasion by nuclear defense, whether through counterforce strikes or ballistic missile defenses, lies beyond the scope of this essay. Only two points need be made. First, those who believed that counterforce targeting against Soviet warfighting potential (military, industrial, and political assets) was necessary to dissuade it from threatening vital U.S. interests insisted on a very large and technically sophisticated nuclear arsenal and support services. Procurement of the panoply of forces (e.g., accurate warheads, survivable delivery systems, durable command and control, civil defense, and air and ballistic missile defenses) required by such a doctrine would have placed

ain, and France, however, credible defenses against even conventional attack by a superpower would have entailed steep opportunity costs that would be especially objectionable during peacetime. The magnitude of the effort that such an independent conventional defense would have required is suggested by the enormous cost to the United States for its *share* of the forces dedicated to defending Western Europe against attack by its Soviet superpower adversary—a sum perhaps five times the total annual military budget of the typical second-ranking power.[33] Moreover, despite deployment of so awesome and expensive a conventional force for defense, doubts about its dissuasive effect led the United States to maintain tactical nuclear weapons and threats of escalation to the strategic nuclear level (i.e., nuclear deterrence) as an essential feature of its strategy for dealing with the Soviet menace in Europe.

Financial considerations aside, limitations of manpower and geography increased the difficulties China, Britain, and France confronted if they wanted to field the sorts of defenses necessary to hold off a superpower adversary's conventional assault. In the post–World War II era, Britain and France faced tight constraints on expanding, indeed even maintaining, the size of their standing armies as their population structure "aged," especially once postwar economic recovery meant that the scarce youth in such affluent societies had attractive alternatives to military service. The relatively small territories of Britain and France also limited their options for defensive maneuvers, though Britain could at least exploit the maritime buffer any adversary would have had to surmount if it chose to stage a conventional assault. And for Britain and France the geographic concentration of population, industry, and military assets further increased the difficulty of defending against the power projection capabilities (especially aircraft and missiles) a superpower adversary could employ. At first glance, manpower and geo-

---

an intolerable strain on the economy of a second-ranking power. Second, many have questioned the security dividend from procuring the sorts of nuclear defenses within reach of even a superpower. Unlike conventional defense, less than perfect defenses against a nuclear armed adversary may not be very helpful. For calculation of the destructiveness of even a limited number of very small nuclear detonations that might result despite imperfect defenses, see Fetter, "Ballistic Missiles and Weapons of Mass Destruction." For a summary of the controversies in the intense Reagan-era debate over ballistic missile defenses, see Steven E. Miller and Stephen Van Evera, eds., *The Star Wars Controversy*. Debates about the cost and effectiveness of ballistic missile defenses against nuclear-armed adversaries intensified once again in the 1990s following the use of the Patriot against Iraqi SCUD missiles during the Persian Gulf War, and as concern about the diffusion of nuclear and ballistic missile technology grew.

[33]See William W. Kaufmann, *A Reasonable Defense*, p. 14.

graphical constraints would seem less severe for a populous and large China. In fact, as will be detailed in Chapter 3, both constraints posed serious, though somewhat different, problems for any Chinese effort at conventional defense.

Dissuasion by defense was, then, not a practical alternative for China, Britain, and France to increase their strategic independence. Instead, the realistic choice (if they were not prepared to accept extreme dependence on a superpower patron) was between two forms of deterrence, conventional and nuclear. Only China seriously embraced conventional deterrence, and trends in its security policy described in the next two chapters suggest this choice reflected short-run necessity at least as much as preference.

Deterrence: Conventional and Nuclear

Without forsaking the possibility of support from a superpower ally, deterrent strategies would enable these second-ranking powers to hedge self-reliantly against abandonment by a patron of uncertain dependability. Unlike the more daunting alternative of dissuasion by defense, dissuasion by deterrence did not require that they impress a superpower adversary with their ability to deny him success on the battlefield, an implausibly demanding requirement. Instead a deterrent strategy called only for the ability to threaten a potential aggressor with unacceptable pain and suffering regardless of outcomes on the battlefield. Two deterrent strategies need to be considered—one that relies on conventional, and one that relies on nuclear military forces as the means for threatening punishment.

The conventional deterrent strategy of interest here threatens a potential adversary with the prospect of confronting a protracted popular resistance, even if he succeeds in attaining his immediate military objectives.[34] The rise and spread of mass nationalism in the twentieth century increased the salience of this strategic alternative by facilitating the mobilization and organization of a country's citizens. Where the punishment of sustained resistance can credibly be threatened, ambitious adversaries must face the risk that even a militarily successful

[34]For reasons elucidated in the appendix, the costs associated with making other conventional deterrent strategies effective, such as those threatening retaliatory strikes relying on nonnuclear explosives, would likely be prohibitively high. Other unconventional, but nonnuclear, deterrent strategies, such as those relying on threats of retaliation using chemical or biological weapons, were economically and technically feasible, but unattractive for practical and ethical reasons that marginalized them as long as the nuclear alternative was within reach.

invasion and occupation will be a painful experience of unknown duration.[35] In principle, such threats can dissuade others from attacking
and, by relying on guerrilla tactics, do so at reasonable cost. For badly
outgunned states incapable of tapping modern technology, this sort of
conventional deterrent may be the most attractive option. It enables
them to translate political support into military power. Moreover, as a
self-reliant alternative it enables leaders constrained by the expectations of the modern nationalist era to avoid unseemly dependence on
foreign patrons. Yet, despite its economic and political sensibility, this
approach is not likely to have great appeal for the leaders of states as
capable as the second-ranking powers discussed here. Five shortcomings of a conventional deterrent strategy rooted in threats to mount a
protracted popular resistance help explain the greater attractiveness of
the nuclear alternative.

First, when relying on conventional deterrence it may be difficult to
convince the adversary he can secure at best a pyrrhic victory. As long as
the enemy knows he need only engage conventional forces, especially if
they are limited to lightly armed "irregulars," a relatively powerful adversary is likely to believe that the risks of testing the balance of capabilities and resolve are manageable; a moderately risk-acceptant decision-maker may see this as a chance worth taking (a point to which I return below). However devastating they may eventually prove to be,
conventional, as opposed to nuclear, deterrent threats do not force a
prospective aggressor to confront the risk of punishment that is almost
instantaneously catastrophic. Given the more modest short-term punishment threatened by conventional, as opposed to nuclear, forces, a determined aggressor can more confidently choose to probe the victim's
resolve.[36]

[35]The classic essays explaining how to rely on the "masses" as part of a strategy
to prevail over a militarily superior adversary were written by Mao Zedong in the
1930s. Though often associated with the harassing tactics of guerrilla warfare, Mao's
People's War strategy actually views guerrilla operations (in which lightly armed irregular forces rely on superior intelligence provided by the sympathetic masses) as
only the first stage in protracted struggle. In the second stage, the dominant military
activity is expected to be mobile warfare by conventional forces, followed by the
third and final stage in which the people's army, relying on well-armed regular
troops, goes on the offensive in set piece battles of annihilation to rout the enemy.
See Mao Zedong, Selected Works of Mao Tse-tung, vol. 2. pp. 79–194. For a discussion in China's recent strategic studies literature, see Yang Xuhua and Cai Renzhao,
Weishe Lun, pp. 384–86, 388, 389, 390; Chen Chongbei, Shou Xiaosong, and Liang
Xiaoqiu, Weishe Zhanlüe, p. 69.

[36]The aggressor may also indulge in wishful thinking about his military prospects, including the belief that the indigenous population will welcome his forces as

Indeed, history suggests that great powers are not easily dissuaded from acting against much weaker states by the risk of confronting popular resistance.[37] One *can*, of course, point to impressive examples of a great power eventually retreating in the face of punishment inflicted by a minor power's protracted "people's war" (e.g., France and the United States in Indochina, the Soviets in Afghanistan). But the fact remains that these great powers were not dissuaded from first attempting to impose their will. Rather, these examples suggest that protracted popular resistance can sometimes effectively serve a strategy of *compellence* (relying on the threat of continuing to inflict pain in order to persuade an enemy to withdraw even when forcible eviction by military offensive is not feasible), not that it has been a powerful deterrent.[38]

Second, conventional deterrence of this sort typically involves trading space for time as opposed to a strategy of forward defense that aims to repulse the adversary's initial attack. But leaders in control of an independent state within defined borders, unlike revolutionary guerrilla movements, are unlikely to embrace a national security policy that requires even the temporary loss of territory under their administration. Although regimes will bend to the need for strategic retreat once a battle has been joined, peacetime planning to do so is likely to be politically unattractive.[39]

---

liberators rather than choose to resist. Therefore, the effectiveness of conventional deterrent threats depends on altering the powerful adversary's assessment of complex, often opaque, political and not just military conditions in a foreign country.

[37]Here one again confronts the notorious problem with assessing the effectiveness of deterrence. Its success is reflected in nonevents. How many great power interventions never occurred, or were never even contemplated, because of the fear of dealing with protracted popular resistance? Answering such a question is difficult and requires close consideration of the foreign policy preferences of particular states. This important matter falls outside the scope of this book. It can be noted, however, that there are at least examples of conventional deterrence failures, something fortunately lacking with respect to nuclear deterrence. For discussion of the vexing problem of demonstrating the effectiveness of deterrence by citing counterfactuals, see "The Rational Deterrence Debate"; Patrick M. Morgan, *Deterrence*.

[38]On the feasibility of small powers successfully compelling the withdrawal of militarily superior adversaries, see Andrew Mack, "Why Big Nations Lose Small Wars." Despite these problems, the lesson seems to be sinking in and great powers are now more risk averse about intervening with ground troops because of the ease with which even poorly equipped resistance fighters may inflict casualties on them.

[39]The response of the West Germans during the Cold War to any compromise of NATO's pledge to forward defense reflected this sort of concern as does South Korea's planning to defend Seoul. On the political definition of a military theater of operations, see Edward N. Luttwak, *Strategy*, pp. 113–15, 127. Threats to take actions unpleasant for oneself as well as the adversary, of course, also characterize nuclear deterrence. The nonnuclear alternative is unappealing to the extent that leaders be-

Third, the economic base of states in the modern world reduces the appeal of a conventional deterrent approach that entails trading space for time. The world's major and many of its minor powers are not peasant societies. To varying degrees they possess an array of fixed industrial assets concentrated in urban settings. Planning for strategic retreat from major cities in preparation for national resistance will, then, involve exercising one of two options. One is to abandon these assets to the aggressor. But doing so will, at a minimum, make the initiation and maintenance of an armed national resistance more costly. It may also enhance the invader's capacity to prosecute a war of suppression. The other alternative is to deny the aggressor these valuable assets by sabotage in conjunction with the strategic retreat. This may increase the logistical problems the invader confronts. It is not likely, however, to have a decisive military impact against a vastly superior adversary able to supply his forces adequately by relying on materiel transported from home. Sabotage, moreover, increases the costs of postwar economic recovery that the leaders in a victimized country hope will follow the eventual withdrawal of the invader's forces.[40] These considerations further diminish the credibility of such conventional deterrent threats.

---

lieve such deterrence is more likely to be tested, and that they may well have to follow through with a planned retreat.

[40]At a time when China was not yet able to deploy a credible nuclear retaliatory force, it undertook two disastrous efforts to offset this economic constraint. Between 1958 and 1960 China's Great Leap Forward was, in part, aimed at creating a country comprised of relatively self-sufficient "people's communes." Each was to possess its own socioeconomic and military infrastructure. Creating this sort of cellular Chinese society (manifesting what Emile Durkheim referred to as "mechanical" as opposed to "organic" solidarity) would make it more difficult for any attacker to achieve decisive victory by striking only a limited number of targets. The Great Leap Forward as implemented became a catastrophic failure, resulted in massive famine, and severely retarded China's economic development. Nevertheless, as China gradually recovered from its effects, Mao Zedong insisted upon a renewed effort to disperse China's industrial assets in order to increase the survivability of an industrial resource base that could support a resistance movement even after China absorbed a superpower attack. This program, known as the "Third Front," was part of an effort to maintain the viability of China's conventional deterrent during the 1960s. Whatever its impact on the credibility of China's conventional deterrent threats against prospective superpower adversaries, its negative impact on economic development was profound. These experiences suggest a trade-off between the economic requisites of modernization and the steps that facilitate conventional deterrence. On the Great Leap Forward, see Franz Schurmann, *Ideology and Organization in Communist China*; Dali L. Yang, *Calamity and Reform in China*; Avery Goldstein, *From Bandwagon to Balance-of-Power Politics*, Part II; Thomas J. Christensen, *Useful Adversaries*, ch. 6. On the third front, see Harvey W. Nelsen, *Power and Insecurity*, pp. 89–90; Barry Naughton, "The Third Front."

Fourth, as the standard of living in a country rises, it becomes more difficult, nationalist pride notwithstanding, to organize the citizenry in the fashion essential to convincing prospective adversaries they will have to face a frightening popular resistance movement.[41] As a smaller proportion of the population is employed in sectors requiring heavy manual labor, the citizenry is less well suited to the anticipated rigors of participation in a people's militia. Regular training to overcome these deficiencies is likely to be constrained by personal and economic concerns that predominate in peacetime. Formal preparations aside, if the potential aggressor doubts the people's ability to persist in the struggle, it will discount the credibility of threatened resistance, undercutting its dissuasive effect. The sharper the contrast between the peacetime standard of living and the hardships that must be endured by those actively or passively supporting a national resistance movement, the greater such doubts will be. This consideration, along with the speed with which they were able to deploy nuclear retaliatory forces, partly accounts for the short shrift Britain and France gave to the conventional deterrent alternative. For China, in addition to the higher hurdles it had to clear before deploying a nuclear retaliatory force, the relatively recent experience its communist leaders had gained during decades of fighting against better armed domestic and foreign enemies in the 1930s and 1940s accounts for the credibility of and initial emphasis on their conventional deterrent strategy of "people's war."

A fifth problem with conventional deterrence reflects what Edward Luttwak terms the paradoxical logic of strategy. If, despite the complications already described, the strategy succeeds, it may become irrelevant.[42] Recognizing the risks of painfully confronting a protracted popular resistance, a militarily superior adversary may be convinced to abandon the option of a total war of invasion and occupation (i.e., a strategic offensive) as a means to achieve the political objective of surrender. But this may only lead him to consider other means for achieving different objectives that nonetheless compromise the weaker state's security. Given the vast resources available to a superpower during the Cold War, for example, China, Britain, and France had to prepare to deal with at least two major alternative threats to their security against which conventional deterrence was likely to be ineffective.

First, relying on its ability to project massive military force, a superpower could attempt to coerce or blackmail its outgunned victim (i.e.,

[41]Luttwak, *Strategy*, pp. 131–40; cf. Gene Sharp, *Making Europe Unconquerable*.
[42]Luttwak, *Strategy*, pp. 18–21.

clear armed states the principal focus was no longer on determining how to use military force to win, or avoid losing, war should it occur, but rather how to forestall a conflict in which either party might at any time inflict unacceptable damage on the other.[47] Because even small numbers of crude nuclear weapons could be used to so punish an adversary, in a world without leakproof defenses close consideration of the likely military results of a conflict between nations with nuclear forces was less important than considering how the fear of a catastrophic outcome could be manipulated to achieve the state's goals without actually initiating hostilities. Decision-makers might yet *hope* that a nuclear adversary could be disarmed in a first strike or somehow convinced to submit despite retaining a retaliatory capability. But the nuclear revolution meant that lingering doubts about the execution of first-strike options and, more importantly, possibilities for miscalculation, accident, or irrationality (discussed below) sharply reduced the expected utility of initiating a conflict that could escalate to the use of these weapons of mass destruction. Consequently, among nuclear states scenarios for using force or the threat of force to serve offensive, or even defensive, strategies, though certainly devised, were highly problematic. On the rare occasions during the Cold War when elaborate plans for nuclear use confronted the reality of a crisis, the strategic logic of dissuasion by deterrence (and to a lesser extent persuasion by compellence) remained dominant.[48]

---

dawned. But even before a balance of terror was established, any plans for an offensive strike as part of a preventive war against the Soviet Union had to consider the implications if the initial salvo failed to produce a surrender. The worry was not simply technical (e.g., because of the limited number and power of the nuclear warheads available early in the nuclear age) but also psychological as the indecisive use of nuclear weapons might undermine the leverage of terror associated with them after Hiroshima. See Richard K. Betts, "A Nuclear Golden Age?"; *Nuclear Blackmail and Nuclear Balance*.

[47]Thus Brodie's now classic 1945 statement that the chief purpose of military establishments in the nuclear age was to avert rather than win wars. See Bernard Brodie, *War and Politics*, p. 377. For a summary of the debate and historical experience that followed in the decades after Brodie's initial comments, see Jervis, *The Meaning of the Nuclear Revolution*. Jervis argues that Brodie's assertion was premature inasmuch as first-generation fission weapons might not have ensured catastrophic damage, especially if the targeted state was large and had many dispersed cities (i.e., the Soviet and American superpowers). The advent of thermonuclear weapons erased doubts about the capability to inflict horrific damage with a relatively small number of weapons. Devin Hagerty suggests that Jervis's argument may overstate the requirements in nuclear deterrent relationships between smaller states, or those with a few densely populated urban areas. In such cases, even fission weapons provide a sufficient capability for inflicting catastrophic damage. See Devin Hagerty, *The Consequences of Nuclear Proliferation*.

[48]Yet during the Cold War some scholars and policy-makers continued to em-

and France faced during the Cold War. This point is most clearly illustrated by the evidence from China's experience detailed in Chapter 3.
What each of these states instead sought was an economically sound yet
self-reliant strategy that would more effectively enable them to cope
with the spectrum of plausible threats a militarily superior adversary
might pose. Because it was a more robust but still affordable strategy,
nuclear deterrence was their preferred approach. The claim that the
twin virtues of robustness and affordability made nuclear deterrence attractive to China, Britain, and France requires some justification. After
all, even the superpowers agonized about the dissuasive adequacy of
their much larger and more diverse strategic arsenals. How, then, could
the relatively small nuclear arsenals within reach of lesser powers satisfy the basic strategic requirement of deterrence—credibly threatening
unacceptable retaliatory punishment? And, even if nuclear deterrence
could be made credible at a bearable cost, in what sense would this constitute a more robust approach for ensuring their vital interests than the
conventional alternative? Answering these questions requires a closer
examination of the logic of nuclear deterrence of the strong by the weak.

DETERRENCE OF THE STRONG BY THE WEAK

IN THE NUCLEAR ERA

The military technology available to states in every historical era shapes
decisions about how resources can best be employed to pursue national
interests. The advent of nuclear weapons technology dramatically altered the military-strategic environment to the point that some labeled
the effects revolutionary.[45] What were the implications of the advent of
nuclear weapons and how did they affect the strategic planning of states
that had the resources to deploy them and sufficient reason to want to
provide for their own military security?

The possession of nuclear weapons fundamentally challenged the
traditional offense/defense calculus in strategic thinking.[46] Among nu-

---

[45]See Michael Mandelbaum, *The Nuclear Revolution;* Robert Jervis, *The Meaning of the Nuclear Revolution.*

[46]Military historians have long discussed the shifting advantage between offense
and defense as weaponry has evolved through the ages. Such analysis entails considering both the objective characteristics of the hardware as well as the subjective beliefs of those who formulate strategies that would employ it. The two may sharply
conflict as is frequently noted in discussions of mistaken beliefs about the advantage
of the offense many asserted on the eve of World War I. The assertion that the nuclear revolution resulted in deterrence supplanting offense and defense is most relevant after the brief U.S. nuclear monopoly ended and the age of mutual vulnerability

clear armed states the principal focus was no longer on determining how to use military force to win, or avoid losing, war should it occur, but rather how to forestall a conflict in which either party might at any time inflict unacceptable damage on the other.[47] Because even small numbers of crude nuclear weapons could be used to so punish an adversary, in a world without leakproof defenses close consideration of the likely military results of a conflict between nations with nuclear forces was less important than considering how the fear of a catastrophic outcome could be manipulated to achieve the state's goals without actually initiating hostilities. Decision-makers might yet *hope* that a nuclear adversary could be disarmed in a first strike or somehow convinced to submit despite retaining a retaliatory capability. But the nuclear revolution meant that lingering doubts about the execution of first-strike options and, more importantly, possibilities for miscalculation, accident, or irrationality (discussed below) sharply reduced the expected utility of initiating a conflict that could escalate to the use of these weapons of mass destruction. Consequently, among nuclear states scenarios for using force or the threat of force to serve offensive, or even defensive, strategies, though certainly devised, were highly problematic. On the rare occasions during the Cold War when elaborate plans for nuclear use confronted the reality of a crisis, the strategic logic of dissuasion by deterrence (and to a lesser extent persuasion by compellence) remained dominant.[48]

---

dawned. But even before a balance of terror was established, any plans for an offensive strike as part of a preventive war against the Soviet Union had to consider the implications if the initial salvo failed to produce a surrender. The worry was not simply technical (e.g., because of the limited number and power of the nuclear warheads available early in the nuclear age) but also psychological as the indecisive use of nuclear weapons might undermine the leverage of terror associated with them after Hiroshima. See Richard K. Betts, "A Nuclear Golden Age?"; *Nuclear Blackmail and Nuclear Balance*.

[47]Thus Brodie's now classic 1945 statement that the chief purpose of military establishments in the nuclear age was to avert rather than win wars. See Bernard Brodie, *War and Politics*, p. 377. For a summary of the debate and historical experience that followed in the decades after Brodie's initial comments, see Jervis, *The Meaning of the Nuclear Revolution*. Jervis argues that Brodie's assertion was premature inasmuch as first-generation fission weapons might not have ensured catastrophic damage, especially if the targeted state was large and had many dispersed cities (i.e., the Soviet and American superpowers). The advent of thermonuclear weapons erased doubts about the capability to inflict horrific damage with a relatively small number of weapons. Devin Hagerty suggests that Jervis's argument may overstate the requirements in nuclear deterrent relationships between smaller states, or those with a few densely populated urban areas. In such cases, even fission weapons provide a sufficient capability for inflicting catastrophic damage. See Devin Hagerty, *The Consequences of Nuclear Proliferation*.

[48]Yet during the Cold War some scholars and policy-makers continued to em-

The advent of nuclear weapons not only elevated the significance of deterrent strategies, it also reinforced the self-help incentive deriving from coexistence in a condition of anarchy that shaped the security policies of China, Britain, and France during the Cold War. First, as mentioned above, vulnerability to thermonuclear destruction subverts confidence in alliances because it exacerbates the fear that self-interested states will abandon one another rather than risk national survival over their partner's vital interests. Second, the relative ease with which horrifying punishment can be inflicted using nuclear weapons supports strategies that do not depend on joint action. In a world where offense/defense balances are key, adding together the capabilities of allies may matter a great deal. In a world where the fear of retaliation turns

---

phasize the importance of offensive and defensive considerations, many of which were incorporated in the expanding array of strategic options contained in the U.S. government's Single Integrated Operational Plan. But despite contrary appearances, even in the most prominent justifications for nondeterrent options, the new core consideration of deterrence remained in a position of logical priority. The classic scenarios challenging the deterrent logic first had to assume that the strategic factors on which deterrence rested were somehow rendered irrelevant. Colin Gray, for example, argued that the Soviet leaders would only refrain from initiating a war that advanced their interests if they calculated that the United States was able to defeat their communist regime, not just devastate the country's population and industry (Colin Gray, "Nuclear Strategy"). His argument, however, depended on *first* establishing that the Soviet leaders were indifferent to the horrifying damage that the United States could at any time inflict on the "socialist homeland" by relying on a small fraction of its nuclear arsenal. Only *after* asserting this premise of indifference (a heroic assumption even about brutal authoritarian rulers who presumably wished a society over which to wield power) could one logically debate the need to move beyond a strategy of deterrence to more traditional considerations of offense and defense. The plausibility of this premise is open to debate, but its central importance for Gray's argument is clear.

Paul Nitze, too, offered a nightmare scenario that seemed to suggest the continuing importance of a focus on offense and defense, rather than deterrence, in the nuclear age (Paul Nitze, "Deterring our Deterrent"). Nitze's concern was the possibility that the Soviets might initiate war by undertaking a well-conceived, limited counterforce first strike leaving the United States with the choice of triggering a suicidal countervalue exchange or submitting to a Soviet aggressor whose action had assured itself of military superiority. This scenario, however, required accepting *first* that the Soviets would be so confident of a measured, rational American reaction based on an accurate interpretation of the size and purpose of the Soviet attack that they would opt to carry out the plan. This assumption was particularly heroic given the historically unprecedented level of destruction even a limited Soviet strike would inflict on the American homeland as well as the fragility of command and control in a nuclearized environment. See Robert Jervis, *The Illogic of American Nuclear Strategy*; Fred Kaplan, *The Wizards of Armageddon*, pp. 377–79; Desmond Ball, "Can Nuclear War Be Controlled?"; Paul Bracken, *The Command and Control of Nuclear Forces*; Bruce Blair, *Strategic Command and Control*.

less on information about the order of battle and more on the choices of national decision-makers, it is neither politically sensible nor militarily necessary to share ultimate control over one's destiny.

Although the superpowers may have believed they could afford to prepare for a wide variety of what seemed to be only remotely plausible contingencies, China, Britain, and France emphasized the simple consequences of a strategic revolution that put deterrent considerations first and raised the premium on self help.[49] But when the prospective aggressor was a superpower, how could the relatively small nuclear forces of the sort within reach of such states satisfy the requirements of credible deterrence?

The basic logic of deterrence through threat of nuclear retaliation is by now familiar. As ever, the credibility of threats is determined by the capabilities at one's disposal and the probability they will be used. Given the characteristics of nuclear weapons technology, acquiring the capability to inflict great pain in short order was a difficult but not insurmountable task for Britain, France and, with much greater effort, even China. The hurdle they had to clear was amassing a punitive force sufficient to create what Devin Hagerty has termed "first-strike uncertainty" in the mind of a vastly more capable adversary.[50] First-strike uncertainty simply means doubt that even the best planned surprise attack will neutralize the victim's ability to launch an unacceptably punishing retaliatory strike. This standard falls far short of the demanding "assured destruction" capability required for deterrence according to U.S. Defense Secretary Robert McNamara's analysts in the mid-1960s. Instead, this more modest standard of strategic adequacy is the deployment of a force that a prospective attacker worries might, even if seriously damaged, be capable of causing the sort of horrific destruction that results from the explosion of even small numbers of nuclear weapons. The McNamaran standard of assured destruction assumed that the state practicing deterrence had to establish the certainty it would retain a large retaliatory capability even after absorbing the adversary's best first strike.[51] The standard of first-strike uncertainty assumes that a potential

[49]It is not surprising that the more elaborate nuclear scenarios emphasizing offensive and defensive strategies and the force structures for carrying them out were the special privilege of the Cold War superpowers. Having easily satisfied the basic requirements of deterrence, they could (or believed they could) afford the luxury of supplementing this with forces to cover a wide variety of expensive contingencies: low-intensity conflict, limited and full-scale conventional war, as well as limited nuclear war.

[50]See Hagerty, *The Consequences of Nuclear Proliferation*, p. 26.

[51]The levels of allegedly necessary destruction were in practice set very high, on

attacker facing a nuclear-armed state will find almost any slippage from
100 percent certainty in successful preemption excruciatingly inhibiting.

The assumption that a nuclear capability satisfying the less demanding standard of first-strike uncertainty will be highly dissuasive reflects
not only the belief that the assured destruction standard vastly over-
states the level of damage that real world political leaders would deem
acceptable. It also reflects an understanding of how states engaged in a
nuclear confrontation are likely view the stakes of the game. Research
in prospect theory suggests that actors value what they already possess
more than what they might hope to gain. Translated to confrontations
between nuclear-armed states, this suggests that both prospective aggressor and victim are likely to recognize that the state interested in
maintaining the status quo will be prepared to run greater risks than the
state aiming to alter it. But it is the aggressor who must take the initial
steps that increase the risk both will pay a heavy price. If, as prospect
theory suggests, gains are not valued as much as losses are feared, then
the prospect of absorbing the horrible, even if not total, losses that
might result from nuclear retaliation will reduce the temptation to seek
gains unless they are inordinately attractive. Put otherwise, this is the
proportional deterrence argument: The possibility of absorbing a handful of nuclear strikes should suffice to dissuade actors from seeking all
but the most valuable prizes.[52]

However, even with a punitive capability in hand, the nuclear

the order of 20 percent of population and 50 percent of Soviet industrial capacity,
partly because at these levels diminishing returns would have set in, enabling
McNamara to portray Pentagon demands for greater nuclear capabilities as excessive. See Kaplan, *The Wizards of Armageddon*, pp. 317–18. Alain C. Enthoven and K.
Wayne Smith, *How Much Is Enough?* Over subsequent decades, McNamara's position seemed to shift in the direction of the belief that deterrence did not require
anywhere near these levels of damage.

[52]See Jervis, *The Meaning of the Nuclear Revolution*, pp. 94–95, 168–72. This
also suggests why claims about deterrence cannot simply refer to levels of tolerance
for absorbing damage. Depending on the prize, one can argue that great gains might
induce a regime to risk huge, if not total, losses. This is essentially the logic behind
Colin Gray's argument that there were circumstances under which the Soviet leadership would have risked sacrificing much of their society if they believed they could
maintain political control over whatever remained (Gray, "Nuclear Strategy"). Minimal deterrence arguments, though reaching different conclusions, also rest on the
assumption that it is difficult to imagine gains worth even the survivable, but horrific, losses that follow from absorbing a small handful of nuclear strikes. The position I set forth focuses not on a comparison of gains and losses, but rather on the fear
that such assessments cannot be made with certainty and that escalation beyond
what might be deemed tolerable losses is always possible.

threats on which deterrent strategies depend are not credible unless the adversary worries that the forces might be used. Many analysts and policy-makers suggested that the probability of states like China, Britain, and France executing a retaliatory nuclear threat against a vastly mightier nuclear superpower was vanishingly small. Indeed, one can argue that the probability of *rationally choosing* to execute the threat was zero. If so, then even the arguments of prospect theory and imbalanced resolve would be insufficient to explain why deterrence of the strong by the weak works. In the following section, I acknowledge that an outgunned nuclear victim cannot rationally choose to retaliate when that would only invite a devastating counterblow by the remnants of the attacker's much larger force. But I will also explain why this does not demonstrate the infeasibility of dissuading a militarily superior adversary by relying on threats of nuclear retaliation. Nuclear-armed states do not need to convince a potential aggressor that retaliation is certain, or even likely, only that it is possible and, most importantly, that *neither* party can safely predict what the actual response will be. This point is central to the viability of the nuclear deterrent doctrines embraced by China, Britain, and France and requires some elaboration.

Security and Possibly Unsafe Actors

Analysts have long noted an unavoidable problem with nuclear deterrent strategies that emphasize the threat of massively destructive retaliation, precisely the sort of threats made by the outgunned powers I examine. Simply put, once each adversary has nuclear forces that cannot be fully destroyed or neutralized with absolute certainty, deterrence cannot be made credible by threatening rationally to execute a large-scale nuclear strike in response to aggression. Under such circumstances, states cannot *deliberately* choose to launch such a strike knowing the result would be retaliation in kind. The inhibitions against nuclear use would be especially strong for a badly outgunned victim of aggression (i.e., the weak facing the strong), since it cannot expect even horrifying retaliatory punishment to eliminate the adversary's ability to launch another, unrestrained wave of devastating strikes. The rationality of not retaliating would seem to hold even if a victimized state faced the prospect of defeat. At worst, defeat might entail the demise of the regime; provoking unrestrained nuclear retaliation would jeopardize not just the regime, but society itself. Although defeat might be a bitter pill to swallow, it leaves open the possibility, however slim, of someday reversing the verdict of the war; choosing national suicide eliminates that possibility. Thus, in a confrontation, the rational choice would always be to prefer the consequences of not launching, however unpalatable, to the far worse outcome of suffering massive destruction—regardless of the balance of forces, the balance of resolve, and peacetime rhetoric or declaratory doctrine (three foci of much of the literature on deterrence).[53]

Recognizing this problem, many analysts argued that in order to be effective, nuclear deterrence requires a state to devise threats that can rationally be executed. Deterrence, it was claimed, must rest on credible threats to resort to one of an array of measures for inflicting punishment, not incredible threats to initiate a suicidal nuclear exchange. Such an approach dissuades the prospective aggressor by confronting him with the threat of an unfolding process of *controlled* escalation in which each party demonstrates its determination to inflict severe but limited damage on the adversary and its willingness to absorb damage in return.[54] The effectiveness of this sort of deterrence, then, depends not just on resolve or absolute destructive capabilities, but also on each state's ability to compete with its adversary in the creation of smaller and more numerous limited nuclear options. Where deterrence rests on a competition in the ability to inflict and endure punishment, the side with the more numerous options, the larger array of punishments, would be more likely to prevail.[55]

[53]See Robert Powell, "The Theoretical Foundations of Strategic Nuclear Deterrence"; "Crisis Bargaining, Escalation, and MAD"; "Nuclear Brinkmanship with Two-Sided Incomplete Information"; *Nuclear Deterrence Theory*; Richard K. Betts, *Nuclear Blackmail and Nuclear Balance*. These issues have also served as foci in the literature on the incentives for and consequences of proliferation. See Michael D. Intriligator and Dagobert L. Brito, "Nuclear Proliferation and the Probability of Nuclear War"; Bruce Bueno de Mesquita and William H. Riker, "An Assessment of the Merits of Selective Nuclear Proliferation"; Bruce D. Berkowitz, "Proliferation, Deterrence, and the Likelihood of Nuclear War." Berkowitz in particular focuses on the difficulties of small states making credible nuclear threats.

[54]Robert Powell, "The Theoretical Foundations of Strategic Nuclear Deterrence," pp. 75–83. The nature of limited damage could range from very small-scale demonstration "shots across the bow" designed to indicate resolve (an idea associated with James Schlesinger when he worked as a RAND analyst), to limited counterforce strikes designed both to signal intent and to encourage mutual self-restraint (an idea associated with RAND analyst William Kaufmann and embodied in the Kennedy administration's flexible response/city avoidance doctrine), to larger but still limited militarily decisive counterforce strikes such as those posited by Paul Nitze in his various assessments of the U.S.-Soviet nuclear balance during the 1970s.

[55]Once a state has run out of limited options and must choose between submitting or using its last option of a suicidal massive nuclear strike, it rationally must

But if deterrence between pairs of nuclear-armed states can only be effective if it is based on the availability of an array of options that each could rationally choose to execute, this raises serious doubts about its viability as a strategy for the weak to dissuade the strong. The burden of competing with a vastly mightier adversary (such as the superpowers China, Britain, and France faced during the Cold War) in the creation of limited strike options would be dauntingly heavy,[56] especially since producing the weapons is only a necessary and not a sufficient condition for the effectiveness of this sort of deterrence. Strategies of deterrence that rely on graduated threats of limited retaliation also require extremely durable command and control.[57] Indeed, this may be the technologically and economically more formidable obstacle for outgunned states facing tight resource constraints. Much of the literature on nuclear deterrence in the waning years of the Cold War questioned whether the highly sophisticated command and control systems that the superpowers deployed at great cost could endure after relatively few nuclear detonations.[58] For smaller states, even those as capable as the Cold War's second-ranking powers, the challenge of deploying command and control that remains durable in a nuclearized environment would be that much greater.

In short, between nuclear-armed adversaries the only deterrent strategies consistent with rational decision-making, those based on the threat to engage in a controlled competition in pain, would seem to be impractical for the weak to dissuade the strong. At a minimum, such strategies significantly reduce the cost advantages of dissuasion by deterrence as opposed to defense, asserted above. In practice, however, neither China, Britain, nor France sought capabilities adequate for the more demanding approaches to nuclear deterrence. How, then, were their nuclear forces of any strategic value? The answer is that they facilitated de-

---

submit since the payoff for so doing always exceeds the payoff of absolute destruction. This logic is explained through a more formal argument in Robert Powell, "Nuclear Deterrence and the Strategy of Limited Retaliation."

[56]Thus the Chinese eschewed counterforce targeting options early in their nuclear weapons program because of the challenge of producing a large enough number of deliverable warheads. See John Wilson Lewis and Hua Di, "China's Ballistic Missile Programs," pp. 21, 30. A similar lack of "chips" partly explains the Soviet Union's rejection of McNamara's suggestion in the early 1960s that the superpowers initially adhere to limited, "no-cities," exchanges in the event nuclear war ever began.

[57]Robert Powell, "Nuclear Deterrence and the Strategy of Limited Retaliation," p. 507.

[58]Ball, "Can Nuclear War Be Controlled?"; Bracken, The Command and Control of Nuclear Forces; Blair, Strategic Command and Control.

UNCONTROLLABLE NUCLEAR ESCALATION [handwritten margin note]

terrence based on the threat of *uncontrollable* nuclear escalation rather than threats to engage in a rational, controlled competition.

Although rational leaders cannot credibly threaten a suicidal act, they can nevertheless threaten to create a risky situation that might slip beyond the control of either party and lead to the same result. In place of clearly drawn threats of massive retaliation, states can resort to what Thomas Schelling called the "threat that leaves something to chance."[59] With such threats, deterrence depends on the adversary's unwillingness to run the risk that events might spin out of control and perhaps result in an unforeseen unlimited nuclear exchange. This begs the question, however: What could possibly trigger an unlimited nuclear exchange when neither side at any stage in the confrontation could ever rationally decide to initiate such action? As Robert Powell has explained, the viability of deterrence based on Schelling's "threat that leaves something to chance" requires the existence of autonomous risk—risk genuinely beyond the control of the parties involved.[60] But what is the source of autonomous risk in the real world of nuclear deterrence?

Powell identifies two sources of such risk that can cause an adversary to worry that its victim might prove to be what I refer to as an "unsafe actor." One source of risk is the technology of the nuclear deterrent arsenal. A prospective aggressor may fear the victim, though rational, would launch a devastating retaliatory strike accidentally. Such an accident might result from an *unauthorized* launch as control over forces placed on crisis alert erodes due either to failures in the command and control system or organizational confusion after nuclear release authority has been delegated to lower levels.[61] Alternatively the acci-

[right margin handwritten note: *T. Schelling "Threat that leaves something to chance."*]

[59]Schelling, *Strategy of Conflict*, ch. 8.
[60]Robert Powell, "Crisis Bargaining, Escalation, and MAD," p. 719.
[61]Robert Powell, *Nuclear Deterrence Theory*, ch. 2; Schelling, *Strategy of Conflict*, pp. 188–90, 201–3; Edward Rhodes, *Power and MADness*, pp. 78–81; Scott D. Sagan, *The Limits of Safety*; Bruce G. Blair, *The Logic of Accidental Nuclear War*. Blair's work, in particular, emphasizes the way such pressures shaped U.S. and Soviet war plans in ways that reduced tight negative control over nuclear arsenals and increased the risks of accidental or inadvertent escalation. Barry Posen, skeptical about the sort of inhibiting effects of feared escalation that I describe here, has portrayed the way the interaction of conventional and nuclear operations for the Cold War superpowers could have lead to inadvertent, though not accidental, escalation. See Barry R. Posen, *Inadvertent Escalation*. Recently declassified documents confirm what circumstantial evidence and logic had already led some analysts to believe was the U.S. response to the threat nuclear weapons posed for durable command and control. By the late 1950s the difficulties of maintaining a coherent national command authority in the wake of a feared Soviet first strike induced even the wealthy and technologically sophisticated United States (that enjoyed the luxury of a well-institutionalized, constitutionally determined statutory line of presidential succes-

dent might take the form of an *authorized* launch based on the mistaken belief, perhaps a result of erroneous intelligence reports or malfunctioning sensors, that the adversary had initiated an unlimited nuclear offensive, the only circumstance under which the inhibitions against massive retaliation disappear, even for a rational decision-maker. The second source of autonomous risk reflects the human element. Deterrence based on the risk of uncontrollable escalation can be effective if the challenger fears that the victim might engage in "the particular irrational act of initiating a massive nuclear strike." It is not sufficient that the challenger worry about the victim's rationality in general or even harbor some vague belief about unpredictability associated with "the fog of war." He must believe there is an unacceptable risk that the victim will engage in this specific irrational act.[62]

Where both parties have nuclear forces, then, deterrence based on the risk of uncontrollable escalation does not work by convincing a prospective aggressor that he faces a rational adversary with the resolve and resources to engage in a competition in pain, or one who would deliberately choose to launch a massive nuclear strike. It works because he is convinced he faces a potentially "unsafe" actor about whose behavior he simply cannot be certain. Is this a reasonable fear? Under normal circumstances, in peacetime, states have strong incentives to minimize the risk of the sorts of accidents outlined above as well as the ability of a potentially irrational leadership to commit national suicide. Technical and institutional safeguards are developed along with nuclear forces to reduce these risks, clearly understood by even modestly sensible re-

---

sion) to opt for the potentially risky, probably unconstitutional, option of predelegation. For documents from the Eisenhower, Kennedy, and Johnson administrations, see "First Documented Evidence That U.S. Presidents Predelegated Nuclear Weapons Release Authority to The Military," Mar. 19, 1998, available at the National Security Archive website, http://www.seas.gwu.edu/nsarchive/news/19980319.htm. Kurt Gottfried and Bruce Blair clarify the distinctions among predelegation, delegation, and (constitutional) devolution. Devolution refers to institutionalized arrangements specifying a line of succession that determines which surviving individual would assume national command authority. Delegation refers to a process by which a surviving leader removes the peacetime negative controls, decides retaliation is warranted, and designates individuals who are granted discretion to decide when and how to launch retaliatory strikes. Predelegation refers to a process by which a leader in peacetime anticipates the possibility of a communications breakdown in wartime, due to death or disruption, and designates individuals who, under specific conditions, are granted the discretion to decide on retaliation even in the absence of the sort of general authorization characteristic of the delegation option. See Kurt Gottfried and Bruce G. Blair, *Crisis Stability and Nuclear War*, p. 80.

[62]See Robert Powell, "Theoretical Foundations of Strategic Nuclear Deterrence," p. 85; Rhodes, *Power and MADness*, pp. 72–77, 164–66, 191–92.

gimes.[63] Provocative actions, however, such as the initiation of a crisis or the infliction of limited destruction by an adversary, especially a vastly more capable adversary, might reduce the effectiveness of these measures.[64] A normally safe actor (i.e., one who strives accurately to monitor the behavior of a potential adversary, maintains control over his own nuclear forces, and cannot credibly threaten to choose the irrational massive retaliatory option) may become less safe as a consequence of aggressive acts by a challenger. To draw on the logic usefully employed by Edward Rhodes, the risk is that the attacker confronts a "contingently" unsafe actor.[65] This risk would seem especially likely to have obtained during the Cold War in any confrontation between a superpower and a nuclear armed second-ranking power.

With regard to the risk of accidental launch, more limited command and control capabilities and smaller, less diverse arsenals make it difficult for an outgunned victim to ensure its continued ability to engage in attack assessment and to maintain tight control over its forces once they are placed on heightened alert or during hostilities. Such problems are even more acute if the national command authority's technical capabilities are degraded by the aggressor's military action, in particular action that creates a less forgiving, nuclearized environment.[66] Superpower coercion against a lesser nuclear power would have increased the danger of accidental launch (authorized or not). Even if he succeeded in the classic decapitating strike, unless the attacker could be absolutely certain of disarming the victim, he would remain unsure about both the extent to which nuclear release authority had been predelegated (a sensible option for states with smaller, more vulnerable forces) and the ability of outraged subordinates to respond independently. Though more speculative, such pressures from a militarily superior adversary might also create conditions that increase the probability of the irrational act of suicidal massive retaliation. At a minimum, students of decision-making have suggested that the extreme time pressures and enormous stakes that would be involved in managing a nuclear crisis (problems

[63]Morgan, *Deterrence*, pp. 161–63; Rhodes, *Power and MADness*, pp. 184–86; Waltz, "Toward Nuclear Peace"; cf. George Quester, "Nuclear Proliferation and Stability."

[64]Schelling, *Strategy of Conflict*, p. 188; Robert Powell, *Nuclear Deterrence Theory*, pp. 22–23; Rhodes, *Power and MADness*, pp. 186–92.

[65]Rhodes, *Power and MADness*. See also Jervis, *The Meaning of the Nuclear Revolution*, p. 87.

[66]Ball, "Can Nuclear War Be Controlled?"; Blair, *Strategic Command and Control*; Rhodes, *Power and MADness*, pp. 139–40; Peter D. Feaver, "Command and Control in Emerging Nuclear Nations."

that would be exacerbated if it actually included limited nuclear exchanges) would adversely affect rationality.[67] This concern, exaggerated or not, would bedevil a prospective aggressor attempting to forecast the response to his actions.

It must be emphasized that I am not arguing that the aggressive acts of a militarily superior adversary make either accidental launch or the dreaded irrational act likely. On the contrary, although a less powerful state's *ability* to preclude a catastrophic outcome would erode, I assume that its *preference* to avoid nuclear annihilation would be unchanged.[68] Attempts to retain control over events would continue and national leaders would not be expected "to commit suicide for fear of death." Instead I am suggesting only that even the mightiest aggressor would have to anticipate that his actions create the contingency that elevates, rather than reduces, the always low probability of either of the unlikely scenarios that could precipitate an unlimited nuclear exchange. This is a concern that facilitates deterrence.

Robustness?

Some who accept this logic of nuclear deterrence based upon a combination of uncertainty and the absolute costs that can be imposed upon an aggressor see its usefulness limited to discouraging only the most extreme, least plausible challenge—full-scale nuclear assault on a state's national territory. Instead, I have suggested that nuclear deterrence appealed to China, Britain, and France during the Cold War, and may appeal to others in the post–Cold War world precisely because it is a robust strategy of dissuasion, more robust than the conventional alternative. Why? In the latter, dissuasion is difficult because an aggressor can plan carefully to monitor the developing costs and benefits of his military campaign. The aggressor can tolerate less than perfect success and perhaps even defeat; the costs of failure are unclear, may be reversible, and are gradually accumulated as the war progresses. Against a nuclear-armed victim the risks of any aggression are not so readily managed; the possible costs of failure are clear and not necessarily distant.[69]

---

[67]Gottfried and Blair, *Crisis Stability and Nuclear War*, pp. 265–68; Rhodes, *Power and MADness*, pp. 135–40.

[68]Thus what would appear to the analyst as irrational behavior might result, without any lapse of rationality on the part of the decision-maker. See Rhodes, *Power and MADness*, ch. 2. For further discussion of distinctions between rationality in the decision-making process as opposed to the apparent rationality of choice, see Frank Zagare, "Rationality and Deterrence."

[69]Waltz, "Toward Nuclear Peace," p. 688.

Some correctly point out that this fear is felt by both parties in a nuclear dyad but conclude that this means nuclear weapons cancel each other out. Security, such nuclear skeptics argue, requires the ability to compete with a prospective adversary at lower, nonnuclear rungs on the ladder of escalation. Although it is true that the possibility of nuclear disaster constrains both parties, the key point about the robustness of the nuclear deterrent strategy is that it succeeds insofar as it makes it difficult for the adversary to "go first." Where the victim is a nuclear power and cannot be confidently disarmed, the onus of initiating a sequence of events that contains the possibility of disaster falls to the aggressor and exerts a powerfully dissuasive effect. The use of force, nuclear or conventional, in ways that jeopardize a nuclear state's vital interests entails risks that simply did not obtain before this revolution in military technology. The robustness of nuclear deterrence is not an absolute guarantee of security. Others may still act in the belief or hope they can control escalation. But the difficulty of entertaining such beliefs or relying on hope is fundamentally transformed by the victim's possession of nuclear weapons.[70] Confronting a weaker, but nuclear-armed state, even the most capable adversary's numerous options—ranging from compellent threats, through limited military assaults, to full scale war—all carry an unknowable risk of escalation to disastrous consequences.[71] The rela-

[70]The way in which nuclear weapons affect the decision-making of prospective aggressors is given a formal treatment in the appendix. The inhibiting fear of escalation that makes nuclear deterrence robust as well as relatively affordable is a result of the strategic consequences of the nuclear revolution, not the particular policies of states. States that have decided to deploy nuclear weapons can, however, act to reinforce its effects. This can be done in part by exploiting the complementarity of nuclear and conventional forces. By denying an adversary the certainty of unresisted aggression, conventional weapons compel an adversary who would challenge vital interests to confront grave risks. Not because they are a tripwire triggering an automatic response, but as Schelling noted because they increase the likelihood of *some* response that might eventually result in unforeseen escalation, conventional deployments by nuclear states serve to dissuade serious, even if initially limited, threats to vital interests. Another step by which states can cause a prospective aggressor to recognize the potentially catastrophic consequences of initiating hostile military action is to respond to crises by placing nuclear forces on a heightened alert status. While of course reducing the vulnerability of weapons, more importantly this step also raises the inhibiting specter of catastrophe by weakening, without eliminating, the tighter peacetime negative controls over nuclear weapons. Regardless of whether control is seriously compromised, the move fosters the sorts of doubts in the adversary's mind that enhance deterrence.

[71]See also Robert Jervis, "Strategic Theory," p. 141. On the cautiousness of U.S. crisis behavior despite great nuclear superiority during the mid-1950s through mid-1960s, see, for example, Richard K. Betts, "A Nuclear Golden Age?"; *Nuclear Blackmail and Nuclear Balance*; Marc Trachtenberg, "The Influence of Nuclear

tively weak may turn out to be a contingently unsafe actor, and this risk enables it to deter the strong. This possibility instills the fear of catastrophic nuclear retaliation despite a severely skewed balance of forces, and despite the implausibility of the outgunned victim ever rationally choosing a nuclear response that would invite national suicide.

Cost-Effectiveness?

During the Cold War China, Britain, and France deemed nuclear deterrence an attractive strategy for dealing with the superpower threat not only because it is robust but also because it is economical when compared with the most plausible conventional alternatives. The economic attractiveness of nuclear forces is not a reflection of their low cost in an absolute sense. Developing and deploying nuclear forces is not cheap. Especially for a poor country like China, the effort is arduous and requires great sacrifice and a husbanding of scarce resources. The relevant assessment of cost-effectiveness, however, is not the absolute amount spent on nuclear forces, but rather the amount that would have to be spent on conventional forces to achieve comparable levels of security. For a country like China, determined to self-reliantly deal with what it believed were serious superpower threats and dissatisfied with its relatively cheap conventional deterrent (i.e., the people's war capability), the choice was between burdensome alternatives—a conventional defensive or a nuclear deterrent capability. The latter offered the more plausibly affordable path to enhanced security.

Relying on conventional forces for deterrence or defense has another economic disadvantage. Conventional deployments usually need to be geared to those of the adversary. The value of an investment in expensive conventional forces depends on ratios of military power (adjusted for qualitative differences) and the skillfulness with which its use is planned. Not only is it difficult to be confident about the outcome of engagements between known forces, but technological change constantly threatens the military value of one's investment.[72] In addition, one must be prepared to counter quantitative and qualitative

---

Weapons in the Cuban Missile Crisis"; Raymond L. Garthoff, *Reflections on the Cuban Missile Crisis.*

[72]The difficulty of the calculation was reflected in the heated debate about the actual balance of NATO and Warsaw Pact forces in Central Europe during the Cold War. See Mearsheimer, "Numbers, Strategy, and the European Balance"; Posen, "Is NATO Decisively Outnumbered?"; Epstein, "Dynamic Analysis and the Conventional Balance in Europe"; Eliot A. Cohen, "Toward Better Net Assessment"; Epstein, "The 3:1 Rule, the Adaptive Dynamic Model, and the Future of Security Studies"; Mearsheimer, "Assessing the Conventional Balance."

improvements in the adversary's capabilities. Precision-guided munitions, electronic countermeasures, stealth technology, and sophisticated armoring are only some of the elements in the clash of modern conventional forces that made them an increasingly expensive gamble and volatile investment as the Cold War progressed. By contrast, where nuclear weapons are involved the calculus is bluntly simple, not agonizingly complex, and the value of the investment is relatively stable. The enduring ability of the most basic nuclear weapons quickly to annihilate military forces or inflict catastrophic damage on society, even in the teeth of massive deployments of technologically sophisticated defenses, remains unchallenged.[73] Until this changes, nuclear weapons will be an economical hedge against obsolescence for states seeking an affordable way to fulfill the requirements of strategies for dissuading highly capable adversaries.

Nuclear forces also represent a prudent security investment because they offer insurance against dramatic shifts in threat perceptions, a point to which I return when discussing the post–Cold War world in the concluding chapter. Investment in conventional forces deployed specifically to defend against aggression by a land-based military power, for example, may be of little value in the event political developments shift one's attention to the threat posed by a naval adversary. By contrast, changes in the adversary's identity are much less likely to diminish the security value of a state's investment in nuclear weapons. Given the requisite delivery capability, states relying on nuclear forces can deal with dramatic shifts in threat perceptions simply by retargeting. China's experience in this respect is illustrative. Beijing originally developed its nuclear weapons to threaten retaliation against American forces and U.S. allies in East Asia. Shortly after it began to deploy the arsenal,

---

[73]This argument is rendered obsolete if a leakproof defense against nuclear weapons is devised. Such a strategically revolutionary system would have to provide confidence in its ability to cope both with traditional delivery methods (missiles and planes) as well as creative delivery methods (smuggling, hidden assembly and deployment). Current technologies offer little hope for addressing either. On the destructiveness of the small numbers of nuclear weapons that might penetrate imperfect defenses, see Fetter, "Ballistic Missiles and Weapons of Mass Destruction." See Miller and Van Evera, *The Star Wars Controversy.* For debate about the effectiveness of the Patriot theater ballistic missile defense as reflected in the Persian Gulf War, see Theodore A. Postol, "Lessons of the Gulf War Experience with Patriot"; Robert M. Stein, "Patriot Experience in the Gulf War" [re: Postol]; Theodore A. Postol, "Correspondence: The Author Replies" [re: Stein]. In the late 1990s, advocates of ballistic missile defenses (both national and theater missile defenses) asserted the improving effectiveness of defensive systems, but only against very limited attacks, or isolated accidental launches.

however, Beijing shifted its attention from the air and naval threat the United States represented to the ground and air threat the Soviets represented. The enemy had changed (as it would again after the Cold War) but with simple retargeting, the usefulness of the nuclear investment was preserved.

Finally, one can also identify links between geographic and manpower constraints and the economic attractiveness of nuclear deterrence. Geographic considerations—such as room for maneuver, available lines of communication, choke points, climate, and location of national assets—affect the feasibility of strategies relying on the deployment and possible use of conventional forces for defensive or deterrent purposes. States without the territory necessary to trade space for time, with few natural obstacles to impede or channel an aggressor's attack, or whose key economic centers are few in number or closely concentrated face daunting challenges in devising strategies relying on conventional forces. Although these challenges may be surmountable, the effort will require a diversion of national resources that returns one to the sorts of financial concerns already addressed. By contrast, the geographic constraints on the usefulness of nuclear weapons are looser. At least with regard to maintaining a punitive retaliatory capability as part of a deterrent strategy, ingenuity with regard to deployment and doctrine can offset problems relating to size and terrain. As will be seen quite clearly in the Chinese case, even without resorting to the expensive option of highly survivable, sea-based deployment, states can confront prospective adversaries with the fear of devastating retaliation by land-based nuclear forces through combinations of mobility and deception that weaken an aggressor's confidence in the effectiveness of preemption. A geographically constrained state can also proclaim an explicit launch-under-warning or launch-under-attack doctrine. But it does not need to do this. Indeed, even if it espouses a no-first-use policy (as did the Chinese), a prospective aggressor must confront the concern that the timing for the use of nuclear weapons will ultimately be the victim's prerogative in an anarchic world, previously espoused doctrine notwithstanding.

Manpower considerations also add to the attractiveness, including the economic attractiveness, of nuclear deterrence. Quantity and quality of available personnel both affect the military effectiveness of alternative strategies for reasons suggested in the discussion of the difficulties of conventional deterrence. To fulfill the personnel requirements of strategies relying on increasingly sophisticated conventional forces for defense, rather than deterrence, may be difficult and expensive. The available pool of recruits must be large enough and skilled enough to

support the deployment of the number and types of units a[c
dealing with the prospective adversary. Some of the manpo[
lems that may arise (and indeed did arise for the three secon[
powers this book examines) include: a small or aging populatio[
to the adversary, a poorly educated population, political const[_____
conscripting as well as economic constraints on recruiting those who
are qualified but would otherwise opt for more appealing civilian employment. Managing a nuclear deterrent force, while certainly requiring
skilled personnel, is simply less likely than the conventional alternatives to bump up against limits set by the size and age distribution of
the available pool of recruits.

Because nuclear weapons introduce an unavoidable risk of catastrophic
escalation, relying on them for deterrence provides a robust solution to
what has historically been a central task of foreign policy, dissuading
aggression against a state's vital interests. Moreover, against foes of
comparable or even much greater capability, they do so at a lower cost
than would be incurred relying on conventional forces. Nuclear weapons also promise a robust and affordable alternative to potentially unreliable and politically unseemly dependence on a powerful ally. In large
measure for these reasons, during the Cold War China, Britain, and
France made nuclear deterrence the keystone of their national security
policies. As subsequent chapters detail, proudly nationalist leaders in
Beijing, London, and Paris worried that they might be excluded from
enjoying the security supplied by a superpower patron's nuclear deterrent. The economic benefits of a free ride notwithstanding, military-
strategic rationality constrained them to hedge against the potentially
disastrous consequences of abandonment. To this end, each sought an
independent national nuclear capability, the only military capability
that offered these outgunned states much prospect of self-reliantly dissuading threats from a superpower adversary. Shouldering the burden of
developing and deploying their own deterrents followed from the fear
that in their moment of greatest need, security provided by a superpower ally's nuclear umbrella could in practice turn out to be the patron's private good, regardless of prior peacetime pledges of extended deterrence. The following chapters on China, Britain, and France examine
the combination of military, political, and economic considerations
that shaped relations between each of these three states and their superpower allies, their decisions to develop independent nuclear arsenals,
the nature of their deterrent strategies, and the types of weapons they
procured.

APPENDIX

Incomplete Information and the Effectiveness of the Improbable

Deterrence based on the threat of uncontrollable escalation depends on the fear of events that are both horrifying and improbable. To work, however, the prospective aggressor must believe that the clearly unacceptable outcome of absorbing a massive retaliatory strike is possible—the probability of uncontrollable escalation cannot be zero. What probability must an aggressor assign the feared outcome in order to be deterred? Some insight can be obtained by considering a simple expected utility model.[74] It suggests why nuclear deterrence based on an improbable escalatory process may be effective even though a rational actor in control of his forces cannot credibly threaten massive retaliation.[75] It also suggests why nuclear deterrence is a more robust strategy of dissuasion than either conventional deterrence or defense. Such a calculation simply highlights the consequences of incomplete information given the clearly understood magnitude of the destruction a state with survivable second-strike forces can always inflict on its adversary.

In deciding whether or not to challenge a state's vital interests, the prospective aggressor must consider not only the utility of prevailing but also the likelihood of the victim retaliating as threatened and the costs of absorbing that retaliation.[76] What difference do nuclear weapons make for the relation between the utilities assigned to the possible outcomes and the probabilities of response that would be sufficient to dissuade?[77] Given the notion of nuclear deterrence used here, let

[74]An alternative expected utility model is presented by Bueno de Mesquita and Riker, "An Assessment of the Merits of Selective Nuclear Proliferation," pp. 295–96. Their model does not, however, hinge on the concept set forth here of the victim as an unsafe actor.

[75]Cf. Berkowitz, "Proliferation, Deterrence, and the Likelihood of Nuclear War."

[76]The meaning of attack may of course vary. Different sorts of coercive measures would be associated with different expected utility calculations. In addition, this reasoning only sets forth the conditions for dissuading attack by a motivated adversary. States may choose not to attack because they simply have no interest in doing so, regardless of the existence or absence of specific threats. To use Patrick Morgan's terminology, this exercise examines the requirements of immediate deterrence rather than general deterrence. See Morgan, *Deterrence*, pp. 40–42.

[77]This of course assumes that the prospective *aggressor's* decision to initiate the confrontation is a deliberate (i.e., rational) choice. If it is not, no strategy can affect his behavior.

Q = utility of the status quo

W = utility of attacking and not suffering punishment (always positive)

D = disutility of attacking and suffering a threatened punishment (always negative)

p = probability that the victim is a "safe" actor (i.e., rational and in control, will not inflict punishment)

1−p = probability that the victim is an "unsafe" actor (i.e., will inflict punishment as a consequence of an accident or an irrational act)

For a state to attack, the expected utility of attacking, $pW + (1–p)(D)$, must be greater than or equal to the expected utility of not attacking (to simplify matters assumed to mean continuation of the status quo).

$$pW + (1–p)D \geq Q$$
$$pW + D–pD \geq Q$$
$$p(W–D) + D \geq Q$$
$$p(W–D) \geq Q–D$$
$$p \geq (Q–D)/(W–D)$$

This means that if $p \geq (Q–D)/(W–D)$ then the adversary is not dissuaded; he can rationally decide to attack; if $p < (Q–D)/(W–D)$, then the adversary is dissuaded; he cannot rationally decide to attack.

How do nuclear weapons affect this probability? Their effect will be highlighted by letting k represent a ratio comparing the magnitude of the payoff from attacking and absorbing the punishment imposed by an unsafe actor $(Q–D)$ and the magnitude of the payoff from attacking and not suffering retaliation $(W–Q)$.

$$k = (Q–D)/(W–Q)$$
$$D = Q(1+k) – kW$$

Substituting in the previous inequality

$$p \geq (Q–D)/(W–D)$$
$$p \geq \{Q – [Q(1+k) – kW]\}/\{W – [Q(1+k) – kW]\}$$
$$p \geq (Q–Q–kQ+kW)/(W–Q–kQ+kW)$$
$$p \geq (kW–kQ)/[W–Q+k(W–Q)]$$
$$p \geq k(W–Q)/(1+k)(W–Q)$$
$$p \geq k/(k+1)$$

This means that as k grows larger, p approaches one. Where nuclear weapons are the threatened means of retaliation, k is likely to be large. Indeed, the difference between the payoffs to continuing the status quo and absorbing a devastating nuclear retaliatory strike $(Q–D)$ is likely to be much larger than the difference between the payoffs to continuing

the status quo and prevailing unharmed (W–Q). This would seem especially true in the sorts of dyads considered in this book. For a superpower, while the gains to be had in prevailing over a lesser power are
smaller than those to be had in prevailing over a superpower adversary,
the potential for devastating losses inflicted by either through nuclear
retaliation may be practically, though not technically, indistinguishable.

If the difference between the utility of the status quo and the disutility of suffering punishment is 10 times the magnitude of the difference
between the utility of prevailing unharmed and the status quo (not an
implausible, probably a conservative assumption about the disutility
actors would assign to absorbing a massive nuclear strike) then, $k = 10$.
Under such circumstances $p \geq 10/11$; to attack, the prospective aggressor must assign a probability of better than 90 percent to the likelihood
that the victim is a completely safe actor. Such a high level of certainty
about one's judgment concerning an adversary's actions in unprecedented circumstances is difficult to imagine. If the prospective aggressor
believes there is even a 10 percent chance that the victim may be an unsafe actor he will be dissuaded. More important, it is also difficult to believe that the magnitude of the disutility of absorbing a massive retaliatory nuclear strike would be seen as only ten times that of the utility of
prevailing unpunished. If, as seems more plausible, k is much larger, the
viability of deterrence based on the risk of uncontrolled escalation is
even more apparent. If $k = 100$, then $p \geq 100/101$ and the prospective aggressor would have to feel more than 99 percent sure of success; he
would have to believe there was less than a 1 percent chance the victim
was an unsafe actor. If $k = 1,000$, that chance must be less than .1 percent.[78]

Compare this sort of calculation with those that would model attempts at dissuasion by relying on conventional forces, whether as part
of a defensive or a deterrent strategy. Two points should be noted. First,
conventional deterrent and defensive threats can be rationally executed.
A prospective aggressor is concerned not with the probability that the
victim is an "unsafe actor" but only whether he is resolute or not. Second, in a conventional world dissuasion is more difficult because of the
smaller difference in magnitude between the utility of prevailing unpunished and the disutility of absorbing punishment (here meaning ei-

---

[78]This line of reasoning, and the significance of the nuclear revolution, is supported also by evidence from research on prospect theory suggesting that "losses
hurt more than gains gratify." See Jervis, *The Meaning of the Nuclear Revolution*,
pp. 169–70, 171.

ther pain inflicted by conventional deterrent forces or the battlefield losses of encountering an impenetrable defense).

In a conventional world it is at least plausible for actors to believe the gains from prevailing unpunished and the losses from absorbing punishment are of a similar magnitude. Thus, if the prospective aggressor judges them equal, $k = 1$ and he can rationally attack if $p \geq \frac{1}{2}$. He need only believe there is less than a 50 percent chance the victim will respond as threatened. If the prospective aggressor is more worried about the punishment that could be inflicted on him, for example believing that the magnitude of the punishment he would absorb is twice that of the benefits from prevailing unpunished, then $k = 2$ and he can rationally attack if $p \geq 2/3$. Dissuasion may be a little easier than in the first case, but the aggressor need only believe there is a less than a one in three chance the victim will respond as threatened for dissuasion to fail. If, on the other hand, the prospective aggressor is relatively unconcerned about the magnitude of the punishment he might absorb, for example believing it to be only half that of the benefit of prevailing unpunished, then $k = \frac{1}{2}$ and he can rationally attack if $p \geq 1/3$. Under such circumstances, dissuasion fails unless the prospective aggressor believes it is quite likely (better than 66 percent chance) that the victim will respond as threatened. Despite incomplete information, where only conventional forces are involved even high probability threats may not suffice.

3

China: Strategic Choices

China's determination to develop nuclear weapons followed
from two beliefs: first, that its alliance with the Soviet Union did not provide adequate security; and second, that a self-reliant strategy of dissuasion by nuclear deterrence would better serve China's national interest than the alternatives of dissuasion by conventional deterrence or dissuasion by conventional defense.[1] Explaining Beijing's decision, then, entails answering two questions: Why did the Chinese lack confidence in the practical value of the Sino-Soviet alliance? Having decided on the importance of self-help, why did the Chinese choose nuclear deterrence over the conventional deterrent and defensive alternatives?

ALLIANCE POLITICS AND THE SELF-HELP IMPERATIVE

The Sino-Soviet treaty of alliance signed in February 1950 is easily understood as China's response to the constraint of bipolarity in the post–World War II international system. As balance-of-power theory would lead one to expect, given the vast capabilities at the disposal of the hostile United States and given the limited resources a war-ravaged, poverty-stricken China could muster in response, Beijing nurtured its only viable means for countering a threat from this superpower, alliance with

[1]This analysis omits treatment of China's strategic interests that may go beyond dissuasion. During the period under discussion, China's principal, though not sole, foreign policy goal was to ensure the political and territorial integrity of the mainland's newly founded revolutionary regime. A viable national security policy had to deal with this problem before addressing others. To the extent Beijing had an interest in expanding its de facto borders (especially by resolving territorial disputes with its regional neighbors) and an interest in assisting communist revolutionaries in the developing world, investment in nuclear forces actually diverted funds that might have been employed to enhance China's conventional power-projection capabilities. Not surprisingly, by the 1980s, *after* China was confident it had satisfied the requirements of its dissuasive strategy, the regime more aggressively began to pursue conventional forces that would support Chinese claims in various territorial disputes with its neighbors.

the armed might of the other. The treaty served as a hedge against the possibility that the United States, despite issuing a White Paper that seemed to signal American disengagement, had not yet reconciled itself to the defeat of Chiang Kai-shek's Kuomintang (KMT), the Chinese Communist Party's (CCP's) bitter rival in China's Civil War that had received Washington's generous support for years. China's leaders worried about three fronts along which the U.S.-led anticommunist Western camp might still pose a serious security threat—the northeast adjacent to Korea, the east coast across from Taiwan and small offshore islands held by the defeated KMT forces, and the southeast bordering Vietnam. Events unfolding after the Sino-Soviet treaty was concluded seemed to confirm Beijing's fears about the dangers the Western camp posed. With the outbreak of the Korean War in June 1950, the U.S. Seventh Fleet positioned itself in the Taiwan Straits and, after initial setbacks, U.S. General Douglas MacArthur's forces advanced toward the Yalu River and Chinese territory. Meanwhile France was engaged in military actions against Chinese-supported insurgents in Indochina. Hostile forces active along the three fronts crystallized Beijing's perception that the United States and its Western allies posed a long-term, serious military threat to China's national interests requiring an alliance with the Soviet Union.[2] How serious was the threat China faced and how useful was its alliance with the Soviets?

Threats and Allies

Because the Chinese Communist Party had demonstrated its ability to organize a protracted war of popular resistance against Japan during the 1930s and 1940s, when its leaders founded the People's Republic of China in 1949 they could be fairly confident that even the American adversary, with vast military superiority, would be unlikely to attempt to

---

[2]On China's concern about the three-front threat, see Shu Guang Zhang, *Mao's Military Romanticism*, pp. 6, 56, 81; Chen Jian, *China's Road to the Korean War*, pp. 93, 94–96. Chen notes that in late 1949 China did not expect the U.S. challenge to emerge immediately in the aftermath of the CCP's victory in the Chinese Civil War, but that eventually a clash between revolutionary China and the "imperialists" would occur. To prepare for the challenge on any of the three fronts, China began to restructure the PLA to make it easier to shift forces to whichever of the three fronts faced the strongest challenge (ibid., pp. 94–96). Zhang argues that China's decision, after hesitation noted below, to intervene in Korea may partly have reflected the CCP's belief that it was the most advantageous of the three fronts in which to face off against the United States (Zhang, *Mao's Military Romanticism*, pp. 6, 56). For a review of the Chinese perception of the threat the U.S. posed in the early 1950s, see Yufan Hao and Zhihai Zhai, "China's Decision to Enter the Korean War." See also Thomas J. Christensen, "Threats, Assurances, and the Last Chance for Peace."

invade and occupy the mainland.[3] Nevertheless, in its first decade of existence the young regime believed the United States posed other plausible and quite serious security risks. In addition to the economic sanctions Washington imposed, the People's Republic of China (PRC) faced an array of dangerous military threats against which alone it could not respond effectively. U.S. power could be used directly or through allied proxies on the periphery of the PRC in ways jeopardizing its national security (e.g., U.S.-backed KMT raids launched from their redoubt on Taiwan could threaten the urban centers of east and southeast China; renewed hostilities on the Korean peninsula could threaten the vital industrial base in Manchuria; and U.S. support for its ally France, engaged in fighting revolutionaries in Vietnam, raised the specter of a Korea-type situation along China's southeastern border). Perhaps most worrisome, President Eisenhower's coercive diplomacy during the closing months of the Korean conflict, as well as the 1954 and 1958 crises in the Taiwan Straits, compelled Beijing to face the possibility that the United States might actually resort to the option of employing nuclear weapons against China to realize American foreign policy goals. U.S. nuclear threats were manifest both in declaratory policy and in the deployment of nuclear capable forces to the East Asian theater.[4] Continuing American rhetoric about rolling back the postwar gains of communism and especially the U.S. decision to sign a security treaty with and to arm the CCP's rivals-in-exile on Taiwan who were dedicated to reversing the verdict of the Chinese Civil War further reinforced Beijing's threat perceptions.[5]

Lacking the ability to deal independently with the conventional power-projection capabilities of the United States and those it supported, or to counter its nuclear threats, Beijing's only realistic choice was to rely on the leverage it hoped an alliance with Moscow provided.[6]

[3]See Chen Jian, *China's Road to the Korean War*, pp. 94–96.

[4]See John W. Lewis and Litai Xue, *China Builds the Bomb*, p. 229; Chong-pin Lin, *China's Nuclear Weapons Strategy*, p. 77; Richard K. Betts, *Nuclear Blackmail and Nuclear Balance*, chs. 1, 2; Marc Trachtenberg, "'A Wasting Asset'"; Roger Dingman, "Atomic Diplomacy During the Korean War"; Rosemary J. Foot, "Nuclear Coercion and the Ending of the Korean Conflict."

[5]See Shu Guang Zhang, *Deterrence and Strategic Culture*; Lewis and Xue, *China Builds the Bomb*, pp. 28–29, 34, 35; also Yuanchao Li, "The Politics of Artillery Shelling." Chinese attempts at a conciliatory approach represented by the short-lived "spirit of Bandung" bore no fruit in terms of dealing with the U.S. threat. See Harvey W. Nelsen, *Power and Insecurity*, pp. 38–40.

[6]The security logic underpinning the Sino-Soviet Alliance was straightforwardly stated in a United States Central Intelligence Agency (CIA) analysis: "Continued US assistance to the Nationalist Government on Taiwan, the US-Japan Security Pact,

But if bipolarity dictated dependence on a powerful ally as the unfolding events in the 1950s suggested, the enduring international condition of anarchy left the Chinese leaders nervous about this arrangement. Specifically, although the existence of the United States as a common enemy established a sound basis for the Sino-Soviet alliance, the allies' national interests threatened by this unifying adversary differed in important ways. The principal concern of the Chinese was the threat U.S. forces in the Pacific posed to their territory along the three interconnected fronts stretching from Northeast to Southeast Asia. The principal concern of the Soviets was the strategic threat American power, particularly airpower, based mainly in Europe and the United States posed to *their* territory, most importantly the Russian heartland far from East Asia. Consequently, short of an unlikely American occupation of China, Washington's actions threatening the PRC would not fundamentally affect the most important Soviet interests. Beijing, therefore, could not be confident that Moscow would choose to face down the United States over Chinese interests in Asia, especially if this entailed risking escalation to a war unnecessarily jeopardizing the Soviet Union. Given the self-enforcing nature of agreements in the anarchic realm of international politics, and recognizing the danger that war in the nuclear age might entail, it was instead reasonable to conclude that during a Sino-American crisis Moscow would have strong incentives to renege on commitments if fulfilling them might prove disastrous, treaties and reassuring peacetime ideological rhetoric notwithstanding.

Even before a formal treaty of alliance was signed, Soviet behavior under Stalin had provided reason for China to worry about the possibility of abandonment. Mao's belief that Stalin had an exaggerated fear of war with the United States that limited his willingness to support the Chinese communists dated at least to the mid-1940s. At the end of World War II, Moscow had argued against the CCP aggressively prosecuting its military campaign against the KMT lest it trigger Western intervention in China that could escalate into a Soviet-American war.[7]

---

and the ever-present apprehension of US action against Communist China itself will tend to draw Communist China and the USSR together" ("Relations Between the Chinese Communist Regime and the USSR: Their Present Character and Probable Future Courses," CIA, Sept. 10, 1952, p. 4).

[7] The continuing flow of previously unreleased documents confirms the depth of the tensions between the Soviet and Chinese communists that actually began as early as the 1920s with disagreements over the best strategy for waging revolution in China. China's communist leaders were intimately familiar with the Soviet track record of bad, sometimes disastrous, advice to the CCP that was tailored to serve Soviet rather than Chinese interests. This history set the stage for Beijing's skepticism

When the Chinese communists ignored this advice and scored a surprisingly rapid victory on the mainland, Stalin nevertheless refused to provide backing for a Chinese assault on Taiwan in the summer of 1949.[8] And despite the conclusion of the Sino-Soviet Alliance in February 1950, these early disappointments were then followed by Stalin's troubling "reluctance to provide direct and immediate military assistance to the Chinese troops in Korea [that] raised Mao's suspicions on the reliability of the Soviet deterrent for China under the terms of the treaty [of alliance]."[9] Indeed, the actual terms of the mutual security pact were less than fully reassuring. After hard bargaining, the firmest commitment Zhou Enlai was able to extract from Stalin was that the Chinese could count on full Soviet support if a "state of war" was declared. Beijing recognized this legal technicality gave Moscow a pretext, if one was desired, to avoid entrapment in military clashes between its ally and the United States as long as the enemy refrained from declaring war.[10] And as the Korean conflict unfolded, Chinese concerns were reinforced when Stalin's initial response to the northward push of United Nations troops was to consider evacuating the Korean communists to northeast China where they could set up a government in exile. This approach suggested the Soviet Union's preference for sacrificing its comrades' interests if that was the only way to avoid a risky military clash with American forces.[11] That Stalin ultimately decided *Chinese* intervention offered a

---

about the wisdom of accepting Moscow's foreign policy advice after 1949. On Sino-Soviet disagreements about revolutionary strategy in the 1920s and 1930s, see Benjamin I. Schwartz, *Chinese Communism and the Rise of Mao*; Chalmers A. Johnson, *Peasant Nationalism and Communist Power*. For evidence of Stalin's reluctance to back the CCP in its final push to power after 1945, see Brian Murray, "Working Paper #12." For Mao Zedong's recounting of Soviet (i.e., mainly Stalin's) mistaken China policies, see Mao Zedong, "Tong Sulian Zhu Hua Dashi Youjin de Tan Hua," pp. 325–27; Mao, "Guanyu Guoji Xingshi de Jianghua Tigang," pp. 599–600. See also Zhang Shuguang, *Deterrence and Strategic Culture*, p. 19; Sergei N. Goncharov, John W. Lewis, and Litai Xue, *Uncertain Partners*, pp. 23, 25, 72, 77, 78.

[8]Stalin was clear about his fears of provoking the United States. Responding to Mao's request for military assistance that would facilitate the defeat of the KMT on Taiwan, Stalin said that while he would not rule it out, "[w]hat is most important is not to give Americans a pretext to intervene" ("Conversation Between Stalin and Mao, Moscow, 16 December 1949," p. 6).

[9]Goncharov, Lewis, and Xue, *Uncertain Partners*, p. 223; see also pp. 69, 208, 175; Zhang Shuguang, *Deterrence and Strategic Culture*, p. 98.

[10]Goncharov, Lewis, and Xue, *Uncertain Partners*, p. 118; see also pp. 69, 208, 175; Zhang Shuguang, *Deterrence and Strategic Culture*, p. 31.

[11]Zhang Shuguang, *Deterrence and Strategic Culture*, p. 95. For a classic early analysis of China's intervention that has stood the test of time (and the new evidence), see Allen Whiting, *China Crosses the Yalu*. Despite the raft of documents released since the 1980s, scholars continue to disagree about the Chinese and Soviet

way to salvage the situation in Korea, and subsequently provided just enough support to embolden Beijing to follow a course of action that Mao believed necessary for China's security, did little to offset festering concerns about Moscow's reliability.[12] On the contrary, as Chen Jian ar-

---

positions on the eve of Beijing's decision to intervene in Korea during October 1950. Chen Jian, drawing on Chinese documents, has argued that although Stalin offered assurances the Soviet Union would protect China's territory and supply military assistance, he refused to provide the expected aircover for the introduction of the Chinese People's Volunteers into the conflict and instead made vague commitments about *future* air support,. According to Chen Jian, China's leaders saw this as "nothing less than a betrayal at a time of real crisis" (Chen, *China's Road to the Korean War*, p. 200). Chen suggests that Beijing decided to intervene despite the risks because the CCP leaders saw vital national interests at stake (ibid., p. 203). Drawing on minutes kept by the Soviet interpreter, Dr. Nikolai T. Fedorenko, Mansourov argues instead that during a crucial meeting with Chinese Premier Zhou Enlai and General Lin Biao in Moscow on October 9–10, 1950, Stalin did pledge timely air cover for Chinese intervention. Alexander Mansourov hypothesizes that Zhou and Lin, who were reluctant about China's intervention, may not have informed Mao of Stalin's promise. Mansourov's documentary sources and his interpretation do confirm Stalin's hesitation about risking Soviet security once the military situation on the Korean peninsula deteriorated after the Inchon landing. But at the time of his meeting with Zhou and Lin, Stalin had come to see Chinese intervention as a better alternative than the disengagement on which he had apparently decided in late September (Mansourov, "Stalin, Mao, Kim, and China's Decision to Enter the Korean War, September 16–October 15, 1950," p. 103).

Is Mansourov's inference that Zhou and Lin sat on information about Stalin's promised support plausible? Although it seems unlikely that these Chinese leaders would have risked withholding such important intelligence from Mao, other archival evidence does confirm that Zhou and Lin were part of a cautious group in a divided CCP leadership that was not yet ready to endorse Mao's bold call to intervene on behalf of the Korean communist forces. Continuing division in the Chinese ranks at the time of the visit to Moscow may also explain why the Chinese and Russian archives have yielded two different telegrams from Mao to Stalin on the subject of China's plans for intervention. The Chinese version manifests Mao's bold risk-acceptance. The Russian version suggests a more risk-averse Mao. Shen Zhihua argues that both may be authentic, and that the Chinese version may have been deposited in the archives but never actually sent because Mao had not yet persuaded his more worried colleagues on the wisdom of intervention and was hoping that the more cautious telegram might induce Stalin to pledge sufficient military support to bring the others (especially Zhou and Lin) on board (Shen Zhihua, "The Discrepancy Between the Russian and Chinese Versions of Mao's 2 October 1950 Message to Stalin on Chinese Entry in the Korean War"). Zhou and Lin may have hoped to stack the decision-making deck in Beijing by withholding encouraging news from Stalin, as Mansourov suggests, but in the end Mao's views carried the day on this, as on most other important matters.

[12]China's leaders may have been especially miffed because the PRC had to pay the heaviest price for involvement in a war on their borders despite the fact that they had not been informed about Stalin's January 30, 1950 "green light" to Kim Il Sung to launch the attack that would provoke the conflict. A new version of a previously re-

gues, "Stalin's incomplete commitment made clear to Mao and the CCP leadership the limitations of the Sino-Soviet alliance." But because a weak, threatened China had no realistic alternative to cultivating Soviet support while attempting to counter the United States in Korea, Mao took whatever Stalin was prepared to deliver. Chen argues that Mao may have had "to swallow the fruit of Soviet 'betrayal'" but he "would never forgive it. A seed of the future Sino-Soviet split had thus been sowed in the process of China's intervention in the Korean War."[13]

Mao's doubts about the usefulness of the Sino-Soviet security treaty because of his Soviet ally's questionable resolve were not unreasonable. Indeed, perhaps most importantly they were shared by those whose thinking and policy choices the treaty was designed to influence. By the end of the war in Korea, the United States Central Intelligence Agency had grown skeptical of Soviet willingness to back the Chinese against American forces, concluding that under most circumstances in the Far East the Soviets would be wary of initiating "general war."[14] Thus, when assessing the likely Soviet response to possible American actions supporting France in Indochina the following year, even the use of nuclear weapons against Chinese targets, the CIA continued to argue that Moscow would provide only limited support. Rather than invoke the Sino-Soviet treaty and risk war with the United States, Moscow was expected to pressure its Chinese ally to negotiate a cease-fire.[15] Similarly

---

leased document from the Soviet archives recounting a meeting between Mao Zedong and Soviet Ambassador Pavel Yudin on March 31, 1956, includes a previously omitted section about the Korean War in which Mao complains both about not being consulted beforehand and about the mistaken judgment regarding the risks war entailed. Mao said, ". . . we were not consulted in a sufficient way. Concerning the Korean question, when I was in Moscow, there was no talk about conquering South Korea, but rather on strengthening North Korea significantly. But afterwards Kim Il Sung was in Moscow, where a certain agreement was reached about which nobody deemed it necessary to consult with me beforehand. It is noteworthy . . . that, in the Korean War a serious miscalculation took place regarding the possibility of the appearance of international forces on the side of South Korea" (Dieter Heinzig, "Stalin, Mao, Kim and Korean War Origins, 1950"). Although Mao may not have been consulted beforehand or informed immediately afterward, Chen Jian indicates that he probably gave tacit approval when Kim, at Stalin's suggestion, visited China. Chen suggests that Mao, too, may have thought that U.S. intervention in the region was unlikely in the winter of 1949–50, making it easier for him to accept the Stalin-Kim agreement (Chen Jian, *China's Road to the Korean War*, pp. 89–90).

[13]Chen Jian, *China's Road to the Korean War*, p. 204 (see also pp. 222–23).

[14]"Probable Effects on the Soviet Bloc of Certain Courses of Action Directed at the Internal and External Commerce of Communist China," CIA, Mar. 9, 1953, pp. 2, 16; "Probable Communist Reactions to Certain Possible UN/US Military Courses of Action with Respect to the Korean War," CIA, Apr. 8, 1953, p. 5.

[15]"Communist Reactions to Certain US Courses of Action with Respect to Indo-

during the first Taiwan Straits crisis the following winter, the CIA argued that as long as the existence of the People's Republic was not in danger, even large-scale clashes of Chinese and American forces would be unlikely to prompt the Soviets to risk war by invoking their treaty with Beijing.[16]

While the Chinese lacked a viable alternative to depending on the Sino-Soviet alliance for security against the presumed American threat, however, they prudently tried to cope with their nagging fear of abandonment. As suggested in the previous chapter, these efforts aimed at encouraging Moscow to focus on the importance of preserving its reputation for resolve in dealing with the United States, a consideration that established a link between the credibility of the deterrent Moscow extended to cover China's interests and the credibility of its primary deterrent designed to cover the Soviet Union's own interests. By adopting a deferential posture toward Moscow and by strongly emphasizing the dangers the common enemy posed, Beijing sought to highlight the Soviet self-interest in supplying security as a collective benefit all members of the socialist bloc, including China, could enjoy.

Deferential Behavior

Although the CCP had long insisted on independence for itself in the international communist movement and apparently supported it for others, until the late 1950s Beijing maintained its deference to the Soviet party's absolute leadership of the socialist bloc.[17] By establishing themselves as one of Moscow's most loyal allies, the Chinese increased the reputational price the Soviets would pay for abandonment even if China's intrinsic military value might be small. China's deference was both stylistic and substantive. When Mao announced his policy of "leaning to one side" (that is, siding with the Soviets in the Cold War) he effusively praised the Soviet Union and Josef Stalin, perhaps to compensate for the long record of strained interparty and interpersonal relations that might have stirred doubts about Chinese loyalty.[18] Deference required not just compromising Chinese pride, but at times more tangi-

---

china," CIA, June 15, 1954, pp. 5, 6; Ian Brodie, "CIA Papers Disclose Plot to Use Bomb on China."

[16]"Communist Reactions to Certain Possible US Courses of Action With Respect to the Islands off the Coast of China," CIA, Jan. 25, 1955, p. 3.

[17]Donald Zagoria, The Sino-Soviet Conflict, 1956–1961, chs. 1, 2, 4; Nelsen, Power and Insecurity, p. 11.

[18]See Zhang Shuguang, Deterrence and Strategic Culture, pp. 28–29. For a somewhat sensationalist account of the tense relations between Mao and the Soviet communist leaders, see Harrison E. Salisbury, The New Emperors.

ble compromises of Chinese autonomy. The latter were especially distasteful because ending infringements on national sovereignty had been touted as one of the major achievements of China's communist-led revolution.

Goncharov, Lewis, and Xue describe the extensiveness of the concessions a fiercely nationalist Mao had to grant the Soviets in order to secure their "support for China's confrontation with the United States and Japan."[19] China had to yield on its demand that the Soviets renounce the "unequal treaty" they had signed with the preceding Kuomintang (KMT) government.[20] And along with the 1950 Sino-Soviet Alliance, China had to ink a separate agreement that gave the Soviets special commercial rights in Xinjiang and Manchuria and restricted China's freedom to allow potential competitors of the Soviets to operate there. This "Additional Agreement" clearly carved out of Chinese territory a sphere of influence for Moscow, a policy so distasteful in light of China's century of humiliation following the Opium War, and so potentially embarrassing, that Mao insisted it be kept secret. Later Mao would tell Soviet emissaries that these deals were "'two bitter pills' that Stalin forced him to swallow" and "that 'only imperialists' would think of imposing such a deal on China."[21] In legal as well as commercial matters, the Soviets replicated the old imperialist practices by insisting on a secret protocol to accompany the 1950 treaty establishing the loathed principle of extraterritoriality: Soviet citizens accused of crimes in China would be dealt with by Soviet, not Chinese, courts.[22] Nevertheless, as long as the PRC believed it required Moscow's backing in recurrent crises with a hostile and powerful United States, it muted its disagreements with the Soviets and, however reluctantly, compromised its principled position on sovereign equality.[23]

[19]Quan Yanchi, *Mao Zedong yu Heluxiaofu* [Mao Zedong and Khrushchev], cited in Goncharov, Lewis, and Xue, *Uncertain Partners*, p. 80. See also Nelsen, *Power and Insecurity*, pp. 7, 11; Thomas J. Christensen, *Useful Adversaries*.

[20]Goncharov, Lewis, and Xue, *Uncertain Partners*, p. 50.

[21]Ibid., pp. 122,124. Goncharov, Lewis, and Xue note also that it seems Stalin slyly sought to manage his China policy to ensure a degree of Chinese dependence that induced their willingness to tolerate such distasteful concessions to Moscow. See also Mao, "Guanyu Guoji Xingshi de Jianghua Tigang," pp. 599–600.

[22]Goncharov, Lewis, and Xue, *Uncertain Partners*, pp. 125–26.

[23]See Mao's angry comments in Mao, "Tong Sulian Zhu Hua Dashi Youjin de Tan Hua," p. 331. A contemporary CIA analysis noted the link between the need for alliance solidarity to "ensure Chinese security from Western counteraction" and China's willingness "to subordinate, at least temporarily, those Chinese national interests which are incompatible with the interests of the USSR . . ." ("Relations Between the Chinese Communist Regime and the USSR: Their Present Character and

New Patron, Old Pattern. The extent to which the constraint of bipolarity rather than Sino-Soviet ideological affinity accounts for Beijing's acceptance of politically unpalatable compromises in the hope of enjoying the security only a superpower could provide, is revealed even more dramatically by the similar, if less pronounced, pattern of behavior that emerged in the late 1960s and late 1970s when China needed to cultivate American support. At the end of the 1960s, the world remained bipolar, but by 1969 the Soviet Union and the United States had switched roles in China's worldview. Beijing turned to Washington to cope with what was seen as the imminent danger posed by Moscow.[24] As relations with the Soviet Union had sharply deteriorated, Mao and his colleagues explored the possibilities for improving relations with the incoming Nixon administration in Washington.

Following armed clashes along the tense Sino-Soviet border in March 1969, Mao tasked a group of China's leading generals, the "four marshals," to undertake a comprehensive re-evaluation of the international situation and the threats to China.[25] In their July 1969 report, the marshals described the emergence of a new strategic context different from both early post–World War II bipolarity and pre–World War II multipolarity. In depicting a situation that western scholars would subsequently refer to as a strategic triangle, the report offered three major reasons it was becoming both possible and advisable to play the United

---

Probable Future Courses," CIA, Sept. 10, 1952, p. 4). After Stalin's death and the conclusion of the Korean armistice, the Chinese leaders gradually addressed the various affronts to their national honor upon which Stalin had insisted, but the enduring condition of bipolarity sharply constrained these efforts. Believing the United States posed a long-term serious threat to China, Mao committed himself to a bold program of military modernization. Because he believed that there was no alternative to relying "heavily on Soviet support" to accomplish this aim, he "would have to compromise China's sovereignty long enough to accomplish his plan ... but no longer than that" (Goncharov, Lewis, and Xue, *Uncertain Partners*, p. 201).

[24]As the official Chinese Communist Party organ, *People's Daily*, put it: "Burning with wild ambition to subjugate China ... the Soviet revisionists never cease brandishing nuclear weapons at the Chinese people. Particularly after the Chenbao Island incident in 1969 [when Chinese and Soviet troops fought a brief battle], they clamored that the Soviet Union possessed 'the world's most powerful nuclear warheads' which can hit 'most accurately' at 'anywhere in the world,' that Soviet troops equipped with nuclear missiles at lake Baikal and on the Sino-Soviet border were 'poised for battle ...'" ("*People's Daily* Article: 'Get Rid of Blind Belief in Nuclear Weapons'").

[25]See "Report by Four Chinese Marshals—Chen Yi, Ye Jianying, Xu Xiangqian, and Nie Rongzhen—to the Central Committee, 'A Preliminary Evaluation of the War Situation' (excerpt), 11 July 1969"; "Report by Four Chinese Marshals—Chen Yi, Ye Jianying, Nie Rongzhen, and Xu Xiangqian—to the CCP Central Committee, 'Our Views About the Current Situation' (excerpt), 17 Sept. 1969."

States off against the more dangerous Soviet threat: (1) the United States, the USSR, and the PRC were locked in struggle, but China could take advantage of the fact that the Soviets would not dare simultaneously confront enemies on two fronts; (2) President Nixon had made remarks suggesting he viewed China as a "potential threat" rather than a real threat; and (3) "[t]he Soviet revisionists have made China their main enemy, posing a more serious threat to our security than the U.S. imperialists."[26]

China still lacked the resources to discourage or frustrate a hostile Soviet superpower's most likely military options. Beijing could not be confident of its ability to dissuade Moscow by threatening retaliation with nuclear weapons since the PRC's arsenal did not yet hold at risk the most valued, key urban targets in the Russian heartland.[27] As had been the case when they faced the U.S. threat, the Chinese could be fairly certain that their ability to wage a People's War made a full scale superpower invasion and occupation unlikely. But vulnerability to other serious and more plausible military options—such as limited air strikes (conventional or nuclear), especially those aimed at China's nascent nuclear facilities, or even seizure of valuable territories adjacent to superior Soviet forces—remained a problem Beijing could not resolve

"Report by Four Chinese Marshals . . . 11 July 1969," pp. 166–67.

[27]Although it had tested its atomic and hydrogen bombs in 1964 and 1967 respectively, in 1968 Mao commented, "Our country, in a sense, is still a non-nuclear power. With this little nuclear weaponry, we cannot be counted as a nuclear country. If we are to fight a war, we must use conventional weapons" ("Conversation Between Mao Zedong and E. F. Hill, 28 November 1968," p. 159). In their September 1969 report, the four marshals stated "our nuclear weapons are still under development" ("Report by Four Chinese Marshals—Chen Yi, Ye Jianying, Nie Rongzhen, and Xu Xiangqian—to the CCP Central Committee, 'Our Views About the Current Situation' (excerpt), 17 September 1969," p. 170). Even in 1975, Mao was telling U.S. Secretary of State Henry Kissinger that compared with the United States, China's international significance remained small "[b]ecause you have atom bombs, and we don't" (William Burr, *The Kissinger Transcripts*, p. 390; see also Mao's belittling of China's nuclear capabilities in his November 12 meeting with Kissinger, p. 182). Although Mao frequently exaggerated his arguments for rhetorical effect, the very real limits on Chinese delivery capability are described in John W. Lewis and Hua Di, "China's Ballistic Missile Programs." Yet doubts about the survivability and penetrability of China's retaliatory forces notwithstanding, if the American experience with "decisive" nuclear superiority from the 1950s and early 1960s is a guide, even with a good chance at a successful first strike, Soviet leaders contemplating an attack on China would have had to worry mainly about what might go wrong as well as the "unconventional" ways in which the Chinese might have been able to deliver nuclear warheads against Soviet targets. For doubts about the value of U.S. nuclear superiority, see Richard Betts, *Nuclear Blackmail and Nuclear Balance*; also Fred Kaplan, *The Wizards of Armageddon*.

independently.[28] China's top military leaders warned that Moscow's intentions were clear and alarming, arguing that a "group of adventurers in the Soviet revisionist leadership want to . . . use missiles and tanks to launch a quick war against China and thoroughly destroy China, so that 'mortal danger' for them will be removed."[29] By late summer 1969 Beijing concluded that the Soviet Union intended to attack China and that it had become imperative to figure out how to cope with this contingency. Recognizing the limited effectiveness of China's own military capabilities, both its regular forces and vast militia, the four marshals emphasized in their report to Mao the importance of playing the American card.[30]

Thus circumstances once again constrained China, as a second-ranking power in a bipolar world, to cultivate the support of a powerful military patron. Despite the strident ideological tone of China's radical domestic politics during the late 1960s, beginning in 1969 Beijing turned to the "capitalist-imperialist" United States in the hopes of free-riding on the benefits of its anti-Soviet deterrent.[31] It would be almost two years before the dramatic breakthrough in Sino-American relations, but after the summer of 1969 parallel concerns were already resulting in a tacit new alignment.[32] And although President Nixon's public opening

[28]See Harlan Jencks, "People's War Under Modern Conditions," pp. 307–8, 309, 316.

[29]"Report by Four Chinese Marshals—Chen Yi, Ye Jianying, Nie Rongzhen, and Xu Xiangqian—to the CCP Central Committee, 'Our Views About the Current Situation' (excerpt), 17 September 1969," p. 170.

[30]Ibid. In a supplement to this report, Marshal Chen Yi emphasized the importance of a breakthrough in Sino-American relations and urged steps more dramatic than continuing the intermittent, long-standing, unproductive talks in Warsaw. In ways that foreshadowed the maneuvers on the U.S. side in 1971, in 1969 Chen boldly (and in Cultural Revolutionary China, dangerously) recommended a high-level Sino-American summit: "It is necessary for us to utilize the contradiction between the United States and the Soviet Union in a strategic sense, and pursue a breakthrough in the Sino-American relations. Thus, we must adopt due measures about which I have some 'wild' ideas. First, when the meetings in Warsaw are resumed, we may take the initiative in proposing to hold Sino-American talks at the ministerial *or even higher levels.* . . . It is possible that if we do not take the initiative, the Americans may make such a suggestion. If that is the case, we should accept it" ("Further Thoughts by Marshal Chen Yi on Sino-American Relations," p. 171, emphasis added).

[31]Robert S. Wang, "China's Evolving Strategic Doctrine," pp. 1043–44; Lowell Dittmer, "The Strategic Triangle," pp. 485–515.

[32]As the report of the four marshals put it: "Several times the U.S. imperialists have expressed a willingness to improve relations with China, which reached a peak with Nixon's recent [July 1969] trip to Asia. The Soviet revisionists are scared by the prospect that we might ally ourselves with the U.S. imperialists to confront them.

to the PRC in 1971 would not result in a formal alliance, Beijing expected to exploit a link between its security and the U.S. determination to check Soviet aggressiveness. The recently declassified transcripts of Henry Kissinger's meetings with the Chinese leaders that William Burr has collected clearly reveal the remarkable extent to which Beijing's initial hopes for a security entente were fulfilled.[33]

But because the tangible security benefits from this partnership were greater for China than for the United States, Beijing also had to worry about the risks Washington would actually run on its behalf in any showdown with a nuclear-armed Soviet Union. In light of this concern, China's leaders, as in the 1950s, sought to deal with their fear of exclusion from the benefit of a superpower-supplied security umbrella in part by deferring to their new patron on what they viewed as a sensitive nationalist issue, in this case U.S. support for the rival KMT regime on Taiwan. Beijing repeatedly stated that reunification was one of the PRC's principal foreign policy goals, and that it was a matter on which they would "brook no interference," one on which there could be no compromise. Yet from the time it decided to cultivate the American connection, Beijing tolerated what it claimed was blatant U.S. interference in this aspect of China's internal affairs. The commentary from Marshal Chen Yi in September 1969 on the strategic imperative of a breakthrough in Sino-American relations is revealing: "... a Sino-American meeting at higher levels holds strategic significance. We

---

... The Soviet revisionists' fears about possible Sino-American unity makes it more difficult for them to launch an all-out attack on China" ("Report by Four Chinese Marshals—Chen Yi, Ye Jianying, Nie Rongzhen, and Xu Xiangqian—to the CCP Central Committee, 'Our Views About the Current Situation' (excerpt), 17 September 1969," p. 170).

[33]For examples of Kissinger's pledges of U.S. support, see Burr, *The Kissinger Transcripts*, pp. 51, 69. The declassified transcripts record the extent to which Kissinger was cultivating a de facto alliance that contrasts with the public posture of greater even-handedness in the Sino-Soviet-American strategic triangle. At times his statements to the Chinese (including offers to share intelligence, preparation of plans for military assistance, and frank disclosures of his private discussions with Soviet leaders) and his memos to President Nixon came close to equating the strategic importance of the U.S. relationships with Western Europe and China (ibid., pp. 73, 112, 113, 136, 144, 171, 204). The most ambitious plans for Sino-American military cooperation raised during the Zhou Enlai–Kissinger meetings in November 1973 (including help improving China's command and control capabilities) apparently failed to materialize, though it is unclear whether the proposals for substantial military ties fell victim to internal debates among the seriously divided Chinese Communist Party leadership, or the diminished interest on both sides as the incentive of the Soviet threat briefly ebbed somewhat during the mid-1970s (ibid., pp. 204–6).

should not raise any prerequisite, which does not mean we have de-
parted from our previous stand on the Taiwan question. The Taiwan
question can be gradually solved by talks at higher levels."[34] Talks on
Taiwan would be a prominent feature of the new Sino-American relationship. But because it needed the security it hoped the U.S. policy of
anti-Soviet containment would provide, in the following years Beijing
repeatedly accommodated the American insistence on continued public
support for the KMT regime on Taiwan. China settled for the largely
symbolic fig leaves of rhetoric to disguise the substance of policy.[35]

The varying emphasis the Chinese placed on the Taiwan issue in its
relations with the United States further reflected the link between this
unpalatable compromise of nationalist principles and the felt need for
the security benefit American military might provided.[36] During the
mid-1970s, when the salience of the Soviet threat receded for a few
years, Beijing more assertively cited the Taiwan issue as the major obstacle that precluded the establishment of fully normal diplomatic relations with Washington. This also reflected the unhappiness of "Maoist
radicals" in the leadership with any compromise of ideological principles.[37] But despite the internal debate and public rhetoric condemning
U.S. inflexibility on Taiwan during the mid-1970s, in private talks with
President Ford and a U.S. Congressional delegation in 1975 both Mao

[34]"Further Thoughts by Marshal Chen Yi on Sino-American Relations," p. 171.

[35]In effect, China had to settle for private assurances from Kissinger, Nixon, and
Ford that the United States would eventually meet its demands on the Taiwan issue,
especially switching recognition from Taipei to Beijing, though for domestic political
reasons the Americans refused to make a public commitment. Kissinger frankly asserted in a memo to President Nixon that China had no strategic alternative to the
United States, and that he believed this interest ensured continuity in Sino-
American ties "even if it means [China's] bending the sacred 'one China' policy . . ."
(Burr, *The Kissinger Transcripts*, p. 116). In his March 2, 1973, memo Kissinger anticipates rewarding China's patience: "The Chinese have been farsighted and patient
on this question [Taiwan]. Their willingness to ease our predicament is now most
dramatically shown in their setting up a liaison office in Washington while we maintain diplomatic relations with the GRC [Government of the Republic of China]. On
the other hand, we have largely bought their public reasonableness with your own
private assurances—to normalize fully our relations by 1976 and to withdraw our
forces from Taiwan now that the Vietnam war is over" (ibid., p. 117).

[36]For a close examination and analysis of the interaction of domestic and international influences that shaped the dynamics of Sino-American cooperation over the
final two decades of the Cold War, see Robert S. Ross, *Negotiating Cooperation*.

[37]For recently declassified documentary evidence on the difficulties of maintain-
ing momentum in U.S.-China relations during the late Nixon and Ford years as the
Taiwan problem festered, see Burr, *The Kissinger Transcripts*, chs. 6 and 8. See also
Harry Harding, "The Domestic Politics of China's Global Posture," pp. 97–102.

and Deng downplayed this allegedly important issue and instead emphasized the fundamental significance of the Soviet threat.[38] When China again grew increasingly anxious about possible Soviet military action against the PRC in the late 1970s, especially as the PRC planned its punitive "pedagogical" war against Moscow's Vietnamese allies, Beijing softened its position, once more hoping to free ride on the deterrent effect of U.S. Cold War policy. After years of haggling over the Taiwan issue, at the end of 1978 full diplomatic normalization finally took place even though the United States would only agree to make ambiguous pledges (despite China's demands for firm commitments) regarding limits on its future support for the island, including arms sales to the KMT regime it was formally derecognizing. Within four months after normalization the U.S. Congress and Executive both reiterated American support for Taiwan (embodied in the Taiwan Relations Act), provoking strident rhetoric from Beijing. In the following years, China repeatedly expressed its unhappiness with the robustness of the unofficial ties the United States maintained with the authorities on Taiwan and especially with the Reagan administration's initially strong pro-Taiwan tilt.[39] Nevertheless, even in the Reagan years, China worked with the United States to prevent the disagreements over Taiwan from scuttling the essential strategic alignment against a powerful and potentially threatening USSR.[40] As long as it believed in the strategic necessity of a counterweight to Soviet pressure, China raised objections but was careful not to forfeit the security benefit they hoped their American connection supplied.

[38]See Robert S. Ross, "From Lin Biao to Deng Xiaoping," pp. 280, 276. A similar emphasis was also evident in comments by Chinese leaders meeting with another U.S. Congressional delegation in late 1976. See ibid., p. 287. For a view that sees the Chinese as sticking to its nationalist principles, see Nelsen, *Power and Insecurity*, pp. 101–2.

[39]As one critical Chinese analyst put it, "[A]lthough we have established strategic relations with the United States, our views are still divergent ... the United States has formulated the so-called 'Taiwan Relations Act' and violated the principle of the establishment of Sino-American diplomatic relations, and reneged on its commitment" (Li Dai, "Independence and China's External Relations," p. A4).

[40]See Ross, "From Lin Biao to Deng Xiaoping," p. 291; Nelsen, *Power and Insecurity*, p. 134. Although Ronald Reagan had been an advocate for reviving official relations with Taiwan during the 1980 presidential campaign, once in office President Reagan basically settled for the formula that he had inherited from his predecessor, ultimately agreeing to the August 17, 1982, Joint Communiqué that established the principle of restrictions on U.S. arms sales to Taiwan. The text of this and other joint communiqués on Sino-American relations are available online at http://www.qis.net/~chinalaw/prclaw4.htm. See also James Mann, *About Face*, ch. 6.

Emphasizing the Common Threat

As suggested in the preceding chapter, a junior partner in alliance with a superpower can also attempt to reduce the risk that its patron will fail to live up to its security commitments by emphasizing the severity of the threat the common adversary poses to all alliance members. Such efforts underscore the superpower's self-interest in avoiding even small losses in the international competition with its rival, especially the loss of a valued ally. While China had no practical alternative to depending on a powerful protector, this approach to fostering alliance solidarity was a prominent feature of Beijing's foreign policy.

During the 1950s China not only promoted socialist bloc unity, but also urged the Soviets to take a hard line against the U.S.-led "capitalist-imperialist" bloc. Beijing was disturbed by lukewarm Soviet support for the PRC in its continuing confrontation with the United States in the Taiwan Straits and more broadly by Khrushchev's shift to what appeared to be a new Soviet international strategy of peaceful coexistence.[41] In response, Mao tried to embolden the Soviet Union to stick with a hard-line policy and stand by its allies, emphasizing what he saw as necessarily rapacious American imperialism. Urging Moscow to lead and bloc members to follow, at the international conference of communist parties in November 1957 Mao made the case that the Soviet Union and its allies had a common interest in more aggressively resisting this mortal threat to the socialist camp.[42]

Growing Disillusionment

Mao may have hoped the payoff for sounding the alarm combined with his unflinching public support for Moscow's leadership would be more reliable Soviet backing on the Taiwan issue.[43] During his November

[41]Gordon H. Chang, *Friends and Enemies*, chs. 4 and 5; Zhang Shuguang, *Deterrence and Strategic Culture*, ch. 8.

[42]See Zagoria, *The Sino-Soviet Conflict*, ch. 4.

[43]In a meeting with Soviet Ambassador Pavel Yudin on the eve of the 1958 Taiwan Straits crisis, Mao noted China's self-restraint in the face of repeated Soviet mistakes in China and emphasized also China's efforts in 1956–57 to maintain the unity of the socialist camp during the upheavals in Poland and Hungary (Mao, "Tong Sulian Zhu Hua Dashi Youjin de Tan Hua," p. 327; see also Mao, "Guanyu Guoji Xingshi de Jianghua Tigang," p. 600). As mentioned above, Soviet willingness to back the Chinese on the Taiwan issue had been weak ever since the summer of 1949 when Stalin balked at providing military assistance to the CCP for its final operation of the Civil War. See Goncharov, Lewis, and Xue, *Uncertain Partners*, pp. 69, 208. A Taiwan Straits crisis in 1954–55 had also failed to elicit a firm Soviet commitment to stand with Beijing against the United States (which, as noted above, was aware of

1957 visit to Moscow, Mao had proclaimed that the newly demonstrated Soviet intercontinental ballistic missile (ICBM) capability heralded an era in which the "east wind prevailed over the west wind" and in which the socialist bloc need no longer be intimidated by American nuclear might. The time had come to exploit a shift in the correlation of forces and seize the initiative in the global competition with the enemies of socialism.[44] But if in October 1957 Mao was hopeful about the prospects for Soviet support, these hopes diminished as relations with Khrushchev soured during 1958. Indeed, Tom Christensen's research suggests that Mao's public posture in late 1957 notwithstanding, privately he was already growing pessimistic about the likely implications for China of a more potent Soviet nuclear deterrent. Although a nuclear deterrent based on rockets in the USSR might increase the security of the Soviet Union, it would further reduce the intrinsic military value of allies (even a major ally like the PRC) for Moscow. To the extent Soviet ICBMs facilitated greater strategic Soviet self-reliance, they reduced the costs of abandoning a militarily less useful China.[45] Khrushchev and his representatives were in fact sending signals that reinforced Mao's pessimistic interpretation, urging the Chinese to be cautious about provoking another confrontation with

---

Moscow's diffidence), disappointing the Chinese. See Zhang Shuguang, *Deterrence and Strategic Culture*, p. 195. See also "Implications for the Free World and the Communist Bloc of Growing Nuclear Capabilities," CIA, Feb. 3, 1959; "Sino-Soviet Relations," CIA, Aug. 9, 1960, p. 15.

[44]Mao's thinking on this score paralleled Western debates about the "stability/instability paradox" in a world of mutual nuclear deterrence: the likelihood that great stability at the level of general war (because of fear of a nuclear exchange) would result in great instability at the level of limited wars (because states safely assume no one would dare escalate). Critics of this argument noted the ever-present risk of escalation in any serious confrontation, and the way this risk would constrain competition even at lower rungs on the "ladder." Mao seemed to believe that Soviet nuclear capabilities after 1957 would so frighten the United States that it could no longer threaten China as it had earlier in the decade. Under the Soviet nuclear umbrella, China could afford to be more assertive. Khrushchev, by contrast, worried about the risk of escalation, and believed that ICBMs provided security because they facilitated deterrence based on threatening the possibility of early use. But this possibility meant that it would be too dangerous to confront the United States over anything less than vital interests. On Mao's and Khrushchev's differing perspectives, see Lewis and Xue, *China Builds the Bomb*, pp. 66–68. For a more general analysis of contrasting perspectives on the stability/instability paradox and the escalation dynamic, see Robert Jervis, *The Illogic of American Nuclear Strategy*. See also "Implications for the Free World and the Communist Bloc of Growing Nuclear Capabilities," CIA, Feb. 3, 1959; "Sino-Soviet Relations," CIA, Aug. 9, 1960, pp. 5, 8.

[45]Christensen, *Useful Adversaries*, ch. 6.

the United States over Taiwan, in which case Beijing might be on its own.[46]

Mao, then, may well have already been losing confidence in the Soviet security guarantee even before he renewed hostilities in the Taiwan Straits in August 1958, fomenting a crisis often cited as the event that produced his strong doubts about Moscow. If so, as Christensen argues, Mao may instead have engineered the 1958 crisis to generate a war scare that would mobilize the Chinese people in the Great Leap Forward, a movement that he expected would yield the resources needed for greater military self-reliance, especially nuclear weapons. Contrary to standard accounts of the 1958 Taiwan Straits Crisis that highlighted Mao's disappointment with the lack of Soviet support once the crisis began, and that saw China's fear of abandonment as a *result* of the crisis, Christensen identifies the fear of abandonment as a direct *cause* of the crisis. The still incomplete release of documents precludes a final choice between these interpretations. But currently available evidence about once obscure events in June and July 1958 is most consistent with the view that Mao's grave doubts about Soviet intentions and level of commitment predated the confrontation triggered in August by China's shelling of the KMT-held offshore islands of Jinmen (Quemoy) and Mazu (Matsu).[47]

In late Spring 1958, China's Defense Minister Peng Dehuai reported to Chairman Mao that Soviet military advisers had raised the idea of setting up a special long-wave radio transceiver in China to facilitate communications with the Pacific fleet. Mao's initial reaction was to insist that a sensitive installation of this sort on Chinese soil must clearly be owned by China. He therefore insisted that China provide most of the funding, though he did not oppose Soviet construction and technical

[46]See Zhang Shuguang, *Deterrence and Strategic Culture*, p. 254. CIA analysts also believed that the Soviets, given their small stakes in the immediate issues involved, were consistently counseling caution to discourage Chinese actions that might provoke "US intervention on such a scale as to call for overt Soviet military participation" ("Probable Chinese Communist and Soviet Intentions in the Taiwan Strait Area," CIA, Sept. 16, 1958, p. 2).

[47]John Lewis and Litai Xue provide an interpretation of events in the first half of 1958 that is also consistent with this argument about fraying Sino-Soviet solidarity prior to the Taiwan Straits Crisis (Lewis and Xue, *China Builds the Bomb*, pp. 61, 70). In addition to material on Sino-Soviet discussions about joint naval forces cited below, see documentary evidence contained in "The Emerging Disputes Between Beijing and Moscow." See also Lewis and Xue, *China Builds the Bomb*, pp. 63–64; Christensen, *Useful Adversaries*, pp. 208–11.

assistance.[48] Within the next month, however, Mao's concern with the issues of ownership and control intensified when Soviet Ambassador Pavel Yudin forwarded a proposal from Khrushchev for China and Russia to establish a joint submarine fleet, and for Premier Zhou Enlai and Peng Dehuai to come to Moscow to hold discussions about the idea. In a tense meeting with Yudin at which Mao responded to these Soviet proposals, the Chairman restated China's position: "First we need to clarify the policy: Are we going to run it with your help? Or will it only be jointly run and if not, then you won't help, in which case you are *forcing us* to run it jointly?"[49] Rather than seeking clarification, however, it seems that Mao had already decided on his own interpretation. As he told Yudin, the Soviets repeatedly insisted that everything in China be jointly run because the Soviets despised the Chinese people, lacked confidence in China's ability to manage modern industrial and military equipment, and worried that China could be a "second Tito" (i.e., politically unreliable).[50] After a long monologue detailing the history of problems in Sino-Soviet relations even before the PRC was founded, and emphasizing the Chinese Communists' alleged self-restraint despite Soviet arrogance, Mao told Yudin that China had decided to forgo Soviet assistance in building a nuclear submarine fleet since the conditions of cooperation would amount to "handing our entire coastline over to you." Instead, Mao argued for separate fleets that could cooperate in wartime under the terms of the Sino-Soviet alliance and supplementary agreements. But even the terms for such wartime cooperation, Mao insisted, had to respect national independence and be based upon absolute equality: Each fleet would only take orders from its home country, must have the right of access to the others' facilities, and must return home after the war is over.[51]

Mao's concerns reflected not so much the technical complications of running a multinational military operation, but rather nationalist sensitivity about China's dependent status in the alliance he believed the Soviet proposals would reinforce. Even though there was little prospect that China would soon have the ability to participate in wartime naval

[48]Mao, "Guanyu Sulian Qingqiu Zai Zhongguo Jianli Tezheng Changbo Wuxian Diantai Wenti," pp. 316–17.

[49]Mao, "Tong Sulian Zhu Hua Dashi Youjin de Tan Hua," p. 322, emphasis added; also, p. 332.

[50]The Chinese phrase Mao used to depict Soviet views of Chinese incompetence, *mao shou mao jiao* (literally cat's hands and cat's feet), means that one is clumsy in handling things (ibid., p. 323). Mao saw the 1958 military proposals as reprising Stalin's insistence on joint economic ventures in the early 1950s.

[51]Ibid., pp. 328, 330–31.

operations on an equal footing, Mao insisted any agreement China negotiated had to embody the principle of equality.[52] In the course of what
must have been a distinctly unpleasant session for the Soviet ambassador, Zhou Enlai and Peng Dehuai chimed in noting that the CCP Polit-
buro was unanimous in support of Mao's stance that the idea of joint
ownership of a submarine fleet and Soviet funding for long-wave radar
posts in China were proposals that could not possibly be justified to the
Chinese people or the rest of the world.[53]

The Soviets must have been shocked. To them, China's reaction
suggested either a worst-case interpretation of Moscow's motives, or a
lack of gratitude for a generous offer of military assistance.[54] Attempting
to limit the damage, Khrushchev quickly arranged to visit Beijing at the
end of July, at which time he tried to reassure Mao that these proposals
were only intended to strengthen the alliance and enhance China's security, not to herald a return to Stalinist-style Soviet domination.[55] Yet
Mao was not easily convinced. Unlike Soviet accounts of the meeting
that emphasize a clearing of the air, Mao's recollection of the visit focused on the strong disagreement expressed and its significance. In 1964
he told Anna Louise Strong

> . . . in 1958 the problem of naval bases occurred. That year, Khrush-
> chev came to Beijing. Why? the Soviet ambassador to China had al-
> ready discussed the question of naval bases with us and the talks broke
> down, Khrushchev had to come himself and clean up the mess. I said
> to him, "How about we give you China's entire coastline." He said,
> "Then what will you do?" I said, "I'll go to the mountains and fight a
> guerrilla war."[56]

Nor did Mao's interpretation of the episode mellow with time (though
his reference to Camp David suggests he may have lost track of the sequence of surrounding events). In his November 12, 1973, meeting with

[52]As Mao put it, "We can also go to your [country] even if we don't go, it has to be
done this way, because this is a question of equality" (ibid., p. 331).

[53]Ibid., p. 329

[54]Mao seems to have anticipated the stunned Soviet reaction, acknowledging
that they would be unhappy (nanguo) with the criticisms after all the help China had
been provided (ibid., p. 330).

[55]This characterization of Khrushchev's comments was offered by Mikhail
Suslov, who was responding to Deng Xiaoping's reiteration of China's resentment
about the 1958 proposals at a September 1960 meeting of communist party representatives. Suslov also asserted that Mao had accepted Khrushchev's explanation of benign generosity with the comment, "If it is so, then all the dark clouds have dispersed." See "The Short Version of the Negotiation Between CPSU and CCP Delegations (September 1960)" (Stenogram July 10, 1963).

[56]Mao Zedong, "Heluxiaofu de Rizi Buhao Guo," p. 515–16.

Henry Kissinger, he recalled:

> We [the Chinese and Soviets] fell out by 1959. We began to fall out in
> 1958 when they wanted to control China's seacoast and also China's
> naval ports. And during my discussions with them, with their Ambas-
> sador, I almost slammed the table, and I gave him hell. (laughter) And
> he reported to Moscow and Khrushchev came. At that time, he put
> forth the notion of a joint fleet, that is for the Soviet Union and China
> to form a joint naval fleet. That was the suggestion he raised. And at
> that time, he was quite arrogant because he had seen General Eisen-
> hower who was then President, and he attained the so-called "spirit of
> Camp David."[57]

The June–July dispute over military cooperation served as the back-
drop for the Taiwan Straits Crisis of August–September 1958. Although
Mao had already decided to put military pressure on the KMT-held
offshore islands of Jinmen and Mazu whenever the international tensions over U.S. military action in Lebanon subsided, he had not briefed
Khrushchev on these plans when the Soviet leader made his July 31 visit
to Beijing.[58] Most likely Mao anticipated that Khrushchev would object
to action that could provoke another dangerous crisis with the United
States at a time when Moscow was interested in putting relations with
Washington on a new footing, an interest that Beijing interpreted as
superpower collusion that could jeopardize Chinese interests.[59] Rather
than permit Khrushchev to complicate China's plans to reactivate the
Taiwan front, or to force a confrontation between allies over this issue
at the same time they were engaged in bitter wrangling over the Soviet
proposals for military cooperation, Mao and his colleagues decided not
to raise the matter. Instead, Beijing only informed Moscow of its plan to

[57]Burr, *The Kissinger Transcripts*, p. 197. Mao ignored the prior conversation
about the fleet, and seems to have confused the July 31, 1958, trip with Khrushchev's
October 1959 visit to Beijing that indeed followed the September 26–27, 1959, Camp
David Summit.

[58]For a summary of the careful planning and politically calculated timing of the
Chinese attacks on Jinmen and Mazu, see Christensen, *Useful Adversaries*, ch. 6.
See also Mao, "Guanyu Bawo Da Jinmen Shiji Gei Peng Dehuai, Huang Kecheng de
Xin," p. 26.

[59]One of the few detailed Chinese analyses of the period claims that Mao did not
tell Khrushchev about his plans during their July meeting because Mao knew the Soviet leader was worried that Chinese actions could ruin his plans for enhancing Soviet-American cooperation (Wei Shiyan, "Eluomihe Guanyu Taiwan Jushi tong Mao
Zedong Zhuxi Tanhua de Huiyi yu Shishi Bufu," p. 137). A decade later, during a
two-and-a-half-hour interview with a Tunisian journalist, Chinese Premier Zhou Enlai reportedly emphasized "US-USSR collusion" and "traced collusion back to
Khrushchev's 1958 refusal to reaffirm that an attack on China would be considered
an attack on the USSR" (FRUS, 1964–68, vol. 30, #252, Apr. 20, 1967).

initiate the bombardment of Jinmen and Mazu.through Soviet military advisers in China shortly before it began on August 23. The Soviets subsequently expressed outrage at what they saw as a failure to engage in timely consultation.[60] The resulting crisis required them to scramble and try to improvise a response that would maintain the credibility of the Sino-Soviet alliance without risking a potentially dangerous deterioration in Moscow's relations with Washington.

On September 4, 1958, Secretary of State John Foster Dulles responded to the Chinese shelling by strengthening the U.S. commitment to Chiang Kai-shek's KMT, invoking the January 1955 Congressional Resolution that called for American support if an attack on the offshore islands in the straits posed a threat to Taiwan.[61] The Soviets could see their worst fears being realized. On September 5 Khrushchev phoned the Soviet embassy in Beijing and asked it to find out whether the Chinese would meet with his foreign minister, Andrei Gromyko, to hear Moscow's assessment of the situation and to confer on the question of a letter to be sent to Eisenhower. Premier Zhou Enlai replied that China welcomed the visit and as preparation provided the Soviet embassy with Beijing's analysis of the situation including an explanation of China's behavior emphasizing that the bombardment was not part of an invasion plan but only an attempt to punish KMT troops and foil the United States' two-China policy. Most important, Zhou reassured the Soviets, "If it results in trouble, China itself will accept the consequences, and won't drag in the Soviets. Please pass this on to the CPSU center."[62] Separately, Mao claimed to be surprised that shelling alone had pro-

---

[60]At a meeting with Deng Xiaoping on July 13, 1963, Iurii Andropov, then head of the CC International Department (socialist countries) stated: "In 1958, the Chinese side did not inform us in a timely fashion about its intentions to carry out the shelling of the coastal islands in the Taiwan straits which was carried out soon after Com. N. S. Khrushchev left Beijing. According to the later admission of Com. Mao Zedong, during Com. N. S. Khrushchev's presence in Beijing the Chinese comrades had already decided on this operation and had prepared it, but you did not consider it necessary to inform the Soviet government about it ("Stenogram: Meeting of the Delegations of the Communist Party of the Soviet Union and the Chinese Communist Party, Moscow, 5–20 July 1963," July 13, 1963). Khrushchev, in short, was miffed not only by China's dangerous brinkmanship, but its decision to initiate and then manage the crisis independently, based on the PRC's own national interest, rather than taking its cues from the leader of the socialist bloc (Vladislav M. Zubok, "Khrushchev's Nuclear Promise to Beijing During the 1958 Crisis," p. 226).

[61]See "Memorandum from the Republic of China Country Director (Bennett) to the Deputy Assistant Secretary of State for East Asian and Pacific Affairs (Berger)," July 11, 1967.

[62]Zhou Enlai, *Zhou Enlai Nianpu*, vol. 2, p. 166; Wei, "Eluomihe Guanyu Taiwan Jushi tong Mao Zedong Zhuxi Tanhua de Huiyi yu Shishi Bufu," p. 137.

voked such a strong international reaction but at the same time adopted a relaxed, almost fatalistic view about where it all might lead.[63] If Mao, as Christensen suggests, was mainly interested in generating a war scare to mobilize the Chinese people in the Great Leap Forward but had no intention of actually initiating a war, his calmness may have reflected confidence that with his limited aim in mind the real risk of war was small and largely under his control.

When Gromyko arrived in Beijing on September 6 and met with Zhou at 2 P.M., the Soviet Foreign Minister acknowledged receipt of the reassuring information passed through the embassy the day before and stated that the CPSU center "completely endorses the Chinese comrades' views and methods."[64] The two sides then exchanged copies of the letter Khrushchev was prepared to send to Eisenhower and discussed China's plan to issue a statement accepting the U.S. offer from early August to resume Sino-American ambassadorial talks. Gromyko, who must have been greatly relieved, reportedly characterized this as an example of close coordination of the two allies' foreign policies. Later the same day, Gromyko met with Mao and restated Moscow's support for the position that Zhou had outlined, boasting that the letter Khrushchev was sending to Eisenhower would "bring the US to its senses."[65]

At first blush, the alliance seemed to have weathered its latest internal crisis. In reality, both sides came away from the experience more skeptical than ever about the value of their partnership. The Soviets were miffed and worried because China had acted as a loose cannon rather than a trustworthy ally closely coordinating policy on this dangerous matter. Moreover, the two days of reassuring conversation, it turns out, were punctuated by a disturbing footnote that apparently reawakened the Soviets' worst fears about their ally. At the evening banquet for Gromyko following the formal meetings on September 6, Mao alarmed his guest by raising a frightening scenario that included Soviet involvement in a war with the United States. In his memoirs Gromyko

[63]On Mao's expression of surprise at the reaction to the shelling, see Mao Zedong, "Zai Di Shiwuci Zuigao Guowu Huiyishang de Jianghua," p. 386. Mao's fatalism was manifest in his view that whether the crisis evolved into nuclear war was a matter out of China's hands, that if nuclear war occurs it occurs, that fearing it would only lead to paralysis, and that the militias being formed along with the Great Leap's People's Communes would in any case make China unconquerable and enable the people to reconstitute a post-nuclear government. See ibid., p. 390; see also pp. 394–95.

[64]Wei, "Eluomihe Guanyu Taiwan Jushi tong Mao Zedong Zhuxi Tanhua de Huiyi yu Shishi Bufu," p. 137.

[65]Ibid., p. 138.

recalled Mao suggesting that if the United States actually attacked China, even if it used nuclear weapons, the Soviets need not react immediately, but rather should wait for China to draw in the Americans, and then while China launched a surprise counterattack in a pincer maneuver, the Soviets could "give them everything [they've] got." Gromyko claimed that he bluntly told Mao that "[s]uch a proposal would not meet with a positive response from us."[66] If Gromyko's recollection is accurate, the exchanges on the evening of September 6 may well have undone much of the fence-mending during the preceding two days. Such an encounter would have simultaneously confirmed Soviet fears of Chinese recklessness that could entrap Moscow in unwanted dangerous confrontations with the United States and confirmed Chinese fears of Soviet diffidence and unreliability, despite Moscow's new intercontinental nuclear forces that Beijing believed gave the Soviets the wherewithal to behave more courageously.

Even without the alarming Gromyko-Mao interaction, the Chinese may well have found the extent of Soviet support during the crisis less than satisfactory. Given Mao's concerns about changing Soviet strategic interests and Khrushchev's desire to improve relations with the United States, the most accurate characterization may be that Soviet support met what by mid-1958 had become China's low expectations. From Beijing's perspective, the sequence of events during the crisis was revealing. Dulles upped the ante on September 4; an alarmed Khrushchev contacted China on September 5 seeking clarification about China's intentions *before* deciding on the message he would convey to Eisenhower; having received assurances about China's limited aims and willingness to defuse the crisis, Khrushchev then offered to back China and warn the Americans. The chronology suggested the Soviets were prepared to stand by their ally as long as the risks weren't too great.[67] At

[66]Andrei Gromyko, *Memoirs*, p. 252. Wei insists that no Chinese present at the meetings with Mao or the banquet recall that he ever asked for the Soviets to launch such a counterattack. Wei is especially critical of the *New York Times* account of Gromyko's text because it misinterpreted "everything you've got" as a reference to nuclear retaliation (Wei, "Eluomihe Guanyu Taiwan Jushi tong Mao Zedong Zhuxi Tanhua de Huiyi yu Shishi Bufu," pp. 135–36, 138).

[67]In a December 1959 report to the CPSU Central Committee covering his October 1959 trip to China, Mikhail Suslov also revealed the following evidence that suggests that the Soviets may have discounted the risks before publicly supporting the Chinese, though the relevance of this comment turns on the date of the intercepted document: "We [in Moscow] regarded it as our internationalist duty to come out decisively in support of the fraternal Chinese people, with whom our country is bound by alliance obligations. *According to secret documents that we had intercepted, it had become clear that the ruling circles in America were already psychologically*

least one Chinese insider's account of the deliberations, though acknowledging Beijing's failure to consult the Soviets beforehand, noted the timing of and conditions on Moscow's strongest backing:

> Khrushchev did not have any idea about our intentions in shelling Jinmen. Afraid of being involved in a world war, he sent Gromyko to Beijing to find out our plans on 6 September. During the Supreme State Conference, Chairman Mao and Premier Zhou met with Gromyko, informing him of our decisions and explaining that we did not intend to have a major war. *After receiving our message, Khrushchev wrote to Eisenhower*, asking the American government to be very cautious in the Taiwan Straits and *warning that the Soviet Union was ready to assist China* anytime *if China was invaded*.[68]

---

prepared to relinquish the offshore islands to the PRC. However, after precipitating an extreme situation in the vicinity of the offshore islands and making far-reaching statements, the Chinese comrades backed down at the critical moment. . . . It is obvious that in backing down, the Chinese comrades squandered things. The perception abroad was that they had caved in" (Mark Kramer, "Declassified Materials from CPSU Central Committee Plenums," emphasis added). Consistent with this Soviet interpretation, Mark Kramer argues that it was China rather than the Soviets who got nervous about the prospect of U.S. military action in September 1958, and that Khrushchev offered China the support due an ally ("The USSR Foreign Ministry's Appraisal of Sino-Soviet Relations on the Eve of the Split, September 1959," pp. 170–85). Yet the documentary evidence on which Kramer and others still indicates that Khrushchev's message to President Eisenhower that the Soviet Union would back China came on September 7, 1958, two days after Zhou Enlai had reassured Moscow about China's intentions and one day after Zhou Enlai announced that China was ready to resume ambassadorial talks with the United States, substantially reducing the risk of escalation.

To be fair, it should also be added that some of Mao's harshest rhetoric also surfaced after the turning point of September 6. See Zhang Shuguang, *Deterrence and Strategic Culture*, pp. 252, 253. Mao's actual cautiousness in the face of U.S. nuclear threats contrasts sharply with his public posture of indifference and defiance. Circumspect behavior could have reflected either Mao's fear of U.S. might or, as Christensen's work suggests, his limited aim of provoking a war scare for domestic consumption, but no war. See Li Yuanchao, "The Politics of Artillery Shelling"; Zhang Shuguang, *Deterrence and Strategic Culture*, ch. 8; cf. Christensen, *Useful Adversaries*, ch. 6. More broadly, Mao's behavior was consistent with his frequently repeated "paper tiger" thesis. Its basic argument (applied sometimes to "reactionaries," other times to nuclear weapons) is that one must respect the enemy tactically, but despise him strategically. In practice this called for refusing to be coerced into abandoning one's long-term goals, but remaining cautious in the means one chooses to confront a militarily superior adversary. See Mao Zedong, "Yiqie Fandongpai dou Shi Zhi Laohu," pp. 371–72.

[68]"Memoir, 'Inside Story of the Decision Making During the Shelling of Jinmen,'" p. 211 (emphasis added), pp. 208–15. Although it does not alter the interpretation, this recollection appears to misstate a couple of facts. As indicated above, the Soviets had been informed of China's position the day before Gromyko's visit and

Nuclear deterrence of the United States, though ostensibly more credible with the advent of Soviet ICBMs, was apparently a security benefit from which China might easily be excluded if Moscow disapproved of its ally's actions or if the adversary's attacks were limited in scope or kind. In the wake of the Taiwan Straits Crisis and the dispute over Sino-Soviet naval cooperation that preceded it, China's leaders stiffened their resolve to reduce their dependence on Moscow at the earliest opportunity. Beijing shifted its emphasis from attempts to reduce the *likelihood* of abandonment (in the hope it could enjoy security as if it were a collective good supplied by the superpower patron) to efforts designed to minimize the potentially dire *consequences* of abandonment and exclusion. The linchpin of this shift was the decision to accelerate the program to develop a nuclear arsenal as the means for independently providing themselves with what they concluded was the private good of national security.

New Patron, Old Pattern. Until Chinese nuclear forces adequate for credible deterrence could be deployed, however, Beijing's preference for greater strategic self-reliance would have to bend to the necessity of coping with the harsh reality of a bipolar world. Although China's weapons development program described in the next chapter successfully tested an atomic bomb in October 1964 and a hydrogen bomb in June 1967, until the late 1970s shortcomings in delivery capabilities limited China's ability to hold each superpower adversary's heartland at risk.[69] Consequently, after 1968 when Beijing began to perceive a serious threat from the Soviet rather than the American superpower, it adopted an approach strategically similar to that of the 1950s—hoping to free ride on the security provided by a superpower patron's deterrent, this time the U.S. strategic arsenal. To this end, China once again empha-

---

the letter was written before, though sent after, his September 6 meetings. Interviews I conducted with analysts in Beijing in 1991 suggest there is room for debate over exactly what the Chinese expected the Soviets to do during the crisis. Clearly, however, the crisis either raised or reinforced doubts in Beijing about Moscow's willingness to stick with an ally determined to retain its foreign policy independence. See Chang, *Friends and Enemies*, pp. 190–94; Nelsen, *Power and Insecurity*, pp. 41–45. See "Possible Changes in the Sino-Soviet Relationship," CIA, Oct. 25, 1973, pp. 3–4.

[69]See "Conversation Between Mao Zedong and E. F. Hill, 28 November 1968," p. 159. It is possible that moderately risk-averse United States and then Soviet leaders may have been leery of confronting China even when it "only" meant putting their allies, troops, and civilians in Asia at risk. But from China's perspective the dissuasiveness of such retaliatory strikes would be qualitatively different than those that threatened vital urban centers in the adversary's homeland.

sized the severity of the common threat both faced. Beginning in the early 1970s, but most prominently between 1979 and 1981, China encouraged the United States (and its allies) to stand up to an increasingly menacing Soviet Union.[70] In a fashion reminiscent of its criticisms of Moscow's interest in peaceful coexistence with the West during the mid 1950s, Beijing warned Washington against being deluded by the prospects of détente or being enticed by militarily insignificant, essentially symbolic arms control agreements with its deadly dangerous rival.[71] While publicly espousing ideologically more palatable rhetoric condemning all superpower hegemony, during the late Maoist years Beijing privately made the case for augmenting American military strength to counter the Soviets. And between 1979 and 1981 a less ideologically constrained post-Mao leadership explicitly called for a strong United Front (whose military teeth would be provided by the United States) against the Soviet threat.[72]

[70]For an unusually explicit Chinese view of the nuclear threat posed by Moscow beginning in 1969, see "People's Daily Article: 'Get Rid of Blind Belief in Nuclear Weapons.'"

[71]Chen Si, "Year Ender"; "France Reorientates Strategy Against Soviet Threat"; "French Public Vigilant Against Soviet 'Détente' Fraud." Such warnings about the mirage of détente were a frequent theme for the Chinese in their meetings with Kissinger, who tried to explain the U.S. rationale for the policy. For one of the more explicit comparisons with the appeasement policy of the 1930s, see Deng Xiaoping's comments to Kissinger suggesting that as in the 1930s, détente was a doomed effort to reduce the threat to the west and direct it eastward (i.e., this time against China) (Burr, The Kissinger Transcripts, p. 384).

[72]See Banning N. Garrett and Bonnie S. Glaser, War and Peace, pp. 57–58, 80. Transcripts of Kissinger's meetings with top Chinese leaders reveal the explicitness with which China was privately making the case in the early 1970s for a virtual united front against the Soviet Union, including closer cooperation between the United States and its European and Japanese allies. For a private posture that contrasted with China's public anti–U.S. imperialism rhetoric in the early 1970s, see Mao's comments during his February 17, 1973, meeting with Kissinger (Burr, The Kissinger Transcripts, pp. 88–89; see also pp. 112, 183–84). As part of this approach, the PRC encouraged the strengthening of NATO, a move that would, of course, limit the Soviets' ability to concentrate its resources against China on the eastern front. See John W. Lewis, "China's Military Doctrines and Force Posture," pp. 183–85; Ross, "From Lin Biao to Deng Xiaoping," pp. 290–91; Gerald Segal, "China's Strategic Posture and the Great-Power Triangle," p. 693; Ya Qi and Jirong Zhou, "Does the Soviet Union Have a Global Strategy," p. C4; Chen Si, "Year Ender." Alarmed at the prospect of spreading support for China's anti-Soviet position, the Central Committee of the Communist Party of the Soviet Union issued the following directive to its ambassadors in communist countries: ". . . Chinese policy, particularly its constant appeals to the USA, Japan, and the countries of Western Europe to unite with China in a 'broad international front' and its pressure on the NATO countries to increase their armaments, including nuclear missiles, is totally and fully directed against the

With conservatives in the United States during the late 1970s airing parallel concerns about an unfavorable balance of power with the USSR, Beijing's clarion call this time fell on receptive ears. Although Sino-American relations would cool in the 1980s, unlike the Sino-Soviet experience of the 1950s, this loosening of strategic ties did not result from disappointment with the superpower ally's provision of security benefits. On the contrary, by the mid-1980s Beijing perceived a United States more actively attempting to contain Soviet influence in the Asia Pacific region.[73] Instead, China's shift to a more independent foreign policy this time reflected a change in Beijing's view of its own security requirements. First, dealing with what they saw as a declining Soviet threat, even before Gorbachev, the Chinese felt less constrained to cultivate U.S. strategic support. During the early 1980s the Chinese began to assert a leveling off in Soviet capabilities that had peaked in the 1970s.[74] Second, the Reagan administration, for its own reasons, already embraced a hard-line anti-Soviet policy fueling a massive American military buildup. This allowed China, without any extra effort, to free-ride on the security U.S. policy toward the common enemy supplied. And third, by the mid-1980s the Chinese could at last be moderately confident of the dissuasive effect of their own small but potent nuclear arsenal, providing themselves with the private benefit of a national deterrent.

In sum, during the bipolar Cold War era China had cultivated a security relationship with each of the superpowers as the only viable exter-

---

socialist states. . . ." In "CPSU CC Directive to Soviet Ambassadors in Communist Countries, 4 March 1980," p. 203.

[73]As one Chinese analyst observed, the Reagan administration had "raised the slogan of 'returning to Asia' . . . [and] forsaken the 'troop transfer strategy' according to which troops are to be transferred from the Far East region to reinforce the European front in wartime. It has instead intensified its military deployment in the western Pacific, engaged in closer military cooperation with Japan and South Korea, and moved the defense line encircling the Soviet Union forward to the country's offshore waters so as to minimize Soviet influence over the Asia-Pacific region" (Wenqing Xie, "US-Soviet Military Contention in the Asia-Pacific Region," p. A2).

[74]See He Zong, "Changes and Development Trends in the International Situation," pp. A3–A5; Xing Shuguang, Li Yunhua, and Liu Yingna, "Soviet-US Balance of Power and Its Impact on the World Situation in the 1980s," pp. A3–A5. The Chinese also began to point out some of the limitations on Soviet power projection capabilities in the Far East owing to geography, the economic underdevelopment of Soviet Asia and the need to cope with awesome American forces in the region. See Wenqing Xie, "US-Soviet Military Contention in the Asia-Pacific Region," p. A5; Jia Bei, "Gorbachev's Policy Toward the Asian Pacific Region," pp. C8–14. In these circumstances the Chinese also felt less constrained to soft-pedal their objections to continued U.S. support of Taiwan. See Ross, "From Lin Biao to Deng Xiaoping," p. 293.

nal counterweight to a threat from the other that it could not parry on its own. Yet doubts about the dependability of needed support from a self-interested partner, however ample its capabilities, often constrained the Chinese to manage relations in ways it hoped would increase the likelihood a superpower patron would provide the strategic benefits Beijing sought. Although it was a necessary accommodation to the reality of China's relatively limited resources, cultivating superpower support required distasteful compromises. The preference to escape the need for such compromises, especially among China's strongly nationalist CCP leaders, and their concern about the ultimate unreliability of support from a self-interested ally in an anarchic international system provided strong incentives to achieve greater strategic independence. The result was China's effort to deploy its own nuclear arsenal, an effort that spanned nearly three decades and was finally bearing the expected fruit just as the Cold War was drawing to a close. What considerations guided China's selection of nuclear deterrence as the most appropriate alternative for achieving greater self-reliance?

SELECTING A SELF-RELIANT ALTERNATIVE

Despite Beijing's deferential behavior toward Moscow in the 1950s, and its promotion of an unyielding socialist bloc stand against American imperialism, from the outset China had harbored serious doubts about the viability of this approach. In a bipolar world, attempts to gain leverage over a superpower ally by artfully managing perceptions could not overcome the basic problem of China's small practical importance for Soviet security. Soviet foreign policy would be made with an eye first to dealing with the American superpower rival, even if a focus on this principal national interest jeopardized the interests of the allies.[75] Khrushchev's foreign policy turn in the mid-1950s, his emphasis on peaceful coexistence and competition with the capitalist world, in fact suggested a diminished willingness to confront the United States over anything less than vital Soviet interests. As noted above, Khrushchev's hesitant support for China when it faced U.S. coercion during the 1958 Taiwan Straits Crisis decisively confirmed China's festering con-

[75]See "Sino-Soviet Relations in the early 1980s," CIA, June 5, 1980, p. 3. See also Kenneth Waltz, *Theory of International Politics*, pp. 169–70. China's intrinsic military value to the Soviet Union was unclear even in conventional terms. In a world of mutual nuclear deterrence between the superpowers the questionable benefit for the Soviets of having China's conventional forces in the socialist camp had to be weighed against the cost of supporting China in confrontations with the United States that risked dangerous escalation.

cerns about the strength and dependability of Moscow's alliance commitment when Chinese interests were on the line.[76] Worried that an accumulating track record of disappointing Soviet behavior justified their fears of abandonment, the leaders in Beijing were increasingly determined to reduce their dependence on a potentially irresolute ally.

But why did China focus on deterrence, and nuclear deterrence in particular, as the key to a more self-reliant policy? China embraced a strategy of dissuasion by deterrence rather than defense because of the resource constraints it faced. China emphasized nuclear rather than conventional forces as the means for fulfilling the requirements of its deterrent strategy, despite its anti-nuclear public rhetoric, because the revolutionary implications of this new military technology suggested that such forces would provide for a more robust yet still affordable means for dissuading the vastly more powerful superpower foes China faced. Nuclear weapons would not provide an absolute guarantee of security. Nor would they be cheap or easy to develop and deploy. On the contrary, the effort would require extraordinary sacrifices and a diversion of resources from other civilian and military projects.[77] The sacrifices that China had to make, and the opportunity costs incurred to realize its nuclear ambitions, were much greater than those required in advanced industrial states like Britain and France. Nevertheless, China's leaders decided that the security dividend from this burdensome effort would far exceed the security dividend from comparably burdensome investments in conventional forces. As noted in the book's concluding chapters, for relatively poor states that believe they face serious threats to their vital interests, such a comparison among costly alternatives may be the relevant calculation that leads some to pursue nuclear weapons. In the following sections, I first explain China's emphasis on deterrent rather than defensive strategies, and then its emphasis on nuclear rather than conventional forces as the preferred means for fulfilling the strategy's requirements.

Dissuasion by Deterrence Rather Than Defense

China's available resources in the two decades after World War II precluded deployment of an effective defensive capability against its prin-

[76]In this vein, Quan Yanchi says Mao referred to the Soviet bomb as "undependable." Cited in Goncharov, Lewis, and Xue, *Uncertain Partners*, p. 348n9.

[77]In the now famous line from foreign affairs minister Chen Yi, China would shoulder any burden necessary to bring the strategic weapons program to fruition, "even if the Chinese had to pawn their trousers for this purpose." Cited in Lewis and Xue, *China Builds the Bomb*, p. 130.

cipal adversary, the United States. The costs of fielding forces in a quantity and of a quality sufficient to dissuade a superpower from threatening Chinese vital interests because its assault would be militarily stymied were simply too high. Establishing credible defenses against the variety of land, air, and naval threats a superpower could pose was not feasible; the attempt would have required an unacceptable diversion of national resources from the pressing task of nurturing an economy that could provide for the basic needs of the Chinese people. Such a military mobilization effort would have had serious implications for the legitimacy of the newly founded communist regime. The CCP's rise to power and its ability to rule without relying solely on coercion depended on fulfilling the twin nationalist promises of its revolution—at last to provide security not just against the sort of foreign interference that had burdened China during the preceding century but also against what for many had become a domestic condition of grinding poverty. Beijing, in short, could not incur the steep opportunity costs of pursuing the vast capabilities that would be necessary for effective defenses against the array of military challenges the American superpower could present.[78]

In the 1950s there was simply no prospect of bolstering the conventional capabilities of the People's Liberation Army (PLA) to a point that they might confidently parry superior U.S. forces, particularly its air and naval forces.[79] And although the Soviets were providing military aid, China could not afford to buy, and the Soviets were unwilling to donate, quantities of conventional arms anywhere near the levels sufficient to offset the American advantage. Indeed, Moscow's aid was limited not only in quantity but also in quality. As John Lewis and Hua Di noted, it was Soviet policy not to "transfer state-of-the-art weapons to allies before it [the USSR] had deployed at least two types of more advanced systems."[80]

The PRC's disadvantage in conventional forces became even more acute following the Sino-Soviet split of the late 1950s that cut China off

[78]On linkages between domestic and international security, see Barry Buzan, *People, States, and Fear*. On the importance of freeing up resources for the essential task of domestic development (as well as the economic advantages of modest nuclear forces), see Sun Mingming and Cai Xiaohong, *Dongdangzhong de Guojia Anquan*, p. 189; Peng Guangqian, Wang Guangxu et al., eds., *Junshi Zhanlüe Jianlun*, p. 168; Chen Chongbei, Shou Xiaosong, and Liang Xiaoqiu, *Weishe Zhanlüe*, p. 29.

[79]As Nie Rongzhen recalled the situation of the 1950s: "[T]he conventional weapons we could produce at the time were far behind, in capabilities and qualities, those of the technologically advanced countries. . . ." Cited in Lin, *China's Nuclear Weapons Strategy*, p. 78.

[80]Lewis and Hua, "China's Ballistic Missile Programs," p. 13.

from its principal foreign source of limited military assistance. Consequently, the impracticality of relying on a strategy of dissuasion by defense persisted even as the probable enemy changed during the 1960s. By the end of the decade, when China concluded that it faced a serious threat mainly from the Soviet Union, Beijing could have little confidence Moscow would view China's defensive capability based on modified Korean War–vintage arms as much of a match for a significantly modernized Soviet Red Army that had increased its deployment on the Chinese border to nearly 30 divisions.[81] And within three years after the armed clashes of March 1969, 45 Soviet divisions were poised for use against China. The PRC was not the only adversary guiding Soviet military planning and motivating this buildup in the Far East. But China could not be sure about Soviet planning or motives during the late Cold War years as Moscow deployed as much as a third of its conventional forces in the region along with advanced theater nuclear weapons.[82]

What would it have taken for the CCP to develop a self-reliant defensive capability based on conventional weapons for dealing with this new threat? The scale of the challenge is suggested by one analysis that estimated the cost of American aid that would have been needed to prepare China to withstand a Soviet conventional attack at $41–$63 billion. This sum almost certainly exceeded the entire annual military budget of the PRC, and may have been two to three times actual military spending.[83] For a country as poverty stricken as China, such a ratcheting up of the PLA's budget was probably infeasible; it certainly would have been unwise, and perhaps disastrous, given the impact on investment in China's civilian sector. Moreover, the required investment for mounting defenses geared to a superpower threat would have been higher still if Beijing insisted on undertaking the bulk of the conventional modernization independently, as seems likely in light of its experience with the Soviet aid cutoff of 1960 and the autarkic policies to

[81]China's pessimism about the conventional force balance at the time of the 1969 Sino-Soviet war scare was evident, though rhetorically softened, in the four marshals' report on the changing international situation: "We have made full preparations, and are ready to defeat any enemy who dares to invade our territory. However, it is more beneficial to us to postpone the war. We should make full use of the time and strengthen preparations in all respects. . . . We must . . . build China into an unshakable proletarian country with stronger economic power and stronger land, naval and air forces" ("Report by Four Chinese Marshals—Chen Yi, Ye Jianying, Xu Xiangqian, and Nie Rongzhen,—to the Central Committee, 'A Preliminary Evaluation of the War Situation' (excerpt), 11 July 1969," p. 168).

[82]Garrett and Glaser, *War and Peace*, p. 14.

[83]Ibid., p. 23. See also Leo Yueh-yun Liu, "The Modernization of the Chinese Military," p. 11.

which China adhered during the Cultural Revolutionary years. In short, debates about its strategic merits aside, during the Cold War China simply lacked the wealth to muster the sort of capability that would be sufficient to discourage a superpower from threatening the country's vital interests by making it clear that any such challenge would be militarily stymied.

Two additional resource problems mentioned in the previous chapter that are related to but distinct from financial concerns, manpower and especially geography, compounded the difficulties China would have faced if it tried independently to pursue the strategic alternative of dissuasion by conventional defense. The PLA recruited its soldiers mainly from China's vast supply of poor peasants. Although this ensured the availability of large numbers at low cost, this pool of recruits represented the least educated segment of society. In an era of increasingly technical requirements for successful performance in combat, the shortfall in quality, if not quantity, of personnel posed a daunting problem for the regime if it would seek to deploy forces able to fend off the assault of a modernized superpower's military. Wise government policy could have addressed the problem of personnel quality through investment in education. But cost aside, in China during the late 1950s and for much of the remaining years of Mao Zedong's life, the leaders in Beijing were not prepared to make the political and financial commitment to an educational system that would significantly elevate the quality of its graduates. Instead, the educational system became a hotbed of political controversy in the ongoing debate about the relative importance of "redness" and "expertise." Especially following the short-lived cultivation of intellectuals during the Hundred Flowers movement in 1956–57, educational standards repeatedly came under fire from the regime's ideologues. In the second half of the 1960s the Cultural Revolution effectively paralyzed secondary and higher education in the PRC. Even when schools and universities began to resume a more normal schedule of classes in the early 1970s, the curriculum was compromised to serve ideological interests, access to world-class scientific knowledge was tightly restricted, and graduate training languished. By the mid-1970s, the sorry state of China's higher education became one of the key battlegrounds between Maoist radicals determined to ensure political purity, and Dengist reformers who sought to improve the quality of available personnel.[84] Until the early 1980s, when Deng Xiaoping consoli-

---

[84]On the debates about education and their role in Deng Xiaoping's second fall from power, see John Bryan Starr, "From the 10th Party Congress to the Premiership of Hua Kuo-feng"; Avery Goldstein, *From Bandwagon to Balance-of-Power Politics,*

dated power and pushed for a thorough reform of academic and intellectual life in the PRC, the weaknesses of China's educational system were
a significant limit on the feasibility of fielding a modern conventional
military.

A regime determined to develop a modern conventional capability
might have chosen to alter its educational policy. But there was not
much China could have done about certain fundamental geopolitical realities that would complicate a strategy of dissuasion by defense.
Throughout the Cold War, Beijing faced two key problems if it hoped to
establish a credible capability to deny a superpower adversary success
on the battlefield. First, the northeastern provinces comprising Manchuria, the nation's heavy industrial base during the PRC's era of Stalin-
ist economics, was an inviting salient vulnerable to being severed from
the rest of Chinese territory through a quick strike for this limited purpose launched by an adversary with conventional superiority. Second,
outside Manchuria, China's most developed regions were concentrated
along the east coast. Though less easily seized, these cities, and Manchuria, too, were highly vulnerable to punishing air strikes against
which the Chinese lacked effective defenses. These two geopolitical difficulties that diminished the appeal of relying on conventional defense
were compounded when the Soviets replaced the United States as
China's principal security concern. At that point, Beijing had to worry
not only about the vulnerability of Manchuria and the eastern cities, but
also about two new problems. First, vast resource-rich territories in
China's west and northwest bordering the Soviet Union were sparsely
populated by minorities of dubious loyalty. Second, Beijing itself was
relatively close to heavily armored Soviet divisions that could strike
from the north and northwest. Topography provided the capital city
with few defensive advantages along the likely axes of Soviet attack in
an age when the Great Wall was no longer much of an impediment to
the enemy's assault. China, then, faced both the threat of strikes for
limited objectives and the threat of a blitzkrieg against the nation's
nerve center.

In short, given its capabilities, China could not deal with the most
plausible threats to its vital national interests by convincing its superpower adversaries that the PLA would deny them their military objectives. As early as the 1950s China's leaders seemed to accept the impracticality of defending the country's most valuable urban assets. In-

---

p. 199. Even in the era of Deng's post-Mao reforms, many have criticized the lack of a
financial, as opposed to a rhetorical, commitment to education.

stead, Mao and his associates decided to devote scarce resources to a futile development plan aimed at reducing their vulnerability by dispersing the industrial base in the country's vast hinterland. This "Third Front" policy, aimed at mounting a passive defense against attack (hiding from, rather than actively attempting to neutralize, the attacking forces), though perhaps not as costly as full-scale modernization of the PLA would have been, had some of the same predictably negative economic and political consequences. The dispersal and duplication of industrial infrastructure diverted scarce resources and employed them inefficiently, contributing to the quarter-century stagnation of the Chinese economy that ultimately undermined the legitimacy of the Maoist development program.[85]

Although China's People's Liberation Army fielded conventional forces useful for ensuring the country's interests if the enemy was a regional adversary, such as India, it could not deploy defensive capabilities sufficient to reliably dissuade the range of dire threats China faced during the Cold War from the American and then Soviet superpowers. Once Beijing decided it needed to hedge against the shortcomings of depending on the support of a powerful ally, the realistic choice was between two forms of dissuasion by deterrence—one relying on conventional and one relying on nuclear forces. Deterrence, by whichever means, was more attractive than defense because it would not require China to field the quantity and quality of forces necessary to frustrate the military assault by a superior adversary. Deterrence required only developing a capability to inflict punishment on the adversary sufficient to convince him that military success on the battlefield would not enable him to escape paying an unacceptable price in the attempt to realize his political objectives. Thus, having decided upon self-reliance, Beijing's relatively limited resources encouraged an emphasis on deterrence. But why, having decided upon deterrence as the more affordable alternative, did Beijing ultimately decide that nuclear weapons were essential for making the strategy sufficiently robust?

Conventional Deterrence as an Alternative to the Nuclear Option

The economic virtues of deterrence are clear. Through the 1970s, however, China's declaratory strategy, unlike that of Britain and France, emphasized deterrence based on a conventional, rather than a nuclear

[85]See Barry Naughton, "The Third Front." See also Nelsen, *Power and Insecurity*, 89–90; Harrison Salisbury, *The New Emperors*, esp. ch. 14.

threat to dissuade its superpower adversaries. Nevertheless, as early as the Korean War, Beijing had begun to recognize some of the deficiencies of its version of conventional deterrence (Mao's strategy of protracted struggle known as People's War) for dealing with the most plausible superpower threats to China's vital interests.[86] This recognition provided an important motive for the program of research and development that would enable the PRC to shift to nuclear deterrence. But until the technical and economic hurdles to the development and deployment of a viable retaliatory force could be overcome, Beijing hoped to maximize the dissuasive effect of threatening aggressors with a People's War. China's experience with this conventional deterrent approach nicely illustrates some of the reasons for its limited appeal.

In the 1950s the threat that China would confront any occupying army with a protracted national resistance movement provided a hedge against the risk of abandonment by a diffident Soviet ally. History certainly provided good reason to believe in the credibility of Beijing's threat to wage a punishing People's War. During the 1930s and 1940s the CCP had demonstrated the impressive political-organizational skills necessary to mount and sustain an effective struggle against an adversary with vast material superiority (both Japan and the U.S.-backed KMT). Although hoping the Sino-Soviet alliance would serve to dissuade the United States, the communist leaders in Beijing could be confident that their country's size and their proven ability to mobilize a sea of peasant resistance fighters would convince the United States that the price of a victorious invasion and occupation would be unacceptably high, whether or not the Soviets came through with promised support. Prior to entering the Korean War, Premier Zhou Enlai made clear his conviction that conventional deterrence would dissuade others: "[T]he unity of our nation and our people is so . . . powerful that any imperialist attempt to invade China would be *frightened away by it*."[87] The subsequent fighting in Korea provided the new Chinese regime with an opportunity to demonstrate once again its willingness to incur grave losses and its ability to inflict severe punishment on a militarily superior enemy when it perceived vital national interests to be at stake. China's bloody participation manifested a resolve that enhanced the credibility of its conventional deterrent threat. Prospective adversaries would have to conclude that China would be even more determined to stay the course in a struggle with foreign forces on its own soil than it had been

---

[86]Lewis and Xue, *China Builds the Bomb*, pp. 8–10.

[87]Cited in Zhang Shuguang, *Deterrence and Strategic Culture*, p. 94 (Zhang's emphasis); see also pp. 22–23.

in a buffer state. Mao indeed argued that the military performance in Korea (including horrific sacrifices resulting from China's seemingly irrational human wave tactics) would have a "lasting deterrent value."[88] In short, China's declaratory doctrine and its actions soon after the regime was founded both strongly suggested that although a more powerful adversary could militarily seize territory on the Chinese mainland, he would find it an excruciatingly difficult place to pacify and govern. Washington's reluctance to widen the war in Korea beyond the peninsula, and its subsequent reluctance to commit itself in Indochina in 1954 indicate the Chinese were probably correct in concluding that the prospect of interminable pain and suffering inflicted by irregular forces and remnants of a retreating PLA could serve to dissuade even the mighty American superpower.[89]

In the late 1960s and 1970s, Beijing once again emphasized this sort of conventional deterrence (rather than conventional defense or nuclear deterrence) when it confronted salient military threats from a superpower, this time the Soviet Union. As noted above, after early border disputes in 1964, Moscow massively built up its forces deployed in the Far East and by 1969 they posed a threat against which the Chinese could not reasonably hope to mount a credible defense.[90] Indeed, the prospects for conventional defense had deteriorated during the 1960s as domestic turmoil and international isolation left China's military technology years behind world standards. Given the impracticality of dissuading Soviet attack by mounting a formidable conventional defense, or flaunting a still dubious nuclear retaliatory capability, and given the ultimate uncertainty about the reliability of the deterrent benefit China obtained from its strategic alignment with the United States, Beijing

---

[88]See Goncharov, Lewis, and Xue, *Uncertain Partners*, p. 223. See also Zhang Shuguang, *Deterrence and Strategic Culture*, p. 146. Deterrence theorists claim that a reputation for irrationality can be a valuable asset for a deterrer. Patrick Morgan, for example, argued that deterrence is enhanced if the potential attacker "holds a highly emotional and exaggerated conception of your military prowess *or your willingness to bear the costs and sacrifices of war*" (Morgan, *Deterrence*, p. 53, emphasis added).

[89]For a CIA analysis suggesting that Korea and Indochina confirmed the U.S. "reluctance to become involved in major war in Asia," see "Communist Courses of Action in Asia Through 1957," CIA, Nov. 23, 1954, p. 7.

[90]"Soviet conventional force levels rose dramatically after 1965, from approximately 17 divisions to 27 divisions by 1969 (and about 48 divisions in the mid-1970s). Moscow also decided to deploy SS-4 MRBMs as well as short-range rockets (SCUD and FROG)" (Christian F. Ostermann "East German Documents on the Sino-Soviet Border Conflict, 1969," *CWIHP Bulletin, The Cold War in Asia*, Issues 6–7, p. 187; see also Garrett and Glaser, *War and Peace*, p. 14).

hopefully reaffirmed its continued confidence in the conventional deterrent doctrine of People's War.[91] And for dissuading their new superpower adversary from considering massive invasion and occupation of
the Chinese heartland, this conventional deterrent may have been effective.[92] Unfortunately for Chinese planners, the awesome resources at
the disposal of the Soviet adversary provided it, like its American predecessor, with a rich set of threatening military options more plausible
than invasion and occupation.

From the 1950s through the 1970s the dubious value of China's conventional deterrent for dealing with the most likely threats to vital national interests reflected the inherent shortcomings of relying on such a
strategy. These shortcomings motivated Beijing's dual approach of cultivating ties with a superpower patron while continuing its ardent pursuit of the independent nuclear alternative. The Korean War had not
only been a showcase for demonstrating Chinese resolve that enhanced
the credibility of conventional deterrent threats. It had also revealed
that the PLA was not yet able to project power beyond the nation's borders against a militarily superior adversary. Once the advantage of surprise had been spent, the Chinese found themselves bogged down in a
stalemate that cost them dearly in terms of lives and treasure.[93] The

[91]During the March 1969 border clashes, Mao ordered preparations be made for
People's War: "Every county should establish a [militia] regiment, this should be
done all over the country. . . . We are now confronted with a formidable enemy. It is
advantageous to have the mobilization and the preparation . . ." ("Mao Zedong's
Talk at a Meeting of the Central Cultural Revolution Group (excerpt), 15 March
1969," pp. 161–62). In his speech at the April 1969 Ninth Congress of the Chinese
Communist Party, Mao indicated that the PLA would only try to resist a limited Soviet attack and that the response to an all-out assault would be to retreat and fight a
People's War: "If it is a small scale invasion the fighting will be waged on the border.
If it is a large-scale invasion, I am in favor of giving up some land. . . . It is easy for us
to fight [an invading enemy] since he will fall into the people's encirclement" ("Mao
Zedong's Speech at the First Plenary Session of the CCP's Ninth Central Committee,
28 April 1969," p. 164).

[92]See Jencks, "'People's War Under Modern Conditions'" p. 309. As ever, the effectiveness of successful deterrent threats is difficult to demonstrate conclusively
because it is reflected in non-events.

[93]This lesson about the importance of the balance of material capabilities was
taken to heart. It may well have confirmed the doubts some of China's military and
civilian leaders expressed during the September–October 1950 debate about the wisdom of intervening in Korea. However supportive its rhetoric, after the experience in
Korea, Beijing was not as eager to come to the aid of their revolutionary East Asian
comrades. In the mid-1960s, when Maoist propaganda was at a fever pitch, Lin Biao
made his famous speech, "Long Live the Victory of People's War." Whatever its in-
spirational value, the speech basically announced to the world's revolutionaries, the
Vietnamese in particular, that their armed struggles must be home grown; in short,

PLA's limited ability to reach out and either defeat *or* punish aggressors beyond China's borders left Beijing vulnerable to superpower coercion that need not entail invasion or occupation. Because it was a country whose limited fixed industrial assets were concentrated in a small number of poorly defended urban settings, China was especially vulnerable to the much greater long-range power projection capabilities the superpowers deployed. During the last months of the Korean War and in the subsequent Taiwan Straits Crises, this point was driven home for Beijing by Washington's nuclear saber rattling. In acting to defuse confrontations with the United States, the Chinese issued rhetorical flourishes about the indecisiveness of nuclear weapons and the effectiveness of People's War.[94] But on the heels of these experiences China actually intensified its own efforts to acquire some of these "indecisive" weapons that could provide the punitive retaliatory capability sufficient to frighten a distant superpower adversary and, thus, dissuade the most serious threats to China's vital interests.

Border clashes with the Soviet Union in the late 1960s served once again to expose the limited value of China's purely conventional deter-

---

they could not count on the direct participation of Chinese troops as in Korea. See A. Doak Barnett, *Uncertain Passage*, p. 270. China *did* provide substantial "semi-covert" support, unacknowledged but just visible enough to dissuade the United States from escalating the conflict in a fashion that might require a Korean War style Chinese intervention: "Beginning in June 1965, China sent ground-to-air missile, anti-aircraft artillery, railroad, engineering, mine-sweeping, and logistical units into North Vietnam to help Hanoi. The total number of Chinese troops in North Vietnam between June 1965 and March 1973 amounted to over 320,000. When the last Chinese troops withdrew from Vietnam in August 1973, 1,100 soldiers had lost their lives and 4,200 had been wounded" (Qiang Zhai, "Beijing and the Vietnam Conflict, 1964–1965," p. 237). For an analysis of China's efforts to rely on deployments to send signals to the United States that predates the details revealed by newly available documents, see Allen S. Whiting, *The Chinese Calculus of Deterrence*. Beijing's *preferences* about intervention notwithstanding, the continuing *inability* of the PLA to project power was once again revealed to Beijing and others by its unsuccessful counteroffensive against Vietnam in 1979. This fiasco, as an editorial in the *Liberation Army Daily* noted, "helped clear away some erroneous ideas" among military thinkers in China who were wedded to the Maoist doctrine of the past. Cited in Segal, "China's Strategic Posture and the Great-Power Triangle," p. 691.

[94]In 1955 Mao had disparaged U.S. nuclear threats by asserting, "the Chinese people are not to be cowed by US atomic blackmail. . . . The United States cannot annihilate the Chinese nation with its small stack of atom bombs." Cited in John W. Lewis, "China's Military Doctrines and Force Posture," p. 163. Chinese analysts interviewed in 1991 continued to deny that U.S. nuclear threats affected Beijing's policy in the 1950s. For a Western view questioning the efficacy of U.S. threats, see Barry M. Blechman and Robert Powell, "What in the Name of God Is Strategic Superiority?," pp. 595–96.

rent and reinforced the desire for its nuclear cousin. Beijing confronted the threat of a variety of Soviet military actions, including threats of a preventive surgical strike against China's minimal nuclear facilities during the 1969 border confrontation. For reasons detailed below, the apparent refusal of the Nixon administration to countenance this more extreme Soviet option helped to defuse the crisis, but Moscow's coercion had compelled China to take the initiative in a diplomatic resolution of the immediate dispute before it got out of control.[95]

After the war scare of 1969, Beijing's insecurity while it lacked confidence in its nascent nuclear deterrent encouraged the diplomatic warming to the West and the United States in particular, as well as limited efforts at easing tensions with the Soviets. Yet the unavoidable risk of relying on an ally for security (the fear of abandonment) made implicit dependence on the American superpower's nuclear deterrent a less than satisfactory, if necessary, stopgap.[96] Moreover, for a strongly nationalist regime, especially one in the throes of a pre-mortem struggle over the succession to Mao, strategic cooperation with the principal capitalist-imperialist power was politically unappealing.[97] The politically more appealing self-reliant alternative, China's vaunted conventional deterrent, was unfortunately a strategy geared to a largely nonexistent peril. Soviet military deployments on the Chinese border, though impressive, never reached the levels suggesting an intention to test Bei-

[95]Richard Wich, *Sino-Soviet Crisis Politics*, chs. 9, 10; Mann, *About Face*, pp. 20–23. China's proposals for reducing tensions that Premier Zhou Enlai presented to Kosygin (who stopped at the Beijing airport while returning to Moscow from Vietnam) called for separating ideological from interstate disputes, avoiding military clashes, and maintaining the status quo while negotiations proceeded on the border dispute (Zhou, *Zhou Enlai Nianpu*, vol. 3, pp. 320–21). On the application of military pressure and the range of options the Soviets considered to coerce the Chinese to agree to resume negotiations during the summer of 1969, see Christian F. Ostermann, "New Evidence on the Sino-Soviet Border Dispute, 1969–71," pp. 186–93. For Mao's anticipation of Soviet preventive strikes against China's nuclear weapons facilities, see "Mao Zedong's Talk at a Meeting of the Central Cultural Revolution Group (excerpt), 15 March 1969," pp. 161–62.

[96]John W. Lewis, "China's Military Doctrines and Force Posture," p. 172. During the years of doubt about its nuclear deterrent, China also attempted to improve its capability for conventional deterrence based on protracted struggle (and perhaps also develop passive nuclear defenses) by dispersing its industrial assets. As noted above, whatever its marginal benefits for security, the economically disastrous consequences of the "Third Front" development policy soon became clear.

[97]Harry Harding recounts the Maoist radicals' charges against relative moderates among the communist leaders in Beijing during the mid-1970s. The latter insisted that China would have to "'wait until we obtain the atom'—presumably a reference to a more credible Chinese nuclear deterrent—before they could 'get tough' with the Kremlin" (Harding, "The Domestic Politics of China's Global Posture," p. 107).

jing's threat to confront an occupying army with a protracted resistance movement. Instead, as Harlan Jencks noted, Soviet forces arrayed in the Far East were more plausibly suited to launching a limited offensive to seal off the industrial heartland of Manchuria or parts of the vast western province of Xinjiang. Easier still would have been Soviet operations with punitive or compellent purposes designed to coerce Chinese policy-makers, especially if the attacks were restricted to air strikes against which the Chinese were largely defenseless. However unlikely such scenarios seem, offensive operations to seal off Manchuria, to bomb or gain a foothold on the eastern seaboard, or to detach western portions of Xinjiang province were far more plausible than an arguably pointless and clearly costly attempt to occupy China's heartland.[98] In such circumstances, should the support of China's informal strategic partner, the United States, waver, a PLA armed with obsolete weapons and an inappropriate doctrine would have had little counter other than perhaps launching annoying, but militarily inconsequential, commando raids into Siberia.[99] Until China could field the forces necessary to make its preferred independent nuclear strategy viable, however, Beijing was left with this uncomfortable combination of a largely irrelevant conventional deterrent, a potentially effective but ultimately uncertain nuclear umbrella supplied by its American quasi-ally, and the hope that the Soviet adversary would not be sufficiently motivated to challenge China's vital interests.

The variety of contingencies against which China's conventional deterrent would be ineffective presented Beijing with an apparently daunting problem during most of the Cold War. Developing a credible defensive capability against the United States in the 1950s and the Soviets in the 1970s was not feasible. Dependence on the nuclear umbrella of a superpower patron was necessary, but strategically risky. Or at least it seemed too risky from Beijing's perspective. But was it really? Soviet

---

[98]Jencks, "'People's War Under Modern Conditions'" p. 309. In his meetings during 1974 with Henry Kissinger, Deng Xiaoping noted that the Soviet Union still had "only" one million troops on the border and that this was not enough even for effective defense, let alone an offensive against China that would require an additional one million. Deng argued that this demonstrated that China remained secure against Soviet attack. Kissinger suggested that the Chinese were ignoring the more likely Soviet strategy—limited strikes, or preemptive attacks on China's nuclear arsenal, rather than invasion and occupation (Burr, *The Kissinger Transcripts*, pp. 282–83, 309; see also Kissinger's exchange with Mao, p. 99). A CIA analysis also saw limited strikes as the most likely form of Soviet military action against China ("Soviet Policy in Asia," CIA, Apr. 15, 1971, pp. 2, 10).

[99]See Jencks "'People's War Under Modern Conditions'" pp. 307–8, 316.

hesitation as it considered launching preventive strikes against China's nuclear weapons installations after the 1969 border clashes and similar U.S. hesitation when it had toyed with the idea earlier in the 1960s suggest that Beijing may not have been quite as vulnerable in the bipolar Cold War world as it feared. Ironically, what appeared to be the tight constraints of a highly forbidding international system may actually have mitigated the danger China faced.

Safe Haven in a Dangerous World?

Chinese leaders naturally worried about the reasons why a strategic partner might renege on security pledges: Anarchy meant that contracts among self-interested states were unenforceable; the advent of nuclear weapons meant that the risks in supporting an ally confronting the other superpower would be inherently grave; and bipolarity meant that a self-reliant superpower need not take grave risks to maintain the loyalty of an ally whose intrinsic military value was small. But as suggested in Chapter 2 there was another, and for China less disadvantageous, implication of the Cold War international system. Although bipolarity provided incentives for the superpowers to avoid entrapment and to abandon allies, to the extent it made international politics more nearly a zero-sum game, it also provided competing incentives for each superpower to worry about its reputation for resolve in the eyes of the other. This consequence of bipolarity was reinforced by the importance of reputational concerns in a nuclear age when strategy rested so much on the credibility of threats. These reputational concerns seem to have provided China with a greater degree of safety against superpower attack than a straightforward consideration of its military vulnerability to American or Soviet strikes might suggest. Because each superpower recognized the other had a self-interest in preserving its international reputation, it had to worry that unilateral action against China (especially if that action entailed as dramatic a step as preventive attack on nuclear weapons installations) might lead its adversary to respond in some unpredictable, potentially dangerous, way. This sheltering effect appears to have been more significant than understandably nervous Chinese leaders appreciated.

In the 1950s, while Beijing worried that it could not count on Moscow to dissuade an aggressive U.S. enemy, the United States worried that extreme measures against China might force a reluctant, but self-interested, Soviet hand. This American concern was not simply the result of specific commitments outlined in the Sino-Soviet treaty, but rather the belief that the Soviets could not afford the appearance of tolerating U.S. unilateralism that challenged Moscow's international commitments in general. Such worries about how Moscow might react to American attacks on China persisted even after the seriousness of the Sino-Soviet split became obvious and the parties to the alliance doubted its usefulness. At the beginning of the 1960s, U.S. intelligence analysts were well aware of the deep disagreements between Moscow and Beijing. But although they expected the alliance to be "from time to time troubled and inharmonious," such contentiousness was not expected to prevent unity against the West in the event of "a major challenge."[100] This conviction among American analysts most clearly induced caution when Presidents Kennedy and Johnson contemplated their options, including military strikes, for preventing China from successfully completing its nuclear weapons program.[101]

On the heels of the Cuban missile crisis, President Kennedy took a strong interest in nuclear arms control and this in turn intensified his concern that a Chinese nuclear weapons test would trigger accelerated proliferation. Serious planning for possible preventive strikes began under Kennedy and continued under Johnson. The option never received approval because the United States decided the action would be ineffective (it could only delay, rather than finally prevent, China from developing weapons, especially once the option of using nuclear weapons in the attack was ruled out), unnecessary (in the future the United States could deter China, like any other nuclear weapons state, from using its arsenal), and most importantly, risky (there was uncertainty about the Soviet response). U.S. nervousness about the Soviet reaction seemed well founded. As he grew more worried about the implications of Chinese nuclear weapons, Kennedy had repeatedly urged his national security team (especially Averill Harriman) to sound out the Soviets about actions that might be taken to prevent the PRC from realizing its nuclear ambitions.[102] The Soviets, sensitive to Chinese accusations of col-

[100]"National Intelligence Estimate: Authority and Control in the Communist Movement," Aug. 8, 1961; "Special National Intelligence Estimate: Communist China in 1971," Sept. 28, 1961.

[101]"Memorandum of Conversation," Jan. 30, 1962. Paul Nitze suggested to Defense Secretary McNamara in May 1963 that the USSR would probably not "stand aside while we defeated China," especially if U.S. strikes included nuclear weapons ("Memorandum from the Assistant Secretary of Defense for International Security Affairs [Nitze] to Secretary of Defense McNamara," May 11, 1963).

[102]For the scattered evidence of U.S. efforts to elicit Soviet cooperation, see "Editorial Note," Jan. 11, 1963; "Editorial Note," June 23, 1963; "Telegram from the Embassy in the Soviet Union to the Department of State, Moscow July 18, 1963, 5 PM"; "Editorial Note," July 15, 1963; "Memorandum of Conversation Between the President's Special Assistant for National Security Affairs (Bundy) and

lusion with the American imperialists, ignored or shot down each U.S. trial balloon. Even during the summer of 1963 when Soviet-American relations were much improved and Sino-Soviet relations were more fractious than ever, the Soviets refused to endorse U.S. proposals aimed against China. As the CIA had anticipated, Soviet self-interest made cooperation unlikely. Although Khrushchev was fully disillusioned with the Chinese, he did not believe he could afford to side with the United States against China "lest this be taken as a sign of weakness which *would embolden the West to take a firmer stand against his demands in other fields.*"[103] In September 1964, as the Johnson administration

the Soviet Ambassador (Dobrynin)," May 17, 1963; "Memorandum of Conversation with Ambassador Dobrynin," Sept. 25, 1964. For U.S. debate about the advisability of preventive strikes against China's nuclear weapons installations (including encouragement and occasional offers to supply personnel for the operation from the government on Taiwan), see "Highlights from Secretary of State Rusk's Policy Planning Meeting," Oct. 15, 1963; "Memorandum from Robert W. Komer of the National Security Council Staff to the President's Special Assistant for National Security Affairs (Bundy)," Nov. 5, 1963; "Memorandum from Robert W. Komer of the National Security Council Staff to the President's Special Assistant for National Security Affairs (Bundy)," Feb. 26, 1964; "Paper Presented in the Policy Planning Council: An Exploration of the Possible Bases for Action against the Chinese Communist Nuclear Facilities," Apr. 14, 1964; "Paper Prepared in the Policy Planning Council: The Implications of a Chinese Communist Nuclear Capability," Apr. 30, 1964; "Memorandum from Robert W. Komer of the National Security Council Staff to the President's Special Assistant for National Security Affairs (Bundy)," Sept. 18, 1964; "Memorandum for the Joint Chiefs of Staff to Secretary of Defense McNamara, Subject: Possible Responses to the ChiCom Nuclear Threat," Jan. 16, 1965; Robert S. Lindquist, "Airgram, from US Embassy, Taipei, Subject: Comments re Effectiveness and Credibility of US Nuclear Deterrent in Far East in Wake of Chinese Communist Nuclear Detonation," Oct. 27, 1964, p. 3. See also "Incoming Telegram, Department of State, Subject: Effect of CCNE on GRC and Implications for US Policy," Oct. 29, 1964; "Incoming Telegram, Department of State"; G. W. Rathjens, "Destruction of Chinese Nuclear Weapons Capabilities" and the recollections of some of the U.S. policy-makers in "Professor Roger Fisher's Comments on Selected Portions of Course III"; Robert H. Johnson, "Letter." For a collection that includes representative positions in the U.S. policy debate, see the declassified documents, including proposals for action, available in *The United States, China, and the Bomb*, National Security Archive Electronic Briefing Book, No. 1, http://www.seas.gwu.edu/nsarchive/NSAEBB/NSAEBB1/nsaebb1.htm. The most explicit proposals to the Soviets came on the eve of China's first nuclear weapons test. For still incomplete evidence on these unproductive contacts with Soviet Ambassador Dobrynin, see "Memorandum of Conversation with Ambassador Dobrynin," Sept. 25, 1964, and the text of the declassified memorandum of consultations on September 15, 1964, among President Johnson, Robert McNamara, Dean Rusk, and John McCone cited in John Lewis Gaddis, *Strategies of Containment*, p. 210 (the nearly complete text of this memo is contained in *The United States, China, and the Bomb*).

[103]"Memorandum Prepared by the Central Intelligence Agency: The New Phase

apparently tried to get one last read on possible Soviet tolerance for U.S. action to prevent the imminent Chinese nuclear test, McGeorge Bundy reported that although Soviet Ambassador Dobrynin had acknowledged the depth of the split with China, when he discussed "American differences with Communist China, *he gently remarked on the continued existence of the treaty between the USSR and the Chicoms.*"[104] Soviet-American rivalry in the bipolar Cold War world, it seems, had provided China with a surprisingly robust safe haven. While China was mainly focused on the Soviet self-interest in avoiding risks and worried that this made it unlikely Moscow would live up to its extended deterrent guarantees, the United States mainly focused on the Soviet self-interest in opposing an American assertion of power on the world stage and wor-

---

of Soviet Policy," Aug. 9, 1963 (emphasis added). Soviet defensiveness at this time is easily understood. While Harriman was floating proposals to his Soviet counterparts at the Moscow talks about a limited test ban treaty in the summer of 1963, the Soviets were nearly simultaneously hosting a meeting with Chinese representatives that amounted to yet another round of ideological jousting about leadership of the international communist cause. By fall 1963 the American view was that although each side was questioning the others' "readiness to fulfill commitments under the Sino-Soviet Treaty of 1950," and although the Soviets now ruled out support for Chinese *initiatives* against India or Taiwan, China risked, but had not yet forfeited, Moscow's "nuclear protection" ("Current Intelligence Weekly Review," Sept. 27, 1963; "Highlights from Secretary of State Rusk's Policy Planning Meeting," Oct. 15, 1963). The intelligence report notes as evidence of a significant split, but not yet a complete rupture, Soviet warnings in a September 21–22, 1963, statement that "quoted the Russian proverb: 'Do not foul the well; you may need its waters.'" In April 1964, Secretary of State Dean Rusk told Chiang Kai-shek, possibly in the context of discussions about proposals for strikes against the mainland, that whatever the nature of the split in the communist camp, in the event of military operations against the Chinese mainland requiring "US forces and possibly nuclear weapons . . . that Khrushchev *would have to* support Mao" ("Memorandum of Conversation: Secretary's Visit to Taipei," Apr. 16–17, 1964, emphasis added).

[104]"Memorandum of Conversation with Ambassador Dobrynin," Sept. 25, 1964. The belief that Soviet interests would require it to react to U.S. military actions against China with unpredictable and perhaps dangerous consequences continued to constrain U.S. decision-making in the opening years of its heaviest involvement in the Vietnam War. See "Information Memorandum from the Acting Deputy Under Secretary of State for Political Affairs (Thompson) to Secretary of State Rusk: China Study," July 15, 1965. For an assessment that notes the dwindling significance, but does not yet assert the complete irrelevance, of Soviet military support for China, see "National Intelligence Estimate: The Outlook for Sino-Soviet Relations," Dec. 1, 1966. Even as late as July 1967, when the United States again sounded out the Soviets and suggested the two superpowers should "exchange views and have discussions about China," "[Ambassador] Dobrynin's attitude seemed to indicate some agreement with these remarks, but he was noncommittal" ("Memorandum of Conversation, Subject: Communist China," July 27, 1967).

ried that this might force Moscow to respond in a dangerously unpredictable way.[105]

The sheltering effect was apparent again after the March 1969 Sino-Soviet border clashes, though the superpower roles were reversed. As nervous Soviet leaders contemplated preventive strikes against China, they worried that the United States might not be willing to tolerate so dramatic a unilateral military initiative. Consequently, they began their own effort to gauge American receptivity to contingency plans for Soviet strikes, or possibly joint action. Given the similar proposals they had heard from American officials just a few years earlier, the Soviets may have hoped that the United States would be receptive. During the spring and summer of 1969, however, the Nixon administration clearly signaled U.S. opposition to a strike against China.[106] The condition of bipolarity apparently had generated Moscow's concern about American reaction well before the dramatic Nixon/Kissinger China initiative in 1971.[107] And once the Sino-American strategic entente took root in 1972, U.S. policy aimed to cultivate this concern. Thereafter, Washington rebuffed Moscow's recurrent anti-China proposals and reassured a

[105]Yet China questioned even explicit Soviet assurances. In the September 1960 meeting of the Chinese and Soviet communist parties shortly after the Soviets had terminated their nuclear assistance to China, Soviet Deputy Frol Kozlov told Deng Xiaoping, "We declare in the name of our country . . . that we will defend you in case of attack with all means [available to us]; but you doubt this." Deng replied, "I ask you that your actions meet your recent statements." See "The Short Version of the Negotiation Between CPSU and CCP Delegations (September 1960)."

[106]See Mann, *About Face*, pp. 21–22.

[107]Even before the 1969 military conflict, the Soviets recognized and worried about the logic of the situation under bipolarity (especially after their August 1968 intervention in Czechoslovakia crystallized Chinese fears about Moscow's intentions). Alarmed by indications that the incoming Nixon administration appreciated the strategic benefit to the United States of rapprochement with the PRC, in December 1968 the second secretary in the Soviet embassy in Washington, Boris Davydov, tried to send a warning through one of Averill Harriman's assistants, Daniel Davidson, known to have connections with Henry Kissinger: "He [Davydov] stated, an attempt to form a U.S.-China alliance would be extremely dangerous and he expressed the hope that I could make the point to anyone of influence I know in the next Administration" ("Memorandum of Conversation, Subject: US-Soviet-Chinese Relations," Dec. 21, 1968). Dinner conversation prior to this comment had covered two articles in the January 1968 issue of *Foreign Affairs*, including one by Kissinger, that hinted at the logic of Sino-American rapprochement as Beijing's and Washington's threat perceptions converged, especially in the wake of Soviet assertiveness in Czechoslovakia (ibid.). The logic of Sino-American cooperation, creating the two-front problem the Soviets feared, was later explicitly articulated in Mao's and Kissinger's discussion on November 12, 1973, cited in Burr, *The Kissinger Transcripts*, pp. 183–84.

skeptical Beijing that American self-interest not only ruled out its acceptance of Soviet strikes against China's nuclear weapons facilities, but actually established a more general U.S. interest in China's security against military threats from the Soviet Union.[108] As Kissinger told China's UN Ambassador, Huang Hua:

> We believe . . . that it is against *our* interests to permit the establishment of an hegemony in Eurasia dominated from Moscow. And, therefore, it is in *our* interest to resist this *without any formal agreement* (with the PRC) *simply out of our own necessity*.
>
> . . . what we have to try to accomplish . . . is to establish enough of a relationship with you so that it is plausible that an attack on you involves a substantial American interest.[109]

It was apparently easier to establish the plausibility in Moscow than in Beijing. Despite Henry Kissinger's frequent and remarkably frank assurances to the Chinese that U.S. self-interest would lead it to respond to any Soviet attack on China, Mao continued to voice his doubts and fatalistically predicted that China would be on its own and stuck with relying on People's War.[110]

[108]Burr, *The Kissinger Transcripts*, pp. 51, 69, 99. Kissinger told the Chinese Ambassador to the United States, Han Xu, about his conversation in Moscow with Brezhnev during which the Soviet leader (in what sounds like a Soviet echo of the arguments the United States had made in the early 1960s about the virtues of joint action against China) allegedly stated that "the Soviet Union and the United States . . . have a joint responsibility to prevent China from becoming a nuclear power. And I [Kissinger] said we recognize no such joint responsibility" (ibid., p. 131; see also pp. 142, 144, 171). A CIA analysis noted the effect the new U.S. relationship with China had on the Soviets. Although it estimated the chances of a Sino-Soviet war at no better than ten percent, the analysis argued that part of the reason for Soviet reluctance to fight China was "uncertainty as to the nature and scope of US reactions" ("Possible Changes in the Sino-Soviet Relationship," CIA, Oct. 25, 1973, p. 1; see also p. 10). Even after the Chinese possessed a somewhat more credible nuclear retaliatory capability, a CIA analysis argued "[t]he Chinese view the United States . . . as at least an ambiguous deterrent in Soviet military calculations about China" ("Sino-Soviet Relations in the Early 1980s," CIA, June 5, 1980, p. 2; see also pp. 5, 12,13, 17).

[109]Burr, *The Kissinger Transcripts*, p. 73, emphasis added. See also pp. 113–14, 136, 386; Burr concludes that Kissinger "treat[ed] the PRC as a de facto *component of the U.S. security system*" (ibid., p. 70, emphasis in original).

[110]See ibid., p. 99. Such worries notwithstanding, China had recognized that there could be a benefit from Soviet worries about the American view. Although the 1969 assessment of the international situation conducted by the four marshals asserted that the Soviet intention to attack China had become clear, and included open threats of "a nuclear strike, and conspiring to launch a surprise attack on our nuclear facilities," it also added ". . . they [the Soviets] cannot reach a final decision because of political considerations. . . . To a large extent, the Soviet revisionists' decision to launch a war of aggression against China depends on the attitude of the U.S. imperialists, which is far from satisfactory to them so far, and this is their utmost worry in

While welcome, then, U.S. support, like Soviet support earlier, could not offset China's belief that it needed to hedge against abandonment in an uncertain world by developing an ability to provide for its own security. But China's beliefs, crucial for understanding its interest in an independent nuclear deterrent, should not obscure the evidence that suggests its situation may never have been quite as dangerous as it thought. Whatever problems bipolarity posed for China's security while it was militarily weak and still striving to deploy its own survivable nuclear arsenal, bipolarity also fed a Soviet-American rivalry that reduced the actual likelihood that either superpower would dare exploit China's vulnerability.

Given the possibly disastrous consequences of abandonment, however, China's leaders focused more on the threat a superpower adversary could pose than on the inhibitions such an enemy might feel, as long as those inhibitions depended on forces and choices Beijing did not control. Thus, to be able to provide for China's security independently and at reasonable cost, Beijing remained determined to deploy a national nuclear deterrent. As long as Mao lived, respect for him as the principal theorist and practitioner of People's War ensured this strategy's preeminence in public rhetoric and precluded public debate about its shortcomings. But the single-mindedness with which China pursued its nuclear weapons program belied the leadership's (including Mao's) satisfaction with his conventional deterrent doctrine as early as the mid-1950s. From that time forward, China began devoting the bulk of its scarce defense modernization resources to the nuclear program.[111] Un-

---

a strategic sense" ("Report by Four Chinese Marshals—Chen Yi, Ye Jianying, Nie Rongzhen, and Xu Xiangqian—to the CCP Central Committee, 'Our Views About the Current Situation' (excerpt), 17 September 1969," p. 170). And, when a delegation of the U.S. Progressive Workers Party asked Chinese Premier Zhou Enlai at the time of the March 1969 border clashes whether war was in the offing, he replied, "Right now we can't say. They have done this to mobilize the people of their own country *and to gauge world opinion*" (Zhou, *Zhou Enlai Nianpu*, vol. 3, p. 285, emphasis added).

[111]For a Chinese account of the emphasis placed upon the development of atomic bombs and the missiles to deliver them, see *Zhongguo Renmin Jiefangjun, (shang)*, pp. 506–29. Mao had publicly announced this priority for the Second Five Year Plan in his 1956 speech "On the Ten Major Relationships." See also Mao Zedong, "Jingji Jianshe he Guofang Jianshe de Guanxi," pp. 365–66; Lewis and Xue, *China Builds the Bomb*, p. 107. For other statements from Mao on the priority he assigned to developing nuclear weapons, see Mao Zedong, "Zhengqu Bijiao Chang de Heping Shijian Shi Kenengde," pp. 358–59; Mao, "Yao Gao Yidian Yuanzidan Qidan," p. 374; Mao, "Ying Zhuajin dui Jianduan Wuqi de Yanzhi Gongzuo," p. 392. See also Zhang Shuguang, *Deterrence and Strategic Culture*, p. 232; "National Intelligence Estimate: Communist China's Military Establishment," Mar. 10, 1965. The estimate for

der Mao's leadership, after 1954 the nuclear weapons program was assigned top priority despite the preferences of some of China's military leaders who would rather have invested in upgrading the PLA's conventional weaponry.[112] The next chapter details China's effort to deploy a nuclear arsenal sufficient for deterring a superpower adversary.

---

the entire cost of producing the first Chinese A-bomb has been put at about 4.1 billion 1957 dollars (see Lewis and Xue, *China Builds the Bomb*, pp. 107–8). Lewis and Xue vividly describe the way in which the Chinese substituted relatively inexpensive manpower for unavailable or unaffordable technology in the course of developing the bomb. Though mass mobilization was not of much value in solving the toughest engineering problems, during the GLF it was apparently helpful in locating and processing the first batch of uranium concentrates, perhaps shortening the development period by one year (ibid., p. 88). Other methods relied upon by the Chinese to save scarce funds were often less laudable as safety measures were sometimes given short shrift. He Zuoxiu, a physicist in the Scientific Division of the Chinese Academy of Sciences who "participates in nuclear strategy decisions with the higher echelons of the Chinese Communist Party leadership" in 1993 claimed that the PRC's tradition of nuclear frugality continued, holding nuclear weapons manufacturing costs to 1–1.5 percent of that of the United States. This was allegedly accomplished by doing "careful calculations and strict budgeting" and using "every cent sparingly at all times . . ." ("Top Physicist Outlines China's Strategy on Nuclear War and Proliferation").

[112]John W. Lewis, "China's Military Doctrines and Force Posture," p. 179; see also Mao Zedong, "Yao Gao Yidian Yuanzidan Qidan," p. 374. In May 1991 I interviewed a figure closely involved with the PRC's early nuclear weapons program who also confirmed that Mao rejected arguments calling for conventional force modernization in the late 1950s because he insisted that scarce available funds for military construction go to the nuclear program, which would have a greater payoff both in terms of status and security.

4

China: Nuclear Deterrent

Although preliminary research began in the late 1940s, China formally decided to develop an atomic bomb at an enlarged meeting of the Central Secretariat of the CCP on January 15, 1955. This meeting was convened in the wake of what Beijing saw as U.S. nuclear blackmail during their initial Taiwan Straits confrontation of 1954–55 and the apparent hardening of U.S. support for the KMT regime on Taiwan embodied in a security treaty Washington had just negotiated with Taipei.[1] China launched its nuclear weapons program with the clear expectation of substantial aid from its Soviet superpower patron to whom it had been a loyal and deferential ally. The PRC's arsenal was to be both a national asset and a contribution to the socialist camp's collective deterrent capability. Thus, although Beijing was determined to maintain national control over deployed nuclear forces, it felt entitled to and anticipated assistance from the Soviet Union.

At first Moscow proved willing to help China develop its nuclear capability.[2] Soon, however, the Soviets began to worry that precipitous action by a Chinese ally about whose prudence they had doubts could entrap them in a dangerous clash with the United States. This prospect seemed ever riskier as the nuclear component of the Eisenhower administration's "New Look" in foreign policy became clear—the threat to launch massive retaliatory strikes against the socialist camp in response to an unspecified set of contingencies. Consequently, military assistance that would make the Chinese feel more secure and perhaps embolden them to confront U.S. forces in East Asia would make the So-

[1]On the role of the 1954–55 Taiwan Straits Crisis as the "proximate cause" for China's formal decision to push ahead with nuclear weapons development, see John W. Lewis and Litai Xue, *China Builds the Bomb*, p. 35; see also pp. 31–42; Zhang Shuguang, *Deterrence and Strategic Culture*, p. 222; *Zhongguo Renmin Jiefangjun, shang*, p. 506; Robert Norris, Andrew S. Burrows, and Richard K. Fieldhouse, *British, French and Chinese Nuclear Weapons*, p. 327.

[2]Soviet assistance was formally specified in six agreements concluded with the PRC between 1955 and 1958. See Lewis and Xue, *China Builds the Bomb*, pp. 40–42.

viets feel less secure.[3] John Lewis and Xue Litai have concluded that by early 1958 Moscow had secretly decided not to deliver on its pledge to supply Beijing with a prototype atomic bomb, reneging on an agreement signed just months earlier.[4] Instead of informing the Chinese who were preparing to accept delivery, the Soviets engaged in a frustrating pattern of stalling that would continue for the next eighteen months. Interested primarily in enhancing Soviet security by improving relations with the United States, Khrushchev apparently had decided to scrap the policy of expediting development of China's independent nuclear capability and instead to promote his ideas on Sino-Soviet naval cooperation described in Chapter 3. Unlike the transfer of technology that would result in an independently controlled Chinese nuclear arsenal, the proposals for joint military operations would enhance Moscow's ability to manage the risks of entrapment in unwanted clashes with the United States. As already noted, in July 1958 Mao and his colleagues, sensitive to their nation's century-long history of international humiliation, vigorously objected to these new Soviet initiatives precisely on the grounds that they would compromise Beijing's decision-making autonomy.[5] China's willingness to escalate tensions with the United States in the Taiwan Straits the following month and its reluctance to consult with the Soviet leaders before, or to defer to their leadership during the confrontation sealed Moscow's decision to end its atomic generosity.[6] During

[3]CIA analysts in 1958 correctly detected the delicate and difficult nature of Sino-Soviet nuclear cooperation, though they underestimated its implications for the durability of an alliance they expected to last. If Soviet nuclear weapons were supplied to China, despite the "potential military risks involved" the American analysts expected they would remain under some form of Soviet control ("Main Trends in Soviet Capabilities and Policies, 1958–1963," CIA, no date, p. 53). And though falling short of predicting the collapse of an alliance that was by then virtually a dead letter, in 1962 CIA analysts noted that Moscow's "partnership with China involves the possibility of being drawn into riskier situations than they wish to contemplate" ("Political Developments in the USSR and the Communist World," CIA, Feb. 21, 1962, p. 15). See also "Implications for the Free World and the Communist Bloc of Growing Nuclear Capabilities," CIA, Feb. 3, 1959, pp. 1, 10, 13; "Sino-Soviet Relations," CIA, Aug. 9, 1960; "Sino-Soviet Relations in the Early 1980s," CIA, June 5, 1980, p. 3.

[4]The New Defense Technical Accord was signed on October 15, 1957. See Lewis and Xue, *China Builds the Bomb*, pp. 41, 61.

[5]In a review of China's foreign policy independence, Li Dai chronicles Beijing's resistance to what it saw as Soviet attempts to interfere in China's domestic affairs and its rejection of Khrushchev's proposal for a "'joint flotilla' along the Chinese coast and a 'long-wave radio' communications network to command the Soviet flotilla in an effort to exercise military control over China" (Li, "Independence and China's External Relations," p. A2).

[6]See Lewis and Xue, *China Builds the Bomb*, pp. 61–65; A. Doak Barnett, *China and the Major Powers in East Asia*, pp. 32–37.

what turned out to be the last months of Sino-Soviet nuclear cooperation, Soviet specialists in China stonewalled their Chinese colleagues on crucial aspects of bomb design.[7] Beijing meanwhile began to suspect that Moscow would never provide any useful assistance to China's bomb project, though it continued to hope otherwise until the decisive cutoff announced in Khrushchev's letter of June 1959.[8]

In short, over the summer of 1958 Beijing had become increasingly suspicious of the motives and thoroughly frustrated with the stinginess of what seemed to be a diffident ally. Moscow, by contrast, fearfully anticipated the dire consequences of an entangling alliance with a nuclear-armed China that might prove less pliable once it was less dependent.[9] Consequently, what had begun in 1955 as a dual track decision by Beijing to combine indigenous efforts with Soviet assistance in developing nuclear weapons to benefit both the PRC and the socialist bloc, soon became a totally self-reliant program to serve China's national interests. China's go-it-alone nuclear effort resulted from a growing unwillingness to endure the compromises on autonomy inherent in its dependent status as junior partner in a Sino-Soviet alliance whose military usefulness was in any event offset by Beijing's concerns about abandonment. This had turned out to be an alliance with what China saw as a reluctant, unreliable partner who, when called upon, acted as if security was a private Soviet, rather than a collective socialist bloc, good. Whatever

[7]Lewis and Xue, *China Builds the Bomb*, pp. 64, 160–63. According to official Chinese sources, prior to the final rupture the Soviets informed the PRC that they were merely holding up on delivery of a teaching model of an atomic bomb and related design materials (*Zhongguo Renmin Jiefangjun, shang*, p. 516).

[8]Following China's refusal to accede to Moscow's demands for closer military integration under the Kremlin's leadership, "[t]he Soviet Union then perfidiously tore up agreements and contracts, recalled its experts and carried out large-scale subversive activities in our Xinjiang region" (Li Dai, "Independence and China's External Relations," p. A2). China's nuclear scientists would name their first atomic bomb "596" in reference to the date of the letter that announced there would be no Soviet prototype weapon delivered to China. During a January 1960 meeting addressing the recent experience, Nie Rongzhen impugned Soviet motives by stating that their "technical aid has become untrustworthy" and that they want "to maintain a considerable gap between China and the Soviet Union in scientific research on the development of new types of weapons and military equipment" (Lewis and Xue, *China Builds the Bomb*, pp. 72, 150). See also "Possible Changes in the Sino-Soviet Relationship," CIA, Oct. 25, 1973, pp. 3–4.

[9]According to Zhang Shuguang's research, Khrushchev had become so concerned about the prospect of the Chinese dragging him into an unwanted clash with the United States over the issue of Taiwan that during a visit to Beijing in fall 1959 he suggested Beijing renounce the use of force against Taiwan, or even acknowledge its independence (Zhang, *Deterrence and Strategic Culture*, p. 266).

its economic merits, free-riding on Moscow's deterrent was not only politically but also strategically unsatisfactory. Soviet attempts to condition continued aid on arrangements that would grant them some control over the PRC's military activities had aggravated Chinese suspicions by touching a raw nationalist nerve. Especially as China's perception of an acute threat from the United States diminished after 1958, the
political price of tepid Soviet support seemed unacceptably high and the
strategic benefits, including nuclear assistance, unacceptably low.[10] Depending on foreigners for technological assistance, in Nie Rongzhen's
words, would keep China "vulnerable to outside manipulation" and always one step behind.[11] In 1959, as Khrushchev announced the termina-
tion of Soviet aid, China accelerated its nuclear weapons program,
which it now saw as a totally self-reliant crash effort to provide the nation with a security guarantee that could substitute for dependence on
what Beijing had decided was a diffident, meddling ally.[12] In two key
meetings (an enlarged meeting of the CCP's Military Affairs Committee
in February 1960 and a Work Conference of the CCP Central Committee at Beidaihe in July–August 1960) China's top leaders confirmed their
decision to push ahead independently. At Mao's urging, shortly thereafter they moved up the target date for the PRC' first atomic weapon test
from 1967 to 1964, a timetable confirmed in August 1962, and met
when China exploded the device on October 16, 1964.[13]

[10]Chong-pin Lin, *China's Nuclear Weapons Strategy*, p. 107. Though CIA analysts as late as 1962 failed to fully appreciate the seriousness of the split, in part because they believed that "China would regard a full rupture [of the alliance] as enor-
mously damaging to its military posture and economic prospects," they did correctly
note that "[t]he dispute . . . has already moved beyond the limit which these considerations, rationally valid as they continue to be, would seem to dictate." Thus it was
recognized that Soviet reluctance to back China's pursuit of its national interests
was frustrating Beijing and that "Peiping may therefore believe that a split, painful as
it would be, would be preferable to meeting Soviet terms" ("Political Developments
in the USSR and the Communist World," CIA, Feb. 21, 1962, pp. 15, 16).
    [11]Lewis and Xue, *China Builds the Bomb*, p. 238.
    [12]Ibid., p. 65.
    [13]*Zhongguo Renmin Jiefangjun, shang*, pp. 510, 516–18. The pattern of an accel-
erating timetable repeated itself in China's development of a hydrogen bomb. In February 1965, under Zhou Enlai's leadership, the regime set 1968 as the target date for
testing a thermonuclear weapon, a deadline beaten by half a year when China tested
such a device on June 17, 1967 (ibid., p. 521). Although the Chinese history of this period asserts that some foreign experts saw the Soviet pullout as a "death blow" that
meant China would be "unable to produce an atomic bomb even after twenty years"
(ibid., p. 516), the American view of these events was actually much less dramatic.
U.S. intelligence estimates in 1960 predicted only that a cutoff of Soviet aid "would
substantially retard China's progress in becoming a nuclear power," still expected
sometime between 1962 and 1964. Only the Assistant Chief of Naval Operations

STATUS, SECURITY INTERESTS, AND CHINA'S
NUCLEAR WEAPONS

Before describing China's nuclear forces and the deterrent doctrine they
served, a few brief comments on some of the motives for the weapons
development effort other than a desire for greater security are in order.
Among those who doubt the military value of smaller nuclear arsenals,
it is often alleged that motives other than security (typically status or
prestige) are the real reasons states unable or unwilling to deploy large,
sophisticated arsenals nevertheless want nuclear weapons. In discussing
the PRC's response to the fear of abandonment, I have already suggested
the way in which China's preference for autonomy was driven not
solely by the self-help imperatives of life in an anarchic realm, but also
by a strong, historically conditioned national preference for political independence. Even if Beijing had been confident of the Soviet *military*
guarantee against the U.S. threat in the 1950s, its *political* uneasiness
with its junior status and the compromises of its sovereignty the alliance entailed would have encouraged the pursuit of an independent
means to provide for Chinese security. In this sense, repeatedly
wounded national pride, and not just a narrow military concern, was an
incentive for the self-reliance that ultimately required a Chinese nuclear capability.[14]

(Intelligence) in a dissenting footnote doubted the Chinese could accomplish much
before the end of the five-year estimate. At the other extreme, the Assistant Chief of
Staff, Intelligence, Department of the Air Force, in his dissenting footnote expected a
Chinese nuclear test in 1962, but possibly as early as late 1961 ("The Chinese Communist Atomic Energy Program," CIA, Dec. 13, 1960, p. 2).

[14]Lewis and Xue similarly suggest that the events of the early 1950s were the
"proximate causes" or specific threats that determined the timing of China's decision to deploy nuclear weapons; a historically conditioned desire to reduce the country's vulnerability to outside pressure was the underlying security concern (*China
Builds the Bomb*, p. 35). In addition to a widely shared concern about national status,
Mao Zedong's concern about his personal status may well have also fueled China's
nuclear ambitions, though it is hard to disentangle individual and national interests
in a case where the leader and many of his followers identified the two so closely. For
a systematic and highly original effort to consider these issues, see Yue Ren, "National Image-Conflicts and the Pursuit of Nuclear Independence." Ren's discussion
of China's weapons program (and his parallel discussion of France's) correctly identifies Mao's and de Gaulle's strong concerns about international image. His analysis,
however, does not demonstrate that image considerations were more important than
security considerations. Instead they were often thoroughly entangled and mutually
reinforcing, if not indistinguishable, as when Mao or de Gaulle asserted that they
needed nuclear weapons in order to be respected, taken seriously, and control their
countries' own fate. See Yue Ren, pp. 5, 100, 125, 139, 262–63, 319–20.

Thus an interest in bolstering China's international prestige did contribute to Beijing's decision to pursue nuclear weapons in the 1950s and retain and modernize them thereafter.[15] Serving this interest was not simple, however, since it required Beijing to limit the harm to its reputation that might follow from the deployment of weapons the Chinese Communists themselves had belittled and that global public opinion had come to disdain.[16] In part Beijing dealt with this difficulty through rhetoric that placed the moral onus for its program on the shoulders of the superpowers whose nuclear threats required China to develop a countervailing capability. Beginning in the mid-1950s Mao asserted what became the PRC's official position—that China needed atomic bombs in order to avoid being bullied by others, a point restated on the occasion of the PRC's first atom bomb test in October 1964, and reiterated by Mao's successors, Hua Guofeng and then Deng Xiaoping.[17] The fear of negative reactions was also addressed by portraying the weapons program as another element in China's international effort to champion the rights of the world's developing states threatened by superpower hegemony. In the interest of international peace, not just national secu-

[15]See Peng Guangqian, Wang Guangxu et al., eds., *Junshi Zhanlüe Jianlun*, pp. 166–67.

[16]The U.S. government, worried about China's program as a stimulus to further proliferation but reluctant to use military force to abort it, hoped to exploit China's embarrassment. In November 1964 one of the papers prepared by the Gilpatric Committee suggesting ways to limit the spread of nuclear weapons listed as its first recommendation: "*Stimulating adverse reactions to the Chinese Communist test.* A continued and aggressive program to encourage the strongest and most universal adverse reaction to the Chinese Communist nuclear test is an essential part of any program for limiting the spread of nuclear weapons. Circular instructions have already been issued to underscore points calculated to produce the above reaction in foreign governments. These instructions have also asked the appropriate posts to protest to certain states which have been less than forthcoming in expressions of condemnation of the Chinese Communist test" ("Program to Limit the Spread of Nuclear Weapons," Nov. 3, 1964, pp. 1–2).

[17]On the eve of China's first atomic bomb test, Mao justified the effort to several foreign guests who had just attended an anti-nuclear World Congress in Japan: "In the future, our country might produce a small quantity of atomic bombs, but we are not preparing to use them. If we are not preparing to use them, why produce them? We will use them as defensive weapons. Today, some big nuclear powers, especially the United States, use atomic bombs to intimidate people" (Mao Zedong, "Shijie Renmin Shi Fandui Yong Yuanzidan Sha Ren de," p. 540). See also Peng, Wang et al., eds., *Junshi Zhanlüe Jianlun*, pp. 166, 167; Chen Chongbei, Shou Xiaosong, and Liang Xiaoqiu, *Weishe Zhanlüe*, p. 209; "Premier Hua Guofeng Discusses China's Development of Strategic Weaponry"; Yang Xuhua and Cai Renzhao, *Weishe Lun*, p. 409. See also Deng Xiaoping's conversation with French Foreign Minister Jean-Bernard Raimond reported in James Miles, "Deng Says Nuclear Arms Necessary for Peace."

rity, China would shatter the superpowers' nuclear monopoly because "... as long as the danger of war still exists, in circumstances where there is no essential guarantee of world peace, our country's nuclear weapons are still an important force for deterrence during peacetime."[18] On these terms, Beijing believed it could square its early anti-nuclear rhetoric with pursuit of its own capability as well as its initial refusal to join the nonproliferation regime. The PRC would consistently profess a willingness to scrap its nuclear weapons as part of global disarmament. But until this ambitious goal could be achieved, China would take the necessary steps to "strengthen its national defenses, safeguard the motherland, and safeguard world peace."[19]

China's arguments were designed to ensure that joining the nuclear club would help, rather than hurt, the country's international status. In any case, the uncertain prestige payoff was at best subordinate to the security motives for deploying nuclear weapons. Although China's leaders certainly anticipated that nuclear weapons would be yet another nationalist symbol of their country's renaissance, the timing and nature of the PRC's effort indicate that practical concerns loomed larger than symbolism. China's formal decision to launch its weapons development program in January 1955 was a direct reaction to the increased U.S. threat, especially the nuclear threat, that Mao and his colleagues perceived on the Taiwan front. Although a fully independent research and development program would have better demonstrated China's greatness, the need for quick results to ensure China's security "forced [Mao] to modify his preference for self-reliance." The sense of urgency to acquire a nuclear counter to the U.S. threat required him to solicit Soviet assistance, rather than undertake a "solo race for the bomb" even if the ultimate goal remained "an indigenous capability."[20] Nuclear weapons that required foreign help to build would clearly be less of a badge of honor than those independently produced, but the time for a program that would serve this purpose as well as China's security needs was a luxury that the leaders Beijing believed they could not afford.

Moreover, if nuclear weapons were valued mainly for their symbolic rather than their security value, demonstrating an ability to produce

[18]Peng, Wang et al., eds., *Junshi Zhanlüe Jianlun*, p. 167. As international anti-nuclear opinion in the 1980s grew in strength, Chinese analysts, though professing sympathy with the abolitionist views of Greenpeace and others, insisted on the need for peace-preserving nuclear weapons in Chinese hands. See Yang and Cai, *Weishe Lun*, p. 408; see also pp. 407, 410.

[19]Peng, Wang et al., eds., *Junshi Zhanlüe Jianlun*, p. 168.

[20]Lewis and Xue, *China Builds the Bomb*, pp. 39, 40, 42.

them should have sufficed. But China, like the other nuclear powers, followed its initial tests with sustained investment in nuclear weapons because they were desired for their deterrent value and China's leaders concluded that a capability serving this purpose required more than mere proof that they had mastered advanced military technology. It required deploying and maintaining the requisite warheads, delivery systems, and command and control infrastructure. After its successful nuclear tests in the mid-1960s, China pressed ahead with the arduous task of fielding a viable, if small, delivery capability. To obtain whatever nonsecurity status benefits were to be had, Beijing could have opted for a variant of the approach India took between 1974 and 1998, demonstrating the know-how to build, but at least formally refraining from deploying, operational weapons.[21] Because the status payoff was desirable but secondary, China moved beyond testing and took the steps it believed necessary to ensure that its nuclear capability provided the expected security payoff.[22]

Indeed, the purported linkage between a demonstrated nuclear capability and China's international prestige in and of itself would hardly have warranted the burden of sustaining a full-blown weapons program since, as it turned out, the nuclear arsenal failed to provide either prestige or increased political influence. From the 1960s through the 1980s, China's nuclear weapons status provided no boost for China in its ongo-

---

[21]And, as the recent literature on opaque proliferation suggests, this strategy would have provided some deterrent value because adversaries could not have been sure about covert weapons deployments. See Avner Cohen and Benjamin Frankel, "Opaque Nuclear Proliferation"; Devin T. Hagerty, *The Consequences of Nuclear Proliferation.*

[22]John Lewis and Litai Xue cite "The Guidelines for Developing Nuclear Weapons," which they believe emerged from a key meeting of the CCP's Central Military Commission between May 27 and July 22, 1958. Of the eight points listing the reasons for pursuing nuclear weapons and the methods to be adopted, none reflected the matter of status or prestige. Instead, the guidelines quite clearly stated the deterrent strategy for which China needed nuclear weapons ("Our country is developing nuclear weapons in order to warn our enemies against making war on us"; "To this end, we have to concentrate our energies on developing nuclear and thermonuclear warheads with high yields and long-range delivery vehicles") and the absolute priority for investment the regime assigned to the development effort ("Any other projects for our country's reconstruction will have to take second place to the development of nuclear weapons"). See Lewis and Xue, *China Builds the Bomb*, p. 70. The importance of this security interest was also reflected in the efforts of the Communist Party's leaders, in particular Zhou Enlai, to insulate to the programs for developing and testing nuclear weapons and ballistic missiles from the disruption the Cultural Revolution caused to most facets of scientific research and development between 1966 and 1976. See *Zhongguo Renmin Jiefangjun, shang*, p. 513.

ing rivalry with the Soviets in the Third World to win the loyalty of various nationalist or communist factions. Nuclear weapons status also did not enable China to supplant Taiwan in the United Nations and on its Security Council. Instead, entry would await the decision by the United States to refrain from blocking China's admission when it decided warming ties with Beijing would give Washington diplomatic leverage in its relations with Moscow. Nor did nuclear weapons status enable China to have a profound effect on the superpowers' nuclear "hegemony" or to advance the cause of nuclear disarmament, as Beijing had claimed it would. On the contrary, China's nuclear capability provided a pretext for the United States in 1968 to announce the deployment of a small force of anti-ballistic missiles (despite their recognized ineffectiveness against the massive Soviet threat and the envisioned limitations of an Anti-Ballistic Missile treaty) and in the 1970s provided incentives for the superpowers to maintain sufficiently large arsenals that China need not enter their complex arms control calculus. Nuclear weapons status did not even enable China to exercise greater regional influence. Instead, as China suffered through the turmoil of the Cultural Revolution and the stagnation of its failed Maoist development policy, Japan and the East Asian newly industrialized countries became the regional economic luminaries, India broke China's regional nuclear monopoly, and Vietnam acted as something of a Southeast Asian hegemon. China's rise to international prominence would eventually accelerate, but only in the 1990s, and as a result of the spectacular economic expansion Deng Xiaoping's reforms produced, not because of a nuclear weapons program that continued to lag behind others'.

Nevertheless, throughout the final decades of the Cold War (and after) China's determination to invest its scarce defense modernization resources in establishing the viability of its nuclear deterrent did not wane. However small the payoff in terms of international prestige, the payoff in terms of enhanced national security was deemed crucial. The Chinese leaders' understanding of the distinctive value of nuclear weapons for fulfilling the requirements of a robust yet affordable strategy of dissuasion by deterrence led them to expect a significant security benefit from deploying even the modest, unsophisticated arsenal that was within their reach.

CHINA'S NUCLEAR DETERRENT

Given China's comparatively limited resources, from the outset the PRC's leaders recognized they would not be able to deploy nuclear weapons on a par with the superpowers. Despite this easily anticipated disadvantage, Beijing believed a heavy investment in developing, deploying, and maintaining nuclear weapons was wise. When the balance in question involved nuclear weapons, traditional notions of inferiority and superiority would not be strategically decisive. In confrontations between nuclear adversaries, deterrence would dominate offensive and defensive considerations and the threat of nuclear retaliation would provide a robust means for dissuading even a vastly mightier foe.[23] The key to success would be to deploy nuclear weapons capable of inflicting terrible pain and suffering and then to maintain "first-strike uncertainty" in the adversary's mind—uncertainty about his prospects for a completely successful preemptive strike disarming China, and uncertainty about the circumstances under which China's clearly horrifying destructive force might be employed. In what sense did the nuclear capability deployed by Beijing meet these requirements? This is a question

[23]For Chinese analysis reflecting on the significance of the nuclear revolution, see Peng, Wang et al., eds., *Junshi Zhanlüe Jianlun*, p. 160; Chen, Shou, and Liang, *Weishe Zhanlüe*, pp. 47, 71; Yang and Cai, *Weishe Lun*, p. 410; Hu Wenlong, Zha Jinlu et al., eds., *Xiandai Junbingzhong Zhanshu*, esp. ch. 11, "Several Important Questions About Nuclear Strategy"; "China Says Its Nuclear Arms Will Deter U.S., Soviet Union"; Miles, "Deng Says Nuclear Arms Necessary for Peace." Strategic thinkers I met in China during spring 1991 typically insisted that China did not practice nuclear deterrence. Follow-up discussions quickly revealed this to be politically necessary rhetoric without much strategic significance. Part of the problem is semantic—the Chinese do not clearly contrast the use of the terms "deterrence" and "compellence." Indeed Chinese usage of "deterrence" sometimes seems closer to what most Western strategists would term "compellence"—the threat to inflict pain (in this case using nuclear weapons) to force a rival to change his position (Yang and Cai, *Weishe Lun*, pp. 120, 138, 139; Chen, Shou, and Liang, *Weishe Zhanlüe*, pp. 2, 257–58, 213–14). Therefore, according to my Chinese interlocutors, nuclear deterrence was a bullying strategy employed only by the superpowers in the Cold War world. They objected to labeling China's policy as nuclear deterrence because they wanted to distinguish it from the aggressive use of coercive capabilities by the superpowers. Instead they claimed that China (and the other medium-sized nuclear powers) possessed nuclear weapons only for purposes of retaliation, to instill in prospective aggressors the fear of devastating destruction. It would be difficult to come up with a strategic statement that more closely fit the standard definition of deterrence. For Chinese descriptions of their nuclear deterrent strategy, see Peng, Wang et al., eds., *Junshi Zhanlüe Jianlun*, pp. 160–62, 165–66, 168–69; Chen, Shou, and Liang, *Weishe Zhanlüe*, pp. 209, 213–15; Yang and Cai, *Weishe Lun*, pp. 408, 409, 410; Chung, "Visit to China's Nuclear Submarine Unit," p. 33; Hu, Zha et al., eds., *Xiandai Junbingzhong Zhanshu*, pp. 244–45. See also John W. Lewis and Litai Xue, *China's Strategic Seapower*, pp. 231–34. In the post–Cold War era, at least some Chinese analysts appear to be increasingly comfortable with the standard usage of "deterrence" to describe the People's Republic of China's strategy. See Alastair Iain Johnston, "China's New 'Old Thinking.'"

best answered by considering first the nuclear forces Beijing deployed, and second, the reasons why a prospective aggressor, however mighty, would have to worry they might be used in response to serious threats to vital Chinese interests.

China's Nuclear Arsenal: Not Much, but Enough

Following its nuclear tests in the mid-1960s, and for the remaining years of the Cold War, China had a relatively primitive nuclear capability, compared not only with the superpowers, but even with the other nuclear second-ranking powers, Britain and France. Although it pursued the full range of weapon types and delivery systems, the PRC lagged behind, both in the quantity and quality of its forces. Nevertheless, by the end of the 1960s China began to deploy powerful bombs well suited to inflicting terrifying pain and suffering on an adversary. Beijing could not provide for the levels of weapons survivability or warhead accuracy the other nuclear states were achieving, and until the late 1970s *probably* lacked delivery systems with range sufficient to reach key targets in the European heartland of the Soviet superpower that had emerged as China's principal adversary. China was, however, able to ensure that even a superpower would have to worry that some of the PRC's multimegaton citybusters might be missed in any preemptive strikes. The availability of such weapons for retaliation was an increasingly frightening prospect to the Soviets who were nervous and uncertain about China's improving delivery capability during the 1970s.[24]

What sort of nuclear weapons did China have? The secrecy surrounding every state's security establishment, combined with Beijing's deliberate attempts at disinformation about its capabilities discussed below, make it difficult to provide a definitive inventory of China's nuclear arsenal. Scholarly research, however, especially the pathbreaking work of John Lewis and his co-authors, provides detail sufficient for the purposes of this analysis.[25]

[24]See Chen, Shou, and Liang, *Weishe Zhanlüe*, p. 3; Peng and Wang, *Junshi Zhanlüe Jianlun*, p. 169; Yang and Cai, *Weishe Lun*, p. 411. Chinese analysts asserted that the aggressor would have to worry about some surviving nuclear retaliatory capability even if he launched a "large scale surprise nuclear attack"(ibid., 410). They also insisted that the fear of devastating retaliation could deter an aggressor despite his deployment of very effective, even 90 percent effective, ballistic missile defenses. See Sun Mingming and Cai Xiaohong, *Dongdangzhong de Guojia Anquan*, p. 193.

[25]See Lewis and Xue, *China Builds the Bomb*; Lewis and Hua, "China's Ballistic Missile Programs"; Norris, Burrows, and Fieldhouse, *British, French and Chinese Nuclear Weapons*; Lin, *China's Nuclear Weapons Strategy*; Bruce Larkin, *Nuclear Designs*.

The warheads loaded onto China's longer range delivery systems were shockingly powerful, even by the standards of the thermonuclear era.[26] The indiscriminate explosive yield of "big and dirty" one-, two-, three-, and five-megaton bombs would have been unsuitable for the more selective, limited nuclear options the superpowers contemplated, but they served Beijing's need to demonstrate an unmistakable capability supporting its terrifying deterrent threat of punishing retaliatory strikes. As was true for the other nuclear powers, most of these potent strategic weapons were first loaded onto bombers. By the mid-1970s, China had deployed more than 100 nuclear-armed bombers, mainly the Hong-6 (a subsonic medium-range Chinese version of the Soviet Tu-16). Each was capable of delivering a one- to three-megaton bomb, though only against Soviet targets east of the Urals.[27] These planes comprised about half of China's available strategic launch platforms as late as 1985, but their relative vulnerability, questionable penetrability, and limited range would gradually diminish their importance.[28] As early as 1959, China's technological shortcomings in aircraft production and the obvious delivery advantages of the rocket-based alternatives others were pursuing (both in terms of certainty of penetrating any defenses and, if properly based, survivability) had led Beijing to plan for a force structure emphasizing ballistic missiles, even though realizing this goal proved to be an arduous task.[29]

Sources disagree about some of the precise dates for initial introduction, pace of deployment, total numbers, and warhead yield for China's various nuclear missile systems, but the broad picture is clear. The People's Republic of China deployed its fifty DF-2s, an MRBM with a 20 kiloton warhead, beginning in 1966. Its range was limited to U.S. bases and allies in Northeast Asia (urgent targets before Sino-American rapprochement), the Sino-Soviet theater of operations, and major Siberian cities. Beginning in 1971, China deployed between 60 and 125 DF-3s, an

[26]Thus China had fielded forces that met one of the main characteristics emphasized in the "Guidelines" for its nuclear weapons program outlined in 1958—"high yields and long-range delivery systems." See Lewis and Xue, *China Builds the Bomb*, p. 70.

[27]See Norris, Burrows, and Fieldhouse, *British, French and Chinese Nuclear Weapons*, p. 359.

[28]Lin, *China's Nuclear Weapons Strategy*, p. 48.

[29]*Zhongguo Renmin Jiefangjun, shang*, pp. 506–29. Though China's leaders recognized the strategic desirability of relying on missiles rather than bombers to deliver a deterrent blow, their efforts to prevent the political turmoil of the Cultural Revolution from affecting missile research and development were only partially successful, and the disruption slowed the refinement of longer-range systems and solid-fuel propellant technology (ibid., pp. 527–28).

intermediate-range ballistic missile (IRBM) with a two- or three-megaton warhead that provided the PRC with a more potent threat against
the Soviet Far East.[30] In 1980 China began deployment of between 6 and
20 DF-4s, a limited range ICBM with a one- or three-megaton warhead,
capable of devastating targets in European Russia,[31] and in 1981 began to
deploy at least four DF-5s, a full range ICBM that could be armed with a
three-, four-, or five-megaton weapon.[32] In April 1981 China took an initial step toward deploying sea-based nuclear forces when it commis-
sioned the country's first ballistic missile–firing nuclear submarine
(SSBN); in October 1982 it successfully tested its JL-1 submarine-
launched ballistic missile (SLBM). The challenges of fielding strategic
submarine forces proved daunting and apparently led Beijing to actually
deploy only one of the first generation Xia-class SSBNs, carrying 12 in-
termediate range JL-1s, each with a single 200–300kt warhead.[33]

Of these forces comprising a nascent Chinese nuclear triad, the land-
based missiles were given top priority during the Cold War. This emphasis, as well as the large fraction of the nuclear arsenal based on
bombers, would seem at odds with the need to ensure the survival of retaliatory forces essential to the strategy of deterrence, especially for a
country with so few weapons. By the 1970s, many security analysts
were beginning to doubt the survivability and effectiveness of penetrating manned bombers and, to a lesser extent, the survivability of immo-
bile land-based ICBMs. Improved air defenses against bombers and the
increasing accuracy of multiple-warhead ICBMs that could be used in
counterforce strikes against land-based missiles, some argued, were
changing the strategic environment that had prevailed during the first
two decades of the Cold War. The superpowers responded to this allegedly new strategic environment by investing in expensive modernization programs. The United States and the USSR sought to deploy large
numbers of ever more sophisticated submarine-based nuclear forces
that were generally regarded as the most survivable of the highly effec-

---

[30]Norris, Burrows, and Fieldhouse, *British, French and Chinese Nuclear Weapons*, pp. 11, 359, 362–63, 380–81.

[31]Ibid., pp. 11, 359, 363, 382–83.

[32]Ibid., pp. 11, 359, 363–64, 384–85.

[33]For various estimates of these capabilities, other than the composite picture of-
fered in Norris, Burrows, and Fieldhouse, *British, French and Chinese Nuclear Weapons*, see John W. Lewis and Hua Di, "China's Ballistic Missile Programs";
Lewis and Xue, *China Builds the Bomb*, pp. 212–14; Lewis and Xue, *China's Strate-
gic Seapower*; Lin, *China's Nuclear Weapons Strategy*, pp. 48–51, 58–59; *The Military Balance 1987–1988*, pp. 145–48; *The Military Balance 1991–1992*, pp. 149, 150,
152, 228.

tive ballistic missile delivery systems. They spent enormous sums of money developing advanced bombers that were expected to have a better chance of penetrating defenses (because of special flying capabilities, electronic countermeasures, or stealthy design) or equipping them with sophisticated long-range cruise missiles whose precise guidance systems would permit their launch in standoff mode (without the crews actually challenging enemy anti-aircraft defenses). Both also tried to reduce the vulnerability of their land-based missiles by investing in costly schemes for making them mobile (on rail or road) or more durable (superhardening silos, or providing them with anti-missile defenses). These sorts of ambitious modernization programs were beyond China's financial and scientific capabilities during the Cold War. Yet China's leaders apparently viewed the relatively small, vulnerable land-based missiles they could deploy as the backbone of their capability. Why? Confidence in the enduring viability of land-based missiles, even as they also worked to develop a modest submarine force and to upgrade the quality of their bomber force, was rooted in their nuclear doctrine. Chinese resources precluded deployment of a nearly invulnerable second-strike capability, such as the submarine forces of the superpowers. And although it might be desirable, one was not necessary. What was necessary was the ability to create first-strike uncertainty in the mind of a mightily armed aggressor. This much could be accomplished relatively cheaply through clever deployment of less sophisticated weapons systems as a stopgap until the day arrived when China's scientific and economic resources would permit a more ambitious modernization program.

The importance of relying on clever deployment, rather than expensive investment, to increase the dissuasiveness of China's meager nuclear arsenal dictated the priority assigned land-based missiles during the Cold War. Neither bombers nor submarines offered similar possibilities for creating and manipulating first-strike uncertainty in the mind of a prospective aggressor about the survivability of China's retaliatory nuclear forces. These other two legs of the Chinese triad could, however, still play a modest deterrent role. Chinese bombers were clearly quite vulnerable to preemptive strikes and had little chance of penetrating Soviet anti-aircraft defenses. But dispersal of aircraft during a prewar crisis during which forces would also be placed on highest levels of alert enabling quicker takeoff, together with inevitable imperfections in the execution of even a well-planned counterforce first strike and unavoidable leaks in defensive systems (not to mention dumb luck), meant that a Soviet planner choosing to attack had to accept the terrifying possibility that one or more of China's obsolete planes would survive and deliver a multimegaton weapon in retaliation.[34] This sort of nagging worry about the Chinese bomber force bolstered deterrence, but short of an expensive aircraft modernization program there was little China could do to increase the concern this leg of the triad created.

China's submarine-based ballistic missiles offered the prospect of a less vulnerable retaliatory force, but the engineering barriers to entry were even higher than for a modern bomber force. Surmounting them would prove expensive, particularly given the requirements for a fleet that would be worth the huge investment. The very small fleet China could deploy during the Cold War (one or two submarines) concentrated many launchers on few platforms, risking the loss of multiple missiles if the boat was destroyed before executing its retaliatory strike. Prudent Chinese leaders could not lightly dismiss the risks of detection and destruction. China's submariners would have to cope with a Soviet antisubmarine warfare (ASW) capability honed in rivalry with a much more sophisticated U.S. adversary. For Soviet ASW forces, Chinese submarines would be relatively easy prey. The well-trained Soviets in their hunter-killer submarines would be out to track and target no more than one or two Chinese SSBNs, an inexperienced fleet that faced daunting operational difficulties introduced by the shallowness of seas and the chokepoints created by island chains off the China coast. Eluding Soviet ASW forces and gaining access to the open ocean would be important not just for concealment and survival, but also because the limited range of China's first-generation SLBMs required they be launched from a location closer to key Russian targets than the western Pacific Ocean.[35] These challenges to China deploying a viable SLBM force could eventually be met. But because the near-term prospects for developing more advanced submarine systems were dim, during the 1970s and

[34]On the dubious survivability and penetrability of China's bombers, see Lewis and Xue, *China's Strategic Seapower*, p. 234. What counts, however, is that an attacker could not tolerate much, if any, slippage in the effectiveness of a counterforce first strike against aircraft before they took off, buttressed by a robust air defense system. This would be difficult to ensure with confidence. Soviet planners would have had to worry about desperate Chinese leaders taking crude but effective steps to degrade air defenses, such as the detonation of nuclear devices near the Sino-Soviet border with the purpose of at least temporarily blinding radar installations. Regarding the various degrading and disabling effects of nuclear explosions on electronic systems, see Desmond Ball, "Can Nuclear War Be Controlled?"; Bruce Blair, *Strategic Command and Control*.

[35]Lewis and Hua, "China's Ballistic Missile Programs," pp. 27–29.

1980s China had to devise some other approach to increasing the first-strike uncertainty of its Soviet adversary.[36]

The shortcomings of its bomber force and the limitations of its SSBN program constrained the PRC to emphasize deployment of land-based ballistic missiles. But in an era of improving satellite reconnaissance and increasingly accurate superpower weapons, how could China enhance the survivability of a small collection of land-based missiles? The Chinese employed a variety of relatively economical means to complicate any aggressor's attempts at first-strike planning, increasing the likelihood that some of its awesome retaliatory forces would be available even after determined attack by a sophisticated and powerful adversary. Although Beijing considered several relatively expensive and complex approaches to making its missiles mobile (on rail or ships), during the Cold War it instead emphasized a cheaper and simpler program of concerted deception designed to frustrate those who would plan counterforce strikes against the PRC's nuclear forces. No adversary was to be sure it had succeeded in locating and targeting all of China's deterrent arsenal.[37]

Deception that created first-strike uncertainty during the Cold War took two forms. First, the distinctively closed nature of Chinese society during the Maoist era helped the PRC ensure great uncertainty about the overall size of its nuclear arsenal. As early as 1971, U.S. Central Intelligence Agency analysts concluded that the Soviets were having problems "estimating Chinese strategic offensive capabilities" and noted that "their apprehensions probably incline them toward worst case estimating."[38] Even with improvements in reconnaissance technology and China's greater openness in the post-Mao era after 1976, the margin for

[36]By the end of the 1980s, however, the commander of the PLA Navy's nuclear submarine unit was openly arguing for the growing importance of the SSBNs, restating the argument that had become standard fare in the other nuclear states, that technical advances were rendering land-based forces unacceptably vulnerable (Chung, "Visit to China's Nuclear Submarine Unit").

[37]Lin, *China's Nuclear Weapons Strategy*, pp. 52, 69. See also Lewis and Hua, "China's Ballistic Missile Programs," pp. 26–27. Toward the end of the Cold War, China also established "round-the-clock alerts" for its strategic forces (Lewis and Xue, *China's Strategic Seapower*, p. 236). Given the difficulties of maintaining liquid-fueled rockets on high levels of alert, it is unclear how meaningful increased alert would have been prior to the deployment of the solid-fueled DF-21s in 1988. For a 1982 U.S. Defense Intelligence Agency estimate that some of the newest Chinese liquid-fueled CSS-3 (DF-4) ICBMs photographed by satellite could be fired in less than *three hours*, see "Weekly Intelligence Summary," pp. 9–11.

[38]"Soviet Policy in Asia," CIA, Apr. 15, 1971, p. 10. See also "Sino-Soviet Relations in the 1980s," CIA, June 5, 1980, p. 17.

error in best estimates remained very large, possibly on the order of two to three hundred percent.[39] China's decision not to participate in arms control regimes meant that Beijing did not have to agree to even imperfect verification schemes or offer an accounting of its forces. This decision therefore limited transparency and increased uncertainty about the number and variety of its nuclear weapons.[40] Second, in deploying their two most potent land-based missiles, the DF-4 (with range to hit Moscow) and DF-5 (China's genuine intercontinental missile), the Chinese adopted basing schemes that increased the targeting problems for Soviet planners. In response to directions from Mao Zedong on May 25, 1975, the Chinese military developed a cave-basing mode for the DF-4 that made these weapons less vulnerable to an attempted counterforce first strike, and perhaps also afforded a degree of secrecy as to number and location. The DF-4s were stored in the caves; if launch was ordered, the missiles would be prepared inside, and then moved outside for final fueling and firing. This basing strategy Zhang Aiping dubbed "shooting a firecracker outside the front door" became operational on August 2, 1980. The survivability of the small handful of DF-5s (perhaps as few as four) was enhanced by building "a large number of bogus silos," "shallow holes disguised to look like the real thing," rather than pursuing the more expensive and technologically challenging alternative of mobile basing (on ships or railcars) or banking solely on the less effective option of camouflaging fixed silos.[41]

Still, ingenuity notwithstanding, given the central role attached to so small a number of relatively vulnerable fixed, land-based forces, some doubted the usefulness of China's Cold War nuclear deterrent. As one analyst put it, the PRC had only a "tentative second-strike capability," and an "assured second-strike capability" would not be attained until it deployed more than 100 ICBMs, ideally with multiple warheads, as well as a fleet of at least six SSBNs.[42] China's leaders also recognized the

[39]Norris, Burrows, and Fieldhouse, *British, French and Chinese Nuclear Weapons*, pp. 358–59, 365. Such uncertainty in estimating the size of China's arsenal persists, as noted in Alastair I. Johnston, "Prospects for Chinese Nuclear Force Modernization," pp. 558–64.

[40]The preference for ambiguity works against transparency arrangements necessary for arms control verification since "it is not in the interests of weak states, who need to keep superior adversaries guessing about their capabilities" (Johnston, "China's New 'Old Thinking,'" p. 31).

[41]Lewis and Hua, "China's Ballistic Missile Programs," pp. 24–25. Lin, *China's Nuclear Weapons Strategy*, pp. 52, 69. For prescient commentary that anticipated these sorts of deceptions by smaller nuclear powers, see Kenneth Waltz, "Toward Nuclear Peace," pp. 695–99.

[42]Robert S. Wang, "China's Evolving Strategic Doctrine," p. 1050.

shortcomings in their force posture. Especially after Mao's death in 1976, they planned for modernization that would move beyond the shoestring measures just described and further reduce doubts about the PRC's retaliatory capability. Even so, the tightness of economic and technological constraints continued to shape planning. Thus the desire for a solid-fueled, mobile missile that would be less of a sitting duck, could be maintained on higher levels of alert, and would have quicker reaction times, was met by developing, the DF-21, a road-mobile adaptation of the JL-1 SLBM. By having the SLBM "go ashore," Beijing was able to salvage the research and development costs for the JL-1, whose range (about 1000 miles) greatly reduced its practical value as a submarine-based retaliatory weapon for use against the Soviet heartland.[43] With deployment of the mobile, solid-fueled DF-21 and the extended range DF-21a, China began to address the major drawbacks of its first generation long-range land-based missiles, the DF-4 and DF-5, whose liquid fueling "require[d] hours to prepare for firing" and whose launch readiness [could] be sustained for only a "limited period."[44] Gradual but determined modernization would continue in the 1990s, as will be noted in Chapter 7.

China's late Cold War push to create a nuclear arsenal that would increase the survivability of its retaliatory forces was understandable. But such efforts should not obscure the importance of China's initially small and relatively vulnerable nuclear capability where it mattered most, in the eyes of its principal adversary. Nuclear deterrence of the strong by the weak rests on the nagging fears that inhibit the powerful from challenging an overwhelmingly outgunned rival. As one Chinese analyst argued, because the superpowers "could not withstand retaliatory blows dealt by medium-sized nuclear powers . . . there is a 'workable' balance . . . in the confrontation between medium-sized nuclear powers and the superpowers" despite the fact that the latter "are in a position to destroy the former. . . . [I]t is neither possible nor necessary for China to compete with the superpowers in quantity of nuclear weapons. . . . Although China's nuclear strength is limited, it is reliable."[45] By the mid-1970s even a remarkably effective Soviet first strike against *known* Chinese forces could not have *ensured* the destruction of all the terrifying weapons it feared Beijing might be able to launch in re-

[43]Lewis and Hua, "China's Ballistic Missile Programs," p. 27.
[44]Ibid., p. 28. See also Harlan Jencks, "Defending China in 1987," p. 277.
[45]Zhang Jianzhi, "Views on Medium-Sized Nuclear Powers' Nuclear Strategy," pp. K32, K33. See also the reflections of a commander of a Chinese missile brigade cited in Lewis and Xue, *China Builds the Bomb*, p. 216.

taliation.[46] Especially with China's determined efforts at deception, Soviet planners, though enjoying substantial qualitative and quantitative
superiority, could not eliminate the risk that Beijing would retain forces
sufficient to inflict devastating punishment. Should a confrontation
spin out of control, the USSR faced the risk of clearly horrifying retaliation. This fear constrained Moscow's conventional, as well as nuclear,
options since military action substantial enough to accomplish its goals
even against an outgunned PRC, would have to be on a scale that necessarily courted "possible escalation that could lead to Chinese nuclear attacks on the Soviet homeland. . . ." [47]

China's Nuclear Credibility: Not Much, but Enough

Yet Chinese nuclear forces, however survivable, would only have an
inhibiting, dissuasive effect if Moscow believed they might actually be
launched. Thus, aside from measures that explicitly aimed at cultivating doubt in the adversary's mind about the sorts of punishment China
might be *able* to inflict in response to aggression, the dissuasive effect
of China's nuclear weapons derived also from uncertainties about behavior, in particular the likelihood Beijing would actually use the capabilities at its disposal. And there are good reasons, noted in Chapter
2, to conclude that a grossly outgunned victim would not choose ragged retaliation after absorbing a first strike. Analysts skeptical of the
durability of deterrence between the United States and Soviet Union,
after all, had asserted the importance of offensive advantages that
might make preemption attractive against a superpower with more
numerous, less vulnerable forces, and more technologically sophisti-

---

[46]The director of the CIA reported in 1978: "Numerous statements have been
made by informed Soviets that attest to a belief that China possesses a small but significant nuclear deterrent." Though a passage is deleted in the sanitized declassified
document, the U.S. analysts seemed to believe that despite uncertainty about the
exact nature of China's nuclear arsenal, Soviet superiority would provide incentives
to attempt a "carefully executed attack on China's nuclear sites . . . in a major conflict, especially one that was not going well for the USSR" in order to limit damage to
the Soviet Union. It is doubtful that decision-makers in Moscow would have been as
confident as Washington's analysts about the feasibility of limiting damage after escalation to the nuclear level. See "Soviet Goals and Expectations in the Global Power
Arena," May 19, 1978, p. 19.

[47]Banning N. Garrett and Bonnie S. Glaser, *War and Peace*, p. 114. Any Soviet
nuclear strike against China would likely have been large-scale. Moscow's fear of a
potential post-nuclear multi-front war in which its country would be threatened by a
still populous China as well as other hostile states that ringed the Soviet homeland
mitigated against anything but massive nuclear strikes on China (ibid., pp. 27–29,
105–6, 108, 115–16).

cated command and control than China possessed. According to such logic, a small and crude nuclear arsenal like the PRC's *a fortiori* should invite preemption rather than bolster deterrence, especially as China's relatively primitive command and control seemed highly vulnerable to decapitation that would render any surviving weapons capability useless. Whether or not a national command survived, what purpose could rationally be served by China's launching nuclear weapons when it would be outgunned at every rung on the ladder of escalation? A small nuclear force would not enable China to engage in a tit-for-tat limited competition in inflicting and absorbing pain, and an unlimited strike would be suicidal because it would invite massive retaliation from an ever capable superpower adversary. In short, though China might not be fully disarmed, China, to use Paul Nitze's term, would be "self-deterred."[48] By this reasoning, China's nuclear investment was far from adequate for deterrence and, therefore, could not provide a very robust security guarantee. Investment in the forces and command and control necessary to eliminate a superpower aggressor's first strike advantage would have required military budgets well beyond China's reach.[49]

Why, then, were the Chinese convinced that the nuclear deterrent they *could* afford was in fact worth the investment? The answer is that they seemed to appreciate that states necessarily operate with incomplete information about the future. If its adversaries could be certain that Beijing would always behave as a rational actor, then it would be true that China's mere *ability* to threaten horrifying retaliation would not enable it to dissuade any attack short of an unrestrained first strike. Under any other scenario, the aggressor could be confident that rational Chinese leaders would recognize that escalation could only worsen their

[48]Paul Nitze, "Deterring our Deterrent."

[49]Economic constraints, rather than conceptual blindspots, provide a more plausible explanation for China's modest nuclear command and control capabilities. China's military thinkers were keenly aware, perhaps by reading the growing western literature on the subject, of the demanding technical and organizational requirements for operating a coordinated nuclear establishment that would have any measure of durability in a hostile "nuclearized" environment and yet remain responsive to civilian leadership. See Hu, Zha et al., eds., *Xiandai Junbingzhong Zhanshu*, pp. 247–48, 254. This was a problem for which China could not afford a solution, even if one could be conceived. Indeed, concern about alleged Soviet first strike advantages and the risks posed for the survivability of U.S. forces and command and control had helped fuel a military buildup during the 1980s that even the vastly wealthier United States found politically difficult to sustain. See William W. Kaufmann, *A Reasonable Defense*; Joshua M. Epstein, *The 1987 Defense Budget*; *The 1988 Defense Budget*; William W. Kaufmann and Lawrence J. Korb, *The 1990 Defense Budget*; William W. Kaufmann, *Assessing the Base Force*.

country's position. But it is precisely because there could be no certainty that China would behave as if it were a rational actor that Beijing could be confident nuclear deterrence and the concomitant risk of escalation to a catastrophic exchange provided so robust a security guarantee, even for a state like China with a small collection of relatively vulnerable and inaccurate, though powerful, weapons.

More specifically, an aggressor would have to worry that, in response to serious provocation, China would turn out to be an "unsafe" actor, an actor whose behavior was inconsistent with the rationality assumption for one of the two reasons set forth in Chapter 2. First, and most important, the adversary would have to worry about the possibility of an accidental launch, that China's behavior would depart from expectations of rationality because decision-makers lost full control over their forces, or because of intelligence failures. Second, an adversary who would bank on cost-benefit analysis inhibiting a nuclear China from choosing escalation would also have to worry about the small, but ever-present, possibility that despite having accurate information and control over their forces, the leaders in Beijing might not choose rationally. Engaged in the sober calculations that would precede action against China, a prospective aggressor could not easily ignore the unpredictable effects on decision-making in Beijing that would follow from the intense pressures of managing a nuclear crisis, particularly given a modestly armed China's small margin for error, together with its historically rooted sensitivity to international humiliation.[50] Even before the PRC had much of a strategic nuclear capability, Moscow's long-standing fears about the recklessness, or at least risk-acceptance, of the leaders in Beijing weighed against lightly treating China's nuclear threats as idle bluffs.[51] As the PRC's nuclear arsenal grew, however, Beijing's credibility was rooted less in its leaders' bravado and alleged impulsiveness than in the usual uncertainties facing a potential aggressor confronting a state with a potentially survivable retaliatory force.

[50]On problems with assuming durable rationality in a nuclear crisis, see Kurt Gottfried and Bruce G. Blair, *Crisis Stability and Nuclear War*, pp. 265–68; also Edward Rhodes, *Power and MADness*, pp. 135–40.

[51]This reflected their experience as allies in the 1950s when, as described above, these fears contributed to the breakdown of Sino-Soviet nuclear cooperation, as well as what Moscow saw as the boldness of the pre-nuclear Chinese Communist revolutionaries and the PRC's international track record of matching words with deeds—from Korea through India to Vietnam. See Garrett and Glaser, *War and Peace*, p. 72. Such a track record would, as Patrick Morgan noted, enhance deterrence if it encouraged a perception of China's leaders as prepared to "bear the costs and sacrifices of war" (Morgan, *Deterrence*, p. 53).

China did not have to *ensure* in advance that it would be an unsafe actor during a crisis in order to benefit from the dissuasive effects of uncertainty about the use of nuclear weapons that could remain after a Soviet first strike. Indeed, efforts to try to create such an expectation would have been implausible. China, like all nuclear states, had strong incentives to establish peacetime controls that minimized the obvious risks that accident and irrationality present.[52] Nevertheless, any aggressor would have to consider the ways in which its provocative actions might elevate the normally low probability that China would cease to behave as if it were a safe, rational actor. The effect of increased military pressure on the leaders' cognitive processes would be hard to anticipate, though one might hope that a confrontation between nuclear states would focus the mind by providing unprecedented incentives for careful deliberation. But unable to rely on hope alone, a prospective aggressor would have to be most concerned about the potentially catastrophic consequences of irrational choice, however unlikely.

In contrast with the uncertain impact of increased military pressure on decision-making, its impact on the risk of accidental launch seems more predictable. Especially for a country like China, with less sophisticated, less durable forces and command and control capabilities, the Soviets had to worry about Beijing's ability to engage in attack assessment and to maintain negative control over its forces during hostilities, in particular if the aggressor's actions created a less forgiving nuclearized environment.[53] An accident that confounded rationality assumptions might, as noted in Chapter 2, take the form of either an authorized or unauthorized nuclear launch. An *authorized* strike could result from Beijing's mistaken belief, based on human or technical intelligence failure, that Moscow had initiated an unlimited nuclear offensive, the only circumstance under which even a rational Chinese leadership would be indifferent to the suicidal consequences of choosing nuclear retaliation. In addition, Moscow had to worry that its actions could provoke an accidental *unauthorized* launch as control over forces placed on crisis alert eroded due to failures in China's command system

---

[52]See Lewis and Xue, *China's Strategic Seapower*, pp. 234, 325n31. Ultimate authority to launch nuclear weapons was formally vested in the Chairman of the Central Military Commission, but China, like other nuclear powers, presumably had contingency plans for devolution of this authority in a crisis or in the wake of attacks eliminating the central leadership.

[53]See Ball, "Can Nuclear War Be Controlled?"; Paul Bracken, *The Command and Control of Nuclear Forces*; Blair, *Strategic Command and Control*; Edward Rhodes, *Power and MADness*, pp. 139–40. Lewis and Hua note China's inability to build a "reliable early warning system" ("China's Ballistic Missile Programs," p. 24).

or organizational confusion after nuclear release authority had been shifted to lower levels.[54] The sorts of concerns analysts raised about the durability of the superpowers' command and control organization and hardware would, of course, be magnified in the case of the technologically less advanced Chinese systems.[55] Moscow might hope that the result of disruption and destruction would be paralysis, but could not ignore the possibility that retaliatory strikes might be launched by those to whom authority had been delegated or predelegated. Even less was known about China's nuclear command and control than about that of the other nuclear states. But prudence would have required an adversary to assume that, at a minimum, some sort of early delegation in a crisis would be China's sensible response to the durability problems deriving from its marked technological inferiority.[56] Whether in fact such procedures had been worked out, one of the PRC's strategists may have intentionally provided a clue as to what Beijing wanted the Soviets to believe about the difficulties of successful preemption:

> He noted that the Soviets—who cannot preempt all of China's nuclear missiles, which are carefully stored in caves or otherwise protected and camouflaged—would have to continue to worry about Chinese retaliation "perhaps hours, days, weeks, months, or even years later. [. . .] Orders could even be sent by foot. The Soviet Union cannot help but be uncertain. . . . China does not need an invulnerable C^3 [command, control, communications] system to ensure the viability of its nuclear deterrent."[57]

Beijing's commitment to develop, deploy, and maintain a nuclear deterrent, then, reflected a belief that the strategic consequences of the nuclear revolution enabled China to provide itself with a credible deterrent by taking advantage of an adversary's uncertainty about the retaliatory forces the PRC would have at its disposal as well as the circumstances under which they might be employed. Could China be sure to retain its punitive capability and would the leaders choose to use it?

[54]Robert Powell, *Nuclear Deterrence Theory*, ch. 2; Thomas C. Schelling, *The Strategy of Conflict*, pp. 188–90, 201–3; Rhodes, *Power and MADness*, pp. 78–81.

[55]Ball, "Can Nuclear War Be Controlled?"; Bracken, *The Command and Control of Nuclear Forces*; Blair, *Strategic Command and Control*.

[56]Indeed, China's limited capabilities and the weakness of its political institutions meant that an adversary had to expect the worst. To a far greater degree than for the better equipped, more politically stable nuclear powers, China's vulnerabilities created strong pressure to opt for some form of predelegation rather than relying on the alternatives of institutionalized devolution or delegation as described in Chapter 2.

[57] Garrett and Glaser, *War and Peace*, p. 129.

Even if the adversary's answer to this question was "probably not," Beijing planned to exploit the fact that this was equivalent to answering "possibly yes." Where nuclear weapons would be involved, a slender possibility powerfully inhibits the initiation of hostilities.

Given a strategy that exploits the effects of ambiguity in the nuclear age, it is ironic that China's most prominent declaratory nuclear policy seemed to prevent it from fully capitalizing on the combination of terror and uncertainty about future behavior that provides for a robust deterrent. At the time of its first nuclear weapons test, and with each subsequent test, China publicly espoused a no-first-use pledge.[58] Though consistent with Beijing's assertion that it deployed nuclear weapons only out of a need to counter superpower hegemony and thus useful for propaganda purposes, this pledge made little strategic sense for a country whose nuclear weapons were fewer in number and more vulnerable than those of its adversary. Instead a doctrine threatening to launch "on warning" would better dissuade a nuclear attack and a doctrine reserving the right of nuclear first use would better dissuade even serious conventional challenges to Chinese security. The reasoning that led NATO during the Cold War to reject a no-first-use pledge and led the United States to retain its prerogative of launch "on warning" or "under attack," would seem even more persuasive for a state, like China, with a comparatively small nuclear arsenal.[59] A shift away from a no-first-use policy would help address the problem of weapons vulnerability and further complicate an adversary's strategic planning. But Beijing apparently did not see these practical benefits as outweighing the symbolic damage to its status as a reluctant nuclear power, especially since it knew that China's no-first-use stance probably would have little actual effect on an adversary's planning or behavior. Precisely because of the incongruity between a no-first-use declaratory doctrine and China's relatively vulnerable retaliatory capability, the Soviets could not safely have counted on Beijing strictly adhering to an unenforceable peacetime pledge in the heat of conflict over vital interests. Indeed, a rare (and undoubtedly pur-

[58]China's no-first-use pledge is: "We will not attack unless we are attacked: If we are attacked, we will certainly counterattack. China will counterattack only when the enemy uses nuclear weapons first." See Zhang Jianzhi, "View on Medium-Sized Nuclear Powers' Nuclear Strategy," p. K33. See also Peng, Wang et al., eds., *Junshi Zhanlüe Jianlun*, p. 167.

[59]In an analysis of the nuclear deterrents of the medium powers, Chinese analysts noted that "In order to strengthen the credibility of the deterrent, some countries reserve the right to use nuclear weapons first" (Chen, Shou, and Liang, *Weishe Zhanlüe*, p. 97). Their specific examples are Britain and France, even though their broader discussion lumps China with them as a medium power.

poseful) public expression of nuclear views in the Chinese military's newspaper during the 1980s suggested ambiguity in operational doctrine about the conditions that might actually precipitate nuclear use. The article indicated that the PRC's nuclear forces enable it "to check an enemy from rashly launching *any war* of aggression *and* from using nuclear weapons against our country. . . ." and listed four functions of nuclear weapons including their usefulness for countering superior conventional forces and discouraging superpower attempts at nuclear blackmail.[60] More recently, Iain Johnston has detected hints in the writings of Chinese strategists that no-first-use might mean only waiting to respond until after confirmation that an adversary was launching an attack against China, not waiting until China had actually absorbed a first strike.[61] Regardless, absent an international authority capable of interpreting and enforcing contracts, during the Cold War Soviet planners would have had to discount China's no-first-use pledge as "cheap talk."

In sum, the exploitation of uncertainty, a contemporary application of Sun Zi's admonition that "[t]he essence of warfare is but the art of ambiguity,"[62] was essential to China's strategy of dissuasion by nuclear deterrence and enhanced its robustness and affordability compared to the conventional alternative. Deterrent threats backed only by conventional forces (to inflict punishment in a protracted popular resistance) would be effective against the least plausible attack scenario, and would have permitted an uncertain adversary to engage in wishful thinking and excessive optimism, overestimating his prospects for success and minimizing the risks of worst-case outcomes.[63] In contrast, the uncertainty associated with threats backed by even relatively meager nuclear forces (uncertainty about both the number of nuclear weapons that might remain after a well-executed counterforce first strike, and uncer-

---

[60]Zhang Jianzhi, "Views on Medium-Sized Nuclear Powers' Nuclear Strategy," p. K33, emphasis added. See also comments by Peng and Wang that China's nuclear weapons provide a peacetime deterrent of possible superpower invasion without reference to the aggressor's military means (Peng, Wang et al., eds., *Junshi Zhanlüe Jianlun*, p. 167); and John W. Lewis, "China's Military Doctrines and Force Posture," p. 163. Chinese strategic thinkers with whom I met in spring 1991 insisted on the sincerity of their country's no-first-use policy, but also acknowledged that a prospective Soviet aggressor had to worry about its sincerity and indicated that such worries were strategically valuable.

[61]Johnston, "China's New 'Old Thinking,'" pp. 21–22.

[62]Lin, *China's Nuclear Weapons Strategy*, p. 69.

[63]For theoretical arguments emphasizing the importance of optimism about the chances of success that drive the decision to initiate wars, see Geoffrey Blainey, *The Causes of War*; Bruce Bueno de Mesquita, *The War Trap*. See also Kenneth N. Waltz, "More May Be Better," pp. 5–8.

tainty about the circumstances under which they might be launched) encouraged fearful thinking, pessimism, and extreme sensitivity to the risks of disaster. As a consequence, the PRC's small nuclear arsenal supported a deterrent strategy that made it difficult for the mightiest of foes to take the first step in challenging China's vital interests.

Whatever Happened to People's War?

The preceding indicates that as early as the 1950s, doubts about the robustness of conventional deterrence against the most plausible superpower threats China faced had led Beijing to assign top priority to developing the forces necessary for nuclear deterrence. Yet while Mao lived, People's War retained its pride of place in China's strategic rhetoric. And until China deployed deliverable nuclear warheads, People's War may have been the only available option in the event strategic alignment with one superpower had failed to dissuade the other. Once Mao died in 1976, however, China's military leaders began more openly to articulate sensible objections to the late Chairman's conventional deterrent strategy that emphasized preparations to lure the enemy deep within China and then to wage a protracted armed struggle against him. Military professionals, who had long doubted the continuing usefulness of People's War for discouraging the superpowers from challenging China's security, called for modernization of both nuclear and conventional forces.[64] But it is noteworthy that even in the context of a more free-wheeling debate, because China was not yet sufficiently confident about its ability to deliver its nuclear retaliatory blow, the priority accorded nuclear weapons over conventional weapons endured. In the early 1980s Defense Minister Zhang Aiping announced that "defense funds should be concentrated on those programs which are badly needed and the most important areas which affect the overall situation, such as strategic guided missiles and centers for producing nuclear fuel and bombs."[65]

The PLA also required more modern conventional forces as a complement to China's fledgling nuclear deterrent, but after 1978 this conventional complement was no longer cast in terms of the traditional Maoist vision of People's War. Instead, should dissuasion by nuclear de-

[64]Renewed calls for military modernization predate Mao's death and were part of Deng Xiaoping's struggle with the radicals that led the Chairman and his radical supporters to sack Deng for a second time in spring 1976 (Harry Harding, "Domestic Politics of China's Global Posture," pp. 110–24).

[65]"Zhang Aiping on National Defense Modernization"; Eric Hall, "Chinese Forces Changing for More Effective Strategic Role."

terrence fail, it was asserted that China needed the ability to at least make it difficult for the Soviets to accomplish their military objectives, an ability to prevent the first wave of invading Soviet divisions from easily seizing key economic and political assets. Strategic retreat might ultimately be required, but Moscow should not be led to believe it could present Beijing with a *fait accompli* (e.g., quickly and painlessly seizing the vital industrial territory of the Northeast and major Chinese cities) without confronting the horrifying risk of nuclear war. On the contrary, China's military leaders in the early post-Mao era indicated a determination to deploy forces that would convince the Soviets they would face initially formidable resistance.[66] This shift reflected a disdain for the conventional deterrent strategy of "retreat, regroup, and resist" and a recognition of the usefulness of even limited forward defenses that require an adversary to launch a larger, more drawn out attack during which it faces an elevated risk of escalation. To achieve this goal, the PLA revamped its plans for conventional operations. Training began to emphasize combined arms operations by regular troops relying on "extensive logistical support from China's industrial centers" that would "block a major Soviet assault before it could penetrate too deeply."[67] Relations between the regular army and militia would be transformed as well. Instead of the army scurrying to organize the militia for protracted struggle against the invader lured in deep, the militia would help prevent the enemy's deep penetration, provide ready reserves to replenish the regular army's ranks, and attempt to defend the cities to ensure "an adequate supply of war material . . . safeguard transport and communications, protect and defend organs of state power."[68]

In addition to openly debated strategic considerations, China's leaders probably also recognized an unspoken risk associated with the traditional People's War strategy that anticipated the surrender of peripheral

---

[66]". . . [D]uring the first stage of a war, we should mainly use positional defensive warfare, with powerful support and co-ordination of mobile warfare in order to gradually consume and annihilate the enemy's strength" (Song Shilun, cited in Harlan Jencks, "'People's War Under Modern Conditions,'" p. 313).

[67]Paul H. B. Godwin, "The Chinese Defense Establishment in Transition," pp. 68, 72. See also Gerald Segal, "China's Strategic Posture," pp. 685–87, 690, 691; Jencks, "'People's War Under Modern Conditions,'" p. 313.

[68]Nie Rongzhen's comments at a speech to a conference on militia work in 1978, cited by Segal, "China's Strategic Posture," p. 690. See also pp. 685–87, 691. Such changes were widely analyzed in the literature on military modernization and reform in the early post-Mao China. See Paul H. B. Godwin, *The Chinese Defense Establishment*; Charles D. Lovejoy and Bruce W. Watson, eds., *China's Military Reforms*; Ellis Joffe, *The Chinese Army After Mao*; Larry M. Wortzell, ed., *China's Military Modernization*.

territories. The military feasibility of Mao's conventional deterrent approach depended on the loyal, if often covert, support of the civilian population in occupied areas. But the allegiance of the minority nationalities in China's vast Southwest, West and Northwest, some in regions near the Soviet Union over which Beijing had struggled to reestablish its authority since 1949, could not be taken for granted. It is questionable whether the Chinese Communist Party would have found these vast stretches of the PRC hospitable for organizing a protracted resistance against Moscow's troops in the event that would ever have been necessary. Prudent policy might well have enabled the Soviets to portray themselves as liberators.

In 1978 China's PLA began referring to its emerging new doctrine as People's War Under Modern Conditions. Its neo-Maoist moniker notwithstanding, the program of military modernization it called for was "designed specifically to avoid a protracted war."[69] The top priority was to deploy deliverable nuclear forces that would dissuade superpower aggression by posing the risk of horrifying retaliation. The next most important purpose of modernization was to deploy conventional forces strong enough to mount a limited forward defense and oblige the adversary to face an escalating risk of retaliation. Dissuasion based on the threat of a protracted People's War was relegated to a "last resort" component of China's security policy geared to the unlikely contingency of full-scale invasion and occupation of the country.[70] China had finally, if tacitly, acknowledged that conventional deterrence, although compensating for material inferiority by enabling the CCP to convert its political support into a military asset, was a less than satisfactory solution to the country's actual security problems. The PRC required an economically sound deterrent strategy that more effectively enabled the state to cope with the spectrum of plausible serious threats it confronted. Because it supported a more robust strategy at reasonable cost, nuclear deterrence was the preferred solution to the difficulties involved in dissuading aggression by a superpower adversary. With the declining importance of conventional deterrence, China's policy began more closely to resemble the Cold War strategy embraced by the British and especially the French that is described in Chapters 5 and 6.

[69]Godwin, "The Chinese Defense Establishment in Transition," p. 73.
[70]See Chen, Shou, and Liang, *Weishe Zhanlüe*, pp. 214–15. As Paul Godwin put it in analyzing China's readiness in the 1970s to deal with the Soviet threat, "[W]hat happens if the Chinese hold a people's war and nobody comes?" ("The Chinese Defense Establishment in Transition," 73).

5

Britain

My treatment of the British and French cases will, insofar as is reasonable, parallel the discussion of China. But the discussion is briefer, in part because the strategic history is a bit less complex. Neither of these European second-ranking powers opted for the conventional deterrent alternative that China had initially embraced out of necessity if not preference. Nor, unlike China, did Britain or France revise its view about which of the two superpowers posed the more serious threat to its vital interests. Instead, clearly worried about the Soviet Union, both made dissuasion by deterrence relying on independent nuclear forces the keystone of their security policies earlier and more openly than did the Chinese. Notwithstanding this and other differences in the evolution of their policies, noted below, all three of these postwar second-ranking powers arrived at the same strategic destination. All three assigned top priority to developing and maintaining national nuclear forces. Alliance arrangements and additional military capabilities were more or less valued supplements, but when political or budgetary considerations forced a choice, national nuclear forces were privileged.

In discussing the British and French cases, as with the Chinese, my aim is not to present a comprehensive historical description of the state's foreign policy, military doctrine, or force structure. Rather my aim is to identify the constraints shaping policy and to indicate how, in particular cases, these constraints—the context of an international system whose structure was anarchic and bipolar, together with the advent of nuclear weapons technology—shaped broad strategic priorities. This chapter begins with an analysis of the alliance dynamics that provided incentives for both Britain and France to develop and maintain a more self-reliant alternative for ensuring their national security.

ALLIANCE POLITICS AND THE SELF-HELP
IMPERATIVE

At the conclusion of World War II, the Allied occupation and division of Germany greatly reduced Britain and France's concerns about a possible revival of the old danger in central Europe, though French worries about managing the German problem persisted. Instead, the creation of puppet regimes in the Soviet-occupied regions of central and eastern Europe, and the awesome military machine Stalin had kept in place after the peace, convinced these two long-standing Western great powers that the massively armed and possibly expansionist Soviet superpower posed the principal foreign threat to their national security. And in the late 1940s Britain and France lacked the means to parry this potentially serious threat. As the reality of a bipolar world became clear, the only viable counter to Soviet power was the armed might of the United States. Only the United States could mobilize the capabilities (conventional and nuclear) sufficient to dissuade Soviet aggression in Europe, through threats either to mount a formidable defense or to inflict unacceptably terrifying punishment in retaliation. Thus Britain and France, together with other Western European nations, actively solicited U.S. participation in the formation of the North Atlantic Treaty Organization.[1] Shared threat perceptions made Washington receptive to this Western European initiative as the United States, too, was increasingly concerned about the postwar international behavior of the Soviets and worried about the possible uses to which the resources controlled by an ideologically hostile country occupying vast stretches of the Eurasian land mass might be put.[2]

Balance-of-power theory readily explains why, given the constraints of a bipolar international system, Britain and France believed it necessary to ally with the United States. External support was required to compensate for their inability to cope independently with the serious threat to their national security that the Soviets represented. The collective goods theory of alliances, too, suggests the economic and strategic reasons for depending on the U.S. military effort. Britain and France, after all, could not decisively affect the conventional balance of forces in Europe and, without nuclear weapons, were not yet able to threaten the Soviets with unacceptable punishment. At the same time, the United

[1]John Lewis Gaddis, *Strategies of Containment*, p. 72.
[2]For an overview of the emerging U.S. focus on the potential Soviet threat, see ibid., esp. chs. 1 and 2.

States' perceived self-interest in containing the Soviet Union was leading it to provide security benefits all allies could enjoy. Thus the rational choice would be to ride free on the combined dissuasive effect of
U.S. theater forces to defend against a Soviet drive westward, and U.S.
strategic forces to deter such aggression by posing the risk that it might
at some point trigger a catastrophic nuclear retaliatory blow. In addition, ideological affinity among these liberal democracies that confronted a rival way of life in the Soviet camp, along with cultural and
historical ties, reinforced the realpolitik underpinnings of the Western
alliance.

However strategically and economically sensible or ideologically
comfortable, the founding of NATO in 1949 and the subsequent forward
basing of U.S. military might (conventional and nuclear) amounted to
an admission by these former great powers that they could no longer do
without the American security guarantee.[3] Such unprecedented peacetime dependence was a distressing position for two countries that had
played a leading role on the world stage over the preceding three centuries. But perhaps more important than the blow to national pride was a
concern about strategic adequacy. How reliable was the security that alliance with this superpower patron provided for Britain and France? Although there was no doubt about the *capability* of the resource-rich
United States to counterbalance the Soviet threat, there was no way to
be sure about U.S. *willingness* to employ its might on behalf of others.
This concern fueled doubts about the true value of the free ride. In short,
the unsettling fear of abandonment in unpredictable future circumstances tempered British and French satisfaction with entrusting their
fates to a NATO alliance whose effectiveness ultimately rested on decisions made in Washington, D.C.

European fears about the wisdom of depending on the United States
in particular were heightened by memories of American strategic aloofness in the years prior to each of the century's major wars, followed by
the entry of U.S. troops into the conflicts only well after the other prin-
cipals had long been engaged. NATO was, after all, the first peacetime
alliance for the United States. The speedy demobilization the United
States undertook after 1945 and early postwar domestic opposition to
the higher levels of military spending that would be necessary for the

---

[3]As Pierre Gallois commented on France's position, in particular, the country's
situation "precluded independence" and as a consequence France's "Military Command progressively learned to rely on others for the defense of the country" (Pierre
M. Gallois, "French Defense Planning—The Future in the Past," pp. 15–16). See also
Wolf Mendl, *Deterrence and Persuasion*, pp. 19, 20, 49.

United States to play a leading internationalist role fueled such concerns. U.S. willingness to court nuclear disaster in order to ensure British or French security aside, there would have been uncertainty about Washington's unprecedented treaty commitment to NATO.

History suggested that the United States preferred to take a "wait and see" attitude when conflict erupted overseas. The U.S. posture evident from history partly reflected the country's advantageous geographic circumstances. Until the mid-twentieth century, geography provided the United States with a natural security buffer, though one whose strategic value was diminishing as technology advanced. For the great powers of Europe and Asia, proximity as well as economic and military interdependence might provide strong incentives to become involved in wars when diplomacy failed to ensure national interests. But for the United States, its distance from the main arenas of international conflict and its continental size, rich resource endowments, and burgeoning domestic market reduced the incentives to risk much to affect the outcome of wars overseas. On the contrary, prior to the transportation and communication revolutions of the mid-twentieth century, sound strategic arguments could be raised in favor of the United States' exercising the utmost restraint and caution before committing itself to causes whose relevance to American interests was not self-evident. Without the impetus of dramatically provocative events (i.e., the sinking of civilian ships, or surprise attack on a U.S. navy base), even strong presidents had encountered stiff popular reluctance to joining the century's two world wars. And early postwar debates in Congress about the wisdom of proposals for a substantial U.S. military and economic role in Europe and Asia provided evidence that at least prior to the war in Korea, not all influential political leaders in the United States had accepted that World War II would herald a new era of American internationalism.[4]

In any case, Britain and France had reason to doubt the dependability of alliances in general, and not just the reliability of an American partner. After all, their own regrettable history of footdragging, appeasement, and buckpassing during the 1930s was a fresh memory and high-

---

[4]Thomas J. Christensen, *Useful Adversaries*, p. 39. Christensen persuasively argues that public attitudes in the United States did not evince isolationism so much as a reluctance to shoulder more than a fair share of the burden in resisting the emerging Soviet threat. Although U.S. military spending during the Truman administration prior to the Korean War fell far short of levels typical during the remainder of the Cold War, as a percentage of GNP it was in fact significantly higher (roughly by a factor of four) than peacetime military spending prior to World War II. See ibid., pp. 34–36, 39–40.

lighted the difficulties alliances can confront in mustering a timely and effective response to a growing threat.[5] The geography lesson from their recent wartime experience also suggested that the dangers of alliance inefficiency might be increasing, especially for France. World War II had demonstrated that technology was greatly enhancing the ability of states to project conventional military power and, as a result, proximity to an adversary increased the risk of quick defeat. Because technology eroded the traditional advantages of distance and strategic depth, the time for post-attack mobilization and regrouping might be short. If allies hesitated, all could be lost. The Nazi blitzkrieg might not have been the sort of quick disaster that nuclear war could be, but it had cost France its sovereignty in a matter of weeks. And though Britain's offshore location still afforded it a measure of protection at mid-century, advances in air and missile power were also diminishing its distinctive geographic advantage even before the dawn of the nuclear age.

Thus, even without the advent of nuclear weapons, early in the postwar era Britain and especially France would most likely still have had reservations about banking too heavily on alliances, especially one whose effectiveness depended on U.S. leadership, to ensure their security against a massively armed, hostile Soviet adversary stationed in the middle of Europe. Yet nuclear weapons did make a difference. Absent nuclear weapons, U.S. behavior matching its treaty commitments (especially the forward deployment of American military personnel and their dependents that began in 1951) might eventually have offset fears about the lessons of history. Worries about a presumed tradition of American isolationism did in fact fade as the United States gradually demonstrated its commitment to internationalism and specifically a surprising willingness to shoulder a disproportionate share of the burden for European security. And absent nuclear weapons, evolving military technology might eventually have tempered fears about geographic vulnerability. Improvements in defensive weaponry along with terrain that limited the plausible westward attack routes through the central front in Europe did in fact provide advantages to the defender that offset fears about the short time for responding to possible Soviet aggression.[6] Fears of abandonment nevertheless persisted. Increasingly they no longer reflected a belief that the United States had a peculiar aversion to interna-

[5]See Barry Posen, *The Sources of Military Doctrine*; Thomas J. Christensen and Jack Snyder, "Chain Gangs and Passed Bucks."

[6]On the advantages for NATO of undertaking defensive actions against a westward blitzkrieg by the Soviet-led Warsaw Pact, see John J. Mearsheimer, *Conventional Deterrence*.

tional entanglement, or simply a recognition that any state is reluctant to become involved in another's conflicts and might delay timely assistance. Instead, during the 1950s the fear of abandonment became firmly rooted in the distinctive new reality of the nuclear age. The effect of nuclear weapons was to ensure that concerns about prompt and effective support from a self-interested, but essential, ally would be deeply held and would persist, notwithstanding changing beliefs about the relevance of history or geography.

Among great powers armed with nuclear weapons, honoring pledges to allies would entail historically unprecedented risks. Staunchly backing Western European interests in a showdown with the Soviets might mean not only American deaths on the battlefields of Europe, the sort of worrisome prospect that had long cast doubt on the reliability of alliances, but more importantly risking the nuclear destruction of cites in the United States.[7] Thus, even though the United States and its European partners agreed that the Soviet Union was their common enemy, the binding force of parallel threat perceptions that had traditionally molded alliances might well prove insufficient if it conflicted with the paramount interest in national survival. In the pre-nuclear era, inefficiencies and miscalculation in the formation and workings of alliances could lead to regrets about wars that might have been avoided or foreshortened. But because a war's final outcome took time to determine and battlefield results could be reversed, states could adjust their policies to cope with the defects of peacetime arrangements. In the nuclear era, alliance inefficiency or miscalculation could be quickly disastrous.

Britain and France, therefore, reasonably worried about the speed and certainty with which the United States would fulfill its treaty obligations during a dangerous confrontation with the Soviet Union. Their worries, however, should not be misinterpreted as evidence that the American nuclear umbrella over NATO was in fact insufficiently credible to deter the Soviet adversary. As in China's case, doubts about the likely U.S. response during a confrontation in Europe had different implications for adversary and ally. For leaders in Moscow, whose principal concern was the fate of the Soviet Union, doubt about the American response might be enough to deter Soviet adventurism. Even if they estimated that there was only a very small probability the United States would act contrary to its rational self-interest and escalate a European conflict to the level of a strategic nuclear exchange, the magnitude of

---

[7]For an analysis that highlights such British concerns, see "Implications of Growing Nuclear Capabilities for the Communist Bloc and the Free World," July 9, 1957, p. 6; on similar French concerns, see ibid., p. 4.

such a disaster meant that only a very small probability of its occurrence could be sufficiently dissuasive. For leaders in London and Paris, however, whose principal concern was the fate of Britain and France, doubt about the American response provided an incentive to hedge their bets and develop the option for self-reliance. Even if they estimated that there was only a very small probability that the United States would renege on its treaty commitments when actually confronting Soviet threats in Europe, the magnitude of such a disaster meant that even a small probability established a strong incentive for purchasing the insurance policy of an independent nuclear deterrent.[8] Because the international political system remained an anarchic realm, there could be no guarantee that at the moment of truth Washington would live up to its treaty obligations, no matter how well crafted and no matter how broadly supported in peacetime by the American public and its foreign policy elite.

Britain and France's determination to develop and maintain independent nuclear arsenals, as described below, reflected this fear of abandonment rooted in anarchy, reinforced by bipolarity, and exacerbated by the advent of nuclear weapons. In this respect their experience paralleled that of China. But before tracing this fundamental similarity in the logic driving the strategic emphasis of these three states, it is worth asking whether Britain and France, like China, also tried to cope with the realities of the post–World War II world by attempting to forestall abandonment. Did they take the sorts of steps that might increase the likelihood their superpower patron would provide alliance security as if it were a collective good from which they would not be excluded? The answer is less obvious than in the Chinese case in part because neither Britain nor France faced incentives as strong as those Beijing faced when it believed it had to accept politically unpalatable compromises for the sake of fostering alliance solidarity.

Although the potential for Soviet military action against these Western European states was enormous, the threat was not as imminent as the superpower dangers China confronted. During the four decades of the Cold War, China had to contend with major U.S. military action and dire warnings of escalation in Korea, the Taiwan Straits, and Vietnam, massive force deployments by and unnerving direct clashes

---

[8]Kenneth Waltz quotes Denis Healey as saying "that one chance in a hundred that a country will retaliate is enough to deter an adversary, although not enough to reassure an ally" (Kenneth N. Waltz, "Nuclear Myths and Political Realities," p. 739; see also Robert Jervis, *The Meaning of the Nuclear Revolution*, pp. 35, 74–76, 206–14, 221).

with the Soviets along the PRC's disputed northern and western borders, and finally a well-armed and battle hardened-Soviet ally in Vietnam willing to grant basing rights to Moscow. By contrast, although
there were several major crises in Eastern and Central Europe, none entailed military action that seriously threatened to spill over into the
West. None in fact fundamentally altered the line of demarcation between the blocs established by the position of the Allied armies at the
close of World War II. In short, because the possibility that a superpower
adversary would jeopardize China's vital interests was higher, the incentive for China to do whatever was necessary to ensure its security,
even if this entailed compromising its nationalist preferences, was
greater.

Still, massive force deployments in the Warsaw Pact countries of
Central and Eastern Europe underscored a potentially grave Soviet
threat that was serious enough for the Western Europeans to cultivate
U.S. support through NATO. Britain and France were sufficiently concerned about the Soviets that they, like the Chinese, sometimes believed it was necessary to take steps to increase the chance their superpower ally would provide for their security despite the risks that such
solidarity might entail.

MANAGING THE RISKS OF DEPENDENCE

British actions, in particular, reflected the need to adjust policy to cope
with the tight constraints under which it operated in a bipolar postwar
world. London's interest in maintaining good relations with its vital
strategic partner, the United States, led it to agree to concessions in its
economic and imperial policies and also to back Washington during the
Korean War.[9] Support for the conflict in northeast Asia reflected a direct
British interest not so much in the war but rather in molding policy to
cement the alliance with the United States:

> No one in the British Cabinet was taking the American connection for
> granted at this time. If the United States was to be persuaded to commit
> its manpower to the defense of Western Europe, then it was felt that
> Britain would have to fight alongside her ally for a cause which Wash-
> ington perceived to be vital to the defence of the west. Even though the
> rearmament programme introduced by the Atlee government brought

[9]On the economic and political frictions in Anglo-American relations in the
early postwar period, see C. J. Bartlett, *"The Special Relationship,"* ch. 2; John Baylis,
Anglo-American Defense Relations, 1939–1984, ch. 2; R. N. Rosecrance, *Defense of
the Realm,* pp. 44–46.

Britain to the verge of bankruptcy, the price was considered to be worth paying to keep the alliance together.[10]

Even after economic recovery and the acquisition of national nuclear forces reduced the extent of its dependence on the United States, Britain's policy evinced a willingness to accept the necessity of "constraints on Britain's freedom of action" in order to retain the security benefits America's key role in NATO provided.[11] Thus, despite asserting the principle of absolutely sovereign control over its own nuclear forces, London would agree to Washington's insistence on the 1962 Athens guidelines and participation in U.S.-dominated NATO nuclear planning that entailed publicly suggesting limits on that independence. Similarly, the asymmetrical "special relationship" (discussed below) that provided Britain crucial access to U.S. nuclear delivery systems technology at bargain basement prices would involve a somewhat embarrassing compromise of the autonomy of an arsenal originally hailed as the symbol of national independence and continued great power status.[12]

France, however, especially after the founding of the Fifth Republic under strong-willed President de Gaulle in 1958, generally eschewed deference as a tactic for retaining the support of what it came to view as an unreliable American ally. Paris bristled at the need for American protection against the Soviet threat because this would require France to "align her policy with that of the United States,"[13] to compromise French policy in the Third World, or, as de Gaulle put it, "to accept a *strategic and consequently a political dependency* in relation to that one of the two giants which is not threatening. . . ."[14] France, then, was less hesitant about openly differing with its superpower ally. But French policy, in practice if not rhetoric, generally reflected a tacit recognition of the importance and benefits of the security supplied by its alliance with the United States. Thus, when withdrawing from NATO's integrated military command in 1966, France stopped short of withdrawing from the alliance and adopting a truly neutral stance. More telling, Paris soon worried about even this limited strategic independence as long as the potential for confrontation with the awesome Soviet military re-

[10]John Baylis, *British Defense Policy*, p. 60.

[11]Ibid., pp. 60–61.

[12]Ibid., p. 63.

[13]From De la Malens and Melnik, *Attitude of the French Parliament and Government Toward Atomic Weapons*, RM-2170-RC (Santa Monica: Rand Corporation, 1958), cited in Wilfred L. Kohl, *French Nuclear Diplomacy*, p. 33.

[14]Ibid., p. 129. See also similar comments by French Premier Raymond Barre in "French Prime Minister on France's Nuclear Policy."

mained. Although in late 1967 Chief of Staff of the Armed Forces Charles Ailleret would briefly talk up the idea of targeting all points of the compass (*tous azimuts*), such strategic aloofness was judged impractical and was not translated into operational plans.[15] The August 1968 Soviet military thrust into Czechoslovakia removed any doubts that the principal threat France faced came from the east.[16] Shortly afterward, France's leaders quietly sought to revive a closer security relationship with the United States and to benefit from American technology and joint military planning—a pattern more similar to that maintained by the British than was openly admitted at the time.[17]

What about the other available technique for managing the risk of abandonment—emphasizing the common threat in order to blur any distinction between the interests of the strong leader of the alliance and its member states, and to discourage appeasement at the expense of one's partners? Here, the British and French experience differs markedly from that of the Chinese. For most of the postwar era Britain and France did not have to work very hard to convince their superpower ally that the Soviets posed a serious threat against which they must stand together. As noted above, in the late 1940s the United States embraced the grand strategy of containment, some variation of which would frame the military-security policy of every administration in Washington from Truman through Bush.[18] Of all the overseas missions associated with containment, preventing Soviet domination of the European continent assumed a position of paramount importance.[19] Indeed, by the last decade of the Cold War it was often the United States rather than the Europeans who promoted the harder anti-Soviet line.

The Europeans' fear of abandonment, then, did not result from the

[15]See David S. Yost, "France's Deterrent Posture and Security in Europe, Part I," p. 6.

[16]See Kohl, *French Nuclear Diplomacy*, pp. 140–48.

[17]Richard H. Ullman, "The Covert French Connection"; Ian Davidson, "France Rejoins Its Allies"; "Nuclear Secrets."

[18]In the immediate postwar years, however, Britain took the lead in rhetoric and policy countering the emerging Soviet threat. See Andrew J. Pierre, *Nuclear Politics*, pp. 68, 82. For the classic survey of the variations on this grand strategic theme through 1980, see Gaddis, *Strategies of Containment*. On the continuing U.S. self-interest in the security of Western Europe during the last decade of the Cold War, see Stephen M. Walt, "The Case for Finite Containment."

[19]Other aspects of containment (U.S. commitments in East Asia, the Persian Gulf, and additional areas of the developing world) and the best means for implementing containment (political, economic, nuclear, and conventional military capabilities) were highly controversial. See Gaddis, *Strategies of Containment*; Barry R. Posen and Steven Van Evera, "Defense Policy and the Reagan Administration."

belief that the United States was insufficiently vigilant about the Soviet threat. Instead, the concern was that *despite* shared interests in containing the Soviets and peacetime commitments, a rational leader in Washington might conclude that the marginal military value of European allies in the nuclear age would not warrant standing by his junior partners in the event of a risky confrontation with Moscow. Given the possibility of a choice between reneging on alliance obligations or running the risk of nuclear retaliation against the United States, Europeans reasonably worried about depending on a president in Washington who might decide that discretion was the better part of valor.[20] Though prudence required Soviet leaders to worry that the United States might live up to its extended deterrent and defensive commitments under the NATO treaty, prudence required the European allies to worry that the United States might abandon them or compromise their interests by cutting a deal with the Soviets. Such concerns fueled calls for tangible evidence of the U.S. commitment to fulfill its alliance obligations. U.S. weapons and troop deployments on the continent allegedly provided such evidence of a close coupling of the superpower to its allies. Soviet aggression in Europe would then necessarily inflict American casualties, thereby increasing the likelihood of a U.S. response. In addition, some believed, the United States would be more likely to respond if it could do so with forces stationed on the continent than it would be if the only option was the cosmic gamble of launching strategic weapons based in North America and aboard nuclear submarines.[21] Whether the approach based on this logic, especially the U.S. stationing of theater nuclear forces on the continent, actually enhanced the security of the Europeans is debatable. Through the end of the Cold War, however, it retained a powerful reassuring symbolism that led NATO allies to insist on the maintenance and modernization of visible U.S. deployments on European soil.[22]

[20]As Thomas Schelling emphasized, there is a fundamental distinction between the commitment to all that is one's homeland, and interests abroad, however vital they are alleged to be. See Schelling, *Arms and Influence*, pp. 56–59.

[21]This argument became prominent during the public debate beginning in the late 1970s, as NATO formulated a response to the modernization of the Soviet Union's intermediate-range nuclear forces in the European theater (deployment of its SS-20s).

[22]The decision to counter Soviet SS-20 deployment with the deployment of U.S. ground-launched cruise missiles and Pershing II intermediate-range ballistic missiles is more easily explained by reference to the symbolic needs of intra-alliance diplomacy than by reference to military requirements. The visibility of NATO's new weapons (though a domestic political liability for the governments in some host states) was preferred to the survivability that could have been ensured by relying on

And yet, despite such attempts at coupling, despite general agreement among NATO allies about the seriousness of the Soviet threat, and despite the ongoing U.S. willingness to spend up to half its military budget to shoulder the largest share of the burden of providing for European security, Britain and France were never fully satisfied with a policy of depending on the United States while managing the unavoidable risks of abandonment. Believing it necessary to prepare for that unlikely but disastrous possibility that they would be on their own, both first deployed and later insisted on maintaining independent nuclear forces, even when this entailed substantial economic sacrifice and led to serious friction with their American ally. The remainder of this chapter examines the evolution of Britain's security policy. France's experience is set forth in the following chapter.

SELECTING A SELF-RELIANT ALTERNATIVE: THE BRITISH EXPERIENCE

Having decided on the need to hedge its bets against the possibility that U.S. support would waver, Britain also concluded shortly after World War II that the only viable self-reliant fallback was nuclear deterrence. Neither dissuasion by defense nor dissuasion by conventional deterrence met Britain's need to safeguard its traditional vital interests— security of the homeland and preventing the domination of continental Europe by a hostile power.

Effective defense against the nuclear and conventional threat the Soviet Union would pose in the postwar era was simply beyond Britain's resources. In the unfolding nuclear age, politically meaningful defenses against atomic and later thermonuclear strikes would have to be virtually leakproof, especially in a country whose population and industry were so geographically concentrated. Leaving aside the question of affordability, nothing on the technological horizon suggested that the requirements for this sort of impenetrable anti-nuclear defense could be

---

sea- and air-based systems. Choosing a visible but vulnerable mode for deployment had two potentially serious strategic drawbacks: (1) it might have encouraged a "use 'em or lose 'em" situation feeding a reciprocal fear of surprise attack, a fear exacerbated by the short warning times Moscow would have had if it did not try to preempt; (2) it might have suggested to the Soviets that these forces were in fact not very important to the United States, weakening their credibility as a trigger for an American response. Visible and vulnerable or not, it was unclear whether the deployment of theater nuclear forces coupled the United States to Europe or actually de-coupled it by facilitating warfighting scenarios that restricted war, even nuclear war, to European targets.

met by Britain or anyone else. Creation of a credible independent defense against Soviet conventional capabilities in central Europe, though not posing the same sort of technological challenge, was prohibitively costly. Resource constraints reinforced the strategic arguments in favor of deterrence rather than defense.

Britain, like most other combatants, had been drained by its participation in World War II, possessed a smaller resource base than the Soviets, and lacked the ruthless, arguably foolish, determination of its adversary to concentrate national wealth on developing its military industrial complex. As the 1950s progressed, the resource arguments that supported a strategy emphasizing nuclear deterrence remained important. The health of the recovering economy and public expectations of rising levels of consumption argued against redirecting government investment to the military. Moreover, skilled manpower for defense work was in short supply, especially in "metal-using industries" essential to the export trade.[23] Thus, even with the postwar recovery, there was no prospect of increasing conventional capabilities enough to preclude Soviet success on the battlefield. By 1955 the Defense White Paper had dropped its usual discussion about preparing for a conventional follow-up to a nuclear exchange in the event of war in Europe and began to emphasize the need to prevent war by threatening massive retaliation against the adversary who enjoyed "massive preponderance."[24] The clear impracticality of the conventional alternative for Britain was restated in the 1958 Defense White Paper, which estimated that it would require Britain to maintain "between 1 million and 1 and ½ million men in the Armed Forces and spend perhaps 1000 million pounds more a year on the defence budget."[25]

The early postwar determination to reallocate scarce resources from conventional to nuclear arms became evident in and was reinforced by practical adjustments in Britain's military posture. In 1957 London ended conscription. Over the next five years the size of the standing army was cut by more than half and the British contingent on the continent underwent a significant, though smaller, contraction.[26] Between the 1950s and 1970s Britain responded to continuing pressures to focus spending on domestic economic concerns and bring policy in line with

[23]Pierre, *Nuclear Politics*, p. 98.
[24]See *Statement on Defence* (1955), cited ibid., p. 92; Peter Malone, *The British Nuclear Deterrent*, pp. 83, 92; Baylis, *British Defense Policy*, pp. 51–52; Martin S. Navias, "Nuclear Weapons and British Alliance Commitments, 1955–56," p. 148.
[25]Malone, *The British Nuclear Deterrent*, p. 92.
[26]See ibid., p. 91; Pierre, *Nuclear Politics*, p. 96.

available resources by scaling back its global military commitments and drawing down the expensive conventional forces they required. In 1966 the British shed their commitment to a fully capable blue water navy, in 1968 their determination to maintain a preeminent position east of Suez, and in 1975 their major Mediterranean and minor Far Eastern presence.[27]

As the share of military appropriations in the national budget was reduced, "unnecessary conventional forces and weapons systems" were cut while funding for "relatively cheap nuclear forces" that fulfilled the UK's deterrent strategy was preserved.[28] The decrease in spending on conventional forces for the Army, Navy and Air Force initiated under the leadership of Defence Minister Duncan Sandys in 1957 helped shrink the large share of Gross National Product that the military had been absorbing in the early 1950s.[29] Military spending declined as a share of GNP from a peak of 9.9 percent in 1952 to 7 percent in 1957 to less than 5 percent by the late 1960s, and as a share of government expenditures from a peak of 32.9 percent in 1953 to 17 percent in the late 1960s.[30] Although Britain continued to deploy impressive conventional forces, they were not designed to be a defensive alternative to nuclear deterrence, but rather a means to ensure that Soviet aggression could succeed only by mounting a challenge large enough to run the risk of triggering nuclear retaliation.[31]

[27]Malone, *The British Nuclear Deterrent*, p. 28.

[28]Navias, "Nuclear Weapons and British Alliance Commitments, 1955–56," p. 148. On the military services' attempts to limit the emphasis on nuclear forces in British weapons procurement policy, see pp. 149, 156–57.

[29]In his statement to Parliament, the Defence Minister emphasized that Britain must prepare for the long haul in dealing with the communist threat, that the health of the economy was the foundation of British power and military strength, and that given the unavoidable vulnerability to devastation in a nuclear world, a nuclear deterrent policy was necessary. Echoing Bernard Brodie's oft-quoted maxim, he insisted ". . . the overriding consideration in all military planning must be to prevent war rather than to prepare for it" ("Enclosure: Defence, Outline of Future Policy," pp. 5–7). See also Leonard Downie, Jr., "U.S. Bombers in Britain Become Superpower Pawns; Britain Sacrifices Conventional Arms in Nuclear Strategy."

[30]Pierre, *Nuclear Politics*, p. 343. And within the military budget, the nuclear deterrent emphasis partly explains the decline in the army's share from about 40 percent in the late 1940s to about 27 percent in the late 1960s. For variations in levels of military spending as a percent of GNP, the defense share of government expenditures, and the pattern of resource allocation among the services, see ibid., pp. 343, 344. See also Lawrence Freedman, "Britain's Defense Policy"; Baylis, *British Defense Policy*, p. 53.

[31]For British Prime Minister Anthony Eden and his military advisers' expression of this view, see Navias, "Nuclear Weapons and British Alliance Commitments, 1955–56," p. 154.

The economic advantages of spending on nuclear-deterrent rather than conventional-defensive weaponry proved compelling not only to the Conservative Party leaders of the 1950s, but also to their Labor Party successors, especially as growing budgetary demands for nonmilitary spending strained government resources. Despite having called for a re-emphasis on conventional defenses in the early 1960s, upon taking office in 1964, Labor instead adhered to the priority accorded nuclear deterrence. This about-face was prudent in light of polls indicating that public support for the independent deterrent had not declined along with the fortunes of Macmillan's Conservative Party. At the time of Labor's victory, 72 percent of those polled thought that it was either very important (55 percent) or fairly important (17 percent) that Britain keep its independent nuclear deterrent.[32] Following the 1964 campaign and for the remaining two decades of the Cold War, the strategic and economic rationale for this doctrinal embrace of nuclear deterrence was clear-cut.[33] Disagreements occasionally arose over plans to procure specific weapons satisfying the national strategy, but the broad consensus that dissuasion by nuclear deterrence rather than conventional defense would have to be the keystone of British security policy endured.[34]

Dissuasion by defense was unattainable against the nuclear threat and unaffordable against the conventional threat that the Soviet Union represented. But what about the low-tech, low-cost alternative to nuclear deterrence, dissuasion by conventional deterrence? Given Britain's historical experience and the contemporary strategic challenges it faced, this alternative held little attraction for leaders in London. Unlike China, and to a lesser extent France, in modern times Britain did not have a glorious tradition of waging a national resistance struggle against an occupying army. For centuries Britain's maritime buffer had afforded

[32]Pierre, *Nuclear Politics*, p. 257.

[33]As Christopher Bertram, director of the International Institute for Strategic Studies in London, summarized the views of its defense analysts: "We have felt for a long time it would be desirable to reduce dependence on nuclear weapons, but the money for conventional forces—the necessary increases in men and equipment has not been there" (Downie, "U.S. Bombers in Britain Become Superpower Pawns").

[34]Malone, *The British Nuclear Deterrent*, pp. 35–38; Baylis, *British Defense Policy*, pp. 53–54, 55. In the early 1980s, for example, controversy did develop over British plans to modernize its aging deterrent. During this defense debate, however, the key issue was not, as in the early 1960s, whether to retain a nuclear deterrent, but whether Britain should spend the extra cash to procure the state-of-the-art Trident II system. Trident II was estimated to cost 50 percent more than the less advanced successor to Polaris originally planned—7.5 billion pounds as opposed to 5 billion (Malone, *The British Nuclear Deterrent*, p. 132; see also Downie, "U.S. Bombers in Britain Become Superpower Pawns").

it unusual natural protection against invasion. Seriously embracing conventional deterrence would have required not only planning for a politically unseemly departure from Britain's proud history of freedom from occupying foreign troops, but also rigorous peacetime preparations for organized resistance among a population eager to return to civilian pursuits after the harrowing military experiences of the first half of the twentieth century.[35] Most important of all, conventional deterrence, for reasons set forth in preceding chapters, would only have enabled Britain to deal with one of the least likely contingencies, a full-scale Soviet invasion. Of all the unlikely scenarios for Soviet aggression against the British Isles, the most plausible would have been attempts at coercion backed by air and missile power, not army and marine divisions. Conventional deterrence would not have been helpful in dealing with these sorts of threats to the homeland. It would also have failed to address Britain's other long-standing vital interest, preventing a hegemon's domination of the European continent. Preparations for popular resistance on British soil could not influence Soviet decisions about taking military action in central Europe.

DISSUASION BY NUCLEAR DETERRENCE:
THE BRITISH EXPERIENCE

British leaders were unwilling to settle for the economically attractive alternative of full dependence on U.S. retaliatory might and its defensive commitment to Europe, and neither independent defensive nor conventional deterrent efforts seemed practical. Instead, more quickly than their Chinese and French counterparts, they concluded that practicing dissuasion by nuclear deterrence was the most sensible approach to prepare for the possibility they would have to deal with a superpower

[35]A reluctance to make it the strategic priority does not mean a national resistance would be ruled out if circumstances required. Any British leader whose efforts at dissuasion or forward defense had failed would undoubtedly repeat some variant of Winston Churchill's famous claim about the sort of unceasing resistance Axis invaders would have faced in World War II. As Churchill put it in his report to the House of Commons on June 4, 1940: "Even though large tracts of Europe and many old and famous States have fallen or may fall into the grip of the Gestapo and all the odious apparatus of Nazi rule, *we shall not flag or fail. We shall go on to the end*, we shall fight in France, we shall fight on the seas and oceans, we shall fight with growing confidence and growing strength in the air, *we shall defend our Island, whatever the cost may be, we shall fight on the beaches, we shall fight on the landing grounds, we shall fight in the fields and in the streets, we shall fight in the hills; we shall never surrender.* ... (Winston S. Churchill, "Wars Are Not Won By Evacuations," June 4, 1940, p. 6231, emphasis added).

adversary by relying on their own resources. Their belief guided Britain's program to develop and then maintain the nuclear weapons that fulfilled the requirements of this strategy.

Developing Britain's Nuclear Weapons

Britain's pursuit of a national nuclear capability early in the postwar era and the effect of this effort on relations with its superpower ally, the United States, differed from China's experience with its superpower ally, the Soviet Union, in ways that reflected the countries' distinctive historical experiences. Yet the two cases also reveal some key similarities attributable to the situation in which both found themselves, an anarchic, bipolar world in which military strategy had been revolutionized by the advent of nuclear weapons.

As pioneers in research on atomic weapons in the early 1940s and then valued partners in the U.S. bomb project, London never confronted barriers to entry to the nuclear club that were as high as for Beijing. Even so, the nuclear sharing agreements worked out between the United States and the United Kingdom during World War II did limit Britain's access to crucial information, hampering its postwar weapons program and straining relations with its superpower ally. Despite the allies' shared wartime goal of quickly realizing what promised to be a militarily decisive weapon, from the start the Anglo-American nuclear relationship was marred by partially conflicting national interests.

After the Japanese attack on Pearl Harbor the United States had begun to forge ahead of the pioneering British in nuclear research. Though it wanted access to the leading edge of nuclear technology, Britain was reluctant to join a cooperative effort whose arrangements placed the Americans in control. British ambivalence and Winston Churchill's preference for continued nuclear independence (through the work of the UK's Tube Alloys Consultative Council) faded only when the costs of autonomy in the desperate wartime years became clearly prohibitive. In addition, however, as early as 1942 those privy to the Tube Alloys project had begun worrying that a postwar American reversion to isolationism and a rising Soviet threat would leave Britain with the "responsibility for keeping the peace in Europe." To meet this challenge, London wanted to be sure it had "full knowledge of the process of manufacturing the ultimate 'police weapons.'"[36] Aware of Washington's reluctance

---

[36]Pierre, *Nuclear Politics*, p. 37. A top figure in the British nuclear weapons program, Sir John Anderson, stated, "We cannot afford after the war to face the future without this weapon and rely entirely on America should Russia or some other power develop it" (Malone, *The British Nuclear Deterrent*, p. 49).

to enter each of the century's major wars, a prudent British leadership could not be certain that the United States would maintain an active interest in the continental balance-of-power after the peace. Thus, given Britain's twin concerns about the war at hand and security in the foreseeable bipolar postwar world, Churchill concluded it was necessary to accept the American conditions for partnership in order to ensure access to nuclear weapons technology, even though the deal outlined in the August 1943 Quebec agreement gave the U.S. president the power to "unilaterally decide" about nuclear sharing after the war.[37]

Despite its importance, the 1943 agreement had not finally resolved the matter of nuclear sharing, and many details were to be ironed out by the Combined Policy Committee it established.[38] In 1944 at Hyde Park, Roosevelt and Churchill signed an executive agreement that reassuringly promised continued nuclear cooperation with Britain. But after the war, the American interest under President Truman soon shifted to molding the new international order, a process that placed a premium on U.S. relations with the Soviet Union and tight control of the U.S. nuclear monopoly. These superpower priorities conflicted with Britain's interest in American aid to its atomic weapons program.[39]

Disagreements about the terms of nuclear sharing during the wartime Manhattan project, then, were followed by a pattern of deteriorating technical exchanges in the immediate postwar months. The uncertainty inherent in a relationship governed by executive agreements was highlighted in 1946 when President Truman, citing the presidential prerogative set forth in the Quebec deal, adopted a narrow view of subsequent promises of assistance and rejected Prime Minister Atlee's request for "technological information" relevant to constructing a "nuclear pile in England."[40] Cooperation collapsed in April 1946 when the U.S. Congress passed the McMahon Act strictly limiting the sharing of American nuclear know-how with other states.

The U.S. cutoff of information and technical assistance that resulted from the McMahon Act had a galvanizing impact not unlike the Khrushchev letter to the Chinese in 1959. It generated a sense of betrayal and distrust that strengthened the British determination to de-

[37]Pierre, *Nuclear Politics*, pp. 31–49; Malone, *The British Nuclear Deterrent*, pp. 45–48; James L. Gormly, "The Washington Declaration and the 'Poor Relation,'" p. 127.

[38]See Malone, *The British Nuclear Deterrent*, p. 49.

[39]Pierre, *Nuclear Politics*, p. 120; Malone, *The British Nuclear Deterrent*, pp. 51–53.

[40]Gormly, "The Washington Declaration and the 'Poor Relation,'" p. 142.

velop an independent deterrent. Although the security rationale was fundamental, the repeated affronts to British pride that accepting dependence on the United States entailed also contributed to the decision to break the American nuclear monopoly.[41] In this respect, British sensitivity differed little from that often noted in discussions of Chinese and French foreign policy. And as for China and France, status considerations reinforced Britain's security motives for developing nuclear weapons. Both security and status concerns encouraged a quest for greater self-reliance and the degree of foreign policy autonomy that it would make possible. Reflecting this belief, Prime Minister Harold Macmillan would claim that Britain's independent nuclear arsenal

> ... gives us a better position in the world, it gives us a better position with respect to the United States. It puts us where we ought to be, in the position of a Great Power. The fact that we have it makes the United States pay greater regard to our point of view, and that is of great importance.[42]

The prestige payoff would prove to be chimerical; deploying its deterrent arsenal failed to arrest, let alone reverse, Britain's fall from the ranks of the great powers. But the security benefit was tangible and enduring. Thus Britain's nuclear weapons procurement policy would reflect the priority accorded security considerations. In subsequent years, as described below, Britain would compromise the prestige-enhancing principle of absolute independence when this was necessary in order to acquire nuclear assistance from the United States.

On January 8, 1947, the Atlee government formally decided to build an atomic bomb. Despite the need to recover from the war's destruction, the British did not believe they could comfortably free ride on security supplied by the United States. Instead, looking ahead to the late 1950s, by which time the hostile Soviets were expected to have a fully deployed nuclear capability, and believing Britain might have to stand alone against this anticipated threat, the leadership in London willingly shouldered the heavy burden of a crash nuclear program.[43] This early postwar period, after all, was a time of U.S. military demobilization and uncertainty about Washington's internationalism. As Prime Minister Atlee later commented on his government's decision:

[41]See Nicholas Wheeler, "The Atlee Government's Nuclear Strategy, 1945–51," p. 135.

[42]Cited in Lawrence Freeman, *The Evolution of Nuclear Strategy*, p. 311.

[43]"The Atlee Government's Nuclear Strategy, 1945–51," p. 135; Jan Melissen, "Prelude to Interdependence," pp. 214–15.

If we had decided not to have it [the atom bomb], we would have put ourselves entirely in the hands of the Americans. That would have been a risk a British government should not take. It's all very well to look back and to say otherwise, but at the time nobody could be sure that the Americans would not revert to isolationism—many Americans wanted it, many Americans feared it. There was no N.A.T.O. then. . . .[44]

British concerns persisted despite events that clarified the U.S. commitment to Europe and reduced the fear of outright abandonment. In 1948 the United States initiated the Marshall Plan and began to base nuclear bombers at East Anglia. In 1949 the United States agreed to participate in NATO and a year later decided to dispatch ground troops to Europe.[45] Even such unprecedented American measures, however, did not eliminate doubts fueled by the anticipation of an increasingly potent Soviet nuclear arsenal that might intimidate the United States. A 1957 CIA analysis acknowledged the consequences of increases in Soviet nuclear capabilities; Britain's enduring determination to retain its own nuclear arsenal had reflected "the reaction against the situation in which the security of the UK, like that of all other non-Communist powers, depends preponderantly on the US. . . . In addition, there has

[44]Cited in Melissen, "Prelude to Interdependence," pp. 214–15. The American public indeed pushed for demobilization of the wartime armed forces to proceed as rapidly as possible, resulting in a startling pace that reduced personnel from 12 million in 1945 to 1.6 million by mid-1947. See *American Military History*, Army Historical Series, Office of the Chief of Military History, United States Army (Washington, D.C.: Center of Military History, United States Army, 1989), pp. 530–31, available on-line, http://www2.army.mil/cmh-pg/books/amh/AMH-24.htm; Gaddis, *Strategies of Containment*, p. 23; Christensen, *Useful Adversaries*, p. 39. The heated debate during the early postwar period about the nature of the overseas role for the United States was undoubtedly reason for concern in London. See ibid., pp. 34–36, 39–40, 44–47, 93–94. The reason why such domestic controversy would have worried British leaders is reflected in Christensen's observation about the state of play in spring 1949: "The [Truman] administration could not take for granted public and congressional support for NATO and MAP [the Military Assistance Program], particularly the latter, more expensive program. Americans liked the idea of helping Europe, but not the real costs and risks involved. For example, if the rather realistic term "promise to go to war" was included in questions about American commitment to the NATO pact, popular support for the treaty dropped to dangerously low levels (40 percent for and 48 percent against)" (ibid., p. 83). Melissen argues that "uncertainty about US policy" and the "the Americans' poor record as a dependable atomic partner" were similarly more important than concerns for "Britain's power status" in 1954 when the Churchill government decided move ahead with development of British thermonuclear weapons (Melissen, "Prelude to Interdependence," pp. 214–15.

[45]See Pierre, *Nuclear Politics*, pp. 70, 75, 76, 79, 112–22; Gaddis, *Strategies of Containment*, p. 114.

been present an element of concern that the US will gradually withdraw its forces from Europe and, as Soviet capabilities against the US increase, become less willing to employ its full force against the USSR in the event of Soviet attacks in Europe."[46]

The British worried not only about exclusion from the collective good of security U.S. nuclear forces supplied, but also about rivalry in its consumption. U.S.-led NATO strategy entailed contingency planning for military action in the event dissuasion by deterrence failed, and planned actions might benefit some allies at the expense of others. Or as Churchill put it, "[We] cannot be sure that in an emergency the resources of other powers would be planned exactly as we would wish, *or that the targets which would threaten us most would be given what we consider the necessary priority in the first few hours.* These targets might be of such cardinal importance that it could really be a matter of life and death for us".[47]

Ironically, perhaps, Britain's fears of abandonment were at the same time compounded by fears of entrapment that could result from its alliance with the United States. General MacArthur's risky adventurism early in the Korean conflict had quickly sensitized Britain to both horns of the dangerous dilemma it faced should a Soviet-American confrontation escalate to full-scale war. On the one hand, London wanted firm commitments from the United States and an American military presence to more tightly couple the allies in the event of Soviet threats to vital British interests. U.S. military intervention in Asia raised the possibility of a diversion of limited American resources away from the European theater that most concerned Britain. On the other hand, if the Korean conflict evolved into World War III, the deployment of U.S. bombers in Britain could pose undesirable dangers. The U.S. presence made British airfields a time-urgent target for Soviet preemptive nuclear strikes; it also raised the possibility of entrapment in an unwanted conflict if these U.S. forces commenced operations on orders from Washington before London was committed to general war.[48] Though

[46]"Implications of Growing Nuclear Capabilities for the Communist Bloc and the Free World," July 9, 1957, p. 6; on similar French concerns, see ibid., p. 4.

[47]Pierre, *Nuclear Politics*, p. 93 (emphasis added), see also pp. 81, 135. Nicholas Wheeler notes that Britain's concerns about possibly divergent priorities in target selection also reflected their experience with its American ally in World War II, during which the United States "had not given priority to attacking the V-1 and V-2 sites in Germany, which posed a threat to the United Kingdom" (Wheeler, "The Atlee Government's Nuclear Strategy, 1945–51," p. 136).

[48]On European, and especially British, concerns about the potentially dangerous consequences of war in Korea, see Christensen, *Useful Adversaries*, pp. 181–82.

less often noted than the need to hedge against the possibility of abandonment, the desire to reduce the extent of British dependence on the United States and, it was hoped, thereby gain some leverage with its ally in situations where entrapment might be catastrophic, also fed the Attlee government's determination to develop the British bomb.[49]

Britain decided on an independent nuclear deterrent as the security insurance it needed and could afford. It must be added, however, that for the UK, nuclear independence was not seen as a full substitute for American backing through NATO. Britain, more openly and consistently than France or China, pursued a dual track policy. London worked hard to maintain close relations with its superpower protector in the *hope* of enjoying security as a collective alliance good supplied by the United States' extended deterrent. At the same time, London worked hard to develop an independent capability to ensure British interests if deterrent-based security turned out to be a private good enjoyed exclusively by those countries possessing their own retaliatory forces.[50] Thus, although early Anglo-American disputes over sharing atomic secrets fueled intra-alliance conflict and encouraged British development of a national nuclear deterrent, they did not culminate in the sort of decisive break that doomed the Sino-Soviet security relationship, or even a partial rupture of the Franco-American sort described in the next chapter. Instead, in an Anglo-American relationship marked by both conflict and cooperation, the latter predominated.

But during the early postwar years following passage of the McMahon Act, the relationship was unusually tense. Mutual suspicion led to the collapse of attempts to negotiate an agreement that would have allowed Britain to test its first atomic bomb at a U.S. site in Nevada. In particular, the U.S. insistence on first examining the British weapon provoked London's concerns about "reciprocity in the exchange of technical information." Remembering the unhappy experience with previous executive understandings and disturbed by the latitude for Washington to interpret the proposed testing agreement, the newly installed Churchill government rejected the plan "because of the limitations imposed by the US."[51] It is easy to understand why the British would be uncomfortably uncertain about American attitudes. Indeed, as

---

[49]Ibid., pp. 137, 138, 143–44. See also Melissen, "Prelude to Interdependence," p. 224.

[50]Baylis, *British Defense Policy*, p. 61.

[51]Steve Connor and Andy Thomas, "How Britain Kept Its Independent Deterrent," p. 4.

late as 1952 even the Chairman of the U.S. Atomic Energy Commission was uncertain about Washington's policy on ". . . the fundamental question of whether we are to encourage an independent effort in the United Kingdom by withdrawal from cooperation and by competing with them, or whether we are, so far as defense matters are concerned, in a joint and cooperative venture. . . . What is the position of the Executive Departments of the United States Government toward cooperation in this field?"[52]

Only after Britain succeeded in testing its first A-bomb at Monte Bello in 1952 was Anglo-American nuclear cooperation gradually reestablished. During the mid-1950s the Eisenhower administration argued that assistance to London was justifiable on the grounds of alliance efficiency.[53] In addition, American concerns about Soviet spies acquiring essential nuclear secrets that had been transferred to an ally seemed less important given what Moscow had already achieved by that time.[54] U.S. Congressional action in 1954 and 1958 (after the British claimed they had tested a thermonuclear device in 1957) eased the McMahon restrictions on sharing nuclear information with countries that had already made "substantial progress in the development of atomic weapons."

[52]Gordon Dean, "Memorandum for the Secretary of State and the Secretary of Defense from Chairman of the U.S. Atomic Energy Commission," Aug. 28, 1952, pp. 2–3.

[53]Though some of his advisers had reservations about the wisdom of sharing classified nuclear data with the British, the President consistently argued for a liberal exchange policy promoting mutual trust and "saving our allies false starts. . . ." (A. J. Goodpaster, "Memorandum of Conference with the President, March 8, 1956; see also A. J. Goodpaster, "Memorandum of Conference with the President, October 25, 1957").

[54]U.S. reluctance to be more forthcoming had reflected not only the desire as leader of the Western alliance to maintain control over this strategically decisive asset but also concern about the vulnerability of Britain's national security establishment to Soviet spies. Revelations in ensuing decades about Soviet atomic espionage suggest that such concerns were reasonable. It should be added, however, that even if Britain (as dramatically revealed in the Klaus Fuchs case) and France may have been more vulnerable, the U.S. nuclear weapons program had not been immune from such penetration. Yet an argument could be made that limiting the diffusion of information limited the opportunities for Soviet penetration and eased the burdens of counterintelligence. On Soviet atomic espionage efforts in the West, see the Venona documents the CIA began to release in 1995 that chronicle intercepted and decoded messages about the early years of Soviet atomic espionage in the West (http://www.nsa.gov:8080/docs/venona/docs.html; also David Holloway, Stalin and the Bomb; Richard Rhodes, Dark Sun; Joseph Albright and Marcia Kunstel, Bombshell). For a prudent warning about relying on any but the hardest evidence in drawing conclusions about the nature and extent of such espionage, see Vladislav Zubok, "Atomic Espionage and Its Soviet 'Witnesses.'"

The 1958 legislation became the keystone for a special nuclear relationship between the United States and UK.[55]

Nevertheless, while Anglo-American nuclear relations were generally cooperative, the allies' sometimes divergent interests ensured Britain's determination to do whatever was necessary to maintain its independent nuclear capability rather than comfortably enjoy a free ride on its powerful American ally. Two episodes in particular reinforced this determination—the Suez Crisis in 1956 (essential also for understanding France's view of its security requirements discussed in the next chapter) and the Skybolt fiasco in 1962.

Suez. During the summer and fall of 1956 the United States and its two principal Western European allies, Britain and France, found themselves mired in deep disagreement about the best way to respond to Egypt's July 26 decision to take over the multinational company managing the Suez Canal.[56] President Nasser claimed that Egypt needed the revenues from operating the canal in order to finance construction of the Aswan Dam. This step was, at least in its timing, a direct result of the U.S. decision announced on July 19 to withdraw its original offer of substantial funding for the dam project. Washington had angrily objected to Cairo's escalating conditions for accepting aid through the World Bank and to its allegedly irresponsible diversion of scarce resources to purchase Soviet military equipment. More important than Nasser's questionable economic justification for nationalization (there

[55]Malone, *The British Nuclear Deterrent*, pp. 57–58; Pierre, *Nuclear Politics*, p. 141. The phrase "substantial progress" apparently referred to knowledge of the Ulam-Teller concept of the thermonuclear bomb. British scientists had demonstrated such knowledge, and in fact a novel version of the concept for designing thermonuclear bombs, in meetings with U.S. physicists in the winter of 1957–58 (see Norman Dombey and Eric Grove, "Britain's Thermonuclear Bluff," p. 10). John Baylis's research of recently available documents contradicts Dombey and Grove's claim that the British "bluffed the Americans into believing they had a thermonuclear capability when they did not" though the Macmillan government may have permitted others, especially the Soviets, to overestimate the success of the early "Grapple" thermonuclear test series in late spring 1957, and to speculate about the distance yet to go in producing a true hydrogen bomb. Prime Minister Macmillan's 1957 claims notwithstanding, the British may not have successfully tested such a bomb until 1958, and a usable weapon was produced only in late 1960 (see John Baylis, *Ambiguity and Deterrence*, pp. 260–68; Tom Wilkie, "First H-bomb Built Amid Safety Fears," p. 3; Robert Norris, Andrew Burrows, and Richard Fieldhouse, *British, French and Chinese Nuclear Weapons*, pp. 32–43).

[56]For brief summaries of the crisis, see Rose McDermott, *Risk-Taking in International Politics*, pp. 135–64. See also Jonathan Kirshner, *Currency and Coercion*, pp. 63–82; Henry Kissinger, *Diplomacy*, pp. 522–49.

was a wide gap between canal profits and the dam's cost) was the way others reacted to what they saw as a political challenge.

However much Washington disliked Nasser's strident nationalism and his willingness to play ball with the Soviets, it was prepared to accept Cairo's control of the canal if, as seemed to be the case, Egypt was able to keep it operating smoothly. From the U.S. perspective the key concern was to prevent a confrontation over the canal from opening the door to greater Soviet influence in this vital region under the guise of support for anti-colonialism. For the British and the French, by contrast, the main problem was not the region's significance as part of the West's global rivalry with the Soviet Union. Britain and France were instead focused on the intrinsic importance of the Suez Canal as a conduit for Western European oil supplies and also their credibility as they struggled with the process of decolonization and the growing forces of nationalism in parts of the Middle East and North Africa where they had been dominant since the nineteenth century.

These different perspectives, especially the extent to which London and Paris believed that their vital national interests required that the status quo ante be restored, led to different responses. Washington advocated a diplomatic solution brokered through the United Nations as the best way to reach an acceptable outcome. The United States did not want to side with Britain and France as they attempted to reassert colonial privilege, a posture that would disadvantage Washington in its Cold War competition with Moscow in the Third World. The United States, therefore, made clear that it rejected the use of force to reverse Nasser's nationalization. Britain and France, however, were leery of the sort of compromise that UN diplomacy would yield and moved ahead with plans for military intervention. Without informing Eisenhower, who they knew opposed the idea, the European allies coordinated preparations with Israel. Israel agreed to participate by attacking Egypt, sensing an opportunity to reduce what it saw as the most serious military threat it faced. After Israel launched its strike on October 29, Britain and France followed their script and issued an ultimatum for both belligerents to withdraw ten miles from the canal. As expected, Egypt refused and Britain and France then used the refusal to justify their October 31 military intervention to seize the canal. London and Paris may have believed that once they had set their plans in motion Washington would prefer to reluctantly support its allies rather than side with the Soviet bloc in opposing them at the UN. They were wrong. President Eisenhower refused to endorse their Suez adventure and instead adhered to a position of working through the UN, beginning with resolutions calling for a cease fire.

Complicating matters further, on November 5 Moscow notified London, Paris, and Washington that the Suez Crisis risked provoking a war in which Soviet nuclear weapons might be used against Britain and France. Moscow may have hoped to divert international attention from its concurrent military suppression of an armed revolt in Hungary, to exploit the obvious split between the United States and two of its NATO allies, and to emerge as the international savior that preserved peace and cowed the latter-day imperialists. President Eisenhower, maintaining his focus on the U.S. overriding interest in its rivalry with the Soviets that had earlier led him to confound his allies, quickly indicated that internal disagreements notwithstanding, the United States would stick with its NATO partners if the Soviets did attack them and also rebuffed Moscow's overtures for bilateral Soviet-American counter-intervention in the region. The United States remained determined to prevent the crisis from yielding the Soviets either a propaganda or a practical advantage.

The American interest in foreclosing Soviet gains, as well as a desire to defuse tensions before they might spin out of control, required a quick end to the crisis. To effect this outcome, the United States, while warning off its adversary, moved to coerce its allies to withdraw from the canal zone and accept the embarrassing necessity of defeat. Jonathan Kirshner has documented the strong economic pressure the Eisenhower administration brought to bear.[57] As Soviet Premier Bulganin rattled his nuclear saber on November 5, the U.S. Federal Reserve exacerbated a run on the pound, and then threatened to make the collapsing currency situation even worse by blocking London's access to its own International Monetary Fund reserves, *unless* Britain went along with a UN-brokered cease-fire and withdrawal. With the British cabinet convinced that economic catastrophe was imminent, it gave in to the U.S. demands. Britain agreed to a cease-fire at the end of the next day, bringing along France, which was less vulnerable to currency manipulation but militarily unable to stay the course without Britain's participation.

The Suez Crisis was a shocking experience for Britain and France

[57]Kirshner convincingly indicates that U.S. currency coercion rather than several alternatives (satisfaction with the results of the operation, looming oil shortages that would result because the United States refused to make up for lost Middle East sources, domestic political opposition, or successful Soviet intimidation) best explains the British reversal of policy (Kirshner, *Currency and Coercion*, pp. 70–81. See also McDermott, *Risk-Taking in International Politics*, pp. 162–63).

that stirred doubts about the wisdom of overdependence on their alliance with the United States. Although it is certainly true that during the crisis the United States reiterated its commitment to respond to direct Soviet aggression against them, these European allies believed that their security interests went beyond merely physical protection of the homeland. From their perspective, the Suez Crisis was not a wasteful adventure but rather a necessary action, however risky, to forestall an increasingly serious challenge to what they defined as vital national interests.[58] As Rose McDermott has suggested in applying prospect theory to the case, Britain and France were operating in the domain of losses, and states are willing to incur grave risks to avoid major losses. For them, the stakes were high: "... if they failed, they stood to lose not only control of the Canal, but loss of men, material, and status in the region, access to vital oil supplies, financial solvency, and even governmental stability."[59] From the U.S. perspective, the stakes were smaller and different: there was not much of an economic reason for opposing Egyptian management of the canal, there was not much of a moral argument for siding with moribund colonialism against the rising tide of nationalism, and there was not much strategic sense in destroying the hope to preserve Western influence in the region by pushing the Arabs into Soviet arms.[60]

The Suez experience also indicated to Britain and France that their security required more than just attempts to manage the risk that the United States might not support its allies if they disagreed about whether vital interests were at stake. During the crisis, Britain and France had in fact attempted to employ one of the above-mentioned methods to try to elicit support from a self-interested patron—emphasizing the severity of the threat to alliance interests in order to generate fear of tolerating even small losses to the common adversary who might then doubt your resolve. Prime Minister Anthony Eden wrote to President Eisenhower in early September, suggesting that Nasser's move was only the first in a planned sequence to "expel all Western influence and interest from Arab countries," a move that the experience with Hitler suggested was best resisted sooner rather than later.[61] French Premier

---

[58]As Kissinger concluded, "What infuriated Great Britain and France in 1956 was not so much legal interpretation as Dulles' strong implication that, in the Middle East, the United States defined its vital interests substantially differently from the way its European allies did" (Kissinger, *Diplomacy*, p. 537).

[59]McDermott, *Risk-Taking in International Politics*, p. 152.

[60]See Kissinger, *Diplomacy*, p. 532.

[61]Cited in McDermott, *Risk-Taking in International Politics*, p. 149.

Guy Mollet similarly tried to stimulate the U.S. aversion to appeasement, drawing parallels with the 1930s and indicating that a failure to
act now might only mean more costly action later.[62] But the attempt to
tap into American fears that Arab nationalism might open the door to
an anti-Western, potentially pro-Soviet turn in the Middle East failed.
Eisenhower shared his allies' broad concern about the future of Western
influence in the region, but believed that the aggressive posture Britain
and France recommended was likely to make the situation worse, not
better. For Eisenhower, backing the allies might hold the prospect of a
marginal gain in terms of alliance solidarity, but it also held the prospect of huge losses by enhancing Soviet influence in the Third World
and, if the worst occurred, dangerous military confrontation between
the superpowers.[63] Opposing Britain and France on intervention in Suez
while supporting them against direct Soviet threats would preserve the
alliance and perhaps yield a small gain by better positioning the United
States in its rivalry with the Soviets for the hearts and minds of nationalists in the Third World. The acceptable price for the United States was
Britain's and France's strong sense of resentment at having been abandoned by their superpower ally at a moment when they required its
support to ensure what they perceived to be important national interests.[64]

The United States may have been correct in its assessment that
European control of the Suez Canal fell far short of a genuine vital interest for which allies should be expected to share grave risks (just as one
can argue that the Soviets were correct in believing that Beijing's desire
to maintain its claim to Taiwan in the 1950s fell far short of a genuine
vital interest covered by the Sino-Soviet alliance). But the message received in London and Paris (as it had been in Beijing) was that the superpower alliance leader was free to decide when support would be forthcoming. Even if there was no immediate evidence that the United States
would fail to fulfill its core NATO commitment (in fact the warnings to
the Soviets provided evidence to the contrary), the Suez experience ensured that a nagging concern would fuel British and French determina-

---

[62]Ibid., p. 153.

[63]And it might be added that prior to the British decision to use force, Eisenhower
warned Eden that military intervention might so antagonize U.S. public opinion that
the commitment to NATO would be at risk. See Kissinger, *Diplomacy*, p. 534.

[64]McDermott notes that French Premier Mollet said, "French opinion was particularly disturbed because they [sic] had the feeling that they were being abandoned
by the US after the US had started the whole affair by their [sic] withdrawal of aid for
Aswan Dam." See reference to Ambassador Dillon's telegram to Dulles in McDermott, *Risk-Taking in International Politics*, p. 153.

tion to hedge their bets against this remote possibility. In unforeseeable future circumstances, interests might diverge, the shadow of nuclear war would raise the risks to be run, and in an anarchic world states would be free to choose to look out for themselves, even at the expense of others. As Henry Kissinger summarized the legacy of Suez:

> The Suez crisis brought home to them [Britain and France] that one of the premises of the Atlantic Alliance—the congruence of interest between Europe and the United States—was at best only partially valid. From this point on, the argument that Europe did not need nuclear weapons because it could always count on American support ran up against the memory of Suez.[65]

Skybolt. U.S. pressure on Britain during the Suez Crisis confirmed London's belief in the need for its own military magic bullet just in case the UK's chief ally should let it down under more critical circumstances.[66] The next episode shaping British thinking about strategic dependence on the United States unfolded in 1962. In October, Washington's failure to closely consult London during the unnerving height of the Cuban Missile Crisis provided a stark reminder for the British that hitching one's fate to the U.S. wagon not only carried the risk of abandonment but also the danger of entrapment.[67] More importantly, the disturbing Cuban Missile Crisis was immediately followed by a renewed Anglo-American dispute over nuclear sharing that seemed to threaten the special relationship in this area forged only four years earlier.

Based on its own cost-benefit analysis of U.S. strategic needs, on December 11, 1962, the Kennedy administration abruptly informed London that it was canceling plans to build the air-launched Skybolt missile and therefore could not deliver this weapon to Britain as promised by President Eisenhower in 1960. In the context of the special relationship with the United States, acquiring the Skybolt system had been viewed as an economical way to extend the future viability of London's bomber-based nuclear forces. Coming so closely on the heels of Defense Secre-

---

[65]Kissinger, *Diplomacy*, p. 547. Henry Kissinger seems sympathetic to the sting the British and French felt, and questions whether or not the United States might have softened the blow: "Yet the gnawing question remains whether America's dissociation from its allies needed to be quite so brutal" (*Diplomacy*, p. 544).

[66]A CIA analysis also noted that Washington's cautiousness in responding to Moscow's 1956 intervention in Hungary at the same time as the Suez Crisis heightened European worries about the United States' willingness to "assume serious risks of Soviet counteraction" ("Implications of Growing Nuclear Capabilities for the Communist Bloc and the Free World," July 9, 1957, p. 7.

[67]Pierre, *Nuclear Politics*, pp. 224–25; Rosecrance, *Defense of the Realm*, p. 13.

tary Robert McNamara's June 1962 Ann Arbor speech belittling the smaller nuclear arsenals of lesser powers, Britain saw the cancellation of Skybolt as part of a U.S. attempt to promote the demise of its ally's deterrent.[68] That interpretation was not unreasonable. After all, during its first two years in office, the Kennedy administration had been engaged in a revision of U.S. grand strategy and nuclear doctrine that boded ill for independent British (and French) nuclear forces. What was the logic of this new American strategy? Why did it make the United States less tolerant of its allies' nuclear forces and contribute to British alarm about the Skybolt decision?

In the 1950s President Eisenhower's nuclear doctrine of massive retaliation had emphasized the deterrent effect of confronting the Soviet Union with the prospect that horrifying destruction could occur shortly after the onset of hostilities. Although Secretary of State Dulles explained that a full nuclear strike would not immediately or automatically be the first U.S. move in a future war, he also emphasized that this possibility was an effective way to dissuade a dangerous adversary from believing it could safely test U.S. intentions. Critics of massive retaliation argued that once the Soviets also possessed a devastating retaliatory capability, the threat would no longer be credible for preventing the communists from nibbling away at U.S. interests, especially in the Third World, or even from challenging more important U.S. interests in Europe as long as they relied on limited, nonnuclear means. Faced with less than the ultimate challenge to U.S. survival, critics argued that massive retaliation would be exposed as a bluff and the United States, lacking alternatives, would be faced with a choice between humiliation or national suicide.

Such criticisms informed the revisions of U.S. strategy that President Kennedy initiated upon taking office in 1961.[69] The purpose of these revisions was to create a diverse array of military options for the United States that ranged from the most limited use of conventional forces to the maximal use of nuclear forces, thereby providing the President with flexibility to choose a response that suited the nature of the adversary's challenge. Creating such options allegedly had two virtues.

[68]On the events surrounding the cancellation of Skybolt, see Richard Neustadt, *Alliance Politics*. McNamara, in his famous line, condemned small nuclear forces as "dangerous, expensive, prone to obsolescence and lacking in credibility as a deterrent" (Malone, *The British Nuclear Deterrent*, p. 156).

[69]For discussions of the logic behind these changes, see Schelling, *Arms and Influence*, pp. 162–63, 190–98; For summaries of the policy process, see Lawrence Freedman, *The Evolution of Nuclear Strategy*, pp. 227–44; Fred Kaplan, *The Wizards of Armageddon*, 248–90.

First, options would provide the president with more credible threats to counter Soviet action in kind, depriving the Soviets of the belief that fear of all-out nuclear war would paralyze a strategically muscle-bound United States and make lesser military operations against Western interests safe. Second, if war nevertheless occurred, the availability of options short of a full nuclear strike would make it possible for the United States and the Soviets to begin the fighting with limited attacks and, it was hoped, negotiate a settlement before escalation resulted in mutual annihilation.

President Kennedy's Defense Secretary McNamara set out to translate what was termed "flexible response" into policy. The United States rewrote its nuclear war plan, developed and deployed a wide variety of more accurate and more survivable weapons better suited to measured and discriminate use, and announced a new declaratory nuclear doctrine. In articulating the shift from massive retaliation to what came to be known as the "city-avoidance" or "no-cities" nuclear doctrine, McNamara noted not only the desirability of the United States having less drastic options, but also that the existence of targeting options would enable both the United States and its Soviet adversary to act on the obvious incentives to hold off on the dreaded unrestrained nuclear exchange for as long as possible, even in the event of a major war. Fundamental questions about its feasibility and sensibility aside,[70] if it was to

---

[70]The logic of flexible response, as well as its shortcomings, reflected the inescapable dilemmas of the nuclear age. On the one hand, once both adversaries possess survivable nuclear retaliatory forces, rationality makes it difficult to credibly threaten nuclear war except as a response to absorbing a full nuclear strike, a step any sensible adversary would avoid. This contradiction between rationality and the credibility of nuclear retaliatory threats encourages the search for limited options and the flexibility they seem to permit. On the other hand, as long as each adversary possesses nuclear weapons, one can never be certain about how and when they might be used. Leaders with available options still face the risk of spiraling escalation and, therefore, are not liberated to employ the many lesser options that they may have available. Advocates of flexible response argued that both parties would recognize the self-interest in managing the risks of escalation even in the context of a war that could, after all, be disastrous if the risks were ignored. Critics insisted that the shift to flexible response was dangerous (by making great power war appear manageable it would reduce the caution induced by the fear of nuclear holocaust) or infeasible (because whatever their self-interest, in the early 1960s the Soviets lacked the quantity and quality of nuclear weapons to engage in a series of limited nuclear exchanges).

The logic of nuclear deterrence offered in this book suggests that the optimism of advocates and the pessimism of critics were both overdrawn. The emerging nuclear history of the Cold War suggests instead that when faced with circumstances that came closest to testing abstract logic, the proponents of flexible response in the Kennedy administration were neither as confident as advocates had hoped, nor as

work, flexible response required tightly centralized control over the selection of options, especially nuclear options, that would be employed in any showdown with the adversary. To send the right signals, a single authority should select the targets, decide on timing of the attacks, and choose the moment for and duration of negotiating pauses as the confrontation unfolds. This organizational imperative would be undermined by the existence of multiple decision centers independently reserving the right to act on their own interests. Consequently, whereas President Eisenhower, embracing massive retaliation, could view British and French nuclear weapons as compounding Soviet uncertainties about triggering catastrophic war, his Democratic successors saw the allies' independent deterrents compounding U.S. uncertainties as it prepared to carefully manage the response to any Soviet challenge. The new U.S. doctrine of flexible response would be jeopardized not only by multiple decision centers but also by vulnerable, hair-trigger weapons, the sort U.S. policy-makers expected smaller nuclear powers to be able to deploy.[71]

---

reckless as critics had feared. The key reality checks were the 1961 Berlin crisis and especially the 1962 Cuban Missile Crisis. With the accumulation of memoirs, interviews with decision-makers, and a steady flow of declassified documents that accelerated once the Cold War ended, the emerging image of President Kennedy during the Cuban Missile Crisis is one that is less tough but perhaps more impressively responsible than the one initially offered in the immediate post-crisis hagiography. For an account that highlights the contrast between the flexibility advocates' confidence when formulating options and their cautiousness when faced with actually choosing among them during the Berlin and Cuba crises, see Kaplan, *The Wizards of Armageddon*, pp. 291–306. For an introduction to the emerging story of actual decision-making during the Cuban Missile Crisis, see Marc Trachtenberg's pioneering effort that drew on some of the earliest declassified documents to rethink the standard version of the events (Marc Trachtenberg, "The Influence of Nuclear Weapons in the Cuban Missile Crisis"). For an overview that contains references to much of the recently available information, see Graham T. Allison and Philip Zelikow, *Essence of Decision*. For a classic early account of the crisis, see Robert F. Kennedy, *Thirteen Days*.

[71] See Ullman, "The Covert French Connection," p. 7; see also Kohl, *French Nuclear Diplomacy*, pp. 217–29. Recently declassified records in Britain reveal the contrasting interests of Britain (wanting independence) and the United States (wanting to maintain control) on the issue of commanding British nuclear forces dedicated to NATO. Britain apparently sought assurances from Washington that London's approval would be secured prior to NATO (i.e., U.S.) commanders ordering British units to use nuclear weapons. "For three years from 1962, the MoD repeatedly tried to get assurances from the Americans who controlled Nato defences in Europe that they would not order British commanders to use nuclear weapons without consulting the Government. But the requests were either ignored or rebuffed at high political level." See Ben Fenton "British Confusion over Cuban Missile Crisis, Newly-released Papers Show Commanders Could Have Ignored Orders to Deploy Atomic Weapons," p. 4.

McNamara's attempt to limit the damage from a predictably negative British reaction to the policy shift in general and his remarks disparaging small nuclear arsenals in particular seemed at best half-hearted. He somewhat confusingly informed the British that he had meant that "limited nuclear capabilities operating independently were dangerous," but that did not mean he was critical of Britain's deterrent since its nuclear weapons "have long been organized as part of a thoroughly coordinated Anglo-American striking force ... although of course their political control remains with the British government."[72] In the event, the unilateral American decision to renege on the Skybolt deal sent a more clearly disturbing message, as Kennedy's advisers seemed to appreciate after the fact. A background paper on the situation in the UK provided to President Kennedy prior to the tense Anglo-American summit at Nassau in December 1962 alerted the president to Britain's deep and growing resentment. It suggested that so soon after a wave of publicly aired criticism in Britain about "inadequate consultation with the United States in connection with the Cuban crisis," the Skybolt fiasco would "seriously harm Anglo-American relations" and that "the effect on the British will be a distinct feeling that the rug has been pulled out from under them."[73] It was in this context, recognizing the potential for a diplomatic disaster and perhaps also the futility of trying to denuclearize a sovereign state, that President Kennedy was persuaded by Prime Minister Macmillan to offer the Polaris SLBM system as a substitute for the cancelled Skybolt.

The Nassau accord preserved the special Anglo-American nuclear relationship and spared Britain the full expense of missile development. Britain, however, was careful to avoid wholesale dependence on the United States.[74] London made sure it not only retained control over the

[72]"McNamara Press Conference."

[73]French President de Gaulle, advisers also warned Kennedy, might well be expected to "point to this episode as proof of the danger of relying on another country for nuclear weapons" ("Kennedy-Macmillan Nassau Meeting, December 19–20, 1962, Background Paper, Current Political Scene in the United Kingdom," Dec. 13, 1962).

[74]"Proposed US-UK Agreement for a Substitute Weapon Incident to Skybolt Cancellation," Dec. 17, 1962. U.S. delivery-systems technology offered a cost-effective solution to guaranteeing Britain's continued ability to field an independently controlled deterrent. Washington granted London's request for access to American SLBMs; these would be fitted with British nuclear warheads and placed aboard British-built submarines (Pierre, *Nuclear Politics*, pp. 224–37). A similar principle was to have guided the canceled Skybolt deal under which Britain would have mated its own warheads with the missiles (Norris, Burrows, and Fieldhouse, *British, French and Chinese Nuclear Weapons*, p. 98).

deployed forces, but also maintained the technological skills to go it alone should a U.S. cutoff ever make that costly course necessary.[75] Recently released British documents indicate that Macmillan took this risk quite seriously. In December 1962 the Prime Minister informed Defence Minister Thorneycroft that he had "doubts about the final outcome of the [Polaris] deal despite successful negotiations with President John F. Kennedy" and was considering moving ahead without American assistance if the arrangement fell through.[76]

The Polaris deal did not fall through but such experiences had a lasting effect, even as an increasingly close Anglo-American relationship developed during the last twenty-five years of the Cold War. British leaders carefully guarded the independence of their national nuclear deterrent, even as they exploited their U.S. connection to help offset the expense of maintaining its viability. Unavoidable uncertainty about the future of the alliance and, more importantly, the possibility that British and American interests might diverge at the brink of disaster meant it was "essential that a British prime minister should control Britain's own nuclear weapons, the ultimate deterrent to any 'tinpot dictator' or would-be aggressor."[77] An independent deterrent would complicate Soviet planning that might focus on estimates of the likelihood the United States could be intimidated into abandoning its ally. Moscow would have to be absolutely certain about the response of two autonomous decision-making centers. As Prime Minister Margaret Thatcher's government put it, ". . . even if [the Soviets] thought at some critical point as a conflict developed that the US would hold back, the British force could

---

[75]John Simpson, *The Independent Nuclear State*, pp. 225–26. Although British Polaris missile submarines were put under NATO command, two key conditions were imposed that substantially weakened the constraint on nuclear independence. First the launching of British nuclear weapons could only be authorized by the British Prime Minister. Second Britain "retain[ed] the right to launch the missiles independently of NATO authorization if the British national interest warrant[ed] such action" (David A. Brown, "British Seeking a Stronger Nuclear Force Capability," p. 263; see also Norris, Burrows, and Fieldhouse, *British, French, and Chinese Nuclear Weapons*, p. 102). Still, the arrangements with the United States did lead Britain to train and deploy forces in ways that it might not have chosen if fully independent. See "U.S. Kept Veto on Polaris; 1964." The determination to resist full dependence on the United States had also been present at the creation of the special nuclear relationship following the 1958 Atomic Energy Act, after which Britain took advantage of U.S. thermonuclear warhead know-how, but also nurtured an indigenous nuclear weapons design capability (Baylis, *Ambiguity and Deterrence*, p. 268).

[76]"Secret Papers from '60s Reveal British Nuclear Strategy."

[77]Comments of British Defence Secretary John Nott in 1982, cited in Bridget Bloom, "Gaullist Sting in Trident's Tail."

still inflict a blow so destructive that the penalty for aggression would have proved too high."[78]

What sort of nuclear weapons did British Prime Ministers control should they need to inflict the destructive blow? And how did such weapons constitute a deterrent against a Soviet adversary with over-whelmingly greater capabilities? Like China, Britain could not match the quantity and diversity of nuclear weapons deployed by its super-power adversary. Yet the British, also like the Chinese, believed that this did not preclude the effectiveness of their strategy of dissuasion by deterrence. Success depended not on a comparison of forces, but rather on creating first-strike uncertainty in the mind of the prospective ag-gressor. As long as the Soviets could not eliminate the British ability to deliver an unacceptably punishing retaliatory blow or be sure the available option would not be exercised, Soviet prudence would inhibit grave threats against vital British interests. By the late 1950s Britain was able meet this deterrent requirement. During the remainder of the Cold War, the potential risks of British nuclear retaliation against the Soviets were awesome, despite the relatively small size of the UK's arsenal and the near impossibility of credibly threatening to undertake the suicidal step of launching those forces that might be available.

Britain's Nuclear Forces: Small but Sufficient

As for China, the economic constraints Britain confronted limited the size of its nuclear deterrent stockpile. But Britain's higher level of eco-nomic and scientific development in the early Cold War years, as well as its cooperation with the United States, meant that the UK was able to deploy nuclear forces (weapons and delivery systems) more potent than those China initially fielded. By the late 1950s British nuclear forces had become powerful enough to hold at risk at least 15–20 million Soviet lives and 15–25 percent of Soviet industrial capacity.[79] What sorts of nu-clear weapons did Britain deploy? What steps did it take to increase the likelihood a sufficiently punishing retaliatory capability would be avail-able even as the Soviet Union rapidly increased the military capabilities it could use in a disarming first strike?

The earliest British atomic weapons (the bulky Blue Danube and

[78]Cited in Malone, *The British Nuclear Deterrent*, p. 94.
[79]Lawrence Freedman, "British Nuclear Targeting," p. 121.

more efficient Red Beard fission devices) were loaded onto the Royal Air Force's nuclear-capable V-bombers (Valiant, Vulcan, and Victor) that became operational between 1955 and 1958.[80] By the early 1960s, however, 100–200 one-megaton thermonuclear devices (Yellow Sun gravity bombs and its variant fitted to the Blue Steel air-to-surface missile carried by the bombers) had entered service as the backbone of an arsenal fulfilling the requirements of Britain's strategic deterrent doctrine of massive retaliation. Although the bomber-based forces provided high confidence in Britain's ability to penetrate and deliver 70–90 warheads against Soviet targets,[81] the emergence of Soviet ballistic missiles posed a threat to the survivability of land-based aircraft prior to take-off. In order to preserve the retaliatory capability aboard its bombers, in 1960 Britain began developing its Ballistic Missile Early Warning Station to provide at least four minutes notice of attack. Together with well-rehearsed scrambling routines and a policy that kept three V-bombers at each main base "fully armed with crews at a 3-minute readiness" (other front-line aircraft were on "15-minute Quick Reaction Alert"), this adjustment effectively deprived Soviet planners of full confidence in the success of any preemptive strike during the 1960s and thereby preserved the deterrent value of a partially vulnerable land-based fleet.[82]

Still, London considered such measures enhancing the viability of a bomber-based deterrent as temporary solutions to a growing problem. Britain, like the other nuclear powers, saw ballistic missiles as the most sensible mode for basing its retaliatory nuclear forces. Ballistic missiles could be made more survivable against improving Soviet counterforce first-strike capabilities and would provide greater confidence than bombers that surviving forces could be delivered on target despite improving Soviet air defenses. In 1955 Britain had launched a program to develop a land-based IRBM, the Blue Streak, but the foreseeable vulnerability of a slow-to-ready liquid-fueled missile in a fixed silo made it hard for an economically strapped government to justify the program's expense. Instead, British leaders opted for an air-launched missile (at first the Blue Steel, later the ill-fated U.S. Skybolt) carried by partially survivable bombers, and then for the sea-launched Polaris ballistic missile.[83]

[80]For detailed chronologies and historical description of the British arsenal, see Norris, Burrows, and Fieldhouse, *British, French, and Chinese Nuclear Weapons*, esp. chs. 2 and 3.

[81]Freedman, "British Nuclear Targeting," pp. 117–19. On the Royal Air Force's (RAF's) strategic bomber force, see also Pierre, *Nuclear Politics*, pp. 145–55.

[82]Norris, Burrows, and Fieldhouse, *British, French, and Chinese Nuclear Weapons*, p. 90.

[83]Ibid., pp. 97–99.

Once the United States agreed in 1962 at Nassau to supply the Polaris in place of Skybolt, a sea-based deterrent was clearly the most sensible choice for Britain's small deterrent force. It combined the strategic advantages of enhanced survivability (mobile, stealthy basing) and penetrability (multiple warhead ballistic missiles) with the economic advantages of American assistance. Once the third Resolution-class SSBN commenced operations in August 1969, the Royal Air Force (RAF) formally surrendered principal responsibility for carrying out nuclear retaliatory strikes to the Royal Navy and its Polaris submarine fleet.[84] Thereafter, London was "capable of destroying Moscow and perhaps ten other major urban-industrial complexes" even in the unlikely worst case where only one submarine with its sixteen multiple warhead missiles was at sea and all bombers had been destroyed on the ground. And in the more plausible case where some strategic warning would be available, the British could credibly threaten to devastate about forty such targets.[85]

Maintaining this submarine-based retaliatory capability over the last two decades of the Cold War was the goal that guided Britain's nuclear force modernization. Confident that its superpower adversary could not be sure of destroying the SLBM force before launch, London's principal concern after the late 1960s was to ensure that surviving forces would pose a sufficiently terrible threat of punishment despite the anticipated Soviet deployment of sophisticated anti-missile defenses. In 1969 Britain initiated an indigenous research and development program dubbed Chevaline that resulted in an ingenious technology combining multiple warheads atop the Polaris with sophisticated decoys (including metallic balloon decoys and penetration-aid carriers that would appear to be warheads).[86] The deceptive value of the Chevaline system was not only that it reduced whatever level of confidence the Soviets might have had in the performance of their anti-missile defenses, but also (in what was probably an unintended payoff) that the package led Soviet planners to overestimate British nuclear capability. In testing, the reentry vehicles gave the appearance of a capability for carrying six warheads when in fact only two forty-kiloton thermonuclear warheads actually accompanied the numerous penetration aids and decoys launched by each Chevaline-tipped Polaris SLBM.[87] Because it satisfied their relatively

[84]Ibid., pp. 100–101.
[85]Malone, *The British Nuclear Deterrent*, p. 101; Pierre, *Nuclear Politics*, pp. 292–97.
[86]Norris, Burrows, and Fieldhouse, *British, French, and Chinese Nuclear Weapons*, pp. 109–13.
[87]Ibid., p. 112.

simple deterrent requirements, the Chevaline upgrade of Polaris enabled the British to avoid the expense of purchasing the U.S. Poseidon SLBM with its multiple independently targeted reentry vehicles, and thereby extended the useful life of the Polaris system until the 1990s, when the Resolution class SSBNs required replacement.[88]

Labor and Conservative governments both agreed on the strategic and economic virtues of maintaining the sea-based backbone of the independent British deterrent. Despite heated controversy focusing on the projected expense of force modernization,[89] extensive discussions begun by Labor Prime Minister James Callaghan in January 1979 and completed under the Conservative Prime Minister Margaret Thatcher resulted in the July 1980 announcement that Britain had decided to purchase the U.S. Trident SLBM and to build four Vanguard-class submarines that were needed to carry the new missiles whose warheads would have multiple, independently targeted re-entry vehicles (MIRVs). The principal advantage of choosing Trident for the post-Polaris fleet, and especially the March 1982 decision to purchase the more advanced Trident II, was not a new strategic interest in increasing the number of deliverable warheads or their accuracy but rather the old economic interest in maintaining "'commonality' with US equipment over the lifetime of the system."[90] Thus, even before the collapse of the Soviet Union led to deep cutbacks in planned warhead deployment, Britain's Ministry of Defence indicated that each Trident missile would be loaded with no more than eight 100 kiloton warheads rather than the possible maximum of 14–16.[91]

A nearly continuous process of modernization facilitated by close

[88]See David A. Brown, "British Seeking a Stronger Nuclear Force Capability," p. 263; Pierre, *Nuclear Politics*, p. 295; François Heisbourg, "The British and French Nuclear Forces," p. 304.

[89]See "Don't Forget the Cheap One." Some, like Colonel Jonathan Alford, Deputy Director of the International Institute for Strategic Studies, suggested that it would be more economical to maintain the Polaris fleet, and supplement it with a large number of "cruise missiles based on lorries, patrol boats or hovercraft" ("The International Institute for Strategic Studies Has Reported to the Commons Select Committee on Defence Evaluating the Various Options for a British Nuclear Deterrent in the Coming Decades," pp. 12, 26).

[90]Norris, Burrows, and Fieldhouse, *British, French, and Chinese Nuclear Weapons*, p. 115.

[91]For varying estimates, see Freedman, "British Nuclear Targeting," p. 124; Heisbourg, "The British and French Nuclear Forces," p. 304; Norris, Burrows, and Fieldhouse, *British, French, and Chinese Nuclear Weapons*, pp. 115–17, 169. As will be indicated in Chapter 7, by the time of actual deployment in the 1990s, the changed strategic environment led to an even greater reduction in the likely loading of the British Trident system.

cooperation with, but never full dependence on, the United States enabled Britain to ensure a discomforting first-strike uncertainty in Moscow, even as the Soviets amassed an increasingly sophisticated and plentiful nuclear arsenal. The modernization effort was consistent with a doctrine that emphasized ensuring the *possibility* of politically catastrophic countervalue strikes, rather than the certainty of militarily decisive counterforce strikes. When budgetary considerations forced London to choose, as noted above, it chose delivery systems that enhanced survivability and penetrability (especially against the politically most valued Soviet city, Moscow) rather than accuracy and extensive target coverage. In the first major modernization program, the highly survivable Polaris was procured as a replacement for the V-bombers, despite a reduction in the total number of independent targets that could be struck.[92] In the second major modernization, the Trident SLBM system was selected over its strongest competitor, cruise missile systems, on the grounds of survivability, penetrability, and cost effectiveness. The chief attraction of cruise missiles, their astounding accuracy, was an advantage that carried insufficient weight given the logic of Britain's deterrent doctrine.[93]

In addition to modernization, however, London also relied on deception, rather than technology per se, to augment the deterrent effect of its limited capabilities. Admittedly less important for Britain than for a more economically constrained, technologically lagging, and more fully self-reliant China, deception was nevertheless one part of the recipe for an outgunned second-ranking power to cultivate doubt in the mind of its superpower adversary about the prospects for nuclear retaliation.

In the late 1940s, when cooperation with the United States was most tenuous, the British government desperately sought an indigenous capability to deliver the atomic weapons it would soon test, since they were expected to be available several years before the V-bombers being developed to carry them. Recently disclosed documents reveal that the stopgap solution designed to maximize the chance that available Lincoln aircraft (retrofitted and armed with nuclear weapons) would reach their targets was a plan to send several of the bombers at a time against the Soviet Union, only one of which would actually be loaded with an atomic bomb. Because the additional 10,000 pound weight of the wea-

[92]Freedman, "British Nuclear Targeting," pp. 117–19.

[93]Ibid., pp. 107–10, 124; Malone, *The British Nuclear Deterrent*, pp. 112, 115–16. On modernization decisions, see also Pierre, *Nuclear Politics*, p. 295; Heisbourg, "The British and French Nuclear Forces," p. 304; Simpson, *The Independent Nuclear State*, p. 233.

pon would preclude a round-trip by the fully armed bomber, its crew would be expected to "bail out 50 miles beyond the target."[94] Many had suspected some such scheme would be Britain's policy based on the logic of the situation, and prudent planners in Moscow would have had to entertain the worrisome thought. As it turned out, after the Soviet A-bomb test in 1949 the United States decided to sell Britain B-29s, and planning for such one-way bombing runs became unnecessary.[95]

A second occasion on which Britain saw deception as a means to compensate for shortcomings in its nuclear capabilities is evident in other documents recently released by the Public Records Office. These papers suggest that Prime Minister Macmillan intentionally deceived the public, including the Soviets, when claiming in May 1958 that Britain had the hydrogen bomb. Initial tests apparently did occur in 1957 but design problems remained to be worked out in further testing, and a usable weapon was not actually produced until late 1960.[96] Undoubtedly hoping that his exaggerated claims would buy some time as Britain furiously worked on its thermonuclear deterrent (in fact the deception apparently went unnoticed for more than three decades), behind the scenes Macmillan rushed the deployment process as much as possible, even to the extent of skimping on safety studies about the risks a planned assembly site at Burghfield in Berkshire posed to nearby Reading.[97]

Deception also played a role in ensuring the deterrent effectiveness of the SLBM program, as noted above. During the 1970s the penetration aids and decoys employed in the Chevaline warhead package led to Soviet overestimates of the size of the British sea-based deterrent arsenal. Such cultivation of doubt about the submarine forces at London's disposal continued in the 1980s as the Trident program was being brought to fruition. The British left unspecified the actual warhead loading, stating only a maximum number that was possible. The Soviets then would have to worry about coping with the challenge the higher figure represented, even though actual loading would likely be smaller.[98]

---

[94]Information discovered in the Public Record by Richard Aldrich of Nottingham University (Michael Smith, "Atom Bomb Pilots Faced One-way Trip," p. 5).
[95]Ibid.
[96]Wilkie, "First H-bomb Built Amid Safety Fears," p. 3.
[97]Ibid.
[98]Norris, Burrows, and Fieldhouse, *British, French, and Chinese Nuclear Weapons*, pp. 115–17, 169.

Britain's Nuclear Credibility: Not Much, but Enough

However potent Britain's surviving nuclear forces would be, or Moscow believed they would be, this capability alone would not have been enough to convince the Soviets that British nuclear threats were credible because they could rationally be carried out. London had neither the ability to prevail in a nuclear war nor the ability to meaningfully limit damage to British society through a counterforce strike. Consequently, it would never be rational for Britain to choose to launch a suicidal massive nuclear strike except in the one circumstance, the aftermath of a full-scale nuclear attack, that prudent Soviet planners would sensibly avoid. Thus, from its earliest days domestic and foreign critics doubted the usefulness of Britain's independent deterrent. When asked against which targets and under what circumstances the nuclear deterrent forces might be employed, British leaders adamantly refused to be specific, arguing that clarification would reduce the nagging uncertainty that dissuaded the Soviets.[99]

But given Moscow's invulnerable nuclear retaliatory capability, how could Britain's apparently suicidal nuclear threats be credible under *any* circumstances? British strategy, critics alleged, would be exposed as a dangerous bluff, and investment in the atomic arsenal as a waste of scarce resources when the government faced the choice between humiliation and national suicide. The classic question posed was whether a "responsible and rational British government" would carry out a suicidal nuclear strike in response to anything short of a highly unlikely total nuclear attack on Britain. The obvious answer was "probably not"— a worrisome thought for a country banking so heavily on the dissuasive power of threatened retaliation.[100] But more important given the purpose of such a dissuasive strategy, in the mind of the potential aggressor "probably not" must mean "possibly yes," a most worrisome thought when retaliation involves nuclear weapons. As emphasized in Chapter 2, the lingering possibility that the British government might prove to be an "unsafe actor," either insufficiently responsible (in the sense that inadvertent or accidental launch might occur) or irrational when seri-

---

[99]Pierre, *Nuclear Politics*, pp. 106–9. See also Malone, *The British Nuclear Deterrent*, p. 92. Speaking in the House of Commons, Deputy Under Secretary of State (policy and programmes) Michael Quinlan stated, "... it has been the preference of Governments to allow [the Soviet Union] to draw their own conclusions rather than to describe precisely what our plans and capability would be in terms of targeting policy" (cited in Freedman "British Nuclear Targeting," p. 109).

[100]Pierre, *Nuclear Politics*, pp. 107, 164, 166, 172–73, 182–83; Baylis, *British Defense Policy*, p. 56.

ously challenged, is logically essential to deterrence of the strong by the weak based on the threat of uncontrollable escalation.

As for the Chinese, the credibility of Britain's independent deterrent against a vastly mightier adversary, then, did not rest most importantly on incredible threats to choose to launch massive nuclear retaliatory strikes based on a cost-benefit analysis. Rather the effectiveness of nuclear deterrence rested on the adversary's fear that Britain might turn out to be an "unsafe actor," one whose behavior failed to conform with predictions based on rational choice. The mere existence of a British nuclear arsenal whose neutralization could not be assured in a preemptive strike constrained decision-makers in Moscow to face the possibility of catastrophic losses in short order imposed by those over whom they could not exercise control and about whose judgment and behavior under conditions of extreme stress they could not be certain. The Soviets had to ponder the possibility that Britain's remnant nuclear forces might be either accidentally launched as a consequence of the loosening of negative controls under crisis or wartime conditions or (less plausibly) irrationally launched as a leadership "overreacted" to a perceived threat to the nation's survival, even though such overreaction could not credibly be threatened in advance. The catastrophic consequences of miscalculation meant that even a very small probability that Britain would turn out to be a contingently "unsafe actor" would suffice to dissuade a Soviet challenge to vital British interests serious enough to elevate the risks of a disastrous response. In this respect Britain's strategy, though reflecting its distinctive national and historical circumstances, paralleled the strategy China ultimately embraced and, as will be described in the next chapter, that embraced by France.

6

France

Economic constraints and proximity to the awesome Soviet conventional and nuclear threat on the European continent made an independent defensive strategy even less feasible for France than for Britain. The viable alternatives from among which French leaders could choose were to rely on the American superpower ally's conventional defensive and nuclear deterrent capabilities or to attempt to independently muster a punitive capability sufficient to dissuade by deterrence an adversary France could not hope to dissuade by defense. After the mid-1950s, French leaders publicly emphasized that dissuasion by nuclear deterrence relying on their own, rather than alliance, forces would constitute the most important, though not sole, guarantee of their national security. Like London, Paris deemed dependence on the extended deterrent supplied by the United States an unsatisfactory, even if economically attractive, option.

SELECTING A SELF-RELIANT ALTERNATIVE: THE FRENCH EXPERIENCE

In pursuing a more self-reliant approach for dissuading the Soviet superpower, France's alternatives to nuclear deterrence were comparatively unattractive on essentially the same grounds highlighted in the British case. Deploying a military force clearly able to frustrate a conventional assault of the magnitude the Soviets could mount, if at all feasible, would have imposed a crushing economic burden on French society. And even a Herculean effort at deploying defenses would not ensure an ability to blunt the damage a growing Soviet nuclear arsenal could inflict on France. The nonnuclear deterrent alternative, resting on a threat to punish an invader by mounting a protracted national resistance struggle, though affordable, would require peacetime sacrifices from a population eager to enjoy a period of postwar prosperity. Aside from the problems of ensuring the dissuasiveness of the threatened punishment noted in Chapter 2, even a well-crafted conventional deterrent strategy of this sort would fail to address the array of more plausible dangerous alternatives, other than invasion and occupation, from among which the Soviets could have chosen in attempting to coerce France.[1] Thus resource constraints combined with the military options created by the advent of nuclear weapons technology led France to eschew the conventional alternatives. Having decided that dependence on the United States was politically unpalatable and strategically risky, French leaders concluded, in General Charles de Gaulle's words, that a national nuclear deterrent was "the only effective way of ensuring [France's] territorial integrity and political independence."[2]

Consistent with this strategic emphasis, France's military budgets during the Cold War gave priority to developing, deploying, and then modernizing the nuclear arsenal. With the exception of a brief controversial attempt to increase spending on conventional weaponry in the mid-1970s under President Giscard d'Estaing (a step that critics immediately condemned as weakening "the deterrent effect of the nuclear force by suggesting that less drastic responses are possible"[3]), France adhered to its nuclear strategic emphasis. Funding for nuclear forces was ensured, even when this conflicted with the desire of some military leaders in France and among its NATO allies to upgrade the country's conventional forces.[4] The budgetary pride of place accorded the nuclear deterrent, the *"force de frappe,"* persisted despite the fact that the cost of maintaining its viability, though a bargain compared to the cost of deploying a dependably dissuasive conventional defense, turned out to be higher than originally expected.[5] Even after France overcame the hurdles of initial research and development of nuclear and thermonuclear weapons, the challenges of modernizing delivery systems resulted in

---

[1] See Pierre M. Gallois, "French Defense Planning," p. 22. Cf. Gene Sharpe, *Making Europe Unconquerable.*

[2] Charles de Gaulle, cited in David S. Yost, "France's Deterrent Posture and Security in Europe, Part I," p. 5; Wilfred L. Kohl, *French Nuclear Diplomacy,* pp. 150–51.

[3] Robert R. Ropelewski, "French Emphasizing Nuclear Weapons"; "French Push Updated Conventional Forces."

[4] See "French Debate Dropping Triad Concept," p. 193; David White, "Paris Gives Priority to Nuclear Arms Spending," p. 1; "France May Rely on Nuclear Weapons for Defense"; David Housego, "French Army Sounds Alarm on Defence Cuts," p. 2; Housego, "Economy Squeezes Future Shape of France's Defence," p. 2. In the early 1980s, when it seemed modernization of the nuclear forces might require significant cuts in conventional forces, Defense Minister Charles Hernu was prepared, if necessary, to reduce the army's size by 10 percent ("France's Draft Defence Budget for 1983 Makes the Country's Nuclear Deterrent the Year's Absolute Priority," p. 11).

[5] "French Debate Dropping Triad Concept," p. 193.

spending on nuclear forces that absorbed up to 20 percent of France's Cold War military budgets, a significantly larger percentage than the 10 percent that was typical for Britain.[6] The costs of maintaining the retaliatory punch of the nuclear deterrent were large compared to Britain's in part because France, as noted below, was at first unable and later unwilling to engage in economically beneficial close nuclear cooperation with the United States, but also in part because France insisted on maintaining the viability of all three legs of its nuclear triad.[7] Its high cost notwithstanding, France maintained the strategic emphasis on nuclear rather than conventional weaponry through the final five-year defense plan (loi de programmation) of the Cold War announced in 1983. Consistent with Defense Minister Charles Hernu's characterization of the nuclear deterrent as an "absolute priority,"[8] the plan accepted that "the emphasis on nuclear forces entailed a draw-down on conventional forces. . . . [C]onventional forces . . . are paying the price for building a strong nuclear arsenal in a period of economic difficulties."[9]

Broad support for the national nuclear deterrent among France's foreign policy elite, including each ruling party, was matched by persistently broad support in the rest of society. Even France's Catholic Bishops, unlike their American counterparts who branded nuclear deterrence inherently immoral, in a 1983 meeting at Lourdes voted 83 to 8 approving a resolution "defending the development and deployment of

[6]Ibid.; "Nuclear Secrets." Although the nuclear share of France's defense budget edged downward in the early 1970s, the expense of modernization following initial deployment of the triad pushed the share back to 20 percent in the 1980s (Robin Laird, "France's Strategic Posture"; see also David Marsh, "The High Price of Independence," p. 14).

[7]France spent more for a larger, more diverse nuclear arsenal, but individual systems were comparably expensive. One estimate of planned modernization of the British and French submarine-based deterrent, for example, pegged the cost of 4 modernized British boats, missiles, and warheads at about 5 billion pounds, and 4 modernized French SSBN systems at about 5.34 billion pounds ("Why France Spends More on Its Nuclear Arsenal," pp. 12ff).

[8]White, "Paris Gives Priority to Nuclear Arms Spending," p. 1.

[9]Michael C. Dunn, "Mitterrand's France Shapes a Nuclear Defense," p. 11; see also Gavin Bell, "French Defence Budget to Upgrade Nuclear Forces." Charles Hernu would reiterate his position when he presented the military budget for 1985: "The heart of our defence is the nuclear deterrent. . . ." (cited in Mary Ellen Bortin, "French Defence Budget to Keep Nuclear Strength Despite Cuts"). Not surprisingly, the sacred cow status of nuclear modernization in the annual budget, especially during the mid-1980s when cuts were the norm, was criticized by those who worried about "an inadequate level of spending on conventional military programmes" (Paul Betts, "French Spending on Nuclear Deterrent Escapes Budget Cuts," p. 22).

nuclear weapons. ..."[10] As late as April 1987, 61 percent of "French adults believe[d] that France should maintain its nuclear strike force even if [as then was becoming likely] Moscow and Washington scrap[ped] their [nuclear] missiles in Europe" under a treaty on intermediate-range nuclear forces.[11] Indeed, until it became clear that the INF Treaty was part of a larger process bringing the Cold War to an end, the official and popular French reaction was that the treaty required *greater* attention be paid to France's own nuclear forces to ensure its ability to dissuade an adversary who had conventional superiority.[12] And even when Paris finally began cutting back on military spending at the end of the Cold War, conventional forces took the initial hit, while nuclear weapons programs were spared.[13]

France's emphasis on dissuasion by nuclear deterrence was clear and durable. The next sections flesh out the process by which the strategy was translated into policy and force deployments.

DISSUASION BY NUCLEAR DETERRENCE:
THE FRENCH EXPERIENCE

In important ways, the history of France's efforts to fulfill the requirements of its national nuclear strategy paralleled Britain's experience, not only in terms of the doctrine espoused, but also in the evolution of relations with its American superpower ally. In both cases there was conflict over U.S. reluctance to share nuclear weapons technology. And in both cases conflict eventually gave way to offers of conditional U.S. assistance. The Franco-American pattern, however, differed from the Anglo-American experience mainly as a consequence of the greater French insistence, at least in declaratory policy and rhetoric, on independence.

[10]David Dickson, "French Bishops Defend Nuclear Deterrence," p. 996.

[11]"French Shun Disarmament Trend, Says Poll." See also Robin Laird, "Mitterrand's New Strategic Vision," pp. 6ff; Bridget Bloom, "Gaullist Sting in Trident's Tail," pp. 12ff.

[12]The 1988 Defense Budget presented by Defense Minister Andre Giraud in November 1987 reflected the perceived need to boost the nuclear strike force. See Simon Haydon, "France Boosts Nuclear Force Amid Worries Over Missile Deal." See also former Prime Minister Raymond Barre's concerns about the possibility of a denuclearized Europe after the INF treaty (cited in "Nuclear Deterrence Vital, Says Former French Prime Minister").

[13]Ian Davidson, "Nuclear Weapons Escape Cuts in French Defence," p. 3; "Nuclear Deterrence Still Priority for France: Chevenement"; "France Upgrading Nuclear Force Despite East-West Détente."

Developing Nuclear Weapons

Shortly after World War II the leaders of the Fourth Republic established the Atomic Energy Commission (CEA) to oversee civilian and military atomic energy matters. During the 1950s, doubts about U.S. willingness to support French interests internationally led this group increasingly to emphasize the military applications of nuclear technology as a route to provide independently for France's security.[14] For France, as for Britain and China, one of the chief incentives for developing an independent capability to deal with the potential superpower threat to its vital interests was skepticism that security provided by the capabilities of a superpower ally was a genuine collective good from whose enjoyment partners could not be excluded. In an anarchic world states have the opportunity to renege on treaty commitments, and given the dangers of war in the nuclear age, a self-regarding, rational state would have strong incentives to do so. For France, American reaction to two events—the siege at Dien Bien Phu in Vietnam in 1954 and the joint military intervention in Suez in 1956—fed the belief that although the United States was a capable ally, it was one whose support could not automatically be presumed. These episodes clinched the French decision that it must have an independent nuclear capability. The previous chapter explored the relevance of the Suez Crisis. For France, the impact of the fiasco in Egypt was heightened in part because it had been preceded by the troubling experience in Indochina two years earlier.

Dien Bien Phu. Franco-American differences over Indochina and especially over the handling of the military emergency that developed at Dien Bien Phu in 1954 were not as dramatic as the subsequent 1956 clash over Suez. Yet the experience in Southeast Asia had raised some of the same troubling questions and nurtured the same sorts of doubts about depending on self-interested allies that contributed to France's determination to develop and maintain its own nuclear forces.

France defined its interest in fighting against Vietnamese nationalist revolutionaries primarily in terms of the precedent being set for managing what remained of its overseas possessions, especially those in North

---

[14]In the immediate postwar years, France had two serious concerns about relying on allies for its security. The more important concern was that it might be abandoned by the United States (and Britain) in the first stages of a future continental war. The other concern was that these allies, though perhaps contributing their air and nuclear power, might expect France (and Germany) to provide the infantry for fighting on the front lines. See Wolf Mendl, *Deterrence and Persuasion*, pp. 92–93.

Africa.[15] As Charles Kupchan has argued, France saw its post–World War
II role as a great power inextricably linked to preserving a modernized
version of the old empire.[16] France's goal was to prevent this first in a series of colonial dominoes from falling, in which case Paris might lose
control over the process of recasting the arrangements between the met-
ropole and its restive colonial territories.[17] Moreover, France surprisingly defined these stakes in the Indochina war as a vital interest no less
important than its security concerns about a potential, but not yet imminent, Soviet challenge in Europe. This distinctive, if questionable,
understanding of its strategic interests in Indochina reflected not only
the French government's desire to tap overseas territories to augment
the limited resources of its homeland, but also sensitivity to the political legacy of the country's humiliating defeat early in World War II.
Kupchan explains how these considerations led Paris to view Indochina
as a vital, rather than a peripheral, interest:

> France's war in Indochina was driven, first and foremost, by a powerful
> strategic image equating the autonomy and sovereignty of the metro-
> pole with the preservation of imperial commitments.
>
> As the overseas territory most threatened by nationalist resistance,
> Indochina emerged as the litmus test of French power in the postwar
> era. French elites ... saw in Indochina the opportunity to rebuild the
> domestic legitimacy of the state. *Imperial success would restore public
> confidence in the discredited institutions of governance.. The defense
> of Indochina thus became associated with the autonomy and inde-
> pendence of France itself.*[18]

The United States defined its strategic interest in Indochina differently, though it too worried about falling dominoes. For Washington,
the reason to support France's military operation against Vietnam's
communist-led nationalists was to prevent the rebels' victory from in-

[15]For a concise summary of these conflicting interests and the policy dilemmas
they produced, see Henry Kissinger, *Diplomacy*, pp. 624–34.

[16]Charles A. Kupchan, *The Vulnerability of Empire*, p. 278.

[17]Because they were operating in the "domain of losses," to use the language of
prospect theory that Rose McDermott employed to analyze decision-making during
the Suez Crisis, France's leaders were willing to incur huge costs and take grave risks
(McDermott, *Risk-Taking in International Politics*). Kupchan's formulation is similar: "Strategic logic [regarding the war in Indochina] was thus infused by belief in
dominoes and the interdependence of commitments, belief attributes commonly associated with high vulnerability and elite efforts to rely on demonstrations of resolve
to offset material inadequacy. Like the British during the 1930s, French elites feared
that the loss of a single territory would lead to the unraveling of the empire" (Kupchan, *The Vulnerability of Empire*, p. 278).

[18]Ibid., p. 287, emphasis added.

spiring communist- (i.e., Soviet-) supported insurgencies elsewhere in Asia, and perhaps beyond. But, as noted with reference to the Suez Crisis, the United States also had an interest in opposing the continuation of colonial rule and instead supporting national self-determination, both because of deeply rooted liberal values and because it was a strategically sensible policy to prevent the Soviet bloc from exploiting the rising tide of nationalism in the Third World. Thus, in the early 1950s, while American forces were fighting in Korea, the United States decided to back France's war in Indochina as part of the regional effort against communist expansion, but urged France to promise Vietnam its independence once the Chinese-backed forces of Ho Chi Minh were defeated. The latter element of this two-pronged U.S. policy clashed with the main purpose for which France was shedding blood in Southeast Asia—preserving the empire. French leaders, therefore, balked at the idea of promising independence for Vietnam and instead hoped to maintain U.S. support by highlighting the contribution their effort was making to regional anticommunist containment (for them at best a secondary interest).[19]

Despite Franco-American policy differences U.S. assistance continued. Yet the war did not go well. Nearly a decade into its costly counterinsurgency campaign, France's military grew frustrated with the indecisiveness of the protracted struggle against evasive Vietnamese guerrilla units. Seeking a strategic breakthrough, in early 1954 France re-deployed some of its best forces to Dien Bien Phu, an isolated spot in northwestern Vietnam, hoping to draw the nationalist revolutionaries out onto an open battlefield where they might be destroyed. The attempt to set the stage for a decisive French victory failed. Instead, by March these French forces found themselves besieged by the Vietnamese who, with unanticipated material support from China, had surreptitiously undertaken a massive military buildup around the encampment. While the Vietnamese pressed their attack, France desperately appealed to its American ally to provide more direct support by intervening with U.S. military power, especially airpower, on a scale that Paris could not muster. President Eisenhower refused. The reasoning behind the U.S. decision in April 1954 against employing the airpower that some military experts believed "could deliver a 'decisive blow'" was especially troubling for France.[20]

[19]Ibid., pp. 282–83.
[20]See discussion of the meeting between the French Foreign Minister Georges Bidault and U.S. Secretary of State John Foster Dulles on April 24, 1954, cited in George C. Herring and Richard H. Immerman "Eisenhower, Dulles, and Dienbienphu," p. 359.

The French pleaded for "armed intervention" . . . warning of ominous consequences to the war in Indochina and to Franco-American relations if nothing were done.

Eisenhower and Dulles peremptorily rejected the French proposal. Dulles advised the administration that because the security of the United States was not directly threatened, the political risk could in no way be justified.[21]

The U.S. decision reflected not just a reluctance to get sucked into another ground war in Asia so soon after the Korean armistice, but also a strong interest in maintaining the American reputation as staunchly anti-colonial. This interest helps account for the alternative approach the United States offered to pursue. Although France was deeply disappointed with the Eisenhower administration's blunt rejection of its specific request for unilateral American intervention, the United States had not categorically not ruled out all support. Instead, Washington proposed a multilateral intervention that it dubbed "United Action." Multilateral intervention, especially as it was to include forces from other nations in the region, might have enabled the United States to preserve its anti-colonial reputation while also acting on its interest in thwarting a Vietnamese revolution that it feared would be just one falling domino in a broad pattern of communist expansion. The U.S. proposal for United Action was cold comfort to French leaders, however, who correctly calculated that the time needed to build a multinational coalition would seal the fate of their position at Dien Bien Phu. As it turned out, the United States was unable to quickly win support for and assemble the forces for multilateral intervention. Consequently, Eisenhower instead emphasized diplomacy at Geneva (where the French had agreed to participate in peace talks proposed by the Soviets) as the most feasible way to try to pursue the dual United States goals of containing communist gains in the region and preserving the United States anticolonial reputation. With United Action still on the drawing board and as peace talks in Geneva began, French forces at Dien Bien Phu fought their losing battle, finally surrendering on May 7.

How did the events in Indochina in the spring of 1954 relate to the motives for France's nuclear weapons development program? The reaction to France's request for support at Dien Bien Phu was a stark reminder that national interests are the basis for cooperation even among allies, and that such interests would not automatically coincide. American priorities had determined the extent and timing of the support it would lend to France in Indochina. Washington preferred diplomacy at

[21]Ibid., emphasis added.

Geneva over unilateral intervention at Dien Bien Phu, even if diplomacy meant sacrificing interests that Paris deemed vital, because Washington expected this approach to better serve the U.S. interest in siding with the struggle against the remnants of colonialism while adequately containing the spread of communism. Worrisome, too, was the fact that France's second most important ally, Great Britain, adopted a stance on rescuing France's position in Vietnam that was no more reassuring than the one the United States took, a position that could only have reinforced the lesson about the uncertainties inherent in alliances among self-interested states. Britain's views on the proper course to follow in Indochina conflicted with those of France, though not over the issue of colonialism. Winston Churchill's rejection of American overtures to participate in United Action on behalf of France was based in part on the politico-military judgment that the place to make a stand against communist expansion in the region was Malaya, and in part on the fear that war in Indochina could escalate to war with China and thus its Soviet ally. The latter concern raised the possibility of entrapping Britain in a conflict that risked Soviet nuclear attacks against U.S. forces stationed in the British homeland (a reprise of London's fears about escalation during the Korean War).[22]

In short, France's two most important allies had demonstrated that there were limits to the circumstances under which they would provide support. The Indochina debacle clearly fell outside those limits, despite its importance to France. Nevertheless, one might doubt the relevance of the decisions made in the spring of 1954 for gauging the dependability of France's allies if more clearly vital French interests were at stake, and thus doubt any connection between these events and France's decision to hedge against a need for self-reliance by developing its own nuclear weapons. After all, events in a remote corner of the world had little to do with the European contingencies for which NATO was formed. It is true that, like the Suez Crisis, the Dien Bien Phu episode was not a direct test of the depth of U.S. commitment to stand by its NATO allies if they were directly challenged. The experience did, however, vividly illustrate an inescapable truth about life in the anarchic international system—the most important determinant of a state's behavior would be its perception of self-interest. And even the most powerful ally's self-interest in backing France would be shaped not only by the value it placed on France, but also on the cost it might have to pay for solidarity. The United States obviously placed a much higher value on the security

[22]Kissinger, *Diplomacy*, pp. 632–33.

of the French homeland than on French holdings in Southeast Asia. But it was also obvious that the costs of horrifying destruction that might result from supporting French interests in a serious confrontation with a nuclear-armed Soviet adversary in Europe far exceeded the potential costs of militarily backing France in Vietnam. As such, it was not entirely fanciful, and arguably prudent, for leaders in Paris to draw broader inferences from their Indochina experience about the wisdom of wholesale dependence on allies, however capable and sincere they might be.

Indeed, concerns about the reliability of the U.S. commitment to stand by its French ally following the Dien Bien Phu episode, however misplaced they may appear to an objective analyst looking at the actual security interests at stake in Southeast Asia, stimulated key decisions in Paris to accelerate the atomic bomb program made in 1954 and 1955, especially the December 26, 1954, decision to provide more funding for the A-bomb effort in the 1955–56 military budget.[23] Norrin Ripsman's research suggests the significance of yet another relevant irritant in Franco-American relations at about this time that may have played a part in the run-up to that decision. In September 1954, the United States increased its pressure on France to reverse its August rejection of the European Defense Community by floating troublesome rumors and issuing public statements about a policy reappraisal that would lead either to the unilateral rearmament of Germany or a peripheral defense of Western Europe with a U.S. presence only in Britain. In the wake of the debacle in Southeast Asia, this strain on Franco-American relations added to concern in Paris about the reliability of the U.S. commitment and its political price.[24] Disturbingly soon thereafter, the French believed such initial doubts about U.S. support were confirmed in a more tangible way. As described in the preceding chapter, during the Suez Crisis Washington not only refused to back Franco-British intervention, but also coerced them into accepting a humiliating defeat on a matter they defined as a vital interest. Eisenhower's position, even though it was accompanied by a clear reassertion of U.S. guarantees against Soviet nuclear attacks on France and Britain, was worrisome because it, "demonstrat[ed] to the French that they could no longer rely on the United States to come automatically to their defense," a belief that "proved

[23]Mendl, *Deterrence and Persuasion*, pp. 95, 100; Yost, "France's Deterrent Posture and Security in Europe, Part I," p. 4; Kohl, *French Nuclear Diplomacy*, pp. 16–20, 35; Norris, Burrows, and Fieldhouse, *British, French, and Chinese Nuclear Weapons*, pp. 183–84.

[24]Norrin M. Ripsman, "The Impact of Decision-Making Autonomy Upon Democratic Peace-Making Policies."

pivotal to French attitudes toward the US strategic nuclear commitment."[25]

With the Suez experience reinforcing the lessons of 1954, France had arrived at the conclusion that it could not be sure of adequate U.S. backing unless vital *American* interests were also at stake.[26] And, of course, no ironclad guarantee that U.S. and French interests would coincide was possible, especially at critical moments of confrontation with France's principal security threat, the Soviet Union. Indeed, in the emerging era of mutual thermonuclear vulnerability between the United States and the USSR, the most vital American self-interest in national survival would likely provide strong incentives to abandon allies during risky confrontations. In this strategic context, prudence argued against policies based on the assumption that a superpower patron's military forces would provide adequate security.[27] Prudence instead required France's leaders to hedge against the small, but potentially catastrophic, possibility that U.S. leaders might either hesitate or reluctantly decide that the risks of entrapment in a showdown with Moscow outweighed the shame of abandoning an ally in its moment of need. Using language strikingly similar to Churchill's cited in the previous chapter, General de Gaulle instead asserted the need for a national nuclear deterrent because "American nuclear power does not necessarily and immediately meet all the eventualities concerning France and Europe."[28] As confidence in the security benefits from alliance with the United States wavered in the late 1950s, France accelerated its drive to develop an independent atomic arsenal.

Franco-American Nuclear Relations

Despite the fact that national nuclear forces were being sought as a means to enhance foreign policy autonomy, the French, like the British and Chinese, initially solicited and expected assistance from their superpower ally. During the Fourth Republic, French nuclear policy was similar to British policy inasmuch as France sought an independent nuclear capability mainly as a complement to, rather than a substitute for, the collective security that the U.S. strategic deterrent supplied for its

---

[25]Norris, Burrows, and Fieldhouse, *British, French, and Chinese Nuclear Weapons*, pp. 183–84, 184n17, drawing on Wynfred Joshua, *New Perspectives in US French Nuclear Relations*, Stanford Research Institute, Research Memorandum SSC-RM-8974-2, Aug. 1972, p. 10.

[26]Mendl, *Deterrence and Persuasion*, pp. 15, 103; Kohl, *French Nuclear Diplomacy*, pp. 35–36.

[27]Kohl, *French Nuclear Diplomacy*, p. 234; see also p. 274.

[28]Charles de Gaulle, cited ibid., p. 234.

NATO allies. But, as with the British (and the Chinese in dealing with the Soviets), French hopes for American aid were both raised and disappointed. The disparity between tantalizing offers of assistance made by Eisenhower in the last years of his administration and the barriers imposed by the U.S. Congress dating to the McMahon Act of 1946 exacerbated Franco-American conflicts. And when Eisenhower pushed for revisions in the McMahon Act in 1954 and 1958 that facilitated sharing nuclear information with allies, the regulations approved by a wary U.S. Congress's Joint Committee on Atomic Energy effectively limited such sharing to Britain by stipulating that recipients must have already "made substantial progress in the development of atomic weapons"[29] As it became clear that this hurdle would soon be cleared by the French, American advisers again emphasized ever-present concerns about communist espionage benefiting the Soviets that France's recent history of political instability only exacerbated.[30]

A restrictive, discriminatory American nuclear aid policy could not help but contribute to French doubts about the dependability of security based on a deterrent to be provided by this same ally. Growing uneasiness with the U.S. approach to exercising its position of nuclear leadership worsened matters. When de Gaulle, as President, proposed the creation of a tripartite decision-making body in which the United States, the UK, and France would jointly manage NATO's nuclear and security policy, the United States resisted. In the view of Chairman of the Joint Chiefs of Staff Nathan Twining, the proposal not only overstepped France's imminent, but yet to be demonstrated and deployed, nuclear capability. It also called for an arrangement that promised to weaken U.S. control and risk confusion in allied decision-making.[31] De Gaulle's biographer, Jean Lacouture, captured the increasing Franco-American tension at the time in his description of a confrontation be-

[29]"Memorandum of Conversation, United States Delegation to the Bermuda Meeting, March 21–22, 1957, Subject: Atomic Energy Items: (1) French Request (2) Test Limitations," p. 6. In a 1957 meeting with representatives of United Kingdom, U.S. Secretary of State Dulles "stated that the US was not disposed to assist the French in a weapons program. If they wanted to produce nuclear weapons, they must do it on their own." The meeting's records also confirm that the French had repeatedly asked for such assistance, "including in the nuclear submarine field," but that they had been told this was prohibited under U.S. law (ibid., p. 5; see also Mendl, *Deterrence and Persuasion*, pp. 55–58; Kohl, *French Nuclear Diplomacy*, pp. 5–6, 64–66, 80–81, 356–57; Richard Ullman, "The Covert French Connection," pp. 5, 6–7).

[30]See "Incoming Telegram: From Paris to Secretary of State, No. 6252, June 28, 11PM."

[31]N. F. Twining, "Memorandum for the Secretary of Defense, Subject: French Proposal for a Tripartite World-Wide Organization," pp. 1–2.

tween de Gaulle and General Lauris Norstad, the Supreme Allied Commander in Europe, after he delivered a briefing on NATO's military.

> De Gaulle congratulated him and asked the American general to tell him the locations of nuclear weapons in France and secondly, what the targets for those weapons were. "I'm afraid I cannot answer those questions unless we are alone," said Norstad. "Very well," said de Gaulle. The entourages of the two generals left. "Well?" "Well General, I'm afraid I can't answer your questions." "General," de Gaulle concluded, "this is the last time, I am telling you, that a French leader will hear such an answer!"[32]

Disputes over nuclear cooperation resulted in French retaliatory measures and a redoubling of their independent research and development effort. During 1959 and 1960 France announced that its Mediterranean fleet would be withdrawn from NATO command in time of war, that they would not allow United States IRBMs under American control to be stationed on French soil, and that no tactical nuclear weapons could be stockpiled in France.[33] In a personal communication to President Eisenhower, de Gaulle explained why he refused to store NATO nuclear weapons on French territory as well as France's determination not to see its nascent nuclear force integrated with an allied command under U.S. control. Dependence on the United States would entail an unreasonable surrender of control over national security in the nuclear age, an era in which dependence on allies carried the risks of both abandonment and entrapment. De Gaulle noted:

> If there were no alliance between us, I would agree that your monopoly on the opening of atomic war would be justified, but you and we are tied together to such a point that the opening of this type of hostilities either by you or against you would automatically expose France to total and immediate destruction. She obviously cannot entirely entrust her life or her death to any other state whatsoever, even the most friendly.[34]

[32]From Jean Lacouture, *De Gaulle: The Ruler, 1945–1970*, trans. by Alan Sheridan (New York: W. W. Norton, 1991), p. 421, cited in Norris, Burrows, and Fieldhouse, *British, French, and Chinese Nuclear Weapons*, p. 188n21.

[33]See Mendl, *Deterrence and Persuasion*, p. 61.

[34]"Letter from French President Charles de Gaulle to US President Dwight D. Eisenhower." At the same time, some of Eisenhower's advisers believed that the carrot of relaxing the restrictions on sharing nuclear information might be used as leverage to convince France to integrate its nuclear forces in a multilateral NATO force. For the United States this would provide a means for controlling France's nuclear forces, precisely the reason why such a proposal would remain unacceptable to Paris. See Robert H. Johnson, "Memorandum, Subject: 422nd NSC Meeting, Thursday October 29, 1959."

As the Fifth Republic became clearly committed to deploying national nuclear forces, President de Gaulle informed Secretary of State Dulles that France was determined to produce such weapons because "[o]nly in this way can our defense and foreign policy be independent which is something we prize above everything else."[35] De Gaulle's comment, it should be added, reflected his belief, like that of his counterparts in China and Britain, that nuclear weapons would yield a prestige as well as a security dividend. Especially for the strongly nationalist de Gaulle determined to reestablish France's "grandeur," a desire for greater status reinforced the security interest in a national deterrent, an interest that was firmly in place prior to his accession to leadership in 1958.[36] Although both mattered, especially to de Gaulle, the tangible benefit of possessing nuclear weapons as the ultimate guarantee of national security was more important than the status benefit. The priority was evident first when France initially sought help from its superpower ally in weapons development rather than aim for the prestige payoff of a weapons program that was totally self-reliant (in this respect similar to both China and Britain), and later when France sought American help with the modernization Paris believed was necessary to ensure the viability of its national deterrent (in this respect similar to Britain). As will be detailed below, even though France made greater efforts than the British to maintain a public posture of adhering to the principle of nuclear independence, privately it established its own sort of special relationship with the United States.

At the end of the fifties, however, France was still openly seeking American assistance despite the disputes over nuclear policy that were driving a wedge between Paris and Washington. And once France had tested its own atomic bomb in 1960, U.S. congressional restrictions need no longer have applied.[37] But unlike President Eisenhower, Presi-

[35]Cited in Yost, "France's Deterrent Posture and Security in Europe, Part I," pp. 13–14; see also Kohl, French Nuclear Diplomacy, pp. 356, 357.

[36]Yue Ren, "National Image-Conflicts and the Pursuit of Nuclear Independence," p. 263, 320. For extensive discussion of de Gaulle's concerns about France's international image, see ibid., chs. 6, 7, 8. See also Lawrence Freedman, The Evolution of Nuclear Strategy, pp. 313, 321.

[37]Lifting restrictions was not automatic, however. The conditions on exchange of restricted data established in the Atomic Energy Act were open to interpretation. As late as 1965, Congressman John Anderson wrote the Executive Director of the Joint Committee on Atomic Energy to ask whether or not it was time to end nuclear discrimination against France, who was a member of NATO's Standing Group along with Britain, a practice that set up "an unfortunate caste system." In an interoffice memorandum, the director's staff counsel indicated that in setting the requirement that the "recipient nation must have made 'substantial progress' in the development

dent Kennedy was not interested in facilitating the weapons programs of qualifying allies.[38] As noted in Chapter 5, the U.S. shift to a strategy of flexible response under Kennedy and McNamara called for more centralized control of nuclear forces. The preceding chapter also discussed the strains this disdain for allied nuclear forces placed on Anglo-American relations. The situation for France was similar, but even tougher, as the United States was not yet resigned to the reality of a French deterrent. France had to move ahead *"[i]n spite of* US efforts" under Kennedy and [his successor President] Johnson to "constantly *thwart* [. . .] France's nuclear ambitions . . . ," part of a nonproliferation policy aimed at persuading Paris to abandon its independent deterrent.[39]

Nevertheless, as with Britain, once France's determination became clear, the United States gradually accepted the irreversibility of its nu-

---

of atomic weapons," the law had "intentionally left the definition of this term quite flexible." Thus, despite the fact that France had tested a weapon five years earlier, it was possible to argue that "there was at least some doubt whether France has made 'substantial progress' within the meaning of the law" ("Interoffice Memorandum, Joint Committee on Atomic Energy, from Leonard M. Trosten, Staff Counsel to John T. Conway, Executive Director, November 18, 1965, Subject: Transfer of Restricted Data to France"). Though sharing could be justified if the United States desired (as Kennedy's 1963 Polaris offer to France revealed), the Atomic Energy Act could be used as a reason for maintaining restrictions if the "progress" hurdle to be cleared was redefined as mastery of particular hydrogen bomb technologies.

[38]President Eisenhower increasingly chafed at these restrictions on nuclear sharing. In a 1960 meeting with Generals Goodpaster and Norstad, he stated: "The US Government seems to be taking the attitude that we will call the tune, and that they [our allies] have inferior status in the alliance." Eisenhower was also reported to have added that "he had considerable sympathy for the point of view of de Gaulle in this question. He is trying to build up his country, and we persist in treating them as second-rate." Eisenhower explicitly referred to the Atomic Energy Act as a "very defective and 'terrible' law, which has done great harm to the conduct of our relations with our allies." When Eisenhower hopefully asked Norstad if de Gaulle would be satisfied with a NATO multilateral nuclear force, Norstad, without addressing the issues of sovereign control, replied that although he might not, at least the "offer would take away every *legitimate* complaint that de Gaulle now has" (A. J. Goodpaster, "Memorandum of Conference with the President," emphasis added).

[39]From a declassified report by Wynfred Joshua, *New Perspectives in US French Nuclear Relations,* pp. 65–66, cited in Norris, Burrows, and Fieldhouse, *British, French, and Chinese Nuclear Weapons,* p. 190n49 (emphasis added by Norris, Burrows, and Fieldhouse). Even prior to the Kennedy administration, restrictions on sharing information were tightened in the last months of the Eisenhower administration as a result of a policy change in March 1960 to attempt "to cut off French access to critical information and equipment . . . which would *directly* assist France in obtaining a strategic ballistic missile delivery capability" ("President's Visit to de Gaulle, Paris, May 31-June 2, 1961, Background Paper: Differences in Release of Information to UK, France and Germany," emphasis in original).

clear weapons program.[40] After the 1962 Nassau agreement with London, Paris was offered the Polaris system on similar terms (formal integration with NATO's nuclear war plans, but with the crucial escape clause allowing reversion to independent control if supreme national interests required). By then, however, de Gaulle's government was extremely suspicious of American intentions. Despite the modest compromise that would be required to secure a major economic benefit, de Gaulle rejected the offer and opted to pay the price he believed would ensure the absolute independence of the French program.[41] Status concerns again reinforced security concerns. De Gaulle apparently rejected the U.S. Polaris because he was worried that using the weapons might somehow require U.S. approval and because he believed that offering missiles, for which France did not yet have submarines or suitable warheads, was a trick to humiliate France by highlighting its technological shortcomings.[42] The enduring legacy of a greater insistence on independence was consistently higher costs for the French, as compared with the British, nuclear effort and a more disputatious Franco-American security relationship.[43]

The U.S. campaign under Defense Secretary Robert McNamara to get NATO to endorse the U.S. doctrine of flexible response added to French doubts about the prudence of relying on Washington's nuclear deterrent umbrella: The view from Paris was that flexible response, by

[40]Yet as late as February 1963 Secretary of State Dean Acheson continued to believe that France would eventually abandon its independent deterrent. American preferences for a flexible response capability for NATO clearly fathered Acheson's wishful thinking when he argued that de Gaulle would come to view a national nuclear deterrent as wasting scarce resources better spent on upgrading the country's conventional forces ("Memorandum by Dean Acheson").

[41]Andrew J. Pierre, *Nuclear Politics*, pp. 238–39; Kohl, *French Nuclear Diplomacy*, p. 233.

[42]German Chancellor Konrad Adenauer's assessment reported in Central Intelligence Agency (CIA), *Adenauer's Attitude Towards de Gaulle*, Memorandum OCI 0749/63, Feb. 4, 1963, pp. 1–2, cited in Norris, Burrows, and Fieldhouse, *British, French, and Chinese Nuclear Weapons*, p. 188n24. Paris had reason to suspect Washington's intentions. In a 1961 meeting with representatives from the Netherlands, President Kennedy plainly stated that the U.S. offers to commit Polaris submarines to NATO ". . . have been made with the thought in mind of discouraging the development of an independent nuclear capability on the part of the French and eventually the Germans" ("Record of Meeting Between President Kennedy and Prince Bernhard and Ambassador von Roijen, the Netherlands Embassy").

[43]On the matter of nuclear budgets, see François Heisbourg, "The British and French Nuclear Forces," pp. 301–20; "Nuclear Secrets"; "Why France Spends More on Its Nuclear Arsenal," pp. 12ff.

attempting to limit the horror of war, undermined a deterrent policy whose success rested on fear of unacceptable damage. Not only would war be more likely, but if it came, a strategy of flexible response seemed to imply the "sanctuarization" of the American and Soviet homelands, or at least their urban centers, as the superpowers sought to refrain from triggering an all-out nuclear exchange.[44] Under this scenario, security would clearly be a U.S.-private, not a NATO-collective, good from whose enjoyment France could be excluded. Perhaps even worse, a Soviet-American conflict could emerge in which France's vital interests were not even at stake but whose destructiveness might be limited to the European theater. These two worrisome possibilities—that U.S. weapons might not be used to ensure French interests or that they might be used to ensure U.S. interests at the expense of French security—strengthened France's determination to deploy and maintain an arsenal of nuclear weapons under its own control. Such an arsenal, as David Yost put it, would have the twin virtues of giving France "the means of self-reliance" (to hedge against the possibility of abandonment in a war serving only French interests) and also "the option of non-belligerency" (to hedge against the possibility of entrapment in a war serving only U.S. interests).[45]

As its nuclear weapons program bore fruit and early Cold War tensions eased somewhat, the French government became less inclined to accept what it saw as the infringements on sovereign choice implied by its role in a U.S.-dominated alliance.[46] In 1966 Paris withdrew from NATO's integrated military command. The strongly negative American reaction only reinforced the independent streak in France's nuclear policy. Paris even briefly flirted with the option of armed neutrality. This was a time when the French nuclear establishment was run by "strong nationalists who had long tended to feel 'that the United States was really the enemy'" seeking to lock France into an inferior international position.[47] The parallels with the Chinese reaction to the deterioration of its relations with the Soviet Union that led to a brief interlude of genuine neutrality in the 1960s are obvious. But mainly because the Soviet threat to France consistently overshadowed problems in France's

[44]Yost, "France's Deterrent Posture and Security in Europe, Part I," p. 5. For a classic account of Franco-American conflict over flexible response versus threats of massive retaliation, see David S. Yost, "French Nuclear Targeting," pp. 147–48.
[45]Yost, "France's Deterrent Posture and Security in Europe, Part I," p. 5.
[46]Ibid., p. 33.
[47]Ullman, "The Covert French Connection," p. 18.

relations with the United States, the French, unlike the Chinese, never completely broke off strategic ties with their superpower ally as part of a policy of dealignment or realignment.[48]

Although U.S. objections to France's independent nuclear force would diminish in time, acceptance was certainly not immediate. Resigned to the impossibility of restoring the American nuclear monopoly within the Western alliance, U.S. Defense Secretary McNamara pursued a second-best option. Seeking a way to regain some centralized control over what he feared were destabilizing independent nuclear arsenals, he proposed establishing a multilateral nuclear force for NATO. But this effort, too, foundered as McNamara was unable to overcome predictable objections to a plan that required surrendering national control over weapons that were at once the ultimate guarantor of and a threat to national survival.[49]

By the early 1970s, the United States had finally developed a tolerance, even an appreciation, of the way its allies' strategic forces deterred the Soviet Union. This understanding of the nature of alliance security supplied by national nuclear arsenals was formally articulated in the Ottawa Declaration of 1974.[50] Afterwards, U.S. nuclear relations with France, as well as Britain, were more cooperative than conflictive. Less openly and efficiently than London, Paris exploited its American connection to economize on research and development costs while avoid-

---

[48]Despite France's formal military independence after 1966, "[b]ehind the scenes, French military men made surreptitious efforts to keep in touch with their opposite numbers in the alliance, but in public almost all such contacts were taboo" (Ian Davidson, "France Rejoins Its Allies," pp. 22ff). Note, however, the 1980 statement by the director of the planning department of France's Foreign Ministry that its nuclear deterrent "guarantees the security of our territory, and the safekeeping of our political sovereignty . . . [and] assures her diplomatic independence in security matters, with respect to the United States as much as the Soviet Union, which is something fundamental" (Yost, "France's Deterrent Posture and Security in Europe. Part I," p. 14). In addition, France's independence was asserted in its refusal, similar to China's, to participate in Cold War arms control regimes they labeled superpower infringements on the sovereign choice of other states. See Yost, "France's Deterrent Posture and Security in Europe, Part II," ch. 3.

[49]On the complicated and conflicting interests fueling the debate over the multilateral force idea, see Freedman, *The Evolution of Nuclear Strategy*, pp. 325–27. A memo written by Walt Rostow clearly indicated that the American concern was to find a way somehow to preserve U.S. control over the decision to use nuclear weapons in Europe in the face of an anticipated push for "a distinct European nuclear establishment, claiming a right to fire independently of the US" (W. W. Rostow, "Memorandum for the President, Subject: The Growing Shadow of a European Nuclear Force").

[50]Peter Malone, *The British Nuclear Deterrent*, pp. 173, 179, 180; Ullman, "The Covert French Connection," p. 8.

ing wholesale dependence on U.S. nuclear technology.[51] Similarities in U.S. nuclear cooperation with these two European allies were generally overshadowed by the public contrast between the special Anglo-American nuclear relationship and France's insistence on nuclear autonomy. As Richard Ullman has made clear, however, the contrast was in some ways more apparent than real.[52] Prestige concerns in Paris dictated a stubborn public posture of independence, but security requirements dictated a pragmatic, if largely invisible, effort to court U.S. assistance that would ensure the continued viability of France's nuclear deterrent.

Covert U.S. nuclear assistance to France began with Kissinger's 1973 initiative designed to allay fears that Soviet-American détente implied a superpower condominium in Europe. Afterward, France secretly benefited from U.S. nuclear technology through the roundabout process of negative guidance, often termed the "twenty-questions approach" (French hypotheses regarding nuclear weapons technology were either confirmed or disconfirmed by U.S. scientists). Such sharing was, however, inherently more limited than the above-board exchanges on weapons design with the UK.[53] In 1985 the highly secretive and cumbersome arrangement was somewhat simplified with the lifting of U.S. legal barriers dating to the McMahon Act and the signing of an agreement specifying areas of cooperation.[54] In addition to such technical assistance, Franco-American cooperation was also evident in their quiet coordination of military planning. Though formally adhering to its 1966 withdrawal from NATO's integrated military command, France, like Britain,

[51]The U.S. Defense Intelligence Agency claimed that France's weapons-related purchases, most significant after the 1985 agreement described below, were driven by considerations of "cost-effectiveness rather than . . . a lack of indigenous capability." See *France's Defense Industry* (partially declassified and released under the FOIA), DDB-1920-215-86, May 1986, pp. ix, 17, 15, cited in Norris, Burrows, and Fieldhouse, *British, French, and Chinese Nuclear Weapons*, p. 193n75.

[52]France's Defense Ministry did not deny Ullman's revelation that the United States had provided covert nuclear assistance, but instead minimized its significance and insisted that it did not result in French dependence on foreign technology. See Ian Davidson, "French Play Down US 'Secret Nuclear Help,'" p. 3.

[53]Ullman, "The Covert French Connection," pp. 10, 11, 13.

[54]The key step in removing the McMahon restrictions was the belated U.S. acknowledgment that France had made "substantial progress" in nuclear weapons development. Together with the 1985 Agreement for Cooperation on the Safety and Security of Nuclear Activities and Installations for Mutual Defense Purposes, this enabled France to benefit from exchanges of information and material with the United States, allowing for "cooperation on warhead design" and even the "transfer . . . [of] . . . nonnuclear parts of atomic *weapons*. . . ." (Norris, Burrows, and Fieldhouse, *British, French, and Chinese Nuclear Weapons*, p. 193, emphasis in Norris, Burrows, and Fieldhouse).

retained two nuclear targeting plans—a joint NATO plan and an independent national plan.[55] Both countries reserved the right of final decision over the use of their nuclear forces, providing for no more than consultations, "time and circumstances permitting." The chief practical difference between the cases was that French forces were not formally integrated with their allies' and thus would not have to be formally recalled from their NATO role.[56]

Despite these similarities in the British and French cases, the legacy of more open conflict gave a distinctive flavor to security relations between Washington and Paris. Greater secrecy surrounding their military cooperation reflected the concern of top French officials who did not want to appear responsible for compromising the national interest in independence when it came to security.[57] And, more vigorously than Britain, France continued to disagree with the U.S. preference for options and flexibility. French doctrine more strictly adhered to its emphasis on the threat of escalation to the strategic nuclear level as the most effective way to deter the Soviets. Thus France did not fulfill U.S. hopes that the economic benefits of nuclear cooperation would encourage Paris to divert funds to building up its conventional forces and thereby contribute to a more credible NATO defense against Soviet divisions in the European theater.[58]

On the contrary, France's deployment of conventional forces continued to reflect its commitment to the strategic primacy of nuclear deterrence. After the early 1960s, France designed its conventional forces chiefly for the purpose of testing the seriousness of the attacker's intentions and warning him of imminent escalation to the strategic nuclear level. In November 1968 de Gaulle laid down the principle: "[T]he basic role of the air and land forces does not consist in joining a battle that they have no chance of winning in view of the balance of forces, but of *obliging the adversary to face the risks of our strategic nuclear response.*"[59] Translated into guidelines for planning, this meant that France only "need[ed] a minimum of conventional forces in order to avoid an adversary being attracted, in an unconscious step, by the ver-

[55]Davidson, "France Rejoins Its Allies," p. 22; Ullman, "The Covert French Connection," pp. 3, 4, 15, 21–22. France and the United States shared their target lists, though "not their timetables for applying them" ("Nuclear Secrets," p. 29).

[56]Yost, "French Nuclear Targeting," pp. 146–47.

[57]Ullman, "The Covert French Connection," pp. 11, 21–22, 24–25, 29–30; Davidson, "France Rejoins Its Allies," pp. 22ff.

[58]Ullman, "The Covert French Connection," p. 27.

[59]Cited in Yost, "France's Deterrent Posture, Part I," p. 6, emphasis added; Kohl, *French Nuclear Diplomacy*, pp. 162, 163.

tigo of a vacuum" and that conventional force deployments "must not sin by default or by excess. . . ."[60]

A similarly distinctive deterrent, rather than defensive, logic guided France's deployment of tactical nuclear weapons. Beginning with the 1972 Defense White Paper their role was defined as delivery of a final warning that would send a clear signal against military targets, stop the enemy in his tracks, and force him to decide on settlement or all-out nuclear war.[61] Since the purpose was to frighten the adversary by signaling the imminence of strategic nuclear retaliation, not defeat him in battle, a relatively modest tactical nuclear arsenal was sufficient.[62] With this role in mind, in October 1984 the Defense Ministry directed that France's tactical nuclear weapons thereafter be labeled "pre-strategic weapons."[63] And consistent with a nuclear posture that emphasized fostering the adversary's uncertainty about the chain of events that could trigger retaliation, France proclaimed that its tactical nuclear weapons might be used for "intervention alone or with allies, before or after the possible collapse of NATO, before or after the use of tactical theater nuclear weapons by the United States. In which place? At what time? There one must deliberately let doubt, uncertainty, and vagueness persist. They contribute to deterrence."[64] Growth in France's tactical nuclear capabilities notwithstanding, in 1987 President Mitterrand indicated there would be no change in their strategic role, rejecting the option of marrying more ample and technologically sophisticated forces to the strategy of flexible response the United States preferred. Instead, he reiterated the traditional French view: "The final warning is the first nuclear warning—and the last. . . . One cannot carve up warnings into small pieces, one cannot dilute them. . . . There is no flexible response strategy for France. . . ."[65] Opposing the idea of planning to control esca-

[60]President Mitterrand's Defense Minister Charles Hernu, cited in Yost, "France's Deterrent Posture, Part I," p. 63.

[61]Norris, Burrows, and Fieldhouse, *British, French, and Chinese Nuclear Weapons*, p. 261.

[62]See Prime Minister Raymond Barre, cited in Yost, "France's Deterrent Posture, Part I," p. 53, and discussion, pp. 53–55.

[63]Ibid., pp. 52–53.

[64]Raymond Tourrain, cited ibid., p. 52.

[65]Mitterrand's comments made in West Germany, cited by Michael Stott, "Mitterrand Says French Nuclear Weapons Only for Massive Strike." France's belief in the fundamental importance of nuclear deterrence was also reflected in its alarm expressed during the run-up to signing the 1987 treaty eliminating Soviet and American intermediate-range nuclear forces. See Housego, "French Army Sounds Alarm on Defence Cuts," pp. 2ff; Haydon, "France Boosts Nuclear Force Amid Worries Over Missile Deal"; "Nuclear Deterrence Vital, Says Former French Prime Minister."

lation on the nuclear battlefield, Mitterrand echoed Bernard Brodie's famous comment by adding that "[t]he object of (nuclear) deterrence is not to win wars, but to prevent them."[66] The enduring strategic emphasis on dissuasion by nuclear deterrence that guided France's military planning was summed up by François Mitterrand's Defense Minister, Charles Hernu:

> The priority is on nuclear weapons, and it is mainly on them that France rests her security.[67]
>   ... he who tells me that he prefers another division of soldiers to a missile-launching submarine has mistaken our epoch. ... France is the only country that has dared to draw all the consequences of her status as a nuclear power. It is to this priority—nuclear weapons programs— that we have sacrificed what was second and had to be economized.[68]

FRANCE'S NUCLEAR DETERRENT

Of the three countries on which this book focuses, France publicly expressed the greatest confidence in, and offered the most explicit justification for, the wisdom of its nuclear deterrent emphasis. Nuclear weapons, the French insisted, made alliances less stable since self-interested states would not jeopardize their national survival for the sake of others. But nuclear weapons also made alliances less important for states that deployed them since they granted their possessors unprecedented security by "sanctuarizing" their national territory. Vulnerability to the "frightful destruction" of nuclear weapons would enable the weak to deter even a much stronger enemy, one they could never hope to defeat.[69] As long as France had the forces necessary to create first-strike uncertainty in the mind of Soviet planners, the overwhelming imbalance in nuclear warheads and megatonnage did not matter. What sort of "frightful destruction" did Moscow have to worry the French might inflict on the Soviet Union?

The *force de frappe* was designed to cause the aggressor "damage

[66]Stott, "Mitterrand Says French Nuclear Weapons Only for Massive Strike."
[67]Cited in David S. Yost, *France and Conventional Defense in Central Europe*, p. 78.
[68]Cited in Yost, "France's Deterrent Posture and Security in Europe, Part I," p. 64. Where shortfalls in defense spending occurred between 1960 and 1975, conventional forces suffered in order to maintain the vitality of the nuclear deterrent. See David S. Yost, "French Defense Budgeting," pp. 581–82.
[69]Gallois, "French Defense Planning—The Future in the Past," p. 17; Yost, "France's Deterrent Posture and Security in Europe, Part I," p. 14; Kohl, *French Nuclear Diplomacy*, p. 152.

'judged superior' to the demographic and economic potential that we represent."[70] The threatened punishment, then, was to be geared to the notion of proportionality, articulated by the influential retired General Pierre Gallois.[71] For Soviet leaders, the stakes in a confrontation with France were inherently smaller than those in the global rivalry with the United States. A capability to deliver a devastating nuclear blow, though not one comparable to that the United States could deliver, would suffice to dissuade the Soviets from threatening France's vital interests. Originally this sufficiency criterion based on proportionality was conceived largely in terms of Soviet fatalities equal to the population of France (about 50 million). By the 1980s, however, the French focus shifted from simply a number of fatalities to the damage inflicted on the Soviet economic and political-administrative capacity. This change did not indicate a French shift to counterforce targeting associated with a nuclear warfighting posture as part of a defensive strategy, but rather a redefinition of countervalue targets that satisfied France's deterrent strategy. The French would aim nuclear strikes against what Colonel Guy Lewin of the Defense Ministry's planning department referred to as the aggressor's *oeuvres vives* (vital works of a ship below the water line) because they would result in damage that Soviet decision-makers would view as *politically* unacceptable.

> The neutralization of the adversary [state's] administrative, economic, and social structures, the destruction of the framework of life and activity of millions of persons constitute damage that would be difficult to accept, even if a part of the population concerned by these destructions escapes immediate death. . . . Would this situation be tolerable for the leaders of a great power that wants to continue to play a preponderant role in the world? Obviously not. . . . [72]

Maximizing the unacceptable political consequences of its nuclear strikes led to a revision of France's proportional targeting requirement from its original anti-demographic to an anti-city focus, simply defined

[70]Cited in Kohl, *French Nuclear Diplomacy*, p. 131.

[71]His ideas are elaborated in Pierre Gallois, *The Balance of Terror*. For a more readily available summary of his views, see Freedman, *The Evolution of Nuclear Strategy*, pp. 314–18.

[72]Cited in Kohl, *French Nuclear Diplomacy*, p. 132. Robert Jervis, too, emphasizes the distinction between the strategic purpose of targeting particular assets (to punish the adversary or protect oneself) as opposed to attributes of the targets themselves (i.e., population, industry, military hardware), a distinction sometimes blurred by simply referring to countervalue and counterforce targets (Jervis, "Strategic Theory: What's New and What's True," p. 138).

as 100–200 vital centers—roughly equivalent to the number of French cities that would be at risk.[73]

This standard for sufficiency, it should be added, suggests one reason why France and Britain were determined to deploy nuclear arsenals during the Cold War that were significantly larger than China's. As advanced-industrial societies, they may have concluded that it was necessary to have arsenals that could impose rather high costs on a Soviet adversary who might hope to extract significant benefits through victory. By contrast, China's smaller retaliatory arsenal, the only sort realistically within reach, may have sufficed for it to impose costs that exceeded any benefits a victor might reasonably envision from defeating a developing country with few valuable prizes. The theoretical importance of such a calculus to explain differences in arsenal size should not be overstated, however. China deployed fewer strategic weapons during the Cold War mainly because of the country's economic and technological limitations.[74]

France's Nuclear Forces: Small but Sufficient

What forces did France procure to fulfill the requirements of its deterrent doctrine? France's pattern of deployment and modernization, like Britain's, aimed to provide a robust and affordable means for ensuring its national security while confronting a prospective adversary whose aggregate military capabilities it could not match. But despite many similarities in their levels of economic development and strategic circumstances, France's nuclear arsenal differed from Britain's in cost and composition because of the Gaullist insistence on greater national autonomy and the related determination to meet the challenge of maintaining a more fully articulated arsenal (IRBMs, bombers, and SLBMs).[75]

Bombers. The first leg of France's nuclear triad came on line in October 1964 with the initial deployment of what at its peak would be a fleet of 36 Mirage IVA aircraft each armed with a 60 kiloton fission grav-

---

[73]Yost, "French Nuclear Targeting," p. 134.

[74]Still, with the bar set lower, China's leaders may have believed the extraordinary effort their nuclear program entailed was worth it, even if the result could only be a rather meager arsenal. And, it should be added, even if China's leaders believed that the requirements of deterrence called for greater retaliatory punch, and could have mustered greater resources, they faced a tougher challenge than Britain or France fielding such arsenal because so many of the high value targets in its superpower adversary's territory (the United States and then the Soviet Union) were comparatively far from bases within China.

[75]Kohl, *French Nuclear Diplomacy*, pp. 5–6, 9; Heisbourg, "The British and French Nuclear Forces," p. 308; David S. Yost, "French Defense Budgeting," p. 604; Ullman, "The Covert French Connection."

ity bomb.[76] Between 1964 and 1971, France took steps to maximize the deterrent value of this relatively small force, dispersing the 36 aircraft at nine separate airfields and maintaining "a rigorous system of permanent ground alert in order to increase the Soviets' uncertainty about their prospects for successfully preempting the *force de frappe*."[77] As IRBMs and SLBMs were activated in the early 1970s, France gradually reduced the numbers of Mirage bombers and the costly burden of keeping them on high-level alert. But the French, apparently embracing the reliability-enhancing virtues of redundancy, also sought to maintain their strategic triad and so took steps to retain a residual deterrent capability in their manned bombers. Dispersal, rotation, and hardened sheltering were undertaken to reduce the vulnerability of the aircraft. And beginning in 1986 eighteen Mirage IVAs were modernized and deployed as Mirage IVPs, each armed with the supersonic medium-range air-to-surface missile (ASMP) carrying a 300-kiloton thermonuclear warhead.[78] Though fewer in number, the overall destructive power of the nuclear forces based on upgraded bombers actually increased from roughly 2,160 kilotons to 5,400 kilotons. Perhaps more important, the prospects for bombers successfully completing the nuclear mission increased because the ASMPs allowed for delivery of these more destructive warheads from a standoff posture rather than requiring aircraft to elude Soviet defenses and fly over their targets.[79] Even as the Cold War waned, France looked ahead to the end of the useful life of the Mirage IVP strike force and began to plan for a successor, the Rafale D, armed with either the ASMP or a more advanced ASLP missile, a decision discussed in Chapter 7. And to ensure continuity in this leg of the nuclear triad, until the new Rafale would be ready early in the 21st century, plans called for some of the Mirage 2000N fleet (previously designated a pre-strategic tactical nuclear force) to be redeployed to the strategic nuclear mission.[80]

IRBMs. In May 1963 the French government decided to develop intermediate-range ballistic missiles for the other two legs of the nuclear triad. The land-based missile program led to the deployment of

[76]For extensive description of the Mirage IVA's deployment, see Norris, Burrows, and Fieldhouse, *British, French, and Chinese Nuclear Weapons*, pp. 225–26.

[77]Ibid., pp. 225, 227.

[78]See "France Qualifies ASMP Nuclear Missile," pp. 21ff.

[79]Yost, "France's Deterrent Posture and Security in Europe, Part I," pp. 18–19; Yost, "French Nuclear Targeting," p. 129.

[80]Norris, Burrows, and Fieldhouse, *British, French, and Chinese Nuclear Weapons*, p. 232n44.

two groups of nine silo-based S2 IRBMs each armed with a single 120-kiloton fission warhead (MR 31), on the Albion Plateau in 1971 and 1972.[81] However impressive this indigenous effort, before the IRBMs became operational French planners recognized that this force would be increasingly vulnerable to preemptive strikes. The Soviet Union commanded an ever larger and more accurate nuclear arsenal whereas France, despite initial plans to deploy 54 IRBMs, never moved beyond the original figure of 18, each based in a fixed, easily targeted silo. Moreover, even if this land-based force were not completely destroyed in a preemptive strike, any surviving IRBMs would confront the emerging anti-missile defensive systems protecting the single most important target for French retaliation, Moscow. How did France deal with these ostensible weaknesses in the IRBM force? It addressed the vulnerability in two ways, both consistent with the economic constraints shaping the strategic choices of a second-ranking power facing a superpower adversary and designed to maximize the dissuasive effect of uncertainty in the nuclear era.

First, Paris insisted that improving Soviet counterforce capabilities could not guarantee instantaneous destruction of France's ability to inflict horrifying punishment in retaliatory strikes. Even if France did not openly embrace a "launch on warning" policy, its IRBMs were solid-fueled rockets with a capability for prompt launch that Soviet planners could not ignore.[82] And regardless of the fate of the IRBMs, in arguments that paralleled its views on the pre-strategic role of its conventional and tactical nuclear forces, France claimed that the magnitude of the preemptive counterforce attack an adversary would have to launch to be confident of success would provide clear evidence of hostile intent and ample justification for retaliation with whatever other elements of its nuclear triad remained on bombers and submarines.[83]

Second, to increase the possibility for at least ragged retaliation and thereby undermine Soviet confidence in the prospects for a fully effective preemptive strike, France began to modernize its land-based IRBM force. Silos and launch control centers were hardened against blast and electromagnetic pulse effects, alert status was improved so that it became possible to launch the entire force on one minute's notice, and the S2s were replaced with a superior missile beginning in June 1980. The

[81]For a detailed history of the French land-based IRBM force, see ibid., pp. 235–44.

[82]Yost, "France's Deterrent Posture and Security in Europe, Part I," pp. 19–21.

[83]See, for example, Defense Minister Pierre Messmer's comments made in 1967, cited in Norris, Burrows, and Fieldhouse, *British, French, and Chinese Nuclear Weapons*, p. 236.

new S3 IRBM, and the further improved S3D version deployed by September 1984, were more survivable because of improved hardening technologies and carried a more potent one-megaton thermonuclear warhead (TN61). Most important, any surviving warheads would have had a better chance than their predecessors of penetrating Soviet defenses permitted under the 1972 Anti-Ballistic Missile (ABM) treaty because they incorporated greater protection against nuclear effects, included penetration aids, had a higher reentry speed, and allegedly offered the "possibility of trajectory 'diversification.'"[84] Just two or three S3Ds escaping preemptive destruction carried megatonnage comparable to that once carried on the entire S2 force and had a better chance of delivering it on target.

Thus the principal responses to the alleged vulnerability of France's IRBM force were to assert the value of a synergistic relationship among the three legs of the deterrent triad and to develop a more sophisticated silo-based missile. Though lacking the resources to compete with the superpowers in terms of number and variety of nuclear weapons, France's resources were greater than those available to China. Paris, therefore, did not need to rely as much as the Chinese did on deception to enhance the retaliatory potential of the land-based forces it was determined to field. In planning the successor to the S3D, which had been scheduled to remain in service until 2000, France continued to explore ways to increase the probability some part of land-based IRBMs would survive. The obvious solution, in light of the presumed costs and technical difficulty of deploying effective hard-point anti-missile defenses against a heavily armed, determined adversary, was to make the fixed missiles mobile.

Beginning in 1976, France debated the merits of a mobile successor for the planned S3D. One option was to deploy more easily hidden and transported cruise missiles, rather than a new generation of ballistic missiles. Because France's strategy called for nuclear weapons to be used as "area weapons . . . against broader population centers," its cruise missiles would not have had to achieve the accuracy typical of U.S. cruise missiles. For this reason, French defense officials argued that cruise missiles were a realistic alternative.[85] Nevertheless, economic constraints, if not technological barriers, required choosing between these missile options rather than following the superpower path of producing both. And, on the basis of cost effectiveness, by 1981 President Mitterrand

---

[84]Norris, Burrows, and Fieldhouse, *British, French, and Chinese Nuclear Weapons*, pp. 216n2, 237, 292–93.

[85]"French Debate Dropping Triad Concept," pp. 193ff.

and the Defense Council had chosen the ballistic missile alternative.[86] Moving beyond this basic decision, however, and selecting a specific design and basing mode for the missile, initially dubbed the SX, led to a succession of false starts not unlike those experienced in the United States as it debated the development of a mobile successor for the Minuteman III system. Over time the focus in Paris shifted from developing a genuinely new S4 IRBM deployed to maximize mobility, to a less costly option of developing a missile that could piggy-back on technologies planned for modernization of the submarine missile force (a cost-saving approach the Chinese adopted), and deploying it in fixed silos while retaining the possibility of making it mobile in a crisis (similar to the rail-garrison plan an increasingly cost-conscious United States had chosen for its MX as the Cold War ended).[87] But before French leaders could reach a consensus on the S4 program, events overtook the debate. The 1986 five-year defense plan reaffirmed the priority assigned to the more survivable and potent sea-based deterrent whose unexpectedly costly modernization required delays in the S4.[88] Shortly thereafter the end of the Cold War cast doubt on the wisdom of heavy investment in IRBM modernization, and by 1996, as noted in Chapter 7, France opted to simply dismantle this leg of its triad.[89]

SLBMs. France's retaliatory ace in the hole was its highly survivable fleet of nuclear missile submarines (SSBNs). The Coelacanthe Program initiated in June 1962 led to the deployment of the first of five Redoubtable-class ballistic missile submarines in 1972.[90] Allowing for training, crew rotation, and equipment servicing, France was able to keep two boats on patrol once its fourth SSBN was launched in 1977, and three on patrol after the fifth was deployed in 1980, with the possi-

[86]Norris, Burrows, and Fieldhouse, *British, French, and Chinese Nuclear Weapons*, pp. 239, 241.

[87]Heisbourg, "The British and French Nuclear Forces," pp. 309, 311–12; See Alan Philps, "French Parliamentary Panel Backs Mobile Missile"; Alan Riding, "France Drops Plans to Build New Nuclear Missile System," p. A6; Norris, Burrows, and Fieldhouse, *British, French, and Chinese Nuclear Weapons*, pp. 239–44.

[88]"The French Cabinet Has Approved a Defence Budget Up By 6% in Real Terms for the Five Year Period From 1987 to 1991," pp. 1, 9; "France: S4 Strategic Missile Project Could Be Shelved," pp. 12ff; Alan Philps, "France Scales Back on Developing New Strategic Nuclear Missile"; Jeffrey M. Lenorovitz, "French Boost 1989 Defense Budget for Conventional, Nuclear Upgrades," pp. 31ff.

[89]On the debate about IRBM modernization in the early post–Cold War era, see Norris, Burrows, and Fieldhouse, *British, French, and Chinese Nuclear Weapons*, pp. 242–44.

[90]For a detailed history of France's submarine-based deterrent, see ibid., pp. 244–69.

bility of getting an additional SSBN to sea on two days notice.[91] What sort of retaliatory punch did this fleet carry for delivery against the Soviet Union? After President de Gaulle's public rejection of President Kennedy's offer to share the U.S. Polaris missile, France pushed ahead with development of its own M1 SLBM, sixteen of which were deployed aboard each of the first two Redoubtable-class SSBNs between 1972 and 1975. The M1 and its successor, the longer-range M2 (deployed on the first three Redoubtable-class SSBNs between 1975 and 1979 and enabling the submarines to expand their areas of patrol) each carried a single 500-kiloton boosted fission warhead (MR41). Recognizing the importance of ensuring the credibility of its sea-based retaliatory threat, in 1970 France began development of a more advanced weapon as a follow-on to the M2. The result was the M20, 64 of which were deployed aboard the fleet of SSBNs between 1977 and 1981. The new SLBM carried a more powerful one-megaton thermonuclear warhead (TN61) that was hardened against nuclear effects and carried penetration aids, all increasing the chances some fraction of surviving French forces would deliver a devastating blow against the Soviet Union in spite of its improving air and ballistic missile defenses. Modernization continued with the M4 SLBM designed to further increase SSBN survivability and warhead effectiveness. The M4 not only had a longer range than the M20, again expanding the fleet's area of patrol, but the M4A and the improved M4B variants both also incorporated more sophisticated technologies for piercing the adversary's defenses. Atop a MIRVed missile with a sophisticated warhead dispersal mechanism, each M4 could carry up to six 150-kiloton thermonuclear warheads (TN70/71) with a smaller radar cross-section, better penetration aids, superior hardening against the various disruptive effects of nuclear explosions, and greater accuracy than its predecessors.[92] First deployed on the technologically improved Inflexible SSBN in May 1985, by 1993 the M4s had replaced the M20s on all four of the newest Redoubtable-class SSBNs through a refitting and updating program. Thus, by the last years of the Cold War, France's sea-based deterrent, its most survivable and penetrable retaliatory force, carried roughly 80 percent of the *force de frappe's* nuclear warheads and 70 percent of its megatonnage.[93] And anticipating advances in Soviet

---

[91]Ibid., pp. 246–47

[92]See ibid., p. 257; "France Qualifies ASMP Nuclear Missile," pp. 21ff.

[93]Though penetration aids reportedly displaced some of the multiple warheads the M4s could have carried, by 1987 the sea-based leg of the nuclear triad (M20s, M4As, M4Bs) was capable of delivering in excess of 200 warheads with a total yield of almost 60 megatons against Soviet targets. See Norris, Burrows, and Fieldhouse,

ballistic missile defenses, in the mid-1980s France sought to ensure the continued reliability of this leg of the triad by initiating the M45 modification of the M4s. Authorized as the Cold War drew to a close, the M45 would incorporate the most sophisticated technologies, especially stealthiness, to improve the penetrability of the warheads carried by France's SSBNs. It was slated for deployment aboard the Triomphant-class submarines that, as discussed in the next chapter, were to begin replacing the Redoubtable-class submarines in the mid-1990s.[94]

France's Nuclear Credibility: Not Much, but Enough

Although the ability to inflict damage outweighing the value France represented to the Soviet leaders was a useful gauge for the sufficiency of forces, it did not ensure the credibility of deterrent threats. As for China and Britain, no capability would be adequate to dissuade an adversary unless the adversary believed the capability would be used. But since forces sufficient for proportional punishment were not sufficient for meaningful damage limitation or a war-winning capability, short of a foolish unrestrained Soviet nuclear assault on France, it would be obviously irrational for French decision-makers to take the suicidal step of launching their weapons knowing this would trigger Soviet retaliation. Though General Gallois, in justifying France's independent deterrent, plausibly argued that the will to risk nuclear war would be greater when one's own national interests, as opposed to an ally's interests, were at stake, acting on this greater resolve would still remain technically irrational.[95] Even in circumstances threatening vital French interests, including scenarios of limited attacks on French territory, unless the Soviets had first blanketed the country with nuclear warheads, Paris could not improve, and most likely would only worsen, its situation by choosing to launch a devastating nuclear strike in reply. Thus, as suggested in Chapter 2, the credibility of France's nuclear deterrent ultimately could not rest on the *certainty* that the country's leaders would choose to carry out clearly specified threats, even thoughtfully calculated proportional threats, rhetoric notwithstanding. Credibility instead rested on the *possibility* that France would prove to be a contingently unsafe ac-

---

British, French, and Chinese Nuclear Weapons, p. 248. On French SLBM capabilities, see also Heisbourg, "The British and French Nuclear Forces," p. 304; cf. Yost, "French Nuclear Targeting," pp. 132–36. Cf. Geoffrey Kemp, "Nuclear Forces for Medium Powers, Part I"; Graeme P. Auton, "Nuclear Deterrence and the Medium Power."

[94]Norris, Burrows, and Fieldhouse, British, French, and Chinese Nuclear Weapons, p. 258.

[95]See Freedman, The Evolution of Nuclear Strategy, pp. 315, 317.

tor, one who when seriously challenged might unleash its awesome capability as a result of accident or irrationality.[96]

The ongoing modernization of France's nuclear triad described above increased Soviet uncertainty about the magnitude of the retaliatory blow it could face, no matter how well-conceived a preemptive strike. Along with measures designed to increase the probability that terrifying retaliatory forces would survive, France also sought to reduce Soviet confidence that a successful decapitating strike against French command and control would render surviving forces useless and to increase their fear that some might be used. A "reinforced command centre [referred to as the Jupiter Room] under the Elysee Palace" was prepared for the French President, whose approval as commander-in-chief was necessary for the authorized use of nuclear weapons.[97] In addition to hardening this and other land-based command and control centers, France responded to a growing Soviet counterforce capability during the 1970s and 1980s by developing an alternative, airborne command post known as *Astarte*.[98] Employing "electronics adopted from the [U.S.] Rockwell Collins Tacamo system," France planned four such alternate command posts to be placed aboard modified Transall C.160 transport aircraft.[99] Like its American counterpart, France's airborne nuclear command, operational beginning in early 1988, provided the technical ability to launch land-based and sea-based missiles even if ground-based command centers were destroyed.[100] Although many analysts doubted the actual durability of such a system even for the better funded U.S. military, especially in a "nuclearized" environment, its mere existence further increased first-strike uncertainty among planners in Moscow. It not only improved the chances a French president could transmit the unlikely decision to authorize suicidal nuclear retaliation after absorbing a limited Soviet first strike, but perhaps more important, confronted the adversary with the likelihood that a threatened French national command would have to predelegate authority, and provide some emergency capability for surviving airborne commanders to launch nuclear

[96]The emphasis on uncertainty and the risks of escalation inherent in a conflict between nuclear-armed states was associated with another leading French nuclear strategist, General Andre Beaufre. For a summary of his views, see ibid., pp. 318–19.

[97]"Mitterrand Shows Military Brass Round Nuclear Control Bunker."

[98]Funding this important aspect of a survivable retaliatory capability was facilitated by reducing the number of Triomphant-class SSBNs scheduled for construction. Yost, "France's Deterrent Posture and Security in Europe," pp. 26–27.

[99]Jeffrey M. Lenorovitz, "French Budget Sets $8 Billion for Equipment," pp. 31ff; "French Nuclear Command Post Enters Operational Service," pp. 78ff.

[100]Ibid.

weapons in contingencies where contact with ground-based authorities was lost.[101] Given the unprecedented confusion, both organizational and electronic, that would likely prevail after even the relatively limited use of nuclear forces, perhaps even after a major conventional attack against French targets, Soviet planners could not lightly dismiss the risk of launches despite the absence of commands from Paris.

Like the British, French leaders acted to bolster the effectiveness of their deterrent by cultivating Soviet uncertainty about the circumstances that might trigger nuclear use. Ambiguity about the sort of challenge that would prompt escalation to a nuclear response kept the Soviets guessing. An aggressor would run the risk of triggering devastating nuclear retaliation whenever it threatened France's vital interests, but these were not clearly identified in the American fashion by creating tripwires (physical or conceptual) the adversary would have to cross. Instead, French leaders encouraged the adversary's doubts about the extent of their nation's vital interests to inhibit him from taking the risk involved in testing their limits. Comments by French officials simply suggested that the nuclear deterrent would probably come into play in contingencies other than the most provocative, and hence least likely, direct nuclear assault on their homeland.[102] The 1972 Defense White Paper stated that "the limits [of vital interests] . . . are necessarily somewhat hazy. . . . France lives in a network of interests which go beyond her borders. She is not isolated. . . . Our vital interests lie within our territory and the surrounding areas. The deterrent strategy covers this geographic zone."[103] And while careful to avoid extended deterrent commitments to its neighbors that might compromise France's strategic autonomy, in a 1977 speech at a nuclear missile base on the Albion Plateau Prime Minister Raymond Barre proclaimed that France's nuclear deterrent "covers not only our territory but also the near-by region, *because an invasion of the near-by region, even before reaching our frontiers will do harm to our vital interests.*"[104] Defense Minister Hernu's

[101]On the sorts of risks introduced by delegation and predelegation, see Kurt Gottfried and Bruce G. Blair, *Crisis Stability and Nuclear War*; Bruce G. Blair, *The Logic of Accidental Nuclear War.*

[102]Yost, "French Nuclear Targeting," p. 150.

[103]Cited in Yost, "France's Deterrent Posture and Security in Europe, Part I," p. 7; see also Heisbourg, "The British and French Nuclear Forces," p. 302.

[104]Cited in "French Prime Minister on France's Nuclear Policy," emphasis added. Any attempt to be very explicit about the scope of French interests covered by the threat of nuclear retaliatory strikes risked charges by domestic critics of compromising French decision-making autonomy. Such criticism was directed at Giscard and his Chief of Staff in 1976 when their reference to an enlarged sanctuary (*sanctuari-*

1982 comments on France's vital interests nicely summarized the belief that uncertainty and caution go hand in hand in a nuclear world:

> Are they [vital interests] tied to geographic, economic, and political criteria? I will respond that we are the judges of that, and not the adversary, who will have to make an inventory of all that we might place in that category. It is up to him to make hypotheses, knowing that an error of analysis could turn out to be immediately mortal.[105]

Such statements fostered the impression among Western analysts, and undoubtedly the concern among Soviet planners, that France's nuclear retaliatory threats during the Cold War covered not just its own national territory, but also that of its key continental allies, especially Germany. Without offering what they had long argued was an incredible promise of extended deterrence in the nuclear age, French comments after the late 1970s suggested that economic interests, political sympathies, and most importantly geographic proximity created a French stake in German security that the Soviets ignored at their own peril. In June 1985 Defense Minister Hernu, speaking at Munsingen, referred to West Germany as "the closest of our allies, from all viewpoints, and we maintain with it the most intense relations in the domain of defense and security. France and Federal Germany share security interests in common."[106]

Ambiguity prevailed not only about the scope of vital interests, but also the wartime circumstances in which French nuclear first use might occur. The adversary would have to worry about the risks of nuclear escalation, even if its challenge to nebulous French interests did not involve nuclear weapons. Preferring the added dissuasive effect of eschewing even a symbolic, Chinese-style, no-first-use pledge, France maintained the public posture that it "has the right to decide when and under what conditions the country can use nuclear weapons."[107] Again, Soviet planners would know that leaders in Paris could not rationally decide to

---

sation elargie) seemed to imply an extended deterrent pledge to France's European allies. See Yost, "France's Deterrent Posture and Security in Europe, Part I," p. 7.

[105]Cited in Yost, "France's Deterrent Posture and Security in Europe, Part I," p. 12.

[106]Cited in David S. Yost, "Radical Change in French Defense Policy," p. 62. See also Yost, "French Nuclear Targeting," p. 152; Malone, *The British Nuclear Deterrent*, p. 181

[107]French President Mitterrand, cited in "Mitterrand Reaffirms Independent Nuclear Deterrent." France's defense minister in 1985 stated that "France does not rule out the use of nuclear weapons to counter a chemical attack on what it considers its vital interests. . . ." (Paul Betts, "France Threatens Nuclear Reply to Chemical Attack," pp. 3ff).

use their nuclear weapons in response to nonnuclear attacks. But Soviet planners could not easily dismiss France's first-use rhetoric as irrelevant bluffing. They had to worry that Soviet military action sufficient to accomplish objectives worthy of the decision to go to war would result in the loosening of peacetime constraints on nuclear decision-making. Because of the risk it might prove to be a contingently unsafe actor, especially in a context where French rhetoric established among subordinates a belief in the legitimacy of nuclear use, dissuasion was more effective than might appear likely if one focused solely on inherently incredible threats to actually decide to retaliate.

As for the other nuclear powers, however, despite broad popular support for and repeated expressions of official confidence in France's nuclear deterrent, the doctrinal emphasis was not without its critics who set forth familiar arguments. Some, like Deputy Chief of Staff of the French Air Force General Etienne Copel, argued that France needed to be ready to fight a conventional war. Because, he alleged, nuclear weapons only deterred the adversary's use of nuclear weapons, France needed to muster the capability for territorial defense in order to dissuade other, more plausible threats to its vital interests.[108] Others doubted that French nuclear weapons were a fully effective counter even to Soviet nuclear weapons. Although France's threat to retaliate in kind might discourage the Soviets from a massive strike against French urban centers, David Yost, a leading expert on France's Cold War security policy, argued that such threats "no matter how sincerely articulated, seem[ed] inherently less credible in deterring attack on French retaliatory forces."[109] Echoing Paul Nitze's criticism of the U.S. deterrent posture in the late 1970s, Yost asserted that with nuclear forces smaller and more vulnerable than those of the United States, leaders in Paris would be self-deterred in the wake of a Soviet nuclear counterforce first strike since a response could only worsen France's position. Because sensible Soviet planners would recognize this, France's nuclear arsenal would not be effective for deterring a determined and militarily superior adversary from undertaking this more discriminating form of aggression. Still others questioned whether France's nuclear deterrent could be effective under *any* foreseeable circumstances. Raymond Aron, for example, saw no need to distinguish among attack scenarios and suggested simply that the obviously suicidal consequences of French nuclear strikes on

[108]See Michael Dobbs, "French General Challenges Cornerstone of Nation's Independent Defense Strategy"; Eiko Fukuda, "General Says French Defence Doctrine a Recipe for Catastrophe."
[109]Yost, "France's Deterrent Posture and Security in Europe, Part I," p. 35.

the Soviet Union would inhibit French leaders from *ever* executing the touted threat.[110]

These various lines of criticism focused on the undeniable irrationality of a massive nuclear response once deterrence failed. Defenders of the official French strategy instead emphasized that their planning was designed to assure the success of deterrence, not prepare for its failure. Yet such a response did not alter the fact that French strategic nuclear retaliation would not be a rational choice under any scenario except the one the Soviets could easily avoid—an indiscriminate attack on France's population and industry. If France's nuclear capability dissuaded the Soviets, then, it was not because of the credibility of official threats to decide to launch a devastating counterblow. Instead deterrence rested on the fact that Soviet leaders could not be certain about French behavior in circumstances where rational retaliation would be inconceivable. The dreaded "clever briefer" in the Kremlin *could* convincingly argue that the probability was quite small that France's leaders would either mistakenly authorize or permit the launch of its nuclear weapons, or irrationally opt for this suicidal act. But because no briefer, however clever, could *guarantee* the complete destruction or paralysis of France's potent nuclear arsenal, even the small risk of devastating retaliation should France turn out to be such a contingently unsafe actor was sufficiently terrifying to dissuade aggression against vital interests. As President de Gaulle had put it, the availability of nuclear weapons "inject[s] into a dangerous world a new and powerful factor for prudence and circumspection."[111] Although France's public pronouncements emphasized the logically untenable threat to deliberately choose nuclear retaliation (what government would want to emphasize the risk of accident or irrationality?), their wording also played on the fear of unpredictable future behavior. Ambiguously, yet ominously, it was asserted that the more perilous the threat an aggressor posed to national security, the more serious the possibility his actions could trigger a desperate military response. To explain their confidence in the dissuasive effect of what they termed "deterrence of the strong by the weak," the French noted that the onus of initiating a potentially disastrous chain of events would be on the powerful adversary's decision-makers.

In a possible conflict between France and the USSR, the latter will always be *the first player*, the party having the initiative and being obliged to decide to pass beyond the prohibition made against his at-

---

[110]Yost, "French Nuclear Targeting," pp. 130–31.
[111]Cited in Gallois, "French Defense Planning—The Future in the Past," p. 17.

tacking our country . . . [a] singularly uncomfortable position for its decision makers, knowing what it would cost to *wager* on nonretaliation
and to lose. . . . The safeguarding of our integrity and our identity is for
us a vital stake, justifying our going all the way and taking extraordinary risks; this confers a nonzero probability, even an elevated one, on
the execution of our threat of nuclear retaliation on the opposing sanctuary.[112]

[112]General Lucien Poirier, cited in Yost, "French Nuclear Targeting," p. 130, emphasis added. See also Kenneth N. Waltz, "A Strategy for the Rapid Deployment
Force," pp. 565–67; Waltz, "Toward Nuclear Peace," pp. 684–89, 695–709.

7

Nuclear Weapons States in the Post-Cold War World

During the Cold War, the principal security concern for China, Britain, and France was how best to cope with the threat from a superpower adversary. This priority established the goal—dissuading the superpower from challenging vital interests—around which they designed their security policies. Primarily interested in preserving the status quo, preferably relying on the indirect, rather than the direct, use of force, these three states could choose between the alternative dissuasive strategies of deterrence and defense, as well as among various means for fulfilling the requirements of the strategy selected. This book has explained why China, Britain, and France opted for dissuasion by deterrence relying on independent nuclear forces. The choice reflected not only the attractiveness of nuclear deterrence, but also the shortcomings of the plausible alternatives. In particular, I have indicated why these states were not satisfied with either the economically appealing option of relying on the dissuasive effect of a more powerful ally's diverse assortment of nuclear and conventional deterrent and defensive capabilities, or with the self-reliant alternatives of dissuasion by defense or deterrence employing conventional forces. The Cold War international system within which they crafted their security policies was, like its predecessors, an anarchic realm in which states might have to fend for themselves. But the Cold War international system was distinguished from those that preceded it because two dominant states had emerged with military capabilities that far outstripped their nearest competitors and because the advent of nuclear weapons had revolutionized the strategic consequences of military technology. The challenge of coping with the potential threat the superpowers could pose and the strategic significance of the nuclear revolution profoundly affected the way China, Britain, and France responded to the concerns that states coexisting under anarchy had confronted for centuries. These distinctive features of the Cold War world determined the effectiveness, feasibility, and robustness of strategic alternatives and encouraged the leaders of China, Britain, and France to emphasize independent nuclear deterrence as the keystone of their security policies. What lessons can one draw from their experience about the choices they and other states are likely to make in the different post–Cold War security environment?

POST–COLD WAR STRATEGIC CONTEXT

One cannot predict with certainty the nature of the international system that will emerge in the early twenty-first century. But four features of the post–Cold War world that seems to be taking shape suggest that the strategic robustness and economic affordability of national nuclear deterrents that have made them attractive will endure.

Polarity. Along the dimensions I have explored, the first and most significant difference between the post–Cold War international system and its immediate predecessor is the end of bipolarity.[1] What will follow

---

[1]The once important role of great power ideological conflict also seems certain to decline. Though ideology is one among many factors shaping a state's foreign policy and has been included here when understanding its influence is essential, this book mainly identifies similarities in security dynamics independent of the ideological attributes of the states studied, aside from the assumption that all have interests rooted in particularistic national beliefs. Two prominent arguments have emerged in the post–Cold War era, however, that suggest the centuries-long era of world politics driven by self-interested states pursuing national interests by whatever means they choose, including the use of force, is drawing to a close. One is Samuel Huntington's thesis that distinct civilizational interests (rooted in cultural ties that are often supranational) are replacing national interests as the basis for global rivalry. His highly controversial argument, even if correct, suggests a change in the size and attributes of the actors who would continue to pursue self-interest within an anarchic realm. If so, the changes he foresees would not fundamentally alter the security logic presented here (see Samuel P. Huntington, "The Clash of Civilizations?"; Huntington, *The Clash of Civilizations and the Remaking of World Order*; cf. Stephen M. Walt, "Building Up New Bogeymen").

A second prominent post–Cold War argument, loosely referred to as "democratic peace theory," foresees the possibility of a still more fundamental change in world politics. With a lineage traceable at least to Immanuel Kant, and more fully elaborated in the contemporary era by Michael Doyle, the logic of this school of thought identifies reasons why the use of force is viewed as neither legitimate nor necessary among a growing community of liberal democratic states (Michael W. Doyle, "Kant, Liberal Legacies, and Foreign Affairs"; Doyle, "Liberalism and World Politics"; Bruce Russett, *Grasping the Democratic Peace*; John M. Owens, "How Liberalism Produces Democratic Peace"). Democratic peace theorists expect that in a world of liberal democratic great powers, the security concerns that prompt the behavior analyzed in this book would no longer prevail. Nevertheless, until that future date when all the great powers (and perhaps also minor powers able to clear the nuclear threshold) develop the attributes required to be labeled liberal democracies, security con-

bipolarity? A decade into the new era, the question remains unanswered.

Continuing growth in China's capabilities, a recovery in post-Soviet Russia, and the reemergence of Japan and Germany (alone or as part of a European federation) as great powers alongside the currently dominant United States could herald the shift to a multipolar international system. Indeed, some variation on this trend seems likely, but not certain.[2] There are doubts about the prospects for each of the candidate great powers in such a future multipolar world to become peer competitors of the United States. China's ascent to true great power status depends on sustaining its recently robust economic growth and maintaining sufficient political coherence so that it can continue along its currently favorable trajectory. Russia must overcome the vexing economic and political legacy of its Soviet past and reverse the precipitous decline that it experienced during the 1990s. Japan and Germany also face hurdles on the path to great power status (not least, reinvigorating Japan's recently stagnant economy and managing the burden of German reunification), though because of their impressive growth during the Cold War the challenges they face seem less daunting.

Given the uncertainties about each of these candidate great powers, it is possible that only one will be up to the task and that bipolarity will be restored. During the 1990s China seemed to be the state with the strongest determination and greatest potential to join the United States as a true great power some time in the twenty-first century. As noted above, however, the distance it has yet to travel suggests caution in judgments about whether or when it will succeed.[3] A third possible outcome, other than recreated bipolarity or a return to historically familiar multipolarity, is perpetuation of the condition that prevailed during the first decade of the post–Cold War era, a condition that some have la-

---

cerns about the possible use of force on which I focus endure. Indeed, if Edward Mansfield and Jack Snyder are correct in arguing that states in the transition from authoritarianism to democracy are prone to adopt more belligerent foreign policies, in the immediate future such concerns may even increase (Edward D. Mansfield and Jack Snyder, "Democratization and the Danger of War"). Other logical and empirical questions about democratic peace theory are raised in Christopher Layne, "Kant or Cant"; David E. Spiro, "The Insignificance of the Liberal Peace"; Henry S. Farber and Joanne Gowa, "Polities and Peace."

[2]For an early post–Cold War analysis that confidently forecasts a multipolar future, see Kenneth N. Waltz, "The Emerging Structure of International Politics."

[3]For discussion of China's changing international role in the 1990s that includes a critical assessment of available evidence and its interpretation, see Avery Goldstein, "Great Expectations." For speculation about revived bipolarity, see Robert Ross, "The Geography of the Peace."

beled unipolarity. Yet the prospects for unipolarity are also unclear. Despite the unchallenged dominance the United States enjoyed at the end of the twentieth century, questions arise because of doubts about the plausibility of a single country managing the world's affairs for more than a short time. Domestic support for shouldering heavy international burdens could flag, especially if Americans come to perceive other states as free-riders. Or other states' resentment of American leadership could encourage them to muster the resources necessary to become peer competitors of the United States.[4]

But whether the structure of the international system in the twenty-first century turns out to be multipolar, bipolar, or unipolar, the appeal of nuclear deterrence for many great and lesser powers will endure. The reasons for this expectation under conditions of bipolarity have been thoroughly explored above. What is to be expected under unipolarity? In a unipolar world, some states would be worried about possible threats from the world's sole remaining superpower and would be attracted to the strategic robustness and economic affordability of nuclear deterrence against an incomparably stronger adversary much as China, Britain, and France had been during the Cold War. Others, not threatened by the world's hegemon, but worried about serious threats from adversaries against whom conventional alternatives seemed inadequate (either because of asymmetric capabilities or because the prospective foe possessed weapons of mass destruction), and who questioned whether a fully self-reliant hegemon would brave the risks to help mount a joint defense or provide a deterrent umbrella, would also appreciate the strategic hedge an independent nuclear arsenal provides. Unipolarity, in other words, would not fundamentally alter and might actually reinforce the reasons why states pursued nuclear weapons under bipolarity.

Multipolarity, however, seems to open up a wider variety of options for security-conscious states. By traditional realist reckoning a shift to multipolarity should revive the importance of alliance formation as an external means of power-balancing and constrain states to stand by their allies for self-interested reasons not operative in a bipolar (or unipolar) world. But the combined effects of the second and third features of the post–Cold War strategic landscape—the enduring consequences of anarchy and the continuing strategic effects of the nuclear revolution—modify this traditional expectation. The availability of nuclear weapons

[4]See Charles Krauthammer, "The Unipolar Moment"; Michael Mastanduno, "Preserving the Unipolar Moment"; cf. Christopher Layne, "The Unipolar Illusion." For the argument that unipolarity may endure, see William C. Wohlforth, "The Stability of a Unipolar World."

for states coexisting in a condition of anarchy will limit the usefulness of alliances among the great powers, even under multipolarity, and preserve the attractiveness of national deterrents. Why will these continuities offset the potentially dramatic effects of a shift to multipolarity?

Anarchy. Barring more fundamental transformations than those that now appear plausible, in the opening decades of the twenty-first century the international system will remain an anarchic realm. Although the system's polarity may change, its ordering principle will not. As long as the international condition of anarchy endures, states will continue to worry about the reliability of self-enforcing alliance commitments and, thus, to doubt that alliance-based security is actually a collective good. States that can feasibly hedge their bets against abandonment by allies and prepare to provide for their own security should be expected to try to do so. Feasibility depends on economic, technological, and political factors. Germany and Japan possessed the economic and technological capabilities of other second-ranking powers during the bipolar Cold War era. But the political constraints imposed on and subsequently embraced by Germany and Japan after their defeat in World War II explain why their security policies radically differed from those of the other three Cold War second-ranking powers examined in this book. Neither developed the full range of military capabilities (especially nuclear weapons) commensurate with their resurgent economic strength. Operating under special conditions resulting from defeat in the war, their foreign-security policies more nearly fit the pattern of attempting to minimize the risk of abandonment by their American ally through deference. As indicated in the next chapter, the logic of this book's argument leads to the expectation that their anomalous posture is likely to change as the special circumstances directly linked to the aftermath of World War II grow more historically distant.

Nuclear Weapons. The post–Cold War world will also still be one in which the availability of nuclear weapons remains the most strategically distinctive feature of military technology.[5] The consequences of

---

[5]Some may contend that the "revolution in military affairs" (RMA) associated with high-technology, precision-targeting capabilities will rival or eclipse the nuclear revolution. Discussion of the strategic consequences of these emerging capabilities indicates, however, that their most profound impact will result from incorporation in defensive and offensive strategies, rather than from their employment in deterrent and compellent strategies for which the punitive capabilities of nuclear weapons of mass destruction remain privileged. The RMA, then, may transform the use of conventional forces, but is not yet the sort of development that negates the revolutionary consequences of nuclear weapons for international security affairs. For

the nuclear revolution reinforce the self-help imperative of anarchy for both providers and recipients of security guarantees. Prospective guarantors will be acutely wary of entrapment in others' disputes if it entails the risk of potentially catastrophic escalation; recipients will worry that allies will be prone to abandon them in their moment of greatest need. The presence of nuclear weapons, regardless of polarity, drives a strategic logic that weakens confidence in security as a collective good supplied through international alliances and encourages the pursuit of an independent deterrent capability as the ultimate guarantee of national security.

National deterrents would remain attractive even if there is a shift to multipolarity not only because the existence of nuclear weapons aggravates doubts about the usefulness of alliances in general, but also because nuclear weapons would be especially helpful for dealing with the greater strategic complexity of a multipolar system in particular. Under multipolarity threats may be harder to anticipate. The basic division of the world's major states into two camps associated with each of the superpowers in the bipolar era has already given way to less obvious, more malleable patterns of alignment.[6] This change foreshadows the strategic

---

states able to clear the steep scientific-industrial-engineering barriers to entry, however, this conventional-technological revolution may negate any lingering attractiveness of small, accurate, or "clean" nuclear weapons in tactical-battlefield or strategic counterforce operations. Although analysts fully embracing the logic of the nuclear revolution doubted the feasibility of such nuclear missions, these nondeterrent roles served as important bases for force planning by the Cold War superpowers. On the meaning and significance of the revolution in military affairs, see Eliot Cohen, "A Revolution in Warfare"; Joseph S. Nye, Jr., and William A. Owens, "America's Information Edge"; "Symposium on the Gulf War and the Revolution in Military Affairs," *International Security*, vol. 22, no. 2 (Fall 1997); Stephen Biddle, "Victory Misunderstood"; Michael O'Hanlon, "Can High Technology Bring U.S. Troops Home?"

[6]The early, classic argument about the strategic implications of the end of the Cold War and its comparatively simple bipolarity is John J. Mearsheimer, "Back to the Future." For a briefer, but geographically more wide-ranging, discussion, see George H. Quester, "The Future of Nuclear Deterrence." It should be added, however, that polarity alone does not determine alignment patterns. As Stephen Walt has explained, a state's leaders interpret changing power relations and the threat they may pose in light of influences such as geography, history, recent behavior, and culture. These, along with the polarity of the international system, condition their behavior, including the choice of alliance partners (Stephen M. Walt, *The Origins of Alliances*). Glenn Snyder, too, suggests that the strategic alignment of states is affected by what he terms "general interests" (conditioned by geography and the structural condition of anarchy) and "particular" interests (conditioned by changes in the capabilities at the disposal of states, domestic politics, and "ideological, ethnic, economic, or prestige values" that may lead to patterns of "conflict or affinity") (Glenn H. Snyder, "The Security Dilemma in Alliance Politics," p. 464). Snyder does argue

ambiguity that may prevail in a multipolar world. Under such circumstances, nuclear weapons provide a useful hedge in two related senses. First, because of the excruciating uncertainties highlighted in the cases of China, Britain, and France during the Cold War, weapons of potentially instantaneous mass destruction in the hands of adversaries induce caution all around, enhancing security regardless of the difficulty of pinpointing the source of future threats. Second, in a more politically complex, multipolar world where the principal threat to vital interests may change, it will be easier, and less expensive, for states to revise nuclear targeting plans and programs than to reconfigure or redeploy massive conventional forces (especially if they have been tailored to cope with the distinctive land-, sea-, or air-based strengths of a particular adversary).[7] States will still have incentives to deploy flexible conven-

---

that alignments in a multipolar world are less likely to be determined by clear and immutable geopolitical concerns and, thus, should more easily be affected by changeable particular interests. Under bipolarity, though conflicting particular interests may strain relations among alliance members, Snyder argues, the prospects for realignment are limited by tight geopolitical considerations (ibid., p. 485; see also Kenneth N. Waltz, *Theory of International Politics*, pp. 163–70). The Anglo-American and Franco-American cases, in which alliances with the superpower were strained but not broken, are consistent with Snyder's (and Waltz's) hypotheses about the rigidity of alignment in a bipolar system.

The shifting alignment of China during the Cold War, however, alerts one to the risk of too readily *assuming* that bipolarity clearly determines threat perceptions. During the 1950s, it was not geography but rather ideology, domestic politics, and especially the unrivaled power projection capabilities of the United States in the immediate postwar years revealed most clearly in Korea, that led China's foreign policy-makers to view the distant Americans as the primary threat to the PRC's security. Their response was to ally with the proximate and powerful Soviet Union, an apparent violation of the expectations about geopolitically determined alignment in the bipolar world. The Sino-Soviet case may simply be an important exception to the pattern Snyder describes. But the Sino-Soviet experience suggests another possibility—that it is interests, rather than polarity, that matter most in patterns of alignment. The Cold War patterns, then, may have had less to do with bipolarity per se than the definitions of national interest in a world in which the United States and Soviet Union were the principal actors. One can easily think of alternatives to the actual postwar world that illustrate the point. A bipolar world in which Germany and Russia were the principal actors, for example, would have had less obvious alignment implications for a self-interested, security-conscious British second-ranking power. Similarly a bipolar world in which Russia and Japan were predominant would have had indeterminate implications for the alignment of a Chinese second-ranking power.

[7]China, after all, initiated its nuclear weapons program with U.S. targets in mind, aimed most of its first-generation weapons at Soviet targets, and after the Cold War has probably redirected many to cover U.S. targets. The United States, too, has added, removed, and restored China as a target for its nuclear weapons as the PRC shifted from Soviet-bloc enemy to anti-Soviet partner to post–Cold War rival. What-

tional forces suitable for offensive and defensive operations in unforeseen minor contingencies, and for testing the determination of an adversary who may probe one's resolve. But for actually dissuading hard-to-
anticipate great power threats to vital interests, nuclear forces best
suited to deterrence will continue to be privileged by their strategic robustness. This consideration also suggests the link between the attractiveness of national nuclear deterrents and a fourth important feature of
the post–Cold War world, the increasing salience of economic considerations.

Economic Concerns. Aside from a change in its polarity, the post–
Cold War international system may well be distinguished from its
predecessor by increased levels of international economic competition.
At the end of the twentieth century such rivalry among the world's leading states has intensified and shows no signs of abating. But what is the
link between such rivalry and military affairs? After all, states seem to
have grasped the obsolescence of conquest as a useful means for en-
richment.[8] Although military action may at times still be necessary to
ensure the supply of key resources, for the most part the route to competitiveness and prosperity is understood to lie with domestic economic
development and mutually beneficial international trade and investment.[9] In such a world, states have strong incentives to pay close attention to the opportunity costs rather than the economic payoffs of high
levels of military spending. At the same time, however, states cannot

ever their default settings, with contingency plans prepared, retargeting modern nuclear weapons takes no more than a few hours, and perhaps as little as ten minutes.
See "A Symbol of Trust"; "New Policy Group Wants Ban on Nuclear Weapons."

[8]The sorry experiences of the great powers trying militarily to impose or maintain their control in parts of the developing world after the spread of nationalism has
clarified the costs of using force to seize and exploit a country that is rich in resources or otherwise economically attractive. In the developed world, the nature of
post-industrial economics has reduced the possibilities for and efficiency of tapping
the productivity of a conquered people. See Steven Van Evera, "Why Europe Matters,
Why the Third World Doesn't." John Mueller argued that the growing recognition
that "war doesn't pay" rendered great-power war itself obsolete after the mid-
twentieth century. Although critics have taken issue with Mueller's bold conclusion, and instead point to the influence of the nuclear revolution or bipolarity as contributing factors to the "long peace," such critics have rarely disputed his assertion
that historical experience has led modern states to focus on the costs, rather than
benefits, of war-fighting. See John Mueller, "The Essential Irrelevance of Nuclear
Weapons"; Robert Jervis, "The Political Effects of Nuclear Weapons"; Carl Kaysen,
"Is War Obsolete? A Review Essay"; John Lewis Gaddis, "The Long Peace." On circumstances in which war may yet pay, see Peter Liberman, "The Spoils of Conquest."

[9]See Richard N. Rosecrance, *The Rise of the Trading State.*

entirely ignore the possibility of threats to their vial interests. How can states sensibly manage this classic guns-butter tradeoff? Free-riding on allies for security is one way to lighten the burden of national invest-ment in military forces. But for reasons set forth above, the economic appeal of the free ride is limited by the riskiness of dependence on others in an anarchic world. National nuclear weapons enable states to satisfy basic security requirements self-reliantly and relatively economically. They are not cheap, but when married to deterrent doctrines nuclear weapons can dissuade even much more powerful adversaries without incurring the high costs of comparably effective conventional defenses. Moreover, where there is uncertainty about the source of threats (as may be the case for great powers in a multipolar world), the security dividends from investment in retargetable nuclear forces with a fairly simple punitive mission seem less volatile than those from investment in conventional forces designed to cope with scenarios whose content depends on the identity and capabilities of a particular adversary. In short, for states interested in focusing their attention and resources on nonmilitary concerns, yet still constrained to cope with the unavoidable uncertainties and insecurities of life under anarchy, national nuclear de-terrents will be economically attractive.[10]

The remainder of this chapter briefly examines the implications of changing polarity, anarchy, nuclear weapons technology, and height-ened sensitivity to economic concerns for the security policies of the ex-isting nuclear weapons states in the post–Cold War world, especially the three states on which this book has focused. The last chapter expands the focus to candidate nuclear states and then concludes by exploring some of the broader implications for international security in the twenty-first century.

[10]These economic considerations also reduce the chance that current nuclear states will move beyond prudent reductions and give up their weapons, disarmament rhetoric notwithstanding. Russian views, noted below, have explicitly highlighted the economic advantages of a nuclear rather than conventional emphasis (Fred Hiatt, "Russians Are Leaning Toward Nuclear Reliance for Security," p. A22). This mirrors the logic of the approach pushed by a cost-conscious Nikita Khrushchev in the late 1950s (Vladislav M. Zubok, "Khrushchev's 1960 Troop Cut"). In the 1990s, as the Russian economy failed to provide the resources to prevent the further deterioration of the army's capabilities, and as a more powerful NATO expanded eastward, the nuclear trump card seemed increasingly indispensable ("Russia Must Drop 'No-first-strike'—Moscow Official"; "Russia May Use Nuclear Weapons First in Self-de-fence"; "Russia Adopts 'Top Secret' Nuclear Document"; "Moscow Makes Crucial Decisions on Nuclear Defence").

EXISTING WEAPONS STATES

China, Britain, and France

In spite of widely differing domestic political circumstances and historical experiences, during the Cold War an interest in developing a robust but economically sound security policy to deal with a superpower adversary led China, Britain, and France each to emphasize a deterrent rather than a defensive strategy, and to rely on nuclear rather than conventional forces to fulfill the strategy's requirements.[11] What does their past experience suggest about their post–Cold War security policies?

The appeal of nuclear deterrence as the means to dissuade serious threats to China's, Britain's, and France's vital interests endures. For reasons outlined in Chapter 2, conventional deterrence (i.e., the threat to mount protracted popular resistance) has become no more appealing. A strategic shift to relying on conventional defense for security is a more plausible alternative. Its economic feasibility, however, depends on the scale of the threats that drive contingency planning. If the Russian successor to the Soviet state remains heavily armed and is perceived as at least a potentially formidable adversary whose importance can vary greatly with changeable intentions, exclusive reliance on conventional defenses will remain prohibitively expensive.[12] Britain and France, then, will continue to face a Russia with the ability (when politically cohesive and economically sound) to spend several times as much as they do on their military. China's principal security concern in

[11]Of course the fit among strategy, doctrine, and forces was never perfect. No state puts all its strategic eggs in one basket. However robust, no strategy is infallible. Leaders concerned with the irrationality of massive retaliation in the event of deterrence failure, therefore, prudently hedge their bets. In addition, domestic politics and powerful bureaucratic interests preclude the smooth translation of strategy into policy. Despite such perturbing influences, the strategic coherence displayed by these three states was impressive, especially compared with the multifaceted, arguably wasteful deployments of the Cold War's superpowers. On the concept of strategic coherence, see Barry Posen, *The Sources of Military Doctrine*.

[12]Implementation of the Conventional Forces in Europe Treaty, the creation of an Eastern European buffer of independent states after the revolutions of 1989, the collapse of the Warsaw Pact, and the rapid decay of the former Soviet/Russian military in the early and mid-1990s together shifted the balance of conventional power from East to West. Thus the difficulties of conventional defenses for Western Europeans derive more from fear of Russian potential than current capabilities. For an explanation of the way dramatic power shifts are at least in part a perceptual phenomenon, see William C. Wohlforth, "The Perception of Power"; Wohlforth, *The Elusive Balance*.

the post–Cold War world has shifted from a much weakened, if potentially strong, Russia to a still powerful, currently dominant United States whose military resource advantages will persist for decades, China's impressive record of economic expansion in the late twentieth century notwithstanding.[13]

For China, Britain, and France, the force requirements of a *robust* defensive strategy continue to weigh against placing full confidence in this option. Yet for each of these states a modest conventional defensive capability will, as ever, remain prudent. Backed by nuclear forces and the inhibiting risk of escalation they pose, even outgunned conventional defenses can mount resistance sufficient, as the French have most explicitly argued, to oblige the enemy to reveal his intentions. By maintaining a nuclear deterrent, the requirements for conventional forces that play a significant strategic role, what Schelling termed a "war-threatening" rather than a "war-winning" role, become more economical. To the extent the post–Cold War era is characterized by negotiated military disengagement and arms reductions in Central Europe and East Asia (a prospect that seemed to be diminishing at century's end), conventional forces filling this limited role would be less costly still. Increased distance and reduced forces mean more time for mobilization and greater opportunity to judge intentions. In any event, as long as the retaliatory capability of nuclear-armed states cannot be neutralized with certainty, even large changes in the qualitative and quantitative balance of conventional forces do not weaken their dissuasive effect when linked to the nuclear deterrent, somewhat easing the need for potentially expensive conventional countermeasures.

Dissuasion by nuclear deterrence, as noted above, remains attractive not only because it is affordable but also because it is strategically robust, especially with respect to changes in the source of threats. If

[13]See Avery Goldstein, "Great Expectations." Even the worst case scenarios implied by the Cox Committee report on Chinese military espionage released in May 1999 suggest a China with a few elements of a modern military rather than a genuine peer competitor of the U.S. possessing forces of comparable quantity and quality. It is, however, unnecessary for China to become a peer competitor in order to complicate U.S. policy in East Asia. Especially with possession of nuclear weapons, China needs only the ability to engage the U.S. military in ways that trigger fears of escalation to unacceptable damage (whose definition may, but need not, include attacks on American cities). See ibid. For the unclassified version of the Cox Committee report, see "The United States House of Representatives Select Committee on U.S. National Security and Military/Commercial Concerns with the People's Republic of China," available online at http://www.house.gov/coxreport/cont/gncont.html.

strategic alignments in the emerging post–Cold War world are destined to be more complex than they were in the bipolar era dominated by the Soviet and American superpowers, China, Britain, and France will continue to prize such robustness. Regardless of patterns of rivalry, in a world where information is inevitably incomplete, weapons of mass destruction clarify the risks for *any* prospective aggressor (including smaller states who may develop the ability to threaten the use of weapon of mass destruction) taking the first step down the road of military confrontation with a nuclear adversary. Given these enduring advantages, China, Britain, and France have all predictably displayed a strong determination to retain their national nuclear deterrents in the post–Cold War world, though the two European powers, with relatively sophisticated arsenals already in place and facing a much diminished Russia, have scaled back what were once highly ambitious modernization plans.

Britain. Britain's response to the end of the Soviet menace has been to plan for a reduction in the size of the nuclear arsenal it will field into the early twenty-first century, without abandoning its commitment to an independent deterrent capability as a sensible way to hedge against unpredictable future threats to the country's vital interests.[14] This doctrinal preference was consistently articulated in the 1990s in terms such as those used at a November 1995 Commonwealth summit when the British delegation refused to endorse a resolution criticizing France's resumption of nuclear testing in the South Pacific.

> [N]uclear deterrence has preserved security and stability over the past half-century. . . . Until security can be assured by other means, and the threat of proliferation removed, it is essential to maintain effective nu-

[14]On British recognition of the value of a national nuclear arsenal as a hedge against an uncertain future, see John Baylis, *British Defense Policy*, p. 121. While the Cold War drew to a close, British Prime Minister Thatcher rejected arguments for the denuclearization of Europe by noting that history had taught that "conventional weapons do not deter war" and that there was "no substitute" for nuclear weapons as a deterrent to war ("No Substitute for Nuclear Weapons as Deterrence, Says Thatcher"). The Liberal Democrats called for deep cuts in military spending, "but reaffirmed their commitment to an independent nuclear deterrent" because it served "as an insurance against the possibility of nuclear blackmail" (Alan Travis, "UK: Defence Spending Could Be Halved Under Liberal Democrats," p. 2). On October 5, 1995, the Labor Party voted to support retention of the Trident-based nuclear deterrent ("U.K. Labor Party Votes to Keep Nuclear Deterrent"). During the campaign leading up to the British elections in spring 1997, Labor reiterated its support for the national nuclear deterrent (Paul Majendie, "UK's Labour Promises Defence Review But No Cuts").

clear deterrence. The existing nuclear powers should take the decisions necessary to achieve this.[15]

Though maintaining its long-standing strategic emphasis on deterrence, Britain's posture has not reflected an obstinate refusal to adjust forces in light of the circumstances of a transformed world. On the contrary, as it soon became clear that a changing international landscape had rendered the initial, modest post–Cold War review (the July 1990 "Options for Change") obsolete, London announced more dramatic military cuts in a July 1993 Defence White Paper.[16] With regard to nuclear forces, the requirements for deterrence were amended in response to altered beliefs about the nature of plausible threats. Though adhering to the plan for four Trident II (Vanguard-class) submarines as the backbone of the national deterrent, Defense Minister Rifkind announced in November 1993 that each boat would not be fitted with the maximum number of warheads their 16 D-5 missiles could carry, but instead would be fitted with no more than a total of 96 warheads and would carry only about the same aggregate explosive yield as the Polaris SSBNs they were replacing.[17] In addition, the sea-based deterrent would fully assume the strategic role it had shared with the air force, as the RAF phased out its WE-177 nuclear free-fall bombs by 1998 and the third Vanguard-class SSBN entered service. Limited warhead-loading together

---

[15]"Britain Angered by Nuclear Test Criticism." See also relevant comments by Prime Minister John Major about the "dangers as well as opportunities" the post–Cold War world presents ("Major Stresses Need of Britain's Nuclear Shield").

[16]Colin Brown, "Navy Bears Brunt of Cuts as Four Submarines Are Axed." Britain also reduced and restructured its conventional forces, notably developing a "Joint Rapid Deployment Force to be drawn from the army, navy, marines and air force" designed to deal with regional contingencies that fall short of threats to vital interests that could be covered by the threat of nuclear escalation ("Britain Announces New Rapid Deployment Force").

[17]Nevertheless, the Trident fleet offers substantial advantages beyond an obvious potential for uploading more warheads should that ever be deemed necessary. Target coverage will be improved as the multiple 150 KT warheads on the Trident can be independently aimed, whereas the cluster of three 200 KT Chevaline warheads on the Polaris would have been dedicated to a single target (Stewart M. Powell, "Britain's Defense Shakeup," p. 50; David Shaw, "Trident Cut 'Won't Harm Our Defences,'" p. 14; Michael White and David Fairhall, "Rifkind Set to Cut Trident Firepower," p. 2). In addition, the Trident, unlike Polaris, can launch its missiles while berthed (Charles Miller, "Reduced Trident Will Still Have Muscle"; James McKillop, "UK: Rifkind to Cut Trident Power as Treasury Wins Price War," p. 2; "Rifkind Maintains Right to Use Nuclear Weapons First"). On August 28, 1996, Britain removed the last of its four Polaris submarines from service. The sea-based nuclear deterrent role thereafter was filled by two Tridents in service, with the final two in the pipeline ("Britain Decommissions Last Polaris Sub").

with improved accuracy would enable the Trident D-5 missile to fulfill both "strategic and substrategic [theater and tactical] nuclear roles."[18]

These changes reflected a recognition that the unexpected collapse of the Soviet Union had greatly diminished the importance of the Trident modernization program's original purpose—"to provide Britain with ultimate insurance [against the Soviet threat] should America ever 'decouple' from Europe." Nevertheless, the perceived need for an independent nuclear deterrent endured. London insisted on maintaining an ability to deal with the risk that the intentions of the existing nuclear great powers (i.e., Russia) might shift over time, as well as the prospective challenge posed by hostile "rogue" states that might develop the means to threaten Britain with chemical, biological, or nuclear weapons. In the early post–Cold War period the United States' willingness to stand with its allies and continue to play a leading role was reassuring, as was the continuing broad international support for the nonproliferation regime. Because there could be no guarantee that such favorable conditions would persist, however, the need for Britain's independent deterrent remained.[19] Cooperation with the United States, and potentially with France, to save on the expense of maintaining a viable nuclear delivery system was still desirable, as were steps to negotiate arms control agreements such as the indefinite extension of the Nuclear Nonproliferation Treaty in April 1995 and the Comprehensive Test Ban Treaty in September 1996 that might slow the horizontal proliferation of nuclear weapons and limit the risks of accidental or inadvertent use. But Britain remained committed to ensuring its ability to field a punitive nuclear force under its own command and refused to embrace the growing anti-nuclear sentiment for diplomatic measures such as a "no-first-use" pledge that might weaken the dissuasiveness of the horrifying

[18]Britain could thus save a projected 2.3 billion dollars by forgoing the planned Tactical Air-to-Surface Missile that had been planned as a standoff replacement for the gravity bombs in the next century ("Farewell WE117: Royal Air Force Jettisons Its Nuclear Capability Ahead of Schedule," p. 9; Charles Miller, "Reduced Trident Will Still Have Muscle"; Jill Sherman and Michael Evans, "Major Faces Battle over Defence Cuts"; "Britain to Scrap Airborne Nuclear Missile"; "Defense Budget: RAF to Lose Tactical Missile—and Its Nuclear Role," p. 4; "Britain to End Air Force's Nuclear Punch by 1998"; Ben Webb, "No Clear Deterrent; United Kingdom's Nuclear Weapons," p. 20).

[19]"Trident's Future." Britain's initial unhappiness with the Clinton administration's decision to extend the moratorium on nuclear testing while working toward renewal of the Nonproliferation Treaty and a Comprehensive Test Ban Treaty may have reflected London's desire for further testing to develop warheads better suited to the variety of anticipated post–Cold War world missions (Alexander MacLeod, "Clinton's Stay of Nuclear Tests Irks Britain," p. 3).

uncertainty any adversary who threatened the nation's vital interests would have to confront.[20]

France. France's nuclear adjustment to the post–Cold War era, though broadly similar to Britain's, was distinguished by the sometimes costly legacy of its traditional determination for greater autonomy in security affairs. Like Britain, France did not waver in its belief in the usefulness of dissuasion by nuclear deterrence as the ultimate guarantee of the nation's vital interests in a changed, but still unpredictably dangerous, world. Despite domestic disagreements about the specific forces and precise wording of strategic doctrine, the commitment to maintaining an independent French nuclear force remained clear.[21] The national deterrent was needed, as ever, not only because "[t]he situation of the weak versus the strong still exists," but also because of the potential threat posed by new nuclear powers.[22] And the basic understanding that dissuasion by deterrence required an ability to launch punitive, countervalue strikes remained firm in the 1994 Defense White Paper, the first France had produced since 1972, though the collapse of the Soviet empire encouraged some adjustments in force structure. Arguments for shifting to an arsenal that could carry out selective, limited, nuclear counterforce strikes were rejected in favor of retaining an ability for horrific retaliation against those who might jeopardize the country's "vital interests, whatever the origin and the form of the threat."[23] In short, broad consensus about the importance of maintaining France's independent deterrent endured in the first decade of the post–Cold War era.

[20]For an early review of Britain's perspective on the prospects for its nuclear deterrent in the post–Cold War world, see Michael Quinlan, "British Nuclear Weapons Policy"; also "Rifkind Maintains Right to Use Nuclear Weapons First."

[21]For a thorough discussion of the often subtle differences of French elite opinion on appropriate nuclear forces and doctrine in the post–Cold War world, see David S. Yost, "Nuclear Weapons Issues in France." Despite criticisms of French non-nuclear capabilities on display during Operation Desert Storm, French President Mitterrand rejected any reallocation of resources that would compromise the continued viability of his country's nuclear deterrent (Alan Riding, "France Concedes Its Faults in War," p. A17).

[22]Defense Minister François Leotard quoted in "French Defense Minister Calls Nuclear Tests Indispensable."

[23]Emmanuel Jarry, "France to Signal Change in Defence Priorities—Sources"; "French Defence White Paper Vague on Nuclear Deterrent." Reaffirming this position at the time of President Chirac's defense review in March 1996, General Jean-Philippe Douin stated that "France's nuclear weapons will be terrifying, massive. . . . They are and must remain weapons that will not be used. If they should become precise and flexible weapons, deterrence would be dead" (cited in "French General Wants French-British Nuclear Ties").

More controversial were France's modernization plans for the *force de frappe* and the related matter of participation in a nuclear weapons test ban. Because France had not explicitly piggy-backed on the nuclear weapons testing program of the United States as had Britain, a decision to forgo additional testing and adhere to the voluntary moratorium announced by President François Mitterrand in April 1992 would have tightly constrained the country's options for deploying new nuclear weapons systems that were on the drawing boards at the end of the Cold War. It might also have required greater dependence on others for technologies to ensure the safety and reliability of existing weapons as they aged. As such, the testing moratorium was inconsistent with the strategic program Mitterrand himself had established for France in the post–Cold War world. Mitterrand had insisted that even in the new era, "[t]he defense of France continues to essentially rely on its atomic force . . . ,"[24] that France would "do what is necessary to keep its nuclear deterrent,"[25] that "nuclear deterrence was at the heart of France's defence and that there was no reason this should change."[26] The difficulty of trumpeting this strategic posture while embracing the moratorium led to pressures to resume testing from conservative politicians (including Jacques Chirac prior to his election as President) and military advisers to Mitterrand who believed in the necessity for a final series of tests prior to France's agreeing to the proposed Comprehensive Nuclear Test Ban Treaty.[27] Mitterrand tried to reconcile his ostensibly conflicting positions by adhering to the moratorium while calling for increased expenditures to perfect simulation techniques that might preclude the need for any more tests. Yet military analysts insisted that more tests were needed, partly in order to master the simulation alternative.[28] Against this background, President Mitterrand's refusal to authorize tests at the end of his term looked like the luxury of a lame duck who could pass the final decision on to his successor. With Jacques Chirac's election as

[24]Eduardo Cue, "Mitterrand Says French Defense Rests on Atomic Bomb."
[25]"France Says Will Maintain Nuclear Deterrent."
[26]"No Europe Nuclear Force This Century."
[27]Prime Minister Edouard Balladur bluntly stated, ". . . we will not sign any definitive test ban as long as we have the feeling that these tests are indispensable to the technical credibility of our nuclear effort" ("France Will Not Sign Nuclear Ban If It Needs Tests"; see also statement by Jacques Chirac in "France Needs Up to 20 More Nuclear Tests—Chirac").
[28]"Mitterrand Predicts Successors Won't Resume N-tests"; "French Defense Minister Calls Nuclear Tests Indispensable"; "France Says Will Maintain Nuclear Deterrent."

president, approval of the military's recommendation for resuming tests in the South Pacific was only a matter of time.

In May 1995, Prime Minister Edouard Balladur provided the justification for what was correctly expected to be a highly controversial decision. Prior to the anticipated conclusion of a Comprehensive Test Ban Treaty during 1996, France would conduct a limited number of tests in order to help perfect simulation technology and to ensure the continued viability of its deterrent.[29] With regard to the latter purpose, the tests would be designed to verify the reliability of weapons detonators and to complete the development of the TN75 warhead for France's newest SLBM.[30] On June 13, 1995, President Chirac announced the country's final nuclear tests, what turned out to be a series of six explosions that took place between September 5, 1995, and January 27, 1996. The international reaction was harshly critical, including riots in Tahiti, diplomatic protests, and calls for retaliatory consumer boycotts of French products. Chirac nevertheless refused to terminate the testing before it had accomplished its key objectives, though he may have pressured the military to find ways to speed up the process and gather the necessary data in fewer tests than originally scheduled. Whatever the short-term political price (again suggesting the priority of security over prestige considerations) the tests accomplished their strategic purpose, setting the stage for France to modernize its national nuclear deterrent while living within the constraints of a comprehensive test ban.[31] According to Jacques Bouchard, head of the military department of the French Atomic Energy Center, the tests' success verified the reliability of the arsenal's detonators, produced the data necessary for confidence in labo-

[29]Premier Balladur also announced that France would build a laser at the Center for Scientific and Technical studies in southwestern France to permit the design of nuclear weapons without testing ("French to Build Laser to Test Nuclear Weapon").

[30]"France Likely to Need More Nuclear Tests—Balladur"; "French Minister Says Experts Want Nuclear Tests."

[31]If Chirac calculated that the storm of protest would have limited lasting effects, he seems to have guessed right. By mid-spring 1996, the process of fence-mending was well under way, and even within French Polynesia the testing controversy was overshadowed by other issues in local elections. See "More Than 60 Percent Turn Out to Vote in Polynesian Elections"; "France Mends Fences with EU Nuclear Critics." And despite Australia's prominent role as a critic of French testing, aside from symbolic boycotts of "some high-profile goods like wine," Franco-Australian trade actually increased. By late summer 1996, the two countries' foreign ministers were meeting to announce that the matter was being put behind them (François Raitberger, "Australia, France Patch Up Nuclear Dispute"; Bernard Edinger, "Australia, France Bury Nuclear Test Hatchet").

ratory simulation in nuclear weapons research, and certified the TN75 warhead for the new generation of French SLBMs.[32] President Chirac claimed that the effort had provided information that would guarantee the country's nuclear deterrent for the next half-century.[33]

The test results engendered the confidence in capabilities that enabled the government to move ahead with steps designed to reverse some of the reputational damage testing had caused. Paris not only confirmed its commitment to join a test-ban regime, but also indicated it would cease producing fissile material and, perhaps of greatest symbolic value, dismantle the land-based leg of its strategic triad.[34] The decision to decommission rather than modernize the 18 S3D IRBMs on the Albion Plateau was part of the adjustment of France's nuclear modernization program to the reality of the post–Cold War world.[35] In a less threatening strategic environment, pressures for the reallocation of resources to nonmilitary purposes were strong. Given the indisputable survivability advantages of sea-based forces and the greater flexibility of sophisticated air-launched missiles, the heavy investment required to ensure the viability of land-based ballistic missiles seemed wasteful rather than sensibly redundant.[36] Instead, consistent with the government's determination to maintain nuclear deterrence as the keystone of

[32]"French Expert Calls Nuclear Tests a Success"; Craig R. Whitney, "France Ending Nuclear Tests That Caused Broad Protests," pp. A1, A4.

[33]"France to Reduce Nuclear Forces."

[34]"France to Scrap Land-Based N-Missiles in September." The missiles remained on 24-hour alert until they were deactivated on September 16, 1996, after which dismantlement began. See "France Shuts Down Nuclear Missile Base This Month"; Thierry Cayol, "Nuclear Silos Empty at Last," p. 13.

[35]A streamlined modernization program was announced by President Chirac in February 1996. For a summary of its significance, see J. A. C. Lewis, "All Change for France," pp. 19ff.

[36]In 1990 Defense Minister Jean-Pierre Chevenement had foreshadowed this decision as France began its review of force requirements in the post–Cold War world when he indicated that across the board modernization was too expensive in the new strategic environment, and that the sensible approach was to invest in new SSBNs and a longer-range air-to-surface missile (Giovanni De Briganti, "Chevenement Indicates French Likely to Scrap Land-Based Nuclear Weapons," p. 5). The shift to a strategic dyad was, however, politically sensitive and proceeded in stages, successively abandoning the idea of a rail- or road-mobile delivery system, then the idea of a distinct MIRVed warhead for the IRBMs, then the idea of dual-use warhead for the land- and sea-based forces, and finally the idea of retaining the forces in any form. See "France: Defence Minister Speaks of Terrestrial Version of New M5 Missile," p. 13; "French Halt Study Work on S45 Nuclear Missile," p. 28; Peter B. De Selding, "France Halts Development of S45 Nuclear Missile," p. 1; Alan Riding, "France Drops Plans to Build New Nuclear Missile System," p. A6; "France Halts Update of Mobile Land-based Missile."

its security policy in an uncertain world, the remaining two legs of the strategic forces would be modernized, though in a fashion consistent with the more relaxed post–Cold War international environment.[37] The alert level of the Mirage-IVs was reduced and as their service life came to an end, their role would be assumed by the Mirage 2000N, whose shorter range would be offset by mid-air refueling and increasing the range of the standoff, air-to-surface nuclear missiles (ASMP) they would carry.[38] Early in the next century it had been expected that the new Rafale fighter equipped with superior ASLP missiles would offer a system better designed for the wider variety of possible threats against which nuclear deterrence might be needed, in particular the prospect of Third World states possessing nuclear, biological, or chemical weapons and the means for delivering them. Though arguably a more fruitful investment than modernization of the IRBM force, the Rafale-ASLP costs were steep, and France had clearly hoped that the expense could be minimized by joint development with Britain, hopes that London ultimately dashed.[39] Nevertheless, reflecting the high priority assigned to maintaining a robust nuclear deterrent within the tighter budgetary constraints the military faced in the post–Cold War world, Paris decided to move forward with the Rafale despite its cost, but opted for an extended-range version of the ASMP (the ASMP+) instead of also shouldering the development costs of the new ASLP cruise missile.[40]

[37]The mission once served by the "pre-strategic" or tactical shorter-range nuclear forces, providing a final warning of imminent strategic nuclear retaliation to an adversary advancing through Germany, had disappeared. At first these missiles were withdrawn from service and plans to deploy a new generation replacement were put on hold; by 1996 it was determined that the short-range forces would simply be dismantled (Robert Norris, Andrew Burrows, and Richard Fieldhouse, *British, French, and Chinese Nuclear Weapons*, pp. 224–25; Julian Nundy, "Hades Missiles Go Into the Cold," p. 11; Paul Webster, "France Nods to Germany and Scraps Hades Missile," p. 10; Joseph Fitchett, "Paris Drops Short-Range Missile"; J. A. C. Lewis, "France to Trim Nuclear Forces, End Conscription," pp. 4ff; J. A. C. Lewis, "All Change for France").

[38]"France to Replace Aging N-bombers."

[39]Giovanni De Briganti, "Britain Ponders Missile Choices," p. 3.

[40]See J. A. C. Lewis, "All Change for France." The Rafale-M is slated to take over the small carrier-based nuclear mission currently assigned the Super-Etendard aircraft. In addition to serving as a deterrent against regional adversaries with weapons of mass destruction, these aircraft could also provide the prestrategic or tactical capability forfeited with the retirement of short-range land-based nuclear missiles. See David Foxwell, "France Weighs Up the Global Price," p. 30. On May 13, 1996, the French cabinet approved a military spending plan for 1997–2002 that made broad cuts even deeper than those envisaged in the early 1990s. It called for ending conscription and cutting troop levels from 500,000 to 350,000 by 2002. Though modernization necessary to support the goal of an improved rapid deployment conven-

The submarine modernization program and the development of a new generation of missiles and warheads to enable this leg of the French deterrent to play its role as backbone of the *force de frappe* proved least susceptible, though not immune, to the pressures for adjustment in the post–Cold War world. In addition to reducing alert levels so that two rather than three SSBNs would be on patrol at any given time, France cut back the projected size of the new Triomphant-class force from six to four, and reduced the planned warhead loading of the missiles, as had Britain, so that there would be little change in the total number of warheads the fleet carries after modernization.[41] But within these limits the modernization program steadily advanced. In addition to the development and testing of the TN75 warhead discussed above, the M45 missile designated to replace the M4 was successfully tested on land in November 1993 and June 1994, at sea in February 1995, and entered service in 1997. While seeking ways to economize on the M45 program, France also moved ahead with the M51 replacement to be phased in beginning in 2008.[42]

Along with changes in the planned composition of France's nuclear arsenal for the twenty-first century, economic pressures and the shifting international political landscape also prompted Paris to make some adjustments in its long-standing practice of minimizing formal military cooperation with its major allies. Three steps were most relevant to the topics covered in this book. First, France moved in the direction of offering to provide a nuclear umbrella to Germany as part of a European policy of "concerted deterrence." Though such professions of good faith marked a change in permissible rhetoric, their real significance is open to question inasmuch as French President Mitterrand also asserted that a joint European nuclear force was unlikely before the next century, and that "[a] nuclear deterrent is difficult to share by its very nature. Before we can talk about a European deterrent, we would have to find common interests."[43] Such ambiguity may not be problematic in a low-threat en-

---

tional capability would proceed, the projected numbers of tanks, planes, helicopters, and artillery were reduced, and the deployment of a second new aircraft carrier was postponed ("French Cabinet Backs Cuts in Defence Budget").

[41]Norris, Burrows, and Fieldhouse, *British, French, and Chinese Nuclear Weapons*, p. 258. By 2003, four submarines should be armed with sixteen M45 SLBMs each capable of delivering its six TN75 warheads at a range of 6,000 kilometers ("France Succeeds in Test-firing New Nuclear Missile").

[42]See J. A. C. Lewis, "France Makes $7b Savings on Projects," p. 4; J. A. C. Lewis, "All Change for France."

[43]"No Europe Nuclear Force This Century"; "France Offers Germany Security"; "Mitterrand Predicts Successors Won't Resume N-tests."

vironment where "cheap talk" can thrive. In more dangerous circumstances, the complementary fears of abandonment and entrapment would challenge both Paris and Berlin to consider the durability of their "common interests." Nevertheless, consultations between France and Germany continued as part of an attempt to work toward a "common nuclear dimension to European defense policy" in which Paris would publicly assert that its deterrent umbrella covered Germany because the two countries' "security interests had become 'inseparable'."[44] In late January 1997, France's media disclosed a December 9, 1996, agreement between France and Germany that restated the closeness of the two countries' strategic interests and the usefulness of France's nuclear deterrent as a supplement to the U.S. extended deterrent guarantee for NATO countries. Despite the dramatic changes in Europe's security environment, this revelation still provoked an outcry in France about a compromise of national independence that recalled the hostile reception in the 1970s to President Giscard d'Estaing's similarly expansive views of France's vital interests.[45]

A second policy adjustment was the effort toward, as British Prime Minister Major put it, "deepening [Franco-British] nuclear cooperation." Such cooperation aims at "strengthening deterrence" and economizing on weapons costs in a post–Cold War world of uncertain threats and tightened budget constraints, "while retaining the independence of our nuclear forces."[46] Britain's decision not to share in the development of the Rafale fighter, though a setback, did not terminate all such cooperation; bilateral agreements were reached to share SSBN technology in ways that should help hold down costs in maintaining these most crucial, but expensive, delivery systems.[47]

---

[44]Craig R. Whitney, "France and Germany to Discuss Joint Nuclear Deterrent," p. 3.

[45]"France, Germany Set Crisis, Nuclear Talks-Paper"; "Franco-German Defense Plan Helps NATO, Minister"; Emmanuel Jarry, "France Denies Changing Nuclear Doctrine"; Jarry, "French Left Charges Defence Sell-out to U.S., NATO."

[46]"France-Britain Deepen Nuclear Cooperation—Major"; Kevin Brown and Bruce Clark, "UK Agrees N-pact with France," p. 1.

[47]In one of the stranger stories on this cooperation, the newspaper *Liberation* reported that "French military sources" indicated a U.S. spyplane overflew French military installations, possibly to track a convoy that "may have been components of nuclear warheads for use on Trident missiles on British submarines, which Washington has refused to deliver to London." U.S. and French officials denied the story ("Paris, US Deny U2 Plane Made Spy Mission"). There were also allegations (denied) that France had shared with London data from its controversial final series of nuclear tests in the South Pacific (Christopher Bellamy, "Chirac Overhauls Missile Arsenal," p. 13).

A third change was France's modification of its long-standing formal aloofness from NATO's military planning. Although as noted in Chapter 6, France had engaged in more or less covert cooperation with its NATO partners even after its 1966 partial disengagement, on December 5, 1995, Paris announced that it was prepared to rejoin the alliance's Military Committee. This policy shift was tantamount to acknowledging the reality of the country's dependence on joint efforts for NATO's conventional operations, such as in Bosnia (and later Kosovo).[48] At the same time French officials adamantly refused to alter their relatively independent stance on nuclear operations, agreeing only to discuss nuclear issues without rejoining NATO's Nuclear Planning Group. As European Affairs Minister Michel Barnier noted in his clarifying statement, "If our European partners want to engage in a dialogue within the Atlantic alliance on nuclear dissuasion, we are ready to participate. . . . [But] France has never proposed entering a debate in the Nuclear Planning Group, or even less of participating in any decision on the planning of (French) nuclear forces."[49] Whatever the political ramifications of shifting French attitudes toward NATO may be, they do not yet suggest any meaningful change in the country's determination to hedge against future uncertainty by retaining the self-reliant option that a national nuclear deterrent provides.[50]

[48]Roger Cohen, "France to Rejoin Military Command of NATO Alliance." On June 3, 1996, NATO foreign ministers agreed to plans that would give the Western European Union the ability to use NATO "assets in European-led military operations in regional crises even when the U.S. did not become involved." One week later President Chirac announced "that France would rejoin all the military structures of NATO from which it pulled out in 1966 if the alliance's decision . . . to give European countries a stronger leadership role was fully carried out" (Craig R. Whitney, "After NATO Overtures, France Is Ready to Resume Military Role," p. 8). The adjustment in transatlantic relations is consistent with both closer Franco-American ties as well as greater independence from the United States for France within the context of working together with its European partners. Yet the reintegration of France into NATO's military command structure has been marked by disagreements over the extent of continued U.S. dominance, reflected most publicly in France's urging that the United States give up control of the alliance's southern command in Naples (Whitney, "France and Germany to Discuss Joint Nuclear Deterrent," p. 13). During Secretary of State Madeline Albright's visit to Europe in February 1997, President Chirac made clear that unless the dispute over U.S. dominance of the commands was resolved, France would not rejoin NATO's military structure, though the matter might be reconsidered in the future (Craig R. Whitney, "Delay Seen in Restoring NATO Role for France," p. 4).

[49]"France Tightens Military Ties with NATO."

[50]Still, the decision to be a more cooperative NATO partner facilitated a nuclear-sharing agreement with the United States signed in June 1996. The pact will ease the transition to a world under the CTBT, in which ensuring the reliability and moderni-

China. In the aftermath of the Soviet empire's decline and col-lapse, China faced its most benign international security environment in many decades. Nonetheless, Beijing soon began to worry about the possibility of new dangers.[51] With the deterioration in Sino-American relations following the crackdown on China's democracy movement in June 1989, and then the breathtaking demonstration of the superiority of American military technology in the Persian Gulf War of 1991, Bei-jing became concerned that a United States no longer constrained by the need to cope with a superpower rival might flex its international muscle in ways that conflicted with China's interests. Divisive issues (includ-ing differing perspectives on regional security, human rights, and inter-national economic arrangements) previously overshadowed by the common interest in opposing the Soviet Union during the 1970s and 1980s seemed bound to resurface after the Cold War. In addition, with the disappearance of the unifying Soviet threat, China expected Japa-nese-American relations to be more seriously tested and initially wor-ried that conflicting interests could eventually result in the reemer-gence of a more fully armed, activist Japan. When such Japanese-American tensions failed to emerge and the allies instead successfully updated their security arrangements for a post-Soviet East Asia, China then worried that it had become the new adversary binding Tokyo and Washington.[52]

In the initially benign early post–Cold War period, however, Beijing saw an opportunity to relax the pace of its investment in an already vi-able, if crude, nuclear deterrent force designed to cope with superpower threats and, as suggested by Defense Minister Zhang Aiping in 1987, at-tend to the modernization of China's long shortchanged conventional forces.[53] Because of the resource constraints on China's military budgets during the Cold War, as well as the technological and ideological handi-caps of the Maoist era, the PRC, unlike Britain and France, had been left without much of a prudent conventional supplement to its small but terrifying nuclear deterrent. Thus, as Beijing set out to cope with the uncertainties of the emerging new world order, it began to tap a more rapidly expanding economy to fund a military establishment that would

---

zation of weapons must take place without nuclear testing ("France Confirms U.S. Nuclear Data-Sharing Pact").

[51]These views were already being articulated in April and May 1991 by Chinese civilian and military analysts with whom I spoke.

[52]See Thomas J. Christensen, "Chinese Realpolitik"; Christensen, "China, the U.S.-Japan Alliance, and the Security Dilemma in East Asia."

[53]"PLA Marching Towards Modernization: Zhang Aiping."

better enable China to use its PLA for offensive power projection as well as defensive maneuvers against regional rivals in Asia.

A decade of events beginning as the Cold War wound down served to reinforce Beijing's belief in the need for more "mobile, quick reaction, ground, air and naval forces capable of conducting sustained, limited operations along and beyond national frontiers."[54] In March 1988, the Chinese military clashed with Vietnamese naval units in the Spratly Islands, triggering greater attention to the potential for armed force to play a role in what became a recurrently salient multilateral dispute over sovereign claims to territory and resource rights in the South China Sea.[55] Early in 1991 the startling display of the advanced West's qualitative military superiority in Operation Desert Storm clarified the price that could be paid in modern combat if a country failed to keep pace with the technological revolutions in conventional capabilities.[56] And in the summer of 1995 and early 1996, tensions with Taiwan and the United States over Chinese prerogatives with respect to the resolution of the island's status resurfaced. The Taiwan Straits confrontation provided an opportunity for the PLA to demonstrate the first fruits of its modernization drive during the Dengist era (especially improved rocketry that might facilitate coercive bombing to intimidate the Taiwanese or their trading partners). But it also drew attention to the enduring shortcomings of China's conventional power projection capabilities (amphibious assault, air and sea forces) even within the country's immediate vicinity.[57]

[54]Tai Ming Cheung, "Beijing Puts Priority Back on PLA," pp. 20ff.

[55]Guy Dinmore, "China's Military Shakes Up for Regional Conflicts." For a summary of China's approach to resolving these disputes, see Gerald Segal, "East Asia and the 'Constrainment' of China"; also Michael G. Gallagher, "China's Illusory Threat to the South China Sea"; Denny Roy, "Hegemon on the Horizon?"; Goldstein, "Great Expectations."

[56]Sheryl WuDunn, "After the War," p. A13.

[57]See "Report Raps China Military." Despite overwhelming quantitative advantages, the severe qualitative disadvantages of China's military when compared with Taiwan's would have prevented Beijing from establishing the air and naval superiority an assault required. Such superiority would have been essential to transport the 300,000 troops allegedly necessary for successful invasion, since China had the ability to transport only about 30,000 troops at a time (Peter Slevin, "China Could Not Easily Overwhelm Taiwan, Analysts Agree," p. A4). To deal with this and other challenges, China has adopted a long-range plan to develop its navy. The plan is to gradually transform an essentially coastal force into a "green-water" fleet (i.e., a regional force able to project power roughly 1,000 nautical miles, out to what the Chinese label the first island chain) by 2000, and then to develop a blue-water fleet (able to operate out to the "second island chain," essentially the entire Western Pacific) by 2020, and finally a genuinely global navy by 2050. See John Downing, "China's

Early in the post–Cold War period, then, a more prosperous China that was attending to a broader range of security interests began to invest in the military assets it needed for contingencies short of great power crisis and war—lingering irredentist claims and territorial disputes as well as growing international commercial interests that demanded some attention to the emerging task of protecting vital sea-lanes. Yet, however impressive the economic strides made since the abandonment of the failed Maoist development model in the late 1970s, for the foreseeable future China would remain at a financial and technological disadvantage relative to the other great powers and candidate great powers of the post–Cold War world.[58] Thus, to be prepared to deal with the remote, but potentially most important, contingency of confrontation with such states, China had to ensure the continued viability of its strategic ace in the hole, its frightening nuclear retaliatory force.

Beijing's determination to maintain its nuclear deterrent as the ultimate guarantee of national security against possibly serious external

---

Evolving Maritime Strategy, Part 1," pp. 129–30. On China's power projection capabilities, see also Paul H. B. Godwin, "Force Projection and China's National Military Strategy"; Godwin, "From Continent to Periphery"; Chong-Pin Lin, "The Power Projection Capabilities of the People's Liberation Army"; Lin, "The Military Balance in the Taiwan Straits"; Goldstein, "Great Expectations."

[58]Even compared to Russia. To improve its air forces during the 1990s China began to import, and planned to co-produce, Soviet fighters (Su-27s) based on upgraded 1970s technology. Although marking a vast improvement in Chinese airpower dominated by 1950s era technology, the limited modernization in this and other areas is indicative of the great gap between China's PLA and other world-class conventional military forces. See Goldstein, "Great Expectations"; Julia A. Ackerman and Michael Collins Dunn, "Chinese Airpower Revs Up," pp. 56ff. During the 1990s China's military budget registered relatively large increases, partly to ensure the political support of the PLA for the communist regime, but partly to continue the daunting long-term task of modernizing China's armed forces in a changing, uncertain post–Cold War security environment in East Asia. See "Asian News: China's Defense Budget to Increase 15 PC"; also comments by CIA director of East Asian Analysis, Martin Petersen, in "Chinese Defense Spending on the Rise: CIA." Estimates on China's expanding defense budgets range from the officially announced $8.4 billion to the World Bank's high-end $52 billion. See also Philippe Massonet, "Exercises Point to True Size of China's Military Budget, Say Experts"; Michael Richardson, "China's Secretive Arms Buildup Is Making Asian Neighbors Jittery." Cf. Shaoguang Wang, "Estimating China's Defence Expenditure." Whatever its exact level, military spending is likely to remain high as Beijing invests in the expensive technologies essential to managing modern military forces, especially advanced electronics for command and control. For example, Zhou Deqiang, Vice-Minister of Posts and Telecommunications, announced a plan to spend $43 billion over five years on items such as satellites, ground mobile receivers, digital microwave and program-controlled switching systems ("China Sketches Out Defense Telecom Network").

military threats has been reflected in the modernization plans designed
to ensure China will have the warheads and delivery systems sufficient
for creating the fear of retaliation in the mind of the most capable adversary. As Deng Xiaoping put it to his colleagues, China's security required that the regime continue developing modern weapons, "including . . . a certain quantity of advanced nuclear weapons."[59] This strategic
requirement shaped not only procurement decisions described below
but also China's evolving position on international arms control and
provided strong incentives for learning as much as possible about leading edge technology by whatever means necessary.[60] During the 1990s
the PRC persisted with a testing program designed to yield a new generation of Chinese strategic forces for the twenty-first century even as it
adhered to its traditional rhetoric of no-first-use pledges and a call for
the abolition of all nuclear weapons.[61] Like the other acknowledged nuclear powers, the PRC agreed to participate in negotiations aimed at
producing a treaty banning nuclear warhead testing. But for a time
China hesitated in joining the voluntary pre-treaty moratorium, noting
that compared with the other four weapons states it had engaged in
much less testing. Such abstinence would have made it difficult for
China to complete its plan to deploy a new generation of more advanced
ballistic missile warheads and to master the computer simulation techniques that would enable Beijing to have confidence in the viability of
its nuclear arsenal under a nontesting regime.[62] Consequently, like

[59]Meng Lin, "Deng Xiaoping Reportedly Comments on Relations with the
United States," p. 41. As Chinese analysts noted, despite deep cuts in the super-
power arsenals, the world has not yet entered a new "nonnuclear era" (Hu Wenlong,
Zha Jinlu et al., eds., *Xiandai Junbingzhong Zhanshu*, p. 244).

[60]The Cox Committee Report the U.S. Congress released in May 1999 alleges
that China obtained significant information from a well-organized espionage program in the United States. Unclear is the extent to which China acquired militarily
useful know-how and hardware from open sources (academic and commercial) as
opposed to classified sources. Also unclear is the extent to which China has been
able to exploit such materials to accelerate a modernization program that proceeds at
a very measured pace. For the unclassified version of the report, see http://www.
house.gov/coxreport/cont/gncont.html. For a declassified U.S. Defense Intelligence
Agency report from 1984 that anticipated China's exploitation of American technology in its modernization program, see "Defense Estimative Brief: Nuclear Weapons
Systems in China," Apr. 24, 1984.

[61]China's representative to the preparatory conference for renewing the Nuclear
Non-proliferation Treaty, Sha Zukang, argued that in the post–Cold War era, with
the demise of the threat once posed by Soviet conventional weapons superiority,
pledges of no-first-use and non-use against non-nuclear states should be even easier
to issue ("Chinese Representative on Nuclear Ban").

[62]China initially set forth numerous conditions for approving a Comprehensive

France, China moved forward with its planned detonations, despite the international criticism it faced.[63] Only after it had completed a final series of tests in 1996 did China announce that it would conduct no more tests and was prepared to agree to the Comprehensive Test Ban Treaty.[64]

Test Ban Treaty (most notable, the call for permitting peaceful nuclear explosions and limits on methods of verification), only agreeing to set the end of 1996 as a target date for completing the negotiations. At first it was unclear whether this posture was designed simply to buy time while China completed its final series of tests and then, like France, fully embrace the CTBT, or was designed to produce a weak regime in which weapons testing could proceed under the guise of scientific and civilian engineering projects, or was designed to scuttle the negotiations. In June 1996, China modified its position and demanded only that the ban on peaceful nuclear explosions be open to review in ten years. This stance may have been viewed as a way to win concessions on the verification dispute, in which China argued that asymmetrical technological capabilities would provide an unfair advantage to the more advanced states if there were no constraints placed on the most sophisticated detection methods. This issue, if mishandled, could have scuttled the treaty since sharp limits on methods would, according to the U.S. Director of the Arms Control and Disarmament Agency, John Holum, "cripple the verification system enabling current or prospective nuclear weapons states to violate the treaty's terms. See Barbara Crossette, "In Concession, China Is Ready to Ban A-Tests," pp. A1, A10; "China Drops Call for 'Peaceful' Nuclear Blasts." On Beijing's evolving views on arms control and especially the prospective Comprehensive Test Ban Treaty, see Banning N. Garrett and Bonnie S. Glaser, "Chinese Perspectives on Nuclear Arms Control"; also "Spokesman on China's Nuclear Testing"; "China Criticised As Bar to Nuclear Test Ban Treaty"; "China Won't Conduct Tests Indefinitely"; "China Test Timed to Avert Criticism but Draws Ire."

[63]Though governments and nongovernmental organizations, in particular Greenpeace, criticized China, the international outrage was mild compared to that France had confronted. See "China Criticised As Bar to Nuclear Test Ban Treaty"; "Greenpeace to Take 'Soft' Approach to China." Part of the difference in international reaction is almost certainly explained by the fact that China conducted its tests within its national borders. See also "China to Hold Nuclear Test Soon, Envoy Hints."

[64]China's final nuclear test was conducted on July 29, 1996, after which Beijing announced it was joining the moratorium on testing ("China Holds Last Nuclear Test Before Moratorium"). Reports quickly indicated that China may have struck deals on information sharing and computer-simulation technology that contributed to this decision and the decision to sign the CTBT (Benjamin Kang Lim, "China Nuclear Halt May Stem from Deal—Analysts"). The one publicly announced compromise was that negotiations with the United States over the CTBT's verification regime had resulted in an accommodation on the number of "executive council members" needed to trigger on-site inspections, clinching China's approval of the treaty ("U.S. and China Make Deal on Side at Nuclear Talks"). Another possible explanation for Beijing's decision is that China had become confident in the viability of its modernization program under the constraints of the CTBT because of the information it had already gained about weapons design or computer simulation not only through its indigenous research and development program, but also through the espionage activities alleged in the Cox Committee Report.

What sort of arsenal is China's nuclear modernization program, with or without testing, designed to yield? Does the program suggest that Beijing is abandoning its Cold War emphasis on a nuclear strategy of dissuasion by deterrence? The country's economic and technological development is gradually providing China's leaders with the *possibility* of pursuing more numerous and more sophisticated nuclear capabilities that could be designed for missions other than punitive retaliatory strikes.[65] But for the foreseeable future, the key elements of China's nuclear modernization do not seem to presage a significant strategic change. China's current modernization plans, even if fully realized, will do little more than improve the survivability of a still-modest deterrent arsenal.

Early in the twenty-first century, deployment of relatively small numbers of solid-fueled, road-mobile ICBMs (the DF-31) and a small fleet of SSBNs armed with a JL-2 SLBM (based on the DF-31) more potent than the limited range JL-1 will reduce, but not completely eliminate, the vulnerability of China's retaliatory weapons when matched against the much more numerous and accurate U.S. or Russian forces.[66]

[65]For a detailed account of predictable interest in such possibilities, see Alastair Iain Johnston, "China's New 'Old Thinking.'"

[66]For an estimate of China's nuclear forces as of 1999, see Robert S. Norris and William M. Arkin, "Natural Resources Defense Council Notebook." On China's view of the importance of mobility as the key to ensuring the survival of retaliatory forces, see Hu, Zha et al., eds., *Xiandai Junbingzhong Zhanshu*, p. 254. Well before the Cox Committee allegations in May 1999, analysts had predicted that the road-mobile, solid-fueled DF-31 system's warhead and missile would be ready for deployment toward the end of the 1990s, filling the strategic role currently played by the handful of slow-to-ready, liquid-fueled DF-4 and DF-5 missiles, relatively vulnerable in their fixed silos ("China Test Fires ICBM Missile, Diplomats Say"). In any event, repeating a pattern evident in earlier forecasts about Chinese weapons deployments, the DF-31 deployment has taken longer than originally expected (now anticipated in the first few years of the twenty-first century). Increasingly available resources in a rapidly developing China and the end of the Cold War make it difficult to predict whether China's preference to invest most heavily in land-based systems will endure. See John W. Lewis and Hua Di, "China's Ballistic Missile Programs," pp. 27–29. Cost aside, as was frequently noted in the debate about modernization of land-based systems in the West during the 1970s and 1980s, the survivability of SSBNs is somewhat offset by the difficulties of command and control while attempting to maintain concealment. Moreover, analysts in Beijing were eager to argue that one of the lessons of Operation Desert Storm was the remarkable survivability of even crude land-based mobile missile forces (referring to the allies' difficulty in locating and destroying Iraqi SCUDs). This experience cast doubt on the allegedly pressing need to give absolute priority to a much larger, very expensive, SSBN force. With extended ranges and improved accuracy for its ICBMs, improved *mobility* rather than sea-basing could ensure the long-term survivability of China's retaliatory forces (author's discussions with military and civilian analysts in Beijing during April–May

And along with development of a new generation of ballistic missiles (including a still longer-ranged ICBM, the DF-41), China may marry a nuclear armed cruise missile with its aircraft to provide a standoff bomber capability at a fraction of the cost of developing a stealthy manned penetrating system. This seems the most viable option if China plans to preserve the air-based leg of its strategic triad.[67] Still, however successful current efforts are, well into the twenty-first century China's modernized nuclear forces will fall well short of providing Beijing with a capability that would be very useful for offensive or defensive nuclear warfighting purposes, even if this proves to be something that elements of the Chinese military establishment want.[68] Though more sophisticated than the arsenal inherited from Mao's China, the relatively small number of warheads China is likely to field (even if MIRVing technology is mastered) may not even result in a significantly larger deliverable punch because of the blunting effect of advanced, though imperfect, ballistic missile defenses that the United States or others may choose to develop and deploy.[69] Moreover, if the Comprehensive Test Ban Treaty

---

1991). Ultimately, of course, resource allocation will reflect budgetary politics as well as strategic sensibility. See John W. Lewis and Xue Litai, *China's Strategic Seapower*, pp. 236–37.

[67]Holly Porteus, "China's View of Strategic Weapons," p. 135. Indeed, vulnerability to anti-aircraft defenses aside, the limited range of China's 120 H-6 bombers (3,100km) makes it questionable whether they are worth considering a strategic weapon.

[68]See Johnston, "China's New 'Old Thinking.'" Johnston describes the views of influential Chinese strategists that suggest a concept of limited deterrence that requires a range of options beyond simple, crude countervalue retaliation. His careful reading of an impressively large sample of Chinese analysts leads him to conclude that they are increasingly "uncomfortable with the assured destruction notion of deterrence," and that the "more common view" is that deterrence requires a usable ability to compete at various rungs on the ladder of escalation, rather than depending on the inhibiting risk of uncontrollable escalation that can be created by Schelling-esque "threats that leave something to chance" (Johnston, pp. 15, 16, 17, 19–20; see also Hu, Zha et al., eds., *Xiandai Junbingzhong Zhanshu*, pp. 245ff). For now, however, the capabilities necessary for a nuclear doctrine emphasizing executable options are so far beyond Beijing's resources that such statements are more wish list than policy prescription, as Johnston notes. That such wishes would be expressed is not surprising, since few analysts in any country, let alone military practitioners, have ever "felt comfortable" with the disturbing implications of relying on a pure nuclear deterrent strategy. More troubling is the indication that the Chinese analysts Johnston cites have latched on to one side of the old Cold War "requirements-of-deterrence debate," one that calls for huge investments in force modernization, without weighing the competing view that questioned the strategic benefits of deploying a vast array of nuclear capabilities.

[69]Thus China has repeatedly stated its concerns about ballistic missile defenses and would almost certainly take steps to ensure that the protection they provide will

to which China agreed in September 1996 clears the remaining ratification hurdles, it will constrain the possibilities for weapons improvement and modernization, at a minimum reducing the already questionable confidence that would be placed in the first-strike or damage-limiting potential of new generations of untested nuclear warheads.[70] Current modernization plans *will*, however, continue to provide Beijing with a useful capability for practicing dissuasion by nuclear deterrence. Increasing the size and survivability of a modest nuclear arsenal will ensure that China can maintain a retaliatory threat sufficient for creating the terrifying uncertainties that fatally compromise the best-laid first-strike plans of even more powerful and technologically sophisticated adversaries. It will also ensure that nuclear rivals will be wary of risking the potentially disastrous consequences of escalation in a major conventional military confrontation with China over its vital interests.[71]

In sum, then, at least for the first decade of the post–Cold War era, the three states this book examined—Britain, France, and China—were not inclined to abandon the nuclear deterrent keystone of their military-security policy. Each retained its doctrinal commitment and devoted the national resources it believed essential to maintain the required retaliatory capabilities, though for China there was the added need for si-

---

remain frighteningly imperfect. See Patrick E. Tyler, "China Warns Against 'Star Wars' Shield for U.S. Forces in Asia," p. 4; Porteus, "China's View of Strategic Weapons," p. 136. For frequently updated coverage of China and its views of missile defenses, see http://www.taiwansecurity.org/TSR-TMD.htm.

[70]See John Holum, "A Powerful Barrier to Future Nuclear Tests."

[71]Early in 1996, as Sino-American tensions over Chinese military exercises in the Taiwan Straits grew, the *New York Times* reported that Chinese officials had informally raised the danger of nuclear escalation (specifically mentioning the vulnerability of Los Angeles) if the United States forced a military confrontation. The veiled threat was conveyed to the Clinton administration "through a former Assistant Secretary of Defense, Chas. W. Freeman, Jr., who traveled to China this winter for discussions with senior Chinese officials" (Patrick E. Tyler, "As China Threatens Taiwan, It Makes Sure U.S. Listens," p. A3). Delivery of the message was eventually confirmed by Assistant Secretary of State for East Asia and the Pacific Winston Lord in a televised interview: "Some Chinese lower-level officials told some visiting American officials that we wouldn't dare defend Taiwan because they'd rain nuclear bombs on Los Angeles." Lord added that the threat was raised with a "high-level Chinese visitor" and denied ("China Aides Gave U.S. Nuclear Warning, Official Says"). Such denial would be the sensible approach to take (to reduce the political price of compliance discussed in Chapter 8) if Beijing were attempting simultaneously to apply the coercive pressure of compellent threats to alter what it feared might be an interventionist U.S. policy, as well as deterrent threats if no U.S. decision had yet been reached. Defense Secretary William Perry's refusal to be specific about U.S. plans, beyond expressed concern, made both interpretations viable. See, for example, "Perry Criticized on Taiwan."

multaneously investing in a significant improvement in hopelessly obsolete conventional capabilities. But is the logic that informed the strategic decision-making of these three countries relevant to the other nuclear weapons states at the turn of the century?

United States and Russia

Beginning with arsenals far exceeding the requirements of a simple deterrent strategy for dissuading adversaries, at the end of the Cold War the U.S. and Soviet/Russian governments initiated a process of deep cuts. As mutual threat perceptions diminished and the power of the former Soviet empire ebbed, planners in Washington and Moscow deemphasized most of the elaborate scenarios for using nuclear forces to fight an unremittingly hostile enemy against whom, it was feared, threats of punitive retaliation might be insufficiently dissuasive. With military conflict between the United States and Russia seeming ever more unlikely, each began the shift to a nuclear force structure that served mainly as a hedge against the remote possibility of confrontation by providing for an unmistakable capability to inflict catastrophic damage on the other or any third party that might seriously threaten its vital interests. In two sweeping arms control agreements (START I and START II), as well as through unprecedented unilateral measures, the leaders of the nuclear superpowers initiated a process that was to cut their inventory of operational warheads from more than 10,000 each to less than 3,500 by early in the twenty-first century. Having heavily discounted the probability they would need to threaten each other with nuclear weapons, let alone launch them at a moment's notice in the face of a surprise attack, Washington and Moscow even agreed to reprogram the weapons' guidance systems so that the default target setting was no longer each other's homeland, but instead no target or, on certain older warheads for which this was technically impossible, remote areas of the ocean.[72]

Although sometimes characterized as fundamentally removing the nuclear sword of Damocles that had been hanging over Russian and American heads since the 1950s, in effect what these modifications in nuclear postures herald is a shift to a nuclear strategic stance somewhat less subject to inadvertent or accidental nuclear catastrophe and strategically more similar to that embraced by the second-ranking powers during the Cold War.[73] Despite occasional rhetoric to the contrary, nei-

[72]"USA and Russia Agree to 'Detarget' Missiles."

[73]Nevertheless, the true significance of changes in force size, default targeting, and rhetoric can only be determined by examining revisions in operational nuclear

ther the United States nor Russia has plans to eliminate their deterrent capability.[74] For both it remains a strategically necessary, economical hedge against an uncertain future.

For Washington, the uncertainty rests on doubts about the political future of Russia and China, as well as concerns about the possible need to deter hostile weaker states who succeed in entering the nuclear club or in acquiring chemical or biological weapons of mass destruction from threatening the United States or other states who have been persuaded to forgo their own nuclear capability with promises of extended deterrence.

For Russia, the affordability as much as the robustness of nuclear deterrence makes maintaining the residual Soviet arsenal indispensable. With wealthy Europeans to the West, and economically vibrant Asian powers rising in the East, nuclear weapons ironically assume a role for Moscow that they once filled for its rivals—they become the equalizer against a prospective adversary's potential superiority in conventional capabilities, though in this case a qualitative more than a quantitative edge. Economically strapped and internally troubled by disputes that tie down conventional military resources, Russia treasures its nuclear trump card. In November 1993 President Yeltsin indicated that Moscow had abandoned even the rhetorical flourish of the Soviet no-first-use doctrine, preferring to maximize Russia's ability to exploit the uncertainty of unpredictable escalation.[75] A determination to continue to en-

---

plans. The sharp divergence between civilian beliefs about the role of nuclear weapons and the actual plans for their use during the Cold War is detailed in Bruce G. Blair, *The Logic of Accidental Nuclear War.*

[74]The U.S. government has left no doubt about its determination to ensure the long-term reliability of the existing arsenal and to retain the option of modernization even under the constraints of the CTBT. See William J. Broad, "Nuclear Arms Builders Move from Creators to Custodians," pp. A1, 14; "Energy Department to Keep Open Experimental Reactor."

[75]See "Nunn: Russia Eyes Nuclear Arms." In the announcement, Yeltsin "for the first time declared his willingness to use nuclear weapons if Russia or its allies were attacked with conventional weapons." The shift was reflected in Russian declaratory doctrine at the time. More recently, as Russia's conventional forces have continued to deteriorate while NATO has expanded eastward, Russia's turn toward a strategy exploiting the compensating advantages of dissuasion by nuclear deterrence in an uncertain world proceeds. In February 1997 Ivan Rybkin of Russia's Security Council stated: "We talk about [the use of nuclear weapons] so that military adventurers do not get tempted by the fact that at this stage our armed forces are being reformed and do not have the might they used to have" (Andrei Khalip, "Russia May Use Nuclear Weapons First in Self-defence"). "Naturally, we are not talking of a preventive nuclear strike, but if an aggressor starts a war against us using conventional weapons, we *may* respond with nuclear ones. . . . Everyone must know that in case of

joy the benefits of a national nuclear deterrent, more crucial for Russia than for a wealthy United States that enjoyed clear superiority in conventional military forces, conditioned Moscow's willingness to reduce its arms during the 1990s. The ample nuclear inheritance from its Cold War research and development efforts did enable Russia, like the United States, to reconcile its strategic interest with approval of the Comprehensive Test Ban Treaty.[76] But, in the course of the decade, while the United States moved closer toward a decision to deploy ballistic missile defenses (even at the risk of putting the 1972 ABM treaty in jeopardy) and as a newly expanded NATO militarily intervened in Yugoslavia, Russian reservations about the strategic wisdom of the START II treaty continued to delay its ratification in the Duma.

THE OPAQUE AND NEWLY DECLARED

NUCLEAR WEAPONS STATES

In addition to the five declared nuclear powers, three additional states— Israel, India, and Pakistan—had developed a nuclear capability by the end of the Cold War but refrained from weapons testing (India conducted a single "peaceful" nuclear explosion in 1974). What purpose did such a recessed capability serve? Why did these three refrain from testing programs that other nuclear states conducted? Why did India and then Pakistan shift gears in 1998 and decide to openly test nuclear weapons and publicly declare themselves nuclear weapons states?

As for the Cold War's second-ranking powers, security concerns pro-

---

a direct challenge our response will be fully-fledged, and *we are to choose* the use of means . . . including nuclear weapons" ("Russia Must Drop 'No-first-strike'—Moscow Official," emphasis added; "Russia Adopts 'Top Secret' Nuclear Document"; "Moscow Makes Crucial Decisions on Nuclear Defence."

[76]Still, when debating the wisdom of agreeing to a Comprehensive Test Ban, some Russian analysts warned against any agreement that would compromise the country's ability to maintain a modern nuclear arsenal because it was necessary to compensate for conventional inferiority, particularly in the realm of high precision technologies, at reasonable cost. As Dr. Radiy Ilkayev of Russia's Federal Nuclear Center articulated the logic: "Currently, Russia is without military allies, and its army, navy and air force have been weakened by the economic crisis. . . . Our nuclear arsenals have become a deterrent against conventional weapons—exactly opposite to the past, when the Soviet Union had the most powerful army in the world, and the West could only rely on nuclear weapons" ("Russians Call for Nuclear Testing"). U.S. Energy Secretary Hazel O'Leary more confidently emphasized that the United States "can maintain an effective deterrent with a smaller nuclear infrastructure, and pathbreaking science and computing can replace nuclear testing and help us achieve a Comprehensive Test Ban" ("Energy Dept. Plans to Shrink Nuclear Weapons Complex").

vided the principal motives for Israel, India, and Pakistan to develop a nuclear deterrent capability to dissuade serious threats from a potentially more powerful adversary. All three chose this course despite their limited economic resources (an especially tight constraint for India and Pakistan), making their decisions more like China's than like Britain's or France's. All three perceived an overriding strategic imperative that justified the expense. In addition, all three believed this strategic imperative offset the price that had to be paid in terms of stiff foreign criticism of their refusal to join the nonproliferation regime established after 1968. With a domestic consensus that the nuclear option was absolutely essential for security, these states were able to muster the resources, withstand external pressures, and press ahead until success was achieved.[77]

Israel initiated its nuclear weapons program in the mid-1950s, a time when it had grave doubts about its ability to rely on conventional forces to ensure its very existence against an encircling coalition of hostile Arab states. Israel's leaders concluded that they required the ultimate

[77]When asked about the strong domestic support for her country's nuclear weapons effort while it was still in its opaque phase, Pakistan's former Prime Minister Benazir Bhutto described both the hope for external assistance and the need to hedge against abandonment: "It's our history. A history of three wars with a larger neighbor. . . . So the security issue for Pakistan is an issue of survival. . . . So given that history, Pakistanis feel, 'Well, we don't have to go all the way. But, God forbid, if there's a threat, at least we have the knowledge to go all the way, *if nobody else comes to our rescue.*' Obviously, we hope somebody else will come to our rescue . . ." (Claudia Dreifus, "The Real-Life Dynasty of Benazir Bhutto," p. 39, emphasis added).

In the years prior to the May 1998 tests, Indian public opinion polls revealed a higher value attached to deterrence of the threats from Pakistan and China than to avoiding international, especially American, criticism. A 1995 poll in *India Today* magazine showed 62 percent favoring, 35 percent opposing a nuclear weapons test ("Indian Parties Bash U.S. over Nuclear Test Report"). And despite changes in governments, India (whose posture was mirrored by Pakistan) continued to eschew the Nuclear Nonproliferation Treaty and the Comprehensive Test Ban Treaty as discriminatory arrangements because no provision was made for the five recognized weapons states to completely destroy their arsenals. See "India Keeps Option to Build Nuclear Arms"; "China Nuclear Test Decision Turns Heat Up on India." India stood by its position in the face of intense lobbying during the summer of 1996 and refused to join the other nuclear-capable states in signing the CTBT, rejecting it as sham disarmament, enshrining the advantage of the declared weapons states, since they could rely on simulation technologies they had already developed ("India Analysts Say Nuclear Test Pact Full of Holes"; "Indian Newspapers Hail Government's Nuclear Stand"; Sonali Verma, "China Nuclear Test Could Harden India Treaty Stand"). In a futile last-minute ploy, France (somewhat surprisingly, in light of its national nuclear heritage) suggested providing India with security guarantees as a substitute for its independent nuclear option ("France Sees Guarantees for India on N-test Treaty").

guarantee against potentially overwhelming adversaries despite two important offsetting concerns—the moral dilemma inherent in planning the use of nuclear weapons for a country distinctively sensitive to the issue of wartime genocide, and the tensions the effort triggered in relations with the United States.[78] Israel's nuclear program yielded a weapons capability by the early 1970s, though its success was not officially acknowledged. On the contrary, while investigative journalists and scholars tried to substantiate claims about a significant Israeli nuclear arsenal, and Israeli leaders sometimes offered ambiguous statements rather than flat denials about the country's capabilities, through 1999 Israel would not officially confirm its nuclear weapons status and instead went to great lengths to conceal hard evidence about it.[79]

India's and Pakistan's reasons to pursue a nuclear capability were closely intertwined. India's decision to move beyond refining technology for a purely peaceful nuclear energy program and to create a nuclear weapons option for itself was triggered by the perception of a potentially massive Chinese threat. China's crushing victory over India in the October 1962 war heightened India's fears about a long-term menace from the north. Beijing's nuclear weapons test in October 1964 sealed New Delhi's resolve to actively pursue the nuclear option.[80] Pakistan's nuclear weapons program resulted from its perception of a serious and growing conventional military threat from a more powerful India in the wake of the 1965 war and then the loss of Bangladesh (East Pakistan) in the 1971 war. The early determination that Pakistan would need nuclear weapons to cope with the Indian threat emerged in 1972 and was decisively reinforced by India's 1974 "peaceful nuclear explosion."[81] As Indo-Pakistani rivalry remained intense and especially as military and perhaps nuclear cooperation between Beijing and Islamabad flowered, Pakistan's bomb program in turn hardened India's belief in the impor-

[78]See Avner Cohen, *Israel and the Bomb*; see also information at the associated National Security Archive web site, http://www.seas.gwu.edu/nsarchive/israel/findings.htm. Cohen's findings confirm that the Kennedy administration pressured Israel, as they had pressured Britain and France, to give up its nuclear ambitions.

[79]The most famous part of this effort was Israel's kidnap and arrest of Mordechai Vanunu in 1986 as he was revealing evidence about the nuclear program to the British press. On the elaborate measures to keep Israel's nuclear capability opaque, see Cohen, *Israel and the Bomb*.

[80]For a concise yet comprehensive overview of India's nuclear weapons program, see Sumit Ganguly, "India's Pathway to Pokhran II," pp. 148–77; see also Devin T. Hagerty, *Consequences of Nuclear Proliferation*, pp. 72–73.

[81]Hagerty, *Consequences of Nuclear Proliferation*, pp. 73–74; on the history of Pakistan's nuclear effort, see Samina Ahmed, "Pakistan's Nuclear Weapons Program," pp. 178–204.

tance of developing its nuclear deterrent that had initially been fostered by the perceived threat from China.

The motives for Israel, India, and Pakistan to acquire nuclear weapons in order to dissuade serious threats from powerful adversaries are clear and follow the deterrent logic detailed in preceding chapters. Their efforts most dramatically differed from those of China, Britain, and France, however, insofar as they developed, but did not openly test and deploy, nuclear weapons. The strong international norm against nonproliferation that developed after 1968 and, perhaps, a military calculus that a secretive effort would be less vulnerable to preventive or preemptive strikes or otherwise less provocative to regional adversaries instead encouraged these three to practice what Avner Cohen and Benjamin Frankel labeled opaque, as opposed to transparent, deterrence.[82] Israel and, prior to May 1998, India and Pakistan exploited the belief that on short notice each could tap a hidden or latent nuclear retaliatory force to punish an adversary. Such opaque deterrence still depends on creating uncertainty in the mind of an adversary about the possibly horrifying consequences of escalation in a conflict over vital interests. But the practice of opaque deterrence differs from its transparent cousin because it relies on creating the fear of retaliation without conclusively demonstrating that one possesses a ready capability to fulfill implicit threats. As with transparent deterrence, adversaries must estimate the probability that the nuclear forces would actually be employed; unlike transparent deterrence, adversaries must be convinced that an ambiguous capability exists. How can this be done? Devin Hagerty suggests that a crucial element in establishing the credibility of opaque deterrents may be the claims that adversaries and the international nonproliferation community make about such states' surreptitious weapons programs, claims that serve to advertise and often provide evidence of a capability that the possessor, for reasons discussed below, chooses not to confirm.[83]

Until May 1998 India and Pakistan, like Israel, apparently found opaque deterrence sufficient—providing the desired strategic benefits while limiting, though not eliminating, the political and economic costs of openly defying the international nonproliferation regime. But this

---

[82]On opaque deterrence, see Avner Cohen and Benjamin Frankel, "Opaque Nuclear Proliferation"; Hagerty, *The Consequences of Nuclear Proliferation*.

[83]Hagerty, *The Consequences of Nuclear Proliferation*. The understandable preference to err on the side of caution in one's estimates about a state's nuclear capabilities undoubtedly contributes to this effect, as may again be demonstrated in the credibility some attributed to the North Korean nuclear program in the 1990s.

similarity ended in 1998. While Israel continued to adhere to opacity at century's end, India and Pakistan shifted course, surprising many who believed that the South Asian rivals had already established the credibility of their nuclear capabilities sufficient for mutual deterrence that would inhibit both in any future confrontation. What explains Israel's restraint and South Asian testing? This topic will undoubtedly receive intense scrutiny in coming years.[84] Here, I only suggest several plausible reasons that serve as a reminder of the distinctiveness of each country's nuclear experience, even when the underlying security motive and strategic doctrine are similar.

One possibility for Israel's continued restraint is that its government has greater confidence in the reliability of its nuclear weapons. This confidence may reflect belief in the sophistication of Israel's scientific-technical community or knowledge of weapons-test data that Israel has acquired, either through espionage or perhaps from a 1979 explosion in the Indian Ocean that many identify as a joint Israeli–South African nuclear test.[85] A second possibility is that Israel sees its opaque posture as useful for depriving regional nuclear aspirants of a simple justification for their own programs. A third, and the most plausible, explanation for restraint is that Israel's security environment has grown more benign than its nuclear pioneers could have imagined—the regional conventional military balance has tilted in Israel's favor and diplomacy has resulted in a series of peace agreements dissolving the unified Arab threat. The changed strategic situation has not made Israel's leaders willing to give up their nuclear deterrent that serves as a hedge against an uncertain future.[86] But by reducing the scale of immediate security threats, the changed strategic situation has muted the incentive that would be necessary for Israel to decide to take the controversial step of testing as a way to increase the credibility of its opaque deterrent.

The calculus for India and Pakistan was different. The underlying

[84]For early post-test analysis, see Ganguly, "India's Pathway to Pokhran II"; Ahmed, "Pakistan's Nuclear Weapons Program."

[85]William B. Scott, "Admission of 1979 Nuclear Test Finally Validates Vela Data," p. 33.

[86]Strong pressures against Israel to renounce its nuclear capability, especially at the time of the renewal of the Nuclear Nonproliferation Treaty in 1995, have been ineffective. Instead, Israel's policy, consistent with the logic presented here, is that it will abandon its right to nuclear weapons only if it feels sufficiently secure. In January 1996, Prime Minister Shimon Peres promised Israel would give up its "nuclear capability" if a comprehensive peace settlement were reached, but added his belief that Arab doubts about Israel's nuclear program have served as a deterrent: "As long as the suspicion itself can serve as a deterrent weapon, let them suspect" ("Peres: ME Should Be Nuclear-Free").

reasons for India's decision to test are clearer than the immediate reasons for the timing of the 1998 decision itself. Two plausible and interrelated trends may explain why India decided to abandon opacity. First, Indian leaders believed that the potentially serious threat from a militarily modernizing and economically vibrant China would increase in coming decades.[87] Second, in the mid-1990s the international pressures on India to abandon its nuclear ambitions were growing and promised to make a decision to test more, not less, difficult in future years. Efforts to portray India as a laggard on nonproliferation at the conference to renew the Nuclear Nonproliferation Treaty in 1995 and in the run-up to the Comprehensive Test Ban Treaty in 1996 meant that even without testing, India was paying a price for its principled refusal to abandon its opaque nuclear option. Such concerns in New Delhi might have prompted a decision to test and make India's nuclear deterrent an irreversible fait accompli as early as 1996. Indeed, there were reports that India was going to test that year, but either internal debate or pressure from the United States delayed a final decision. That India ultimately decided to act on its incentives to test in 1998 is most likely linked to the victory of the Hindu nationalist party (BJP) that brought Prime Minister Vajpayee to power.

Vajpayee's decision to test quickly reflected not only the underlying reasons noted above but also a domestic political interest in fulfilling the policy pledges contained in his party's platform. Testing would clearly result in a wave of international condemnation, but recognizing the popularity of the nuclear option within India, Vajpayee could also anticipate a domestic political boost for his party's tenuous position of leadership. He was right on both counts. In the short run, as was true for the initial tests by each of the declared nuclear weapons states, the May 1998 tests did lead to an upsurge of nationalist pride that benefited the ruling party. And, as in the case of China, Britain, and France, the Indian government proudly announced that the tests would enable India to assume its rightful, respected place among the world's great powers.[88] Yet, as with the other nuclear weapons states, the prestige benefits of entry into the nuclear club were fleeting. Briefly the world paid great attention to India, but there was no lasting boost for the country's international status. And soon, domestic exuberance about the successful tests

[87]In a recent report to the parliament, India's defense ministry pessimistically claimed "it was 'too late' for India to match the air-power of its giant neighbour, China . . ." ("Indian Air Force Cannot Take on China, Pakistan in War: Report").

[88]The hope that others would take India more seriously may have reflected resentment at the attention others lavished on China during the 1990s.

faded. Within a year the BJP was in electoral trouble because of unrelated pocketbook economic issues. Nevertheless, because security considerations were paramount in India's thinking about its need for a nuclear deterrent, such disappointments did not shake the government's determination or the consensus among the public and elite about the importance of keeping the now openly acknowledged capability.[89]

For four interrelated reasons Pakistan decided almost immediately to match India in testing. First, if Pakistan did not test, some might have questioned whether it actually had the capability many attributed to it. Second, a decision not to test would have led to intense domestic political pressures on the government to demonstrate that Pakistan's opaque deterrent was not based on a bluff.[90] Third, Pakistan faced the same pressures from the international nonproliferation regime that India faced and may have believed that the window for testing could soon close. Fourth, and perhaps most important, India's test had created a golden opportunity to justify a Pakistani test as an unavoidable response forced by the provocative actions of its regional adversary. The Pakistani tests, like India's, predictably resulted in an upsurge in nationalist pride and a wave of international condemnation. Although the domestic political payoff for the ruling party was short-lived and the sanctions imposed by international economic partners were painful, Pakistan, like India, has remained determined to do what it believes necessary to preserve the credibility of its nuclear deterrent.[91]

Although their patterns of deployment have varied, each of the seven declared nuclear states and opaquely nuclear Israel have decided that

[89]On the first anniversary of the tests, Uday Bhaskar of India's Institute for Defence Studies and Analysis argued, "We have crossed the rubicon and we should not be apologetic about something we should have done decades ago. We have to carry the whole thing forward." See "India's Nuclear Blasts Lose Their Impact."

[90]When rumors of an impending Indian nuclear weapons test had circulated in early 1996, Pakistan's foreign minister, Assef Ahmad Ali, though preferring to maintain an ambiguous nuclear status that he claimed had "warded off the possibility of war in South Asia for the last 25 years," promised a tit-for-tat response to Indian action ("Pakistan Vows Tit-for-tat Nuclear Reply to India"). In 1998, this promise was fulfilled.

[91]Pakistan's former army chief, General Mirza Aslam Beg, stated: "Maintaining a minimum nuclear deterrence is the life-saving drug, which despite its attendant side effects, is deemed necessary to keep breathing" ("Pakistanis Pin Blame for South Asian Nuclearisation on India"). Subsequent negotiations to remove the U.S.-led international sanctions effort have focused on policy adjustments Pakistan and India might undertake, including constraints on the types of arsenals they will deploy and acceding to the CTBT. Their willingness to consider such agreements has been sharply limited by their overriding security concerns.

they require these strategically revolutionary weapons because they provide a robust and affordable means to dissuade potentially serious military threats to vital interests. Not all states have reached this conclusion, however. Some have even abandoned their nuclear weapons or weapons development efforts. Sweden abandoned its program early in the Cold War. In 1990, Argentina and Brazil agreed not to produce nuclear weapons, aborting their covert weapons development efforts.[92] In 1993, South Africa claimed it had built six nuclear bombs but had dismantled them in 1989 as the Cold War ended and the threat of Soviet-backed military pressure on the apartheid regime evaporated.[93] In 1996, Jurg Stussi, the Swiss government's senior military historian, reported that Switzerland had run a secret nuclear bomb program. From 1945 through 1988 Switzerland (despite signing the NPT in 1970) had accumulated a secret stockpile of uranium for 400 nuclear warheads that could be used on aircraft, artillery, and guided missile systems. The principal fear seems to have been the possibility of a German nuclear weapons capability.[94] And during the first post–Cold War decade, Belarus, Kazakhstan, and Ukraine each turned over the nuclear weapons they inherited from the Soviet arsenal to Russia. Why have some states chosen to develop and retain nuclear weapons while others have not? What does the experience of the existing weapons states, especially that of the three countries most closely examined in this book suggest about the continuing role of nuclear weapons in international politics during the post–Cold War era? The final chapter addresses these questions.

[92]The agreement came at the end of "a decade of improving relations between the two countries—after years of competition for political and economic influence in South America" and in response to pressure from some of the countries' key nuclear industry suppliers (Gary Milhollin and Jennifer Weeks, "Keeping the Lid on Nuclear Arms; Nuclear Arms Control in Argentina and Brazil," p. 26).

[93]"Africans Adopt Treaty to Create Nuclear Free Zone."

[94]"In an anarchic world we were prepared in case we needed it. . . . If Germany developed nuclear weapons, then we would have built one to keep ourselves alive" ("Swiss Kept Atomic Bomb Option, Magazine Says"; see also Robert Uhlig, "Swiss Kept Nuclear Arms Secret for 43 Years," p. 10).

8

Legacy of the Nuclear Revolution
for the Twenty-first Century

My study of the security policies of China, Britain, and France highlighted the interaction of international and national influences that encourages states to pursue a nuclear weapons capability. The structure of the international system, especially its persistent condition of anarchy, provides incentives for self-regarding behavior and undermines confidence in international guarantees, even ostensibly firm military alliances, as a means for ensuring security. On practical strategic and normative political grounds, states prefer autonomy to dependence and search for ways to provide for their own security. The search, however, is influenced by national attributes (economic, geographic, and demographic) that may limit the possibilities for security independence and shape the strategy and forces that states can realistically select. This constrained search for a practical means to provide for a measure of self-reliance in security policy is also influenced by beliefs about how current military technology shapes the strategic environment. The argument in this book is that states have sought to develop nuclear weapons primarily because they provide a hedge against the most serious threats to vital national interests that is not only more reliable than dependence on external assistance, but also more strategically robust and economically affordable than the available independent alternatives. Yet anticipating the future place of nuclear weapons in international politics requires explaining not only why some seek nuclear weapons, but also why others may eschew them. This chapter begins, therefore, by considering the incentives that face prospective, or candidate, nuclear powers and illustrates their importance by reference to three cases in the immediate post–Cold War era—Ukraine, Japan, and Germany.

TO HAVE OR TO HAVE NOT

Why have some states remained nonnuclear? Instead of attempting to provide an exhaustive list of possible factors that would account for the wide variety of particular historical circumstances that might determine nuclear abstinence, I suggest a set of core reasons.[1] Thus a state would not be expected to seek a nuclear capability if (1) it were satisfied with its security, either because it perceived no serious threats or were comfortable with existing international security guarantees (from allies or international organizations) and any compromises of autonomy that might be necessary to ensure sufficient levels of such external support; (2) its economic, geographic, and demographic resources made it feasible to deploy nonnuclear forces to cope with the most important threats to its national security; or (3) its economic, industrial, and scientific capacity were inadequate for exploiting nuclear technology. Brief consideration of these reasons why a state might not seek nuclear weapons will further illuminate the implications of this book's argument for the prospects of their continued spread.

The third in the list of reasons a state may not develop nuclear weapons reflects common sense rather than theoretical argument. Despite the revolutionary strategic implications of nuclear weapons that may make them attractive, some states will be unable to produce them. As the absolute costs of exploiting the technology drop and knowledge disseminates, however, the number of states that simply cannot produce nuclear weapons will shrink. If so, this limit on growth in the number of nuclear weapons states depends on attempts to deny states essential radioactive fuels as well as relevant engineering capabilities. The diplomatic conventions of the current nonproliferation regime are part of just such an effort to limit the options available to states rather than their choice among options.[2] Preventive or preemptive military

---

[1]For a recent classification of three approaches to explaining how states decide whether to become nuclear-armed, see Scott D. Sagan, "Why Do States Build Nuclear Weapons?" My analysis clearly falls within Sagan's "security model," at least in terms of the causes I identify as most important. While I disagree with Sagan's weighting of alternative causes in the cases I have examined, I agree with him that domestic-political and normative considerations play a varying and sometimes important role, especially for states not tightly constrained by external security concerns. See also the range of explanations contained in Zachary S. Davis and Benjamin Frankel, eds., *The Proliferation Puzzle*.

[2]Commenting on the significance of one such agreement, the Comprehensive Test Ban Treaty signed in September 1996, Director of the United States Arms Control and Disarmament Agency, John Holum, highlighted this rationale: "... [o]ne major effect of the test ban will be to help prevent the spread of nuclear weapons to

strikes against incipient nuclear powers may also be employed in support of this effort. Given the difficulty both of enforcing international agreements in an anarchic realm and ensuring the lasting effectiveness of military action, however, measures of this sort are more likely to slow than to stop the spread of a technical capability some states may have strong strategic incentives to pursue.[3] Nevertheless, such attempts to ensure that membership in the nuclear club expands at a measured pace may be desirable if one believes that keeping the barriers to entry high increases the care with which this most valuable national security asset will be managed.[4] As indicated below, scholars continue to disagree about the chances that new nuclear states, especially those in the developing world, will be as circumspect in their nuclear behavior as the existing weapons states have been. Even those who are most optimistic, however, base their optimism on the assumption that these new members of the nuclear club will have the ability to maintain effective peacetime control over their forces. To the extent that high barriers to entry

---

more countries. Without testing, it is much harder to make a weapon small enough to load on an aircraft, fit atop a rudimentary missile, or conceal in a terrorist's luggage. So the test ban backs up other agreements, including the Nuclear Non-Proliferation Treaty, to keep shrinking the number of states with a usable nuclear option" (John Holum, "A Powerful Barrier to Future Nuclear Tests").

[3]For example, Israel's air strike in the early 1980s, and more massive U.S. military and international diplomatic efforts in the early 1990s, not to mention Iraq's accession to the NPT, have slowed but may yet not prevent Baghdad from realizing its nuclear ambitions. Despite all such efforts, rumors of a resurgent, covert Iraqi nuclear weapons program surfaced in 1995. Though many suspected the rumors lacked foundation, the difficulty in dismissing them out of hand reflected a recognition of the problems of preventing a highly motivated state from surreptitiously pursuing a nuclear capability. The International Atomic Energy Agency adopted tougher inspection rules in 1995, but they "will cover only nuclear sites that were already accessible to the agency" (Christopher S. Wren, "Making It Easier to Uncover Nuclear Arms," p. A6). As IAEA Director Hans Blix acknowledged, no matter how tough the rules, the agency would be unable to confirm that a nuclear weapons program does not exist. "We say we have seen no evidence of diversion or misuse. . . . We happen to live in a world of sovereign states. . . . We cannot parachute in or shoot our way in. . . . The IAEA could raise the alarm but further action would be up the Security Council" (ibid.).

[4]The relative optimism of two of the more prominent visions of the consequences of the continued spread of nuclear weapons derives in part from such a belief. See Kenneth N. Waltz, "More May Be Better," pp. 1–2, 42 (an updated version of Waltz's seminal statement on the likely consequences of a slow increase in the number of nuclear weapons states, "The Spread of Nuclear Weapons: More May Be Better"); also John J. Mearsheimer, "Back to the Future." For representative strongly pessimistic views, see Lewis Dunn, "What Difference Will It Make?"; Scott D. Sagan, "The Perils of Proliferation"; Sagan, "More Will Be Worse"; cf. David J. Karl, "Proliferation Pessimism and Emerging Nuclear Powers."

limit membership to those able and interested in developing this expertise along with the weapons, counterproliferation measures, though imperfect, may pay significant dividends. Most important among the benefits would be a reduction in the chances that growth in the number of nuclear weapons states will markedly increase the risk of inadvertent or accidental use, or the illicit transfer to terrorist groups or organized crime.[5]

The other reasons listed as to why states may not pursue nuclear weapons bear on the choices of those who *could* make the effort. My central argument has focused on insecurity as the principal motive for developing such a capability. Obviously, then, a state unconcerned about external threats would lack this key reason to pursue nuclear weapons. Few states, however, behave as though they believe they can afford the luxury of indifference, even during periods of low international tension. The vast majority instead hedge their bets against the risks of an uncertain future by pursuing some sort of military capability. More interesting, then, is the possibility that security-conscious states might decide not to exploit their nuclear potential because they are satisfied with external security guarantees or alternative nonnuclear, but self-reliant, strategies.

If a state believes alliances or international organizations ensure its national interests against foreseeable threats, it may not seek much of an independent capability, nuclear or nonnuclear. Kathleen Bailey has suggested, for example, that the nonproliferation regime, though formally discriminating against nonweapons states, in practice may well serve their security interests by slowing the spread of nuclear weapons to potential adversaries and strengthening "international norms against their use or threat of use."[6] For some states, the benefits of abiding by the NPT may well exceed the costs of a more self-reliant military capability. For others, however, doubts about the wisdom of placing too much confidence in international norms, even those backed by assurances from the leading members of the United Nations, will arise.[7] In-

[5]The possibility of a loss of control can never be completely eliminated, and indeed, as emphasized in this book, for states this possibility plays a central role in creating the deterrent effect of nuclear weapons, whose use is hard to reconcile with fully rational decision-making. Steps that maximize control during peacetime, however, do not eliminate this possibility.

[6]Kathleen Bailey, "Why We Have to Keep the Bomb."

[7]In order to encourage non-weapons states to agree to an indefinite extension of the Nuclear Nonproliferation Treaty in April 1995, the members of the U.N. Security Council passed a resolution giving such states "assurances of unspecified assistance," and promises to act "immediately in accordance with the relevant provisions

deed, one of the lessons from the experience of China, Britain, and France during the Cold War is that even when economic rationality and common interests with a powerful ally indicate the attractiveness of free-riding on others' military efforts, states still worry about the dependability of rather specific bilateral security guarantees. The ultimate unenforceability of international commitments leads states to ponder what might happen if their interests and those of their security patrons diverge. During the bipolar Cold War, allies' threat perceptions, though not identical, were largely similar. Nevertheless, China, Britain, and France were concerned enough about possibly conflicting interests to want a hedge against the potential unreliability of alliance guarantees. Such worries will likely be even stronger for states that might depend on diffuse collective security guarantees against unspecified adversaries in the post–Cold War era, as will be noted below. Since this concern ultimately results from the constraint of anarchy, short of a transformation of this enduring feature of the international system, there is little that can be done to decisively control this structural incentive for self-reliance that contributes to nuclear proliferation.

It is also possible, however, that a state, though discounting the dependability of relying on others, may believe its conventional defensive or deterrent capabilities will be sufficient to dissuade the threats prospective adversaries pose. If so, the state could forgo nuclear weapons. In this case, the leaders may conclude that challenges to its security do not merit a nuclear weapons program that would divert additional national resources from more productive peacetime uses and perhaps also trigger international military, economic, or diplomatic sanctions, or domestic political opposition. The widespread objections to France's last series of nuclear tests and the widespread condemnation of India and Pakistan's testing in May 1998 suggest the sort of response leaders can anticipate.

---

of the Charter of the United Nations." These promises were combined with statements by the five acknowledged nuclear powers giving "'security assurances against the use of nuclear weapons to non-nuclear-weapon states,' that are signatories of the NPT." The presumed beneficiaries of the security assurances objected to the vagueness of the commitments the weapons states were willing to put in a formal resolution ("U.N. Council Gives Assurance to Non-nuclear States"). Provision of security guarantees was also a central feature of U.S. non-proliferation strategy from the mid-1960s, as suggested in the recently declassified papers of the Gilpatric Committee. Though it was hoped that such assurances would provide an acceptable substitute for national nuclear forces, the committee's discussion at the time acknowledged the difficulty of crafting pledges that were acceptable to the guarantor (not risking unwanted entrapment), and yet adequate for the guarantee (not risking feared abandonment). See "Security Guarantees and Non-Proliferation of Nuclear Weapons"; R. Murray "Problems of Nuclear Proliferation Outside Europe (Problem 2)."

But for strategic reasons detailed in the Chinese, British, and French cases, states facing highly capable adversaries—prospective foes with vast conventional superiority or armed with nuclear, biological, or chemical weapons—are unlikely to be satisfied with the dissuasive effects of conventional forces and more likely to be prepared to pay the price necessary to undertake a nuclear weapons development effort. Again, the question is not simply one of the still-hefty price tag for a nuclear weapons program. The economic burden of developing nuclear weapons may be quite heavy, especially for states outside the advanced industrial world. The relevant question facing the leaders of some such states, however, will not be whether to bear a heavy burden to cope with what they perceive as serious threats to vital interests, but rather which heavy burden they (and their countrymen) choose to bear.

For insecure states, the difficulties of making threats restricted to the use of conventional forces sufficiently dissuasive, a matter of the speed and certainty with which destruction can be inflicted, are compounded by economic concerns. The costs of modern conventional forces sufficient for a robust strategy of dissuasion either by defense or deterrence continue to escalate in the era of high technology. Defensive and retaliatory conventional forces must cope not only with straightforward build-ups in the adversary's capabilities, but also with an ever-changing array of countermeasures. The expense entailed, as well as doubts about military effectiveness, will encourage states facing serious threats to consider the economic and strategic virtues of the more robust nuclear alternative for which variations in quantity and quality are much less crucial.[8] The pace and extent of the spread of nuclear weapons, therefore, will depend not just on the price paid for violating the norm of nonproliferation, but also on the opportunity costs of adherence to the norm, a consideration that reflects the affordability and reliability of dissuasion by conventional forces. In principle, at least, limitations on advanced weapons technology transfers and conventional arms control that yielded defense-dominant regional balances could reduce the incentive to go nuclear. But the difficulties of maintaining an international technology control regime in the porous global economy, and the complexities involved in stabilizing a conventional arms competition between mutually suspicious adversaries constrained to coexist in an anarchic realm (i.e., fostering cooperation under the security dilemma) must temper any hopes for exercising such control.[9] Efforts of this sort

[8]See Bailey, "Why We Have to Keep the Bomb," pp. 30ff.
[9]See Robert Jervis, "Cooperation Under the Security Dilemma." For a reconsideration of the severity of the security dilemma and a realist rationale for greater op-

seem most likely to work where least needed, in settings where threat perceptions are weak and modest conventional forces are thus already deemed adequate.

In sum, then, given the incentives and constraints identified in this book, the number of nuclear states should be expected to grow, though at a pace determined by the particular circumstances candidate states confront. Only a change in the anarchic structure of the state system that rendered international commitments enforceable, a technological breakthrough that negated the strategic consequences of the nuclear revolution, or a transformation of interests that led all states to rank adherence to global norms against possessing nuclear weapons above preserving national autonomy would decisively weaken the incentives to deploy nuclear weapons. Short of such unlikely changes, policies to limit the spread of nuclear weapons will address the symptom rather than the causes of proliferation. As already noted, such symptomatic treatment, even if only successful in slowing the pace, may be advisable. But given the underlying causes, few major states with important international interests should be expected to eschew nuclear weapons indefinitely. One instead should expect that the durability of nuclear abstinence among states able to surmount the declining barriers to entry and free to choose for themselves will depend on the seriousness of perceived threats to vital interests.

Thus far I have emphasized the significance of continuity in the military effects of nuclear technology and the political constraints of coexistence in an anarchic international realm that will shape candidate states' decisions about joining the nuclear club in the post–Cold War world. But while the current strategic context is marked by these important continuities, as the previous chapter indicated, it is also marked by an important change, the end of bipolarity. What are the likely effects of such a change on prospective nuclear states if, as many analysts contend, multipolarity emerges in the new century? Chapter 7 suggested reasons why the existing weapons states are likely to want to retain their nuclear weapons in a multipolar world.[10] For at least three reasons, such a change in the polarity of the international system would also encourage additional states to pursue a nuclear capability.

First, in an emerging multipolar world, a desire for strategic flexibil-

---

timism about the prospects for arms control, see Charles L. Glaser, "Realists as Optimists."

[10]Should unipolarity instead endure, candidate states would face its somewhat different strategic incentives discussed in Chapter 7.

ity provides an incentive for candidate nuclear states that perceive potentially serious threats to vital interests to move toward a nuclear weapons capability. As noted for the existing nuclear states, to the extent strategic alignments are less clearcut than in the bipolar era, complexity in threat assessment makes the robustness of nuclear deterrence appealing. Retargetable nuclear weapons provide a valuable hedge against the strategic and economic risks of changes in the source of threats to vital interests, as well as the obsolescence of a costly conventional force structure tailored to a specific adversary's current capabilities. Increased concern with economic competitiveness and attention to the opportunity costs of high military spending in the post–Cold War world, as noted in Chapter 7, will reinforce this consequence of a shift to multipolarity.

Second, in a multipolar world, military competition among the great powers is unlikely to be as intensive and extensive as it was under bipolarity. In a bipolar world, there were clear incentives for each of the duopolists to respond to any change that might work to the advantage of its adversary.[11] Consequently, lesser powers in the Cold War system could often exploit Soviet-American rivalry to garner military aid and protection. In a multipolar post–Cold War world, such states may find they must figure out how most effectively to draw on their own resources. According to the logic of the argument presented above, for some the self-help imperative is likely to foster an interest in nuclear weapons as affordable security insurance.

A state deciding whether to pursue its nuclear option in a multipolar world, however, might also face an important new disincentive. The absence of the close competition between superpowers that transformed many other states into clients and proxies under bipolarity means that great power preventive military action against post–Cold War nuclear aspirants would pose fewer risks of escalation. In a multipolar world candidate nuclear states might then refrain from pursuing their nuclear ambitions if they anticipate decisive military action that could thwart their efforts. Would such action be much more likely in a multipolar world than it was in the bipolar past?

Under bipolarity militarily marginalized allies worried about abandonment, but each superpower understood that the other had a self interest in preserving its reputation for resolve and therefore faced incen-

---

[11]See Karl W. Deutsch and J. David Singer, "Multipolar Power Systems and International Stability"; Richard N. Rosecrance, "Bipolarity, Multipolarity, and the Future"; Kenneth N. Waltz, "International Structure, National Force, and the Balance of World Power."

tives to stand by allies even if this meant risking entrapment in grave confrontations. Because each had to worry that the other's concern for its reputation might override the temptation of abandonment, extended deterrence was probably more effective than nervous allies believed. As most vividly illustrated in the case of China, for states that drew the superpowers' attention, bipolarity may in fact have resulted in safe havens within which lesser powers could develop, deploy, and modernize their nuclear arsenals. By contrast, in a multipolar world unilateral military action by one among several great powers would not *automatically* engage the interests of the others. A great power contemplating preventive attack on an aspiring nuclear state might still hesitate because of fears that the strike could engage the reputational concerns of a self-interested great power benefactor and trigger a dangerous response. But unlike the relatively focused competition of bipolarity, under multipolarity such fears would be less certain and would more likely vary with particular circumstances (such as ties between the great and lesser power rooted in geography, history, or culture). Diminished prospects for safe havens under multipolarity seemingly opens the door to a sturdy, coercive counterproliferation fallback for the diplomacy of the nonproliferation regime that might discourage some nuclear aspirants. Under multipolarity as under bipolarity, however, the implications of international structure are not that straightforward. Multipolarity results in a diffusion of responsibility as well as diminution in competition. While great power self-interest may provide fewer safe havens for nuclear aspirants, great power self-interest may also not lead any one of them to take the initiative in launching preventive counternuclear strikes. In line with the logic of collective action, unless the threat posed by an aspiring nuclear state is clearly focused, potential enforcers may rationally delay undertaking costly preventive military measures, hoping that others will do the job for them.[12]

A third, and related, effect of multipolarity is that it may further weaken the credibility of always problematic political assurances that security patrons can offer candidate states as a substitute for independent nuclear capabilities. States might refrain from pursuing the nuclear

[12]Indeed, only Israel, perceiving a clearly focused threat from Iraq, has launched an unvarnished, counter-nuclear preventive strike. The United States did seize the opportunity created by Operation Desert Storm to attack Iraq's reconstituted nuclear program. But in peacetime the United States has displayed little enthusiasm for shouldering the burden and risks of preventive strikes against the incipient nuclear capabilities of even presumably hostile, worrisome states like North Korea or Iran, let alone friendly and responsible states like India and Pakistan.

option if they had confidence in an umbrella of protection supplied by others (whether in practice this turns out to be the United States, NATO, or other international organizations). The upshot of this book's argument is that such an approach confronts serious obstacles.[13] Especially when considered together with the end of the ideological rivalry that reinforced the competitiveness of bipolarity during the Cold War, the diffusion of responsibility in a multipolar world makes it difficult to limit the spread of nuclear weapons by encouraging states to rely on questionable guarantees from allies or international organizations.

During the early decades of the Cold War, the superpowers had relatively large and growing nuclear arsenals and ostensibly strong commitments to their allies based not merely on common threat perceptions but also ideological affinity. Despite such propitious conditions for free-riding, three of their principal allies (China, Britain, and France) were sufficiently concerned about the possibly exclusive, as opposed to collective, character of the nuclear deterrent fielded by a superpower partner that they opted to shoulder the burden of developing, deploying, and maintaining their own nuclear arsenals as private insurance. If the benefits of external security guarantees were not readily treated as a collective good among close allies during the 1950s and 1960s, the prospects seem even bleaker in the post–Cold War world. To the extent ideological affinity among Cold War allies (with the exception of the Sino-American entente) acted as a moral constraint on callously abandoning partners in the Manichaean struggle between East and West, reinforcing the reputational constraint that reflected the competitiveness of bipolarity, the fear of exclusion should have been somewhat tempered. In the post–Cold War world this normative constraint on purely self-interested behavior may be lost along with the reputational constraints of bipolarity. And since security commitments are designed for circumstances that will entail facing grave risks, the foreseeable clash of self-interest and ethical concerns arising from purely formal, as opposed to ideologically rooted, prior obligations weakens confidence in the credibility of security guarantees as a reason for candidate states to remain nonnuclear.

In sum, then, in the post–Cold War world the list of candidate nuclear states (i.e., states who could deploy a national deterrent but currently do not) is likely to grow. Some states that could deploy nuclear weapons may decide they do not need them, or may choose to rely on assurances and inducements offered as a substitute. Others, however,

[13]See also Avery Goldstein, "Understanding Nuclear Proliferation."

will decide that they have good reasons to tap their potential. Among the many candidate states are a number of small and medium-sized countries (e.g., North Korea, Iraq, Iran, Libya) that have drawn much attention in the literature on nuclear proliferation because of their apparent determination to pursue the nuclear option and especially because of concerns about their potential for disruptive international behavior. The issues raised by such cases will be addressed below. First, however, I briefly examine three candidate states whose current nonnuclear status seems to be at odds with the argument I have presented. Ukraine, Japan, and Germany. Ukraine's experience in the 1990s, when circumstances required it to grapple with the decision about its nuclear status, illustrates some of the key concerns that will inform debates in states considering a national nuclear deterrent. Japan and Germany are of special interest, not only for theoretical reasons, but also because of their potential to re-emerge as great powers in the next century.

Ukraine

Ukraine's decision to divest itself of the remnants of the Soviet arsenal it had inherited suggests that it is possible to put together a package of incentives that convinces a state to forgo the nuclear weapons it might otherwise deploy. The circumstances surrounding Ukraine's decision, however, also suggest the inherent limits to this approach.

Following the disintegration of the USSR, Ukraine agreed to turn over its Soviet-era nuclear forces in exchange for international financial assistance and great power security assurances.[14] The extraordinary economic pressures on Kiev in the early 1990s, the moderate foreign policy behavior of the initial post-Soviet Russian regime, and the difficulties involved in gaining effective control over and then modifying Soviet weapons that had been designed for intercontinental missions, together explain this decision. Well into the post–Cold War period there has been little reason for Kiev to reconsider its "nuclear free" pledge and forfeit valuable foreign economic assistance (as well as the plaudits that go with nuclear abstinence) simply to be among the ranks of the nuclear powers. The Russian economy continues to stagnate, the Russian mili-

[14]Russia promised supplies for nuclear power reactors; the United States promised funds to help dismantle the SS-19 and SS-24 missiles, to transfer the warheads to Russia, and the release of economic and technical assistance held hostage to Ukraine's nuclear disarmament; the European Union also promised economic and technical aid. "In light of the drastic problems that the Ukrainian economy was suffering, this Western (and Russian) assistance was of no small importance, especially at a time when serious economic reforms were finally being considered" (Mark Kramer, "Realism, Nuclear Proliferation, and East-Central European Strategies," p. 49).

tary continues to atrophy, and Russo-Ukrainian relations continue to be amicable. Put simply, in light of Russia's current capabilities and intentions Ukraine's security environment remains relatively benign.

Should it perceive a more serious threat from Russia in the future, however, would Kiev be comfortable with the heavily qualified nature of external security assurances that have been provided thus far? The concerns that arose in the debate about giving up the Soviet weapons provide reason to doubt the durability of the arrangements under less favorable circumstances, especially since Ukraine retains the personnel and technological infrastructure that would smooth the path to a restored nuclear capability.[15] Even as Ukraine chose to surrender the portion of the Soviet nuclear arsenal left on its soil, some questioned the wisdom of its decision. During the debate, deputies to parliament worried about the practical value of verbal security pledges offered by the existing weapons states.[16] And Ukraine's subsequent initial criticism of NATO's eastward expansion reflected an enduring fear of abandonment. Would NATO's eastern boundary be interpreted as a dividing line for the seriousness of the West's security guarantees (indicating that Ukraine fell outside the alliance's sphere of vital interests)?[17] Kiev's political elite not only must ponder the risks inherent in relying on external assurances, but also the difficulty, perhaps infeasibility, of Ukraine deploying conventional military forces sufficient to defend against the range of options that would be open to a resurgent and potentially threatening Russia.[18]

[15]On May 19, 1997, Ukraine refused to halt production of its short- and mid-range missiles, insisting on the need to maintain the ability to produce strategic missiles, though for now the focus of production would be on the space program. Shorter-range missiles "can be used to defend the borders." Volodymyr Horbulin, Ukraine's top security official, stated: "Ukraine is not abandoning the idea of having strategic missiles. . . . We cannot give up the products of our brains, knowledge and hands. . . . Why should we guarantee that in 2010 we wouldn't produce a missile able to fly to Mars. Maybe it will be a strategic missile . . . I don't think that there will be a need for this but why should we limit our options?" (Rostislav Khotin, "Ukraine to Keep Making Missiles Despite U.S. Pressure").

[16]"Ukrainian Deputies Criticize Security Assurances." Milder reservations about disarmament were expressed in Kazakhstan as well. See Edith M. Lederer and Sergei Shargorodsky, "New Reluctance on Giving Up Their Nuclear Arms," p. A3; John F. Cushman, Jr., "Senate Endorse Pact to Reduce Strategic Arms," pp. A1, A6.

[17]Anthony Goodman, "Ukraine Worried About Potential Nuclear Neighbors." For analysis of the Ukrainian nuclear disarmament debate, see also John J. Mearsheimer, "The Case for a Ukrainian Nuclear Deterrent." For the counterarguments, see Steven E. Miller, "The Case Against a Ukrainian Nuclear Deterrent"; also Kramer, "Realism, Nuclear Proliferation, and East-Central European Strategies."

[18]"Ukrainian officials are under no illusions that their conventional forces can

Even in a more dangerous setting, Ukraine might still choose to lean heavily on support from others, perhaps even a nuclear umbrella provided by other European states or the United States. But for reasons illuminated by the Chinese, British, and French experience during the Cold War, and because that bygone era's reputational and normative constraints on abandonment have faded, prudent Ukrainian leaders would face strong incentives to doubt the reliability of peacetime pledges of extended deterrence whose fulfillment would require allies to run the risk of dangerous military conflict with Russia. Under more threatening circumstances nuclear deterrence of the strong by the weak would be a powerfully attractive option for ensuring continued Ukrainian autonomy, even if its realization entailed shouldering a heavy economic burden.

Japan and Germany

Inasmuch as Japan and Germany were second-ranking powers confronting superpower-sized threats, they had nonnuclear Cold War security policies that seem anomalous when viewed from the perspective offered in this book. Yet their posture is not hard to explain. External constraints established by the victors of World War II and domestic political constraints reflecting sensitivity to the lessons of that war narrowed the range of military-strategic options these two countries considered.[19] Most importantly, such limits precluded serious consideration of the nuclear alternative, though each did test the waters in limited ways.[20]

---

dependably repulse a full-scale Russian attack. The key problem for Ukrainian military officials, therefore, has been how to make a prospective attack so costly that Russian leaders would not want to pay the price of 'victory.'" (Kramer, "Realism, Nuclear Proliferation, and East-Central European Strategies," pp. 33–34). The extraordinary costs of high-tech nonnuclear weapons reduce the viability of relying on Ukrainian qualitative superiority to offset Russian quantitative advantages in conventional forces (ibid., pp. 47–48).

[19]These constraints are manifest in the pacifist constitutional provisions (Article 9 for the Japanese, Article 26 for the Germans) frequently cited as reasons why Japan and Germany cannot undertake a variety of military actions.

[20]On German pledges of nuclear abstinence in the 1950s, see Wilfred Kohl, French Nuclear Diplomacy, p. 312. Having forsworn an independent national nuclear arsenal, Germany supported various multilateral nuclear arrangements within NATO. And in 1957 discussions with France were leading to an arrangement for joint Franco-German nuclear weapons efforts, but these were aborted in 1958. At the time it joined the non-proliferation regime (1969), and when discussing its support for indefinite extension in 1995, Germany's analysts noted that such agreements did not preclude participation in "a European nuclear defense option" or even an independent option if, as Article 10 of the NPT permits, Germany decided to quit the treaty because "it found that its 'supreme interests' were in jeopardy" (Mark Hibbs,

U.S. security guarantees, of course, helped reduce the incentive for Germany and Japan to go nuclear, but it is not clear why such pledges alone would have been much more decisive for these allies than they were for China, Britain, or France. Entering the post–Cold War era, however, the constraining legacy of World War II is fading, and the appropriateness of a U.S. nuclear umbrella is less obvious. As doubts about the compatibility of interests in a Soviet-less world develop, and as disagreements about international affairs inevitably arise, Japan and Germany will be freer to consider a wider array of foreign policy alternatives.[21] To the extent Japan and Germany come to value foreign policy

---

"Tomorrow, a Eurobomb?," pp. 16ff). In the 1990s France and Germany renewed a security dialogue touching on nuclear matters in the context of developing a common defense policy for the European Union (Craig R. Whitney, "France and Germany to Discuss Joint Nuclear Deterrent," p. 3).

Japan, for historical and domestic political reasons, was more circumspect in its enjoyment of the U.S. nuclear umbrella during most of the Cold War. Nevertheless, recently declassified background papers for the Gilpatric Committee on nuclear proliferation indicate that the U.S. government believed in 1964 that despite public revulsion at the idea, "some Japanese leaders are likely to advocate nuclear weapons of Japan for the same set of reasons that de Gaulle has used. . . . According to intelligence reports, Prime Minister Sato and other leaders of the dominant LDP Party [sic] have been privately urging that Japan soon undertake a crash program to develop nuclear weapons. On December 29, Sato privately told U.S. Ambassador Reischauer that Japan could easily build such weapons, and that the Japanese public would have to be educated to accept them." Because such a step would evoke a public outcry in Japan, the analyst expected Japan to opt for "an indigenous 'peaceful' nuclear power reactor program, which would facilitate a military program at a later date . . ." ("Comments on Non-Proliferation Background Papers of December 12, 1964," pp. 3, 4). And in 1969, a highly secretive debate about the possibility of a Japanese nuclear deterrent was conducted. *Mainichi Shimbun* reported that in 1969 the Japanese foreign ministry drafted a report entitled "Prerequisites of Japan's Foreign Policy" in which it was suggested that Japan "should make sure it could produce (nuclear arms), if needed, no matter what foreign pressure were applied." Kazusuke Miyake who took part in the meetings, stated that the report was part of an internal government consensus that the country would "be weak if it did not hold such options. . . ." ("Japan in 1969 Ensured Nuclear Arms Potential—Daily"). Such opinions persist. Michio Royama, another of the participants in the covert debate of the late 1960s, recently reiterated the importance of retaining the option, though he continues to oppose moving forward at present: "We don't know the future. Let's not close that path." Hideshi Takesada, professor at the National Institute for Defense Studies, similarly does not see any imminent change, but emphasizes uncertainties about security in a changing world that mean "the important thing is never to say never" ("Japan Ponders Building Nuclear Weapons").

[21]As early as December 1994 a survey by CBS, the New York Times, and Tokyo Broadcasting System revealed declining Japanese confidence in the United States as a reliable military ally. 53 percent of Japanese surveyed favored revising the section of their "American-written Constitution" tightly limiting Japan's military capabilities, an increase from 42 percent in 1993, and, in the view of Japan specialist Richard

autonomy, and to discount the reliability of continued U.S. promises of protection, especially if they no longer share an obvious common adversary, the emergence of serious threats to Japan's and Germany's vital interests would provide incentives to consider fielding an independent nuclear deterrent.

Such a Japanese or German decision to pursue the nuclear option would not, however, be likely simply because of beliefs about the prestige value of such weapons though, as has been the case with the other nuclear weapons states, arguments of this sort might be used to rationalize a decision made for substantive strategic reasons. Indeed, if the decision turned primarily on status considerations, there would be little reason to expect Japan or Germany to follow in the military-strategic footsteps of their nuclear predecessors. Despite the initial hopes and early pronouncements made by the leaders of China, Britain, and France, their subsequent experience during the Cold War clearly revealed the weak link between nuclear capabilities and international prestige. Indeed, among the second-ranking powers Japan and Germany were the rising stars over the last three decades of the Cold War, their nonnuclear status notwithstanding. In addition, as the Israeli, Indian, and Pakistani experience suggests, since the norms of the nonproliferation regime have taken root after the mid-1960s, the prestige costs of a decision to go nuclear may exceed the benefits. Thus, if Japan and Ger-

---

Samuels, a "dramatic change from the past . . . Fifteen years ago, you could not talk about a change in the Constitution" (cited in David E. Sanger, "Poll Finds Japanese Less Sure of Future," p. A8). Japan's debate about the appropriate role for its military in the post–Cold War world became even more wide-ranging (including consideration of ballistic missile defenses and an independent reconnaissance satellite capability) following the North Korean Taepo Dong missile launch across Japanese territory on August 31, 1998. See Cameron W. Barr, "Weak by Design, Japan Ponders Its Missile Gap"; "Japan Says It Can Attack Nkorean Launch Site If Hit By Missile"; Cameron W. Barr, "North Korea's Missile Show Tests Japan's Tolerance." This catalyst sparking debate came just four months after Japan pondered the implications for Asian security of regional reactions to the South Asian nuclear tests. See Pierre-Antoine Donnet, "Japanese Strategists Warn of Renewed Nuclear Arms Race."

In August 1995, French proposals for extending the coverage of its *force de frappe* as part of a "concerted deterrent" for its European allies appealed to some German officials, who stated in "off-the-record discussions" that for the first time they were being floated in a post–Cold War era in which the U.S. "nuclear umbrella ceased to exist." At a time when domestic pacifism still precluded discussion of a German nuclear option, shifting from an American to a European extended deterrent might be viewed as a prudent hedge against uncertainty. As Freidbert Pfluger, spokesman on disarmament affairs for the CDU/CSU, put it, "No pacifist or well-intentioned idealist on this planet is going to convince me that in five, or maybe in two or three years, some dictator won't rule in the Kremlin who is holding 25,000 nuclear weapons. Nobody wants that, but who can exclude it?" (Hibbs, "Tomorrow, a Eurobomb?").

many decide that the possession of national nuclear forces is prudent in the post–Cold War world, it will most plausibly be because they serve tangible security interests and not just a desire for status. Their decision to go nuclear, like others' described in this book, would be taken because an independent deterrent promises significant security benefits at reasonable cost for states facing ill-defined but potentially serious threats, even those from vastly more capable adversaries.

Although perhaps not as important a constraint on choice for these two relatively wealthy countries as it was for the Cold War second-ranking nuclear powers, economic considerations will nonetheless significantly shape Japan's and Germany's security policies in the early twenty-first century. If perceived threats warrant a more self-reliant military effort, economic considerations will contribute to the attractiveness of the nuclear option. Indeed, Japanese and German leaders should be especially sensitive to the opportunity costs of unnecessarily high levels of military spending, inasmuch as their nations' remarkable post–World War II prosperity was facilitated by relatively modest defense expenditures.[22] As they contemplate the military-strategic component of more independent national security policies, both are likely to recognize one of the few clear truths about the nuclear era: Over time, maintaining nuclear forces sufficient for retaliatory threats as part of a deterrent strategy (perhaps a fleet of three or four SSBNs together with a small number of quick-reaction aircraft equipped with air-launched cruise missiles), though far from cheap, is less costly than maintaining comparably effective conventional forces to deny a great power adversary its military objectives as part of a defensive strategy. Reinforcing the economic appeal of a nuclear deterrent emphasis will be its above-mentioned strategic robustness in a more complex, possibly multipolar, world in which threat perceptions may be less determinate than those of the Cold War.

What, if anything, can be said about the time frame within which expectations about Japanese and German nuclear forces might be fulfilled? The absence of obvious major threats to vital interests in the immediate post–Cold War period provided these candidate nuclear great powers with little incentive to overhaul their long-standing nonnuclear commitments. The argument of this book leads to the somewhat vague prediction that serious consideration of the nuclear alternative will be prompted by as yet unforeseen challenges to Japanese and German vital

---

[22]Since at least the time of the Meiji reforms of the late nineteenth century, Japan has recognized economic health as an essential aspect of a comprehensive definition of national security.

interests that underscore the importance of self-help in an uncertain and dangerous anarchic world.[23] At that point, the principal barrier against Germany and Japan deploying nuclear weapons as an economical and robust national security guarantee will be domestic and international opinion (preventive military action by others seems improbable).[24] In the sort of threatening circumstances that would prompt such a major revision of foreign policy, the effectiveness of such constraints is doubtful, as the recent experience with India and Pakistan suggests. If the security concerns are genuine, the force of international opinion will not likely be decisive. And if the security concerns are genuine, domestic opinion against a nuclear capability that other states have deemed necessary for themselves may well crumble, especially as the original historical justification for Japan's and Germany's nuclear abstinence becomes ever more remote.[25]

[23]For Japan, at least, growing Chinese power and its more assertive behavior in regional territorial disputes contributed to a rethinking of the country's security requirements, as reflected in the 1996 Defense White Paper (Brian Williams, "Japan Sees China As Growing Military Challenge"; Nicholas D. Kristof, "Tension With Japan rises Alongside China's Star," p. E3). Although, as noted above, a more open debate about Japan's future military role has emerged in the late 1990s, for two reasons the process unfolds slowly. First, Japan's security concerns have been somewhat muted by strong U.S. reassurances about its commitment to remain militarily engaged in East Asia and the related updating of the United States–Japan defense guidelines for the post–Cold War era. Second, the debate is muted because Japan's elite are wary of provoking the fears of and eliciting criticism from many East Asian states, most importantly China, who suffered at the hands of a more militarily active Japan in the past.

[24]The technical hurdles are low. The skills and materials are readily available and a decision to move forward with nuclear weapons production in Japan reportedly could bear fruit in as short as a matter of weeks. Indeed, since actual weapons testing would be unnecessary (as for Israel), and since reports have circulated that Japan has already obtained nuclear triggers, it is unclear whether others would be aware of a modest development program ("Japan Ponders Building Nuclear Weapons"). For the notion that Japan might possess a "virtual" rather than an "opaque" deterrent, see Andrew Hanami, The Military Might of Modern Japan, pp. 127–41. Yet the easily anticipated reaction to such a decision is a concern that cannot be ignored. Fifty years after World War II, most other East Asian countries remain remarkably wary of any Japanese shift toward a more activist, militarily significant international role. In 1987 China reacted with alarm when Japan's defense budget for the first time barely exceeded the symbolically important ceiling of one percent of GNP ("Deng Warns over Japan's Defense Spending"). Such concerns, especially in China and Korea, endured well into the post–Cold War era despite Japan's continued impeccable behavior in the region. See Nicholas D. Kristof, "Japanese Look at the Possibility of a Military Role in Asia," p. A8; Thomas J. Christensen, "Chinese Realpolitik"; Gerald Segal, "China Takes on Pacific Asia"; "China Media Say Japan Shrine Boost to Militarism."

[25]Japan already has a constitutional justification for possessing nuclear weapons;

Thinking about the Japanese and German cases, as well as the Ukrainian situation, suggests the expected broader pattern of nuclear spread. States will consider the match between their available resources and the threats they face, and then determine whether their security concerns warrant the decision to buck the international norm of non-proliferation and incur any sanctions that may be placed on them. The balance of such considerations will in each case determine the feasibility of international efforts to limit membership in the nuclear club. Success is most likely where perceived threats are modest and where international sanctions, especially multilateral economic sanctions, would be most effective.[26] But the inference from the analysis offered here leads to the conclusion that the number of nuclear states will continue to grow, even if slowly, because some capable states facing serious threats will deem a national deterrent necessary, and the costs of its pursuit tolerable. The murky North Korean nuclear program and nuclear testing in South Asia provide fresh evidence that even poor states are willing to suffer the hardship of economic sanctions and incur the wrath of international public opinion if they believe their national interests require development of a nuclear capability.[27]

---

they have been deemed permissable as long as they are used to fulfill a deterrent role. See "Japan Ponders Building Nuclear Weapons," and Mike M. Mochizuki, "Japan's Search for Strategy." The Japanese debate about permissible military activities and the desirability of revising the "peace constitution" continues to unfold slowly, but its scope has clearly expanded, as noted above. Fear of a potential military confrontation with North Korea over its suspected nuclear weapons program in the mid-1990s helped focus the debate, as did the April 1996 summit between President Clinton and Prime Minister Hashimoto to discuss U.S.-Japan security ties, and especially the August 31, 1998, North Korean Taepo Dong missile test. A less threatening context for the great powers in Europe than that found in the post–Cold War Pacific has provided fewer incentices for Germany to reconsider its defense planning. It remains to be seen whether German debate will be ignited by a new external threat, or by the requirements of formulating a common defense policy for the European Union as mandated in the Maastricht Treaty.

[26]See David A. Baldwin, *Economic Statecraft*; Lisa L. Martin, *Coercive Cooperation*; Edward D. Mansfield, "Review—Coercive Cooperation: Explaining Multilateral Economic Sanctions."

[27]The North Korean case is most difficult to interpret. It is possible that Pyongyang's highly opaque nuclear research effort has been aimed less at developing a working weapon and more at providing a credible bargaining chip it can use to exploit proliferation concerns and extract economic assistance and political concessions from concerned regional actors, especially the United States and Japan.

A NUCLEAR FUTURE: PESSIMISM OR
TEMPERED OPTIMISM?

This book has focused on the reasons why states decide to pursue nuclear weapons, highlighting their attractiveness as a robust and affordable means for coping with potentially daunting threats to security. It has most closely examined the Cold War experience of China, Britain, and France, in which modest numbers of nuclear weapons were carefully deployed to serve deterrent strategies that aimed to preserve the status quo. If, as the preceding discussion suggests, the number of nuclear-armed states is likely to continue to grow, will the newer members of the club deploy their weapons as prudently and for similarly benign purposes? In short, what are the probable consequences for international politics of a world with a small but growing number of nuclear states?

The overwhelmingly dominant view of the consequences of any spread of nuclear weapons is strongly pessimistic. The argument and evidence presented in this book, however, supports the more sanguine minority view, suggesting room for tempered optimism. The chief concerns about the spread of nuclear weapons are familiar. New nuclear states, it is often asserted, (1) may be led by fanatical, ambitious leaders or self-interested military groups who would callously employ weapons of mass destruction to achieve their preferred goals; (2) may be unable to deploy invulnerable forces and so, in a crisis, be tempted to launch before a nervous adversary can mount a preemptive strike (the "use'em or lose'em" mentality); or (3) may be unable to maintain effective control over their forces, raising the risks of inadvertent or accidental use, especially once they are put on alert in a crisis, as well as the chance of illicit transfer to criminal or terrorist elements (the "loose nukes" nightmare).[28]

These are certainly troubling possibilities and, given the stakes of

---

[28]See Sagan, "The Perils of Proliferation"; Peter D. Feaver, "Command and Control in Emerging Nuclear Nations"; Feaver, "Neooptimists and the Enduring Problem of Nuclear Proliferation"; Bruce G. Blair, *The Logic of Accidental Nuclear War*, pp. 10–12; Devin T. Hagerty, "Nuclear Deterrence in South Asia"; Steve Fetter, "Nuclear Deterrence and the 1990 Indo-Pakistani Crisis"; Devin T. Hagerty, "The Author Replies." For discussion of some of the troubling concerns about nuclear weapons as a tool for terrorists, as well as the difficulties that such actors would face in incorporating them in their repertoire, see Robert J. Art, "A Defensible Defense," pp. 25–28; Thomas C. Schelling, "Thinking About Nuclear Terrorism"; Brian M. Jenkins, "Is Nuclear Terrorism Plausible?" For an extensive bibliographic overview and reconsideration of the debate about proliferation optimism vs. pessimism, see Karl, "Proliferation Pessimism and Emerging Nuclear Powers."

the game when nuclear weapons are in play, understandably encourage policy-makers to undertake strong counterproliferation efforts.[29]
Though political leaders sensibly err on the side of caution, what does
scholarly analysis suggest about the likelihood of the more frightening
possible consequences of nuclear proliferation? A minority view among
scholars asserts that the usual fears are exaggerated and offers three basic
reasons.[30] First, even ruthless, purportedly irresponsible leaders, it is argued, will behave with uncharacteristic caution once they possess nuclear weapons because they recognize the potentially catastrophic consequences of nuclear adventurism. Such leaders may not be perfectly rational or peace-loving, but they are not interested in the self-destruction
of their cause, be it secular-national, religious, or ideological, and will
easily recognize that this is a very real possibility should their nuclear
recklessness provoke retaliation in kind, especially when, as is often the
case with the more worrisome candidate states, that retaliation would
be launched against a homeland with no more than a small handful of
major metropolitan centers.[31] And in the unlikely event that a leader entirely disconnected from reality could achieve and maintain control of a
state's political system, that would not ensure his ability to have military officers carry out nuclear orders inviting national suicide.[32]

[29]Even the optimistic Kenneth Waltz recommends a case-by-case policy toward
new proliferants, "sometimes bringing pressures against a country moving toward
nuclear-weapons capability and sometimes quietly acquiescing" ("More May Be Better," p. 44).

[30]Two leading scholars identified with these contrasting visions directly address
each other's arguments in Scott D. Sagan and Kenneth N. Waltz, eds., *The Spread of
Nuclear Weapons*. See also Art, "A Defensible Defense," pp. 24–28

[31]It is worth recalling that on the eve of China's first nuclear detonation, U.S.
analysts predicted that China would be more confrontational in its relations with
the United States in Asia as it deployed nuclear weapons. See the recently declassified "China as a Nuclear Power (Some Thoughts Prior to the Chinese Test)," Oct. 7,
1964. China's subsequent foreign policy instead reflected both the caution-inducing
effects of nuclear possession as well as the importance of influences other than armaments that shape a state's international posture.

[32]Kenneth Waltz argues that orders inviting national suicide would not be
obeyed since a leadership's authority collapses when defeat seems imminent. He
cites as supporting evidence the refusal of German generals to launch gas warfare in
early 1945 (Waltz, "More May Be Better," p. 29). By contrast Scott Sagan argues that
the real danger may not be the execution of civilian orders, but weak civilian control
that allows an offensive-minded military organization to act on its parochial preferences rather than according to a broader definition of national interest (Sagan, "More
Will Be Worse," pp. 48–49). Hard evidence on this, as on many nuclear nightmare
scenarios, is fortunately lacking, but the circumspect behavior of the Soviet nuclear
command and control system during the August 1991 coup is at least encouraging.
See Blair, *The Logic of Accidental Nuclear War*, pp. 82–86.

Second, nuclear optimists suggest that the "use'em or lose'em" concern may simultaneously understate the inhibitions against nuclear use (choosing to risk suicide for fear of death) and overstate the difficulty of fielding nuclear forces whose survivability is strategically adequate. Creative deployment and concealment of actual weapons and decoys, an approach reflected in China's handling of its relatively small, vulnerable arsenal during the Cold War, can instill uncertainty about target coverage in the mind of an adversary contemplating a preemptive first strike whose expected effectiveness must approach 100 percent to be a realistic option against a nuclear-armed state. Even in what is often believed to be the more dangerous case of confrontation between relatively poor and small regional nuclear rivals, first-strike uncertainty mitigates the vulnerability problems that pessimists emphasize. As Jordan Seng has argued, such states have more limited reconnaissance capabilities for locating and targeting the adversary's nuclear forces and a lower threshold for unacceptable retaliatory damage.[33]

Third, nuclear optimists assert that states with the resources to develop and deploy a nuclear arsenal will also possess the rudimentary organizational and technological capabilities necessary to maintain control over what are likely to be relatively small numbers of weapons. And because these weapons are not only a regime's most prized military asset, but one whose possession and possible use by renegade officers, criminals, or terrorists could invite catastrophic retaliatory punishment, the state will have powerful incentives to devise the means for ensuring such control.[34] Bruce Blair and Scott Sagan, disagreeing with such optimism, have described how bureaucratic routines designed to cope with the unforgiving realities of nuclear war increase the risk that any nuclear use will be spasmodic rather than carefully managed.[35]

[33]See Jordan Seng, "Less Is More."

[34]Moreover, the Cold War experience cautions against the belief that great technological sophistication is either necessary or sufficient for this task. Despite having a less advanced technological base than its American rival, the Soviet Union appears to have established tight and redundant negative controls over its nuclear arsenal. On this comparison, see Blair, The Logic of Accidental Nuclear War. Indeed, organizational interests may well trump technological capabilities. For decades the U.S. Navy successfully resisted the installation of permissive action links (PALs) on its submarine-launched ballistic missiles, emphasizing the potential loss of positive control and asserting the reliability of its submarine officers as a means for ensuring negative control. Only in 1995 did the Navy agree to have PALs installed during 1996–97 (David Wood, "Navy Subs Give Washington Control Over Nuclear Missiles," p. 6A).

[35]Sagan, "The Perils of Proliferation" and "More Will Be Worse"; Blair, The Logic of Accidental Nuclear War.

Their work suggests a terrifying loss of control once the dynamics of escalation begin. Optimists offer two countervailing considerations. One is that the pessimists may be correct in their characterization of the organizational risks when the linked adversaries were the overarmed Cold War superpowers, but wrong to impose their logic on other nuclear states. For states other than the superpowers, the small size of the arsenals, along with simple doctrines for weapons use, render irrelevant many of the organizational pathologies that the pessimists detail.[36] The other optimist counter is that fear of the very dynamic the pessimists describe may well be an important consideration discouraging leaders from greatly easing tight peacetime controls, even in a crisis, lest they set in motion standard operating procedures that prove irreversible. Fearing even a small probability of inadvertent disaster discourages recklessness in confrontations among nuclear-armed states. Doubt about one's actual ability to manage alerted nuclear forces, or to exercise sustained positive control over the use of nuclear weapons in a military conflict, like doubt about an adversary's actual ability and willingness to launch a nuclear retaliatory strike, tips the balance further in the direction of war avoidance and encourages a reluctance to loosen controls.[37]

[36]See Seng, "Less Is More." Cf. Feaver, "Neooptimists and the Enduring Problem of Nuclear Proliferation"; Seng, "Optimism in the Balance." See also Barry R. Posen, *Inadvertent Escalation*. Though hardly constituting evidence decisively settling this debate, it is worth noting that since becoming declared nuclear weapons states both India and Pakistan have publicly asserted their understanding of the importance of command and control issues. See Pratap Chakravarty, "India Counting Days to Become a True Nuclear-weapons State"; "Pakistan Setting Up Nuclear Command and Control System."

[37]States can manage, but not eliminate, the risks involved in trying to cope with the sometimes conflicting requirements of maintaining both positive control (use when ordered) and negative control (no use, if not ordered) over their nuclear forces. Bruce Blair, for example, reported that the Soviets had responded to the growing concern about a U.S. option to launch a decapitating strike by deploying an automated retaliatory system, the "dead hand" doomsday machine. Blair was alarmed by what he saw as a system that could automate a response during a crisis and result in an accidental or inadvertent nuclear exchange. But Valery Yarynich, "a retired colonel in the Russian Strategic Rocket Forces who spent his career working on command and control systems," responded to Blair's concerns by clarifying the escalation-dampening purpose of the "dead hand" and the redundant negative controls designed to prevent its premature activation. According to Yarynich, the system was developed so that "Russia's top military commanders will not be forced to launch nuclear missiles immediately after receiving a signal that Moscow is under attack" and instead could depend on launch orders being issued by an underground radio crew, but even then only if three criteria were met: "preliminary sanction for an attack from the Russian general staff"; "full loss of communication with top military commanders"; and

Despite such plausible and, to some, logically persuasive arguments indicating that pessimism about the consequences of growth in the number of nuclear states may be overstated, given the stakes involved most scholars, policy-makers, and citizens prefer to err on the side of caution and support attempts to prevent the spread of this capability.[38] But since there are strong reasons to believe that counterproliferation will not be fully successful, it is important to keep in mind that there is room for tempered optimism in thinking about the consequences of nuclear spread. Indeed, to the various reasons for tempered optimism just mentioned, one can add that both logic and the experience of the Cold War (especially as illustrated in the Chinese, British, and French cases) suggest that nuclear weapons may be a stabilizing influence on international politics because they are most easily married to strategies designed to preserve the status quo, and not easily employed for other purposes. For most, as this book has explained, an interest in preserving the status quo will in fact provide the decisive motive for acquiring nuclear weapons. But even those whose nuclear ambitions are fed by more aggressive desires will find it difficult to incorporate their new capability in strategies with much prospect of altering the status quo. Why?

Nuclear Weapons and the Status Quo

As noted in Chapter 2, despite parallels in their logic regarding the indirect use of force, there is an important difference between dissuasive strategies to maintain, and persuasive strategies to alter, the status quo. A state practicing dissuasion (by deterrence or defense) need do nothing unless the adversary initiates a challenge. Inaction is the desired response to dissuasive threats and signifies the strategy's success. A state practicing persuasion (by compellence or offense), in contrast, cannot simply tolerate inaction. It visibly signifies the strategy's failure and, worse, could lead others to discount future threats as idle bluffs. Yet inaction may well be the adversary's most likely response, especially if acceding to the demanded revisions in the status quo will be politically embarrassing or militarily imprudent. Visibility raises the domestic as well as international political costs of compliance for the targeted

---

"evidence of nuclear explosions." And even in circumstances where all three conditions were met, a launch order could "be transmitted only by the crew—that is, an attack cannot be launched automatically." See Bruce G. Blair, "Russia's Doomsday Machine," p. A35; Valery Yarynich, "The Doomsday Machine's Safety Catch," p. A17.

[38]For an argument that presents the case for hedging one's bets about the possibly benign effects of the spread of nuclear weapons capabilities, see Art, "A Defensible Defense," pp. 28–30.

state's foreign policy elite.[39] Short of abandoning its goals, what can a state practicing persuasion do if results are not forthcoming? The alternatives are to carry out the threat or to attempt to make the threat more effective. If nuclear weapons are in play, neither choice is attractive.

The first of these choices, carrying out a threatened strike, though perhaps useful for sending a message of credibility to future adversaries, is not a plausible means for achieving the immediate objective and may be unacceptably risky if the rival has its own retaliatory capability or may be able to tap that of an ally. The second choice, attempting to make nuclear persuasion more effective, is also problematic. Thomas Schelling's seminal works on coercion and bargaining suggested the appropriateness of the use of limited force to demonstrate credibility and increase pressure on an adversary to comply with one's demands. But, as Schelling recognized, however logically straightforward, in practice devising appropriate catalyzing actions is likely to be difficult. How does one strike the correct balance between restraint and severity, especially when nuclear weapons are the military means behind a strategy of persuasion by compellence or offense?[40] With regard to compellence, nuclear forces provide evidence of an unmistakable *ability* to inflict horrifying punishment, but not the willingness to do so, evidence that may well be required in order to prompt costly visible compliance. Capabilities notwithstanding, a state's moral or political inhibitions on the use of force, its fears of uncontrollable environmental damage if the adversary is a regional neighbor, or concerns about third-party retaliation in kind[41] may lead the targeted state to heavily discount nuclear compellent threats. With nuclear compellence, unlike nuclear deterrence, the burden of taking dangerous first steps rests with the party making the threats of catastrophic damage. This is not easily done. Resort to catalyzing actions that entail only conventional munitions, for example, or even very small nuclear explosions in remote areas in an attempt to sig-

[39]On the links between an elite's domestic and international political concerns, see Robert D. Putnam, "Diplomacy and Domestic Politics." For a nuanced application of such two-level considerations to the case of Sino-American relations, see Thomas J. Christensen, *Useful Adversaries: Grand Strategy, Domestic Mobilization, and Sino-American Conflict, 1947–1958.*

[40]See Thomas C. Schelling, *The Strategy of Conflict;* Schelling, *Arms and Influence.*

[41]This consideration may well be the most important. The one clearly successful case of nuclear compellence, the bombing of Hiroshima and Nagasaki, required U.S. decision-makers to worry only about their ability to inflict punishment, the scale of punishment to be inflicted, and their own moral concerns. There was no need to worry about possible Japanese retaliation in kind or retaliation by a nuclear-capable ally.

nal the determination to take stronger steps, is unlikely to eliminate doubts about credibility. The choice of clearly safe opening gambits is more suggestive of the reluctance of a bluffer, rather than the resolve of the ruthless. In response, the victim can simply sit tight, effectively pushing the ball back into its adversary's court.[42]

If nuclear munitions are not easily used in compellent strategies to alter the status quo, they are even less plausibly linked with strategies of persuasion by offense. A strategy of persuasion by offense must convince the adversary that one has the requisite military capability and resolve to forcibly alter the status quo if it does not comply. Essentially the message one seeks to send is that resistance is futile; victory for the offensive is a foregone conclusion and, therefore, actually engaging in armed struggle is pointless. In theory, either nuclear or conventional forces can serve as the means to clearly demonstrate one's decisive military advantage that lies at the heart of a strategy of persuasion by offense. But the questionable usefulness of nuclear weapons for achieving battlefield objectives, as opposed to inflicting punishment, undermines their credibility for offensive threats. Even against a nonnuclear, nonaligned adversary where worries about retaliation in kind are irrelevant, nuclear weapons are not easily married with offensive strategies. Nuclear weapons, with few exceptions, produce collateral damage, both blast and radiation effects, that may irretrievably degrade the object of contention—whether it is disputed territory beyond one's borders, or national territory one seeks to win back from an aggressor.[43] Their dis-

---

[42]The catalyzing actions in support of a persuasive strategy, if they must be very large-scale, effectively evolve into offensive operations to alter the status quo through the direct use of force or punishment inflicted for vengeance after compellence has failed. Fred Kaplan discusses this complication in describing the Nixon administration's attempts by James Schlesinger to translate the idea of a nuclear warning shot into a practical targeting guideline, and also Henry Kissinger's dissatisfaction with alternative proposals (deemed either too strong or too weak) for limited nuclear use in the event of a Soviet invasion of Iran (Kaplan, *The Wizards of Armageddon*).

[43]And, it must be remembered, some objectives (a change in policy or behavior) are not the sort that can be directly seized (such as disputed territory or natural resources), with nuclear or conventional forces. But even for objectives that can be seized by force, only the most advanced nuclear weapons with specially tailored effects (e.g., enhanced radiation bombs) can avoid some of the counterproductive consequences of nuclear use. To the extent such devices can more effectively accomplish the missions serving an offensive strategy without the residual side-effects of cruder nuclear weapons, the special problems of nuclear use disappear. Still, depending on perceptions about the importance of a clear distinction between nuclear devices and all other weaponry, belief that their use could entail significantly greater risks of escalation than those already presented by the engagement of conventional

tinctively destructive effects on both natural and human resources make it hard to convince an adversary that one could directly employ nuclear weapons to achieve political objectives.[44] This not only undermines persuasive strategies relying on threats to stage offensive actions, but also greatly diminishes the feasibility of forcibly altering the status quo through the direct use of nuclear force should persuasion fail.[45]

---

forces might undermine the credibility of threats to use such "clean mini-nuclear weapons."

Assuming one has the economic and technological wherewithal, it is more credible to threaten the use of conventional forces (especially with the advent of precision guided munitions) as part of an offensive strategy. To say it is plausible is not to say it is easy. As with compellence, persuasion by offense will require the adversary to comply with demands in a visible fashion that may carry steep costs in terms of international or domestic political prestige. And if the means for carrying out the strategy are most suitably non-nuclear, the target of one's persuasive efforts may be inclined to test one's vaunted military prowess. Where only conventional weapons are to be confronted, an adversary can expect that he will have the time to comply with the original demands after the battle has been joined, if in fact it becomes obvious that the outcome of the military struggle will be unfavorable. Unlike nuclear detonations, the consequences of the use of conventional forces can be hard to estimate. The difficulty in practicing compellence relying on conventional threats is reflected in the now-familiar checkered history of conventional strategic bombing campaigns during the twentieth century. For a summary of strategic bombing debates in the pre-nuclear and nuclear era (many of whose themes were reprised in debates about the 1991 Persian Gulf War and the 1999 campaign in Yugoslavia), see Lawrence Freedman, *The Evolution of Nuclear Strategy*. See also Robert A. Pape, *Bombing to Win*. Moreover, the potential victims of conventional attack can hope to avail themselves of imperfect active and passive defenses whose level of effectiveness against nuclear punishment would be deemed unacceptable. See Bailey, "Why We Have to Keep the Bomb"; Robert Jervis, *The Meaning of the Nuclear Revolution*.

[44]This last consideration would be especially relevant if one is considering the possibility of relying on a compellent strategy to persuade an invader to withdraw from one's occupied homeland as part of a people's war of national resistance. Though potentially stymied by similar considerations, non-nuclear forces may more plausibly be married to strategies of persuasion through compellence or offense. Still, the difficulty of conventional compellence is revealed by the fact that even in the cases where the strategy has succeeded, most notably against the French and Americans in Indochina, success was slow in coming. It requires an organization capable of mobilizing and organizing a sustaining population for the long haul. Put simply, as Mao Zedong explained, victory in people's war is achieved only after a protracted struggle. Historically, few political movements have been able to meet the strategy's stiff requirements.

[45]Offensive strikes with nuclear weapons simply to destroy the adversary may be viable against a nonnuclear foe. Under such circumstances a ruthless leadership unmoved by the fate of the human and natural resources of an adversary could act. Two minimal conditions would have to be met, however. The environmental consequences of attack would have to be acceptable to the attacker (in terms of radioactive fallout, effects on the water supply, refugee flows), and the attacker would have to be certain that the victim would not be able to call on a nuclear state to carry out re-

A related reason for tempered optimism about the consequences of continued slow growth in the number of nuclear weapons states is its likely effect on diplomacy in disputes that threaten the status quo. Among nuclear states, the difficulties of relying on the indirect or direct use of force to alter the status quo constrains leaders to work harder to discover political rather than military resolutions to such disputes. Although force and diplomacy have long been recognized as alternative means for achieving foreign policy goals, the nuclear revolution fundamentally alters expectations about the feasibility of the military option.[46] Geoffrey Blainey has argued that war results when states are unable to reach negotiated resolutions of their disputes because they disagree about their relative power and because both sides are optimistic that they can improve their bargaining position by fighting a war to demonstrate their strength.[47] Nuclear capabilities makes such demonstrations unnecessary and optimism difficult. Once adversaries possess a survivable retaliatory capability, comparisons of nuclear forces are irrelevant within wide margins and even comparisons of conventional capabilities must be heavily discounted inasmuch as a disadvantaged party can exploit the risk of escalation to the top rung on the ladder of military force.[48] Although diplomacy may yet fail, the ever-present possibility of nearly instantaneous catastrophe in a war against a nuclear adversary about whose behavior one cannot be absolutely certain provides historically unprecedented incentives for negotiators to discover a way to avoid risking national survival.[49] Distasteful diplomatic com-

---

taliatory strikes on its behalf. Although the allies of nuclear states, for reasons stated above, naturally worry most about abandonment, aggressors worry most about the possibility, however small, that a nuclear patron will in fact respond. And in most cases, other obvious considerations would come into play, such as the political fallout, both domestic and international, that would also affect a leadership's plan to execute an offensive, nuclear war plan against a nonnuclear adversary.

[46]On the ways in which vulnerability to thermonuclear destruction fundamentally transformed strategic logic and the relation between diplomacy and the use of force in international relations, see Jervis, *The Meaning of the Nuclear Revolution*, esp. ch. 1.

[47]Geoffrey Blainey, *The Causes of War*; see also Waltz, "More May Be Better," pp. 5–8.

[48]Robert Jervis, *The Illogic of American Nuclear Strategy*.

[49]The nuclear revolution dramatically alters a decision-maker's calculus of expected utility that is based on the combination of preference for alternative outcomes and the estimated probability of their coming to pass. The classic statement, subsequently revised and refined, applying the expected utility model to the study of international politics is Bruce Bueno de Mesquita, *The War Trap*. For a wide-ranging discussion that assesses the claims about the reasons states may rationally decide to go to war, see James G. Fearon, "Rationalist Explanations for War."

promises that would have been rejected in favor of war in the pre-
nuclear era (when catastrophe was merely a long-term possibility, often
hard to envision, and whose arrival could be prevented through either
military action or renewed negotiations) appear today as the lesser evil
when the alternative requires accepting even the small possibility of
triggering a series of events that at any moment could result in prompt
national disaster.[50]

Yet, it might be noted, during the Cold War the superpowers did at
times attempt to gain bargaining leverage from their nuclear arsenals. In
terms of lessons for the post–Cold War world, however, their experience
in this regard is far from discouraging. Nuclear weapons provided diplomatic leverage in cases where the interests of just one nuclear state
were directly involved, or where the nuclear state issuing threats did so
to press for the limited goal of a return to the status quo ante. Eisenhower used nuclear threats to persuade China to accept a Korean Armistice (essentially ratifying the prewar division of territory on the peninsula), and later to cease pressure against the offshore islands in the Taiwan Straits (maintaining the status quo there). Kennedy used threats of
unpredictable escalation to persuade the Soviets to reverse their nuclear
deployment in Cuba (in return for a U.S. pledge to preserve the pre-crisis
status quo). And Soviet threats of preventive strikes against China in
1969 were only useful to persuade China to live with the de facto Sino-
Soviet border and agree to negotiations. The most noteworthy Cold War
attempt to gain bargaining leverage from saber-rattling to significantly
alter the status quo where the vital interests of nuclear states clashed,
was a spectacular failure—Khrushchev's threats in support of the re-

---

[50]The evidence from South Asia since India and Pakistan were nuclear capable in
the late 1980s, even before the 1998 tests, suggests that fear of nuclear escalation
sharply constrains even highly antagonistic rivals. Devin Hagerty makes a persuasive case that opaque nuclear deterrence prevented the India-Pakistan Kashmir crisis
of 1990 from spinning out of control. See Hagerty, *The Consequences of Nuclear Proliferation*, ch. 6. Those who asserted that nuclear weapons made South Asia a more
dangerous place often alarmingly noted that India and Pakistan had fought three
wars since 1947, but omitted the equally important observation that none had been
fought since the two sides became undeclared nuclear weapons states in the late
1980s. The future evolution of their relations, and especially the handling of their
dispute over Kashmir, will provide a strong test of the war-inhibiting effects of nuclear weapons. Even as India carried out military strikes against Kashmiri insurgents
in late spring 1999, leaders in both countries eagerly sought to preclude escalation.
Hagerty's argument notwithstanding, some regional experts even during the 1999
confrontation doubted whether either country actually had a usable nuclear capability. Yet these expert opinions were speculative and characterized by enough uncertainty that political leaders could not escape the inhibiting fears of nuclear escalation. See Pratap Chakravarty, "Nuclear India, Pakistan Incapable of Atomic War."

peated Soviet efforts to unify Berlin. In Berlin the risks of nuclear escalation instead facilitated a successful U.S. strategy of dissuasion by deterrence, not the Soviet strategy of persuasion by compellence.

Another reason why the possession of nuclear weapons is unlikely to encourage attempts to alter the status quo is that their possession sharply reduces the intrinsic military value of territory.[51] To the extent that states rely on threats of nuclear punishment to dissuade challenges to their vital interests, security depends less on geographic considerations relevant to the time and space necessary for offensive or defensive maneuvers, and more on the modest requirements of deployment sufficient for ensuring that potential aggressors will be uncertain about their ability to execute a fully effective preemptive strike. As the practice of the smaller nuclear states reveals, creativity in modest mobile deployments, stealth, and deception can compensate for material disadvantages linked with geography.

For two reasons, however, this change in the military value of territory for nuclear states reduces, rather than eliminates, its importance as a cause of interstate conflict to alter the status quo. First, for political reasons states may yet be reluctant to abandon long-standing irredentist claims to what they perceive as sacred national territory that call for action to overturn the status quo. And second, for military reasons states may be reluctant to abandon a desire for territorial advantage. Even if leaders are inclined to embrace the centrality and robustness of nuclear deterrence, given the high stakes of international politics, few will happily place all their eggs in a single strategic basket. With an eye to preserving their strategic options in an uncertain future, prudent military and political leaders are unlikely to entirely discount conventional warfighting considerations and related territorial concerns. But, by sharply reducing the importance of battlefield requirements that would be crucial for security policies emphasizing conventional defensive or offensive strategies, nuclear weapons weaken the incentives to take grave risks to acquire disputed territory.[52]

Despite the aforementioned reasons for tempered optimism, one particular scenario is often viewed as especially worrisome—the emergence of nuclear-armed regional bullies. Even if such states recognize

---

[51]See Kenneth N. Waltz, "The Spread of Nuclear Weapons."

[52]The diminished intrinsic military value of territory may make diplomatic concessions easier. One suspects, for example, that in the absence of the security guarantee supplied by national nuclear arsenals, it would have been even more difficult for Israel to yield territories occupied in the 1967 war, and for Mikhail Gorbachev to tolerate the evaporation of the Soviet/Russian buffer zone in Eastern Europe.

the futility of employing nuclear weapons for offensive or compellent purposes to alter the status quo, they might believe that their robust deterrent shield frees them to undertake aggressive military action relying on a conventional sword. How likely is this disturbing scenario?

An offense-minded regional bully of the sort envisioned would have to amass substantial conventional capabilities as a complement to its nuclear deterrent. The greater the capabilities it possesses, and the more threatening it appears, the more likely others would notice its buildup and respond.[53] Moreover, once it acquires or is even suspected of possessing a nuclear capability a regional bully might enjoy a powerful deterrent shield, but by attracting the concern of the world's great powers, it would most likely also confront greater obstacles to realizing any hegemonic ambitions. When a potential regional bully possesses nuclear weapons, regional *and* extra-regional actors are more likely to focus on its menacing behavior and growing capabilities and to worry about the long-term threat it may pose. The range of predictable responses by local actors includes the organization of a countervailing regional nonnuclear coalition facilitating a policy of dissuasion by conventional deterrence or defense, the development of a countervailing nuclear capability facilitating a strategy of dissuasion by nuclear deterrence, or soliciting extended deterrent or defensive guarantees from extra-regional actors (either great powers separately or through international organizations).[54] How plausible are these options? Wouldn't a regional bully with a nuclear shield be confident it could use its conventional sword and victimize isolated rivals before an effective response was forthcoming? For two reasons this seems unlikely.

First, in the short term, dissuasion by conventional defense can more easily and at lower risk be made robust against regional rather than global powers. Regional conventional balances would not quickly be altered just because one state acquired nuclear weapons. To the extent a potential aggressor's nuclear deterrent shield enabled it to redirect military investment from defensive to offensive conventional forces, potential victims would have both the incentive and time to respond, through forming defensive coalitions, recruiting extra-regional allies, or

---

[53]The response is predicted both by balance-of-power theory (Kenneth N. Waltz, *Theory of International Politics*) and balance-of-threat theory (Stephen M. Walt, *The Origins of Alliances*).

[54]In April 1995 the nuclear great powers suggested their support for this last alternative in their promise to aid any signatory of the NPT threatened by a nuclear state ("U.N. Council Gives Assurance to Non-nuclear States"). See also Waltz, "More May Be Better," pp. 8–17.

developing a nuclear deterrent of their own. A second reason to doubt that regional nuclear bullies would be strongly tempted to act on their more aggressive impulses is the effectiveness of extended nuclear deterrence. As noted above, although the fear self-interested states will refuse to run grave risks on behalf of others may mean that extended deterrent guarantees are unlikely to be sufficiently reassuring to their recipients, this does not mean they are insufficiently threatening to adversaries. Where nuclear weapons are in play, even a small probability that dubious deterrent pledges will be fulfilled is highly dissuasive.[55]

Still, states *may* act foolishly, failing to respond in timely fashion or to warn aspiring bullies about potential risks. On this score, the behavior of regional actors, U.S. inattentiveness, and the messages Washington's representative apparently conveyed to Iraq just prior to the invasion of Kuwait are not encouraging.[56] Presumably, if Iraq had already been a nuclear power, the U.S. government would have had much

[55]Unfortunately, this also means that low-credibility, ostensibly irrational threats from nuclear-armed bullies will be useful for preserving the status quo and constraining military countermeasures against them, in particular granting them security that makes it too dangerous to push for the unconditional surrender of even the most despised, internationally reckless regimes. See Waltz, "More May Be Better," p. 29.

[56]Janis Gross Stein's review of the available evidence indicates that the United States did not focus attention clearly on the seriousness of Saddam Hussein's intentions prior to Iraq's invasion of Kuwait and failed to seize the opportunity to practice deterrence when he probed U.S. resolve and attempted to gauge a likely U.S. response, most importantly when he summoned American ambassador April Glaspie. At best, Saddam was sent mixed messages in public and private statements, including those conveyed by Glaspie. Though Glaspie claims she sternly warned the Iraqis, her language was apparently neither sufficiently clear nor sufficiently threatening to serve as a deterrent message at a moment when Saddam was almost certainly taking a final read on the probability of a forceful U.S. response. Stein quotes a comment by Iraq's foreign minister Tariq Aziz who was at the Glaspie meeting with Saddam: "*She spoke in vague diplomatic language* and we knew the position she was in. Her behavior was a classic diplomatic response and we were not influenced by it." From Interview of Tariq Aziz by Milton Viorst, "Report from Baghdad," *The New Yorker*, June 24, 1991, pp. 55–73, cited in Janice Gross Stein, "Deterrence and Compellence in the Gulf, 1990–91," p. 154, emphasis added by Stein. In summarizing her review of the signaling that went on prior to the August 2, 1990, invasion, Stein concludes that Bush administration claims to the contrary notwithstanding, "The diplomacy of deterrence was inconsistent, incoherent, and unfocused in the critical two weeks preceding the invasion. Had Saddam been deterrable, it is unlikely that he would have been stopped, given the confusing signals from Washington" (ibid., p. 155). Bush's Secretary of State claims that the U.S. position should have been clear enough to Saddam Hussein, but also notes that American foreign policy attention was focused elsewhere, on shifting Soviet-American relations and the resulting changes in Europe (James A. Baker III, "The Politics of Diplomacy," pp. 52ff).

stronger incentives to analyze Iraqi intentions closely and monitor its behavior as well as stronger incentives to manage more carefully the views its diplomatic representatives expressed. At least in the wake of the Persian Gulf War, the lesson of inattentiveness to such cases seems to have been taken to heart and incorporated in U.S. policies toward North Korea and Iran.[57] Nevertheless, as noted above, the reluctance to entrust one's fate to others makes it unlikely that potential victims of prospective regional bullies who have the wherewithal to develop their own nuclear shield will comfortably settle for complete dependence on extra-regional promises of support.

LIVING WITH THE LEGACY

Though the future behavior of states cannot be predicted with certainty, there are multiple reasons to believe that nuclear weapons will continue to contribute to the peacefulness of international politics by limiting the attractiveness of military action to achieve foreign policy goals, especially to alter the status quo. Some might object, however, that peace means more than the existence of a sturdy buffer against war, or even the absence of war for extended periods.[58] A more demanding perspective sees peace as a condition in which the very possibility of war has been eliminated and human energy is fully directed toward improving the quality of life. Will the spread of nuclear weapons contribute to peace in this broader sense? Nuclear weapons are certainly not an absolute guarantee against war, since the possibility of war derives not from technology but rather the permissive structure of an anarchic international system populated by states that place a high priority on retaining

---

[57]Even with respect to a nonnuclear Iraq, lessons from the summer of 1990 have been learned. When the Clinton administration was unsure how to interpret Iraqi troop maneuvers during October 1994, it clearly transmitted its deterrent signals: "Administration officials said that even while Mr. Hussein's intentions are far from clear, the experience of August 1990 had taught that it would be folly to risk under-reaction. 'We are not going to allow the mistakes of the past to be repeated,' Leon E. Panetta, the White House chief of staff, declared in a television interview today. While Secretary Perry was announcing that dozens of American warplanes were heading to the region, Secretary of State Warren Christopher was warning from Jerusalem that Iraq would be made to pay 'a tremendous price' if it dared launch another invasion. Those statements were crafted to be as different as possible from the conciliatory messages that Ms. Glaspie and Mr. Bush sent to Iraq in the last days of July 1990" (Douglas Jehl, "Threats in the Gulf," p. A1).

[58]The less demanding definition of "peace" is consistent with John Lewis Gaddis's relabelling the Cold War, the Long Peace (John Lewis Gaddis, "The Long Peace"; cf. Daniel Deudney and G. John Ikenberry, "After the Long War").

their independence. Indeed, the argument offered here about the pacifying effects of nuclear weapons depends on the fear that war remains possible.

The presence of nuclear weapons may, however, do more than just reduce the likelihood of war. The availability of nuclear weapons may, as the more demanding definition of peace suggests, help limit the diversion of human resources to huge military establishments even while states continue to believe their security requires them to maintain arms. Because the retaliatory requirements of a deterrent strategy do not entail close comparison with the adversary's forces, nuclear states need not maintain large weapons inventories or engage in intense arms racing to ensure their security.[59] Nor do states emphasizing nuclear deterrence need to field massive (and comparatively expensive) conventional forces designed to fight a protracted war, since their main purpose is to preclude quick and easy gains for the adversary and oblige him to confront the unacceptable risk of unpredictable escalation.[60]

Yet states may not embrace the strategic logic of the nuclear revolution. The behavior of the superpowers during the Cold War suggests that when resource constraints are loosened, states choose to deploy nuclear and conventional forces that exceed the simple requirements of dissuasion by deterrence. Driven by a combination of prudent bet-hedging, political status concerns, the parochial interests of military and economic organizations, and a belief that larger, more sophisticated nuclear arsenals might possibly provide a real warfighting advantage, the superpowers engaged in wasteful nuclear spending. Thus the nuclear revolution does not eliminate the possibility of states diverting national wealth from civilian to military purposes, any more than it eliminates the possibility of war. It does, however, offer a sound strategic rationale, as opposed to merely an ethical or political rationale, for the side in national debates that seeks prudently to limit investment in military forces.

This assertion that nuclear weapons are likely to mute the incentives for arms racing and to free up national resources for more productive purposes contrasts with one of the standard worries about the spread of nuclear weapons to additional states—that states least able to

[59]Waltz, "More May Be Better," pp. 29–31, 32–33; see also Hagerty, The Consequences of Nuclear Proliferation.

[60]Beyond this pre-nuclear role, conventional forces may be required for the comparatively less challenging need to deal with regional foes in contingencies where limited offensive and defensive capabilities may be useful, or for peripheral conflicts where the vital interests covered by the risk of nuclear escalation are not clearly established. See Waltz, "More May Be Better," pp. 32–33.

afford it may engage in arms racing. The typically pessimistic view linking nuclear weapons and wasteful arms racing was vividly displayed in the wake of the 1998 South Asian nuclear tests. Seemingly without hesitation, observers labeled the bilateral military dynamic in South Asia a nuclear arms race. Exactly what did this mean? Arms racing implies a competition in which the parties are trying their utmost to outdo one another, pursuing rapid and large-scale improvements in the quality and quantity of the weaponry they possess. The United States and Soviet Union engaged in this sort of nuclear arms race after the early 1960s. By contrast, although India and Pakistan are likely to compete, they are unlikely to race in the usual sense of the term. Their governments face very tight domestic economic and political constraints that limit their ability to divert much more of their scarce national wealth from the challenges of development to superfluous nuclear weapons programs, particularly while coping with the effects of the international economic sanctions their tests elicited. Shortly after their tests, both India and Pakistan clearly stated that they had no intention of pursuing the sort of nuclear buildup normally labeled an arms race and instead set forth their intention to undertake the arduous, but affordable, effort to deploy sufficient retaliatory forces. Best estimates are that in the near future Pakistan may deploy tens of nuclear warheads, and India perhaps more than a hundred. Over time each will undoubtedly undertake reasonable steps to minimize the vulnerability of their modest arsenals (dispersal, concealment, mobility, etc.). Pakistan will most likely emphasize mobile, land-based systems (missiles and aircraft); India may well add a highly survivable sea-based component. Do such efforts constitute an arms race? The numbers envisioned (in the end perhaps a couple hundred) would seem to fall far short of the usual meaning of the term. Domestic political and bureaucratic interests may drive each to deploy more than the absolute minimum militarily necessary, but neither can afford to indulge in the foolishness that characterized the Cold War superpowers' nuclear extravagance. Instead, like the Cold War's economically more tightly constrained second-ranking powers (Britain, France, and most clearly China), India and Pakistan are likely to seek arsenals sufficient for the military requirements of security-enhancing deterrence. Where nuclear weapons are possessed, absolute amounts of punishment that can be threatened are more important than comparing relative numbers of warheads or launchers.

In addition to affecting national decisions about the allocation of resources to the military, a strategic emphasis on nuclear deterrence may also improve the prospects for international arms agreements that constrain military spending. Nuclear deterrence may facilitate arms control in three ways. First, although it is difficult to define the absolute minimum of retaliatory power necessary for deterrence, it is easier to recognize that one has achieved a sufficiently redundant, if not wasteful, punitive capability.[61] For states embracing a nuclear deterrent strategy, the economic benefits of avoiding strategically pointless spending creates a self-interest in arms control agreements that mitigate the political pressures to compete with the adversary.[62] Second, the robustness of nuclear deterrence also facilitates arms control agreements by making it easier to achieve acceptable levels of verification. The difficulty of overtly, let alone covertly, deploying a force sufficient to confidently neutralize a rival's punitive retaliatory capability reduces the chances for strategically meaningful cheating.[63] And third, to the extent states rely on the dissuasiveness of nuclear deterrence, the importance of retaining massive nonnuclear forces is diminished, opening the door to economically beneficial agreements to limit them as well. The escalatory risks created by the availability of nuclear weapons limit the roles for conven-

[61]Ivo Daalder suggests that the bare minimum should be determined by concerns for a stable deterrent balance among the existing weapons states (i.e., preserving the risk of mutual vulnerability to unacceptable punishment), maintaining a nonproliferation regime (i.e., discouraging aspirants who might believe nuclear superiority was achievable, or reassuring those who require the reassurance provided by extended deterrent guarantees), and safety (i.e., a quantity and quality of weaponry over which negative control can confidently be exercised) (Ivo H. Daalder, "What Vision for the Nuclear Future?," pp. 134–39).

[62]On the mitigation of the classic "guns/butter" tradeoff in the nuclear era, see Robert Powell, "Guns, Butter, and Anarchy." Even if formal arms control agreements are not of major strategic significance, they may yield economic benefits insofar as they enable states to avoid the opportunity costs of investing in superfluous forces. These costs could, of course, be avoided through unilateral choice in a strategic environment in which even exorbitant levels of spending cannot fully eliminate the risk of retaliation. Nevertheless, despite the robustness of such a mutual deterrent relationship, by increasing transparency and undermining procurement arguments rooted in worst-case scenarios, formal agreements can help leaders enmeshed in the two-level game of foreign policy decision-making to sell a policy of restraint to relevant domestic audiences. See Bernard Brodie, "On the Objectives of Arms Control." For consideration of various strategic and political aspects of international arms control, see also Thomas C. Schelling and Morton H. Halperin, with the assistance of Donald G. Brennan, Strategy and Arms Control.

[63]An effective CTBT would be another barrier to investment in the development of new weapons for war-fighting rather than punitive purposes. As John Holum, Director of the U.S. Arms Control and Disarmament Agency, noted, "Through computer modeling, subcritical experiments, and other techniques, we keep existing weapons safe and reliable without tests. . . . But it's a far different thing to develop new kinds of weapons that can be confidently relied upon. . . . That, absent testing, we cannot do" (Holum, "A Powerful Barrier to Future Nuclear Tests").

tional land, sea and naval capabilities to possible tests of resolve among the major powers and fighting lesser regional adversaries. Conventional arms build-ups may continue for other reasons, but the international-strategic rationale for intense racing is weakened.[64]

Why, however, were these beneficial effects of nuclear weapons not evident in the arms control experience during the Cold War? Indeed, with the exception of the 1972 treaty limiting ballistic missile defenses, the various Soviet-American agreements did more to shape a relatively intense arms race than to preclude wasteful spending. Clearly the superpowers deployed nuclear capabilities that exceeded the requirements for inflicting catastrophic damage on each other. Yet neither embraced the simple logic of deterrence as an adequate guideline for deploying forces. With the massive resources they were able to devote to military purposes, they instead chose to prepare for a wide range of unlikely war-fighting scenarios and to seek a numerical edge that might yield some uncertain diplomatic advantage. Will others, if they have the wherewithal, simply repeat the Cold War superpower experience of serious arms racing and ineffective arms control?

Even if deterrent logic weakens the strategic motive for expanding arsenals, because military strategy is not the only consideration that drives states' investment in military research, development, and deployment (parochial political, bureaucratic, and economic interests play important roles), effective arms control will remain difficult. But the Cold War experience itself, together with the economic pressures noted above, may bolster the position of those who advocate arms control as a prudent way to avoid obviously superfluous nuclear deployments. Just as nuclear learning may account for the more careful management of superpower confrontations in the later decades of the Cold War, perhaps one of the last lessons of the Cold War is a clearer recognition of the extent to which superpower nuclear arsenals exceeded any reasonable understanding of the requirements of the strategy for which those forces proved useful, dissuasion by deterrence. The arms control experience at the end of the Cold War is somewhat encouraging on this score. Although the most important reason for the negotiated reductions con-

[64]Of course, subjective beliefs, as well as objective realities, matter. If, despite the apparent inability of the two superpowers to gain much advantage from changes in the strategic nuclear and conventional balances during the Cold War, states continue to believe that a warfighting capability is achievable, or that numerical comparisons are politically important regardless of military significance, then a rationale for arms racing, limited only by domestic economic and political considerations remains available.

tained in START I was the diminution in Soviet-American tensions, the confidence of both sides in the deterrent sufficiency of what would remain also contributed to the relative ease with which they agreed to sharp cuts. Indeed, the huge arsenals that would remain after START I facilitated movement toward START II, a document more fully embracing the logic of relying on nuclear weapons solely for their deterrent value.[65]

The preceding suggests that the twin desiderata of peace and prosperity may be served, even if imperfectly, by states embracing nuclear deterrence as the core of their security policies. But wouldn't these ends be even better served by nuclear disarmament? Though implausible during the Cold War, in its immediate aftermath this possibility received renewed attention in conjunction with the bilateral reductions in the old superpower arsenals, the reassertion of the disarmament pledges contained in the terms of the nonproliferation regime, and the negotiations leading to the CTBT. [66] The debate over the merits of total nuclear disarmament ever since 1945 has spawned a literature whose substance cannot be rehearsed here.[67] Instead, it will suffice to note some of the

[65]Start II became a harder sell partly because some saw it cutting too close to the bone despite the clear end of the Cold War. Administration officials in both Washington and Moscow faced a stiff battle convincing those who were skeptical of the wisdom of the treaty. To ease fears of extravagant cuts, U.S. Defense Secretary William Perry's Nuclear Posture Review made clear that even under Start II the United States would retain a large reserve of roughly 3,500 warheads that could be used to upload ICBMs and SLBMs if future international conditions warrant (Robert S. Norris and William M. Arkin "U.S. Strategic Nuclear Forces, End of 1994," pp. 69ff). For a list of Russian concerns and the responses by a treaty supporter, see Sergei Rogov, "Several Questions to the Treaty." As the issue of NATO's eastward expansion aggravated Russian security concerns about an uncertain future, the prospects dimmed for parliamentary approval of START II without a "sweetener" such as pledges on the outlines for more attractive terms in START III. See Ivan Rodin, "Russian Legislators Back New Arms Cuts, Oppose START"; Jonathan Clayton, "U.S. Works on Nuclear Deal with Russia." Even so, the visions for alternative future arrangements come closer to force structures consistent with the requirements adequate for dissuasion by deterrence rather than the more ambitious, often Byzantine, offensive and defensive nuclear strategies that justified the superpowers' huge Cold War arsenals.

[66]An upsurge in the call for eventual nuclear disarmament occurred with General Lee Butler's public promotion of the idea during the mid-1990s. On February 19, 1997, prominent supporters of this goal announced the formation of The Committee on Nuclear Policy ("New Policy Group Wants Ban on Nuclear Weapons").

[67]For some early post–Cold War consideration of its merits, See Daalder, "What Vision for the Nuclear Future?"; Bailey, "Why We Have to Keep the Bomb." On the history of the international nuclear disarmament movement see Lawrence S. Wittner, *The Struggle Against the Bomb*, vols. 1 (*One World or None*) and 2 (*Resisting the Bomb*).

chief shortcomings of denuclearization that reflect the intertwined problems of feasibility and desirability.

Assuming that states find unilateral disarmament imprudent for international security and domestic political reasons, denuclearization would require the negotiation of far-reaching, multilateral arms control treaties. A key difficulty in reaching agreement would be the problem of satisfactory verification. As states approach very low numbers of nuclear weapons, isolated instances of cheating could once again become strategically decisive and states would almost certainly require foolproof verification of compliance. This standard is hard to meet in most cases, and especially one involving weapons as easily concealed as nuclear weapons or their components. Even if a verification regime could be negotiated, fears about its possible imperfections would provide strong incentives for a sub-rosa security dilemma to play itself out, in which even states valuing the treaty would believe it necessary to hedge their bets by hiding a fallback deterrent against small-scale cheating.

Moreover, if a presumptively verifiable agreement could be reached (and, of course, absent universal amnesia, the best such treaty could only render renuclearization very difficult, not impossible), it would create a window of opportunity for conventional war. Indeed, the more robust the safeguards against renuclearization, the greater the possibility that the leaders of states in conflict may be able to conjure up scenarios for the large-scale use of conventional forces leading to victory or more acceptable negotiated settlements before renuclearization occurs. Such a situation would muddy the clarifying pressures of the nuclear revolution rooted in its distinctive fear of nearly instantaneous national catastrophe. Increasing the expected utility of actually employing military force makes war a more plausible alternative to diplomacy. This outcome is unfortunate not only in terms of the peacefulness of international politics, but also in terms of the likely diversion of additional national resources to military investment.[68] States would see a need to bolster their conventional capabilities to compensate for the lost dissuasive effects of the nuclear deterrent they had forsaken. Among cautious, relatively secure states this outcome would be troublesome

---

[68]To the extent wars, however unlikely, were expected to remain non-nuclear, military planners would return to a strategic environment where relative comparisons of men and material were crucial. Determined to compensate for the loss of the nuclear equalizer, states might well be faced with steep increases in military spending, especially as conventional weapons incorporate increasingly sophisticated technologies entailing higher procurement costs and higher personnel costs to ensure the availability of troops qualified to use the weapons.

enough. Of greater concern, however, is the possibility that if renu-clearization were expected to be difficult, adventurous leaders, or sim-ply those who saw their state in an irretrievably desperate position, might be tempted to gamble on a long-shot war-fighting strategy in the belief it could be altered or aborted well before facing a distant moment of nuclear truth.[69]

Perhaps most disturbing is the possibility that crises that slipped into conventional war in such a formally denuclearized world would be more, not less, likely to lead to disastrous outcomes than a similar proc-ess unfolding in a world of existing nuclear states. Once hostilities had erupted, confidence in the verification regime that undergirded the dis-armament treaty would likely plummet. Fearing the consequences of unreciprocated self-restraint, adversaries would have strong incentives to reconstitute a nuclear capability, if only as a deterrent. In the more opaque intelligence environment of a crisis or war, worst-case planning would be seen as merely prudent. Maximum suspicion and minimum empathy would drive an arms race in renuclearization. Whether one state would at some point feel tempted to use what it believed was a fleeting nuclear monopoly in a preemptive strike, or be inhibited by the fear that its adversary might in fact already have an undetected nuclear retaliatory capability, is an open question. It does, however, highlight the Achilles heel of denuclearization proposals as long as the knowledge and materials for assembling the weapons cannot be eliminated or states refuse to subject themselves to an international authority with re-liably effective enforcement powers.[70]

In short, despite the dramatic changes in international relations that have accompanied the end of the Cold War, proposals for full nuclear

[69]There is certainly precedent for such risk-acceptant behavior in the pre-nuclear era, most notably Japan's attack on Pearl Harbor. A deteriorating strategic posture in the face of tightening natural resource constraints, combined with the influence of ultra-nationalist elements favoring an aggressive foreign policy in East Asia, led To-kyo to embrace a strategy whose success depended on a stunned, under-mobilized United States preferring a negotiated settlement to a long war. The inability of the Japanese government to cut its losses and end the war once the failure of its gamble became clear indicates the dangers of overestimating the manageability of events even in a purely conventional context.

[70]See Daalder, "What Vision for the Nuclear Future?," pp. 132, 133. For a care-fully reasoned version of nuclear disarmament that would entail building republican institutions of governance at the global level to which states would entrust a re-cessed, residual deterrent force, see Daniel H. Deudney, *Pax Atomica*. Though its in-ternal logic is hard to fault, the plan's feasibility depends on sovereign states choos-ing to cede decision-making powers in a process that seems unlikely to unfold for the foreseeable future.

disarmament are problematic at best; they carry with them the risk of creating more, not fewer dangers. This assertion, however, should not be seen as a Panglossic conclusion that we live in "the best of all possible worlds." Though the existence of national nuclear arsenals has much diminished the probability for war among states possessing these weapons of mass destruction, better worlds are conceivable, and some may be within the realm of practical political action. How can a world made less war-prone by the presence of nuclear weapons be made safer still? The argument contained in this book suggests that one of the first steps endorsed by recent advocates of nuclear disarmament may be a good place to start, though the argument offered here also suggests that at least for the foreseeable future, the first step may be a good place to stop.

Disarmament advocates, as well as those who are optimistic about the peacefulness of a world in which states retain nuclear weapons, can agree that it is feasible and wise for states to negotiate agreements that further reduce the small chance and terrible consequences of accidental or inadvertent nuclear launch.[71] Because even the largest and most sophisticated attacker could not fully eliminate the possibility that some of its rival's retaliatory capability might survive a first strike, the deterrent effects of uncertainty are easily established and self-regarding states can prudently embrace organizational and technological improvements that help guard against unwanted nuclear use. Nuclear states, therefore, need not prime their forces for prompt retaliation (as was most clearly the practice for the United States and the Soviet Union during the Cold War). They need only meet the less challenging standard of maintaining an adversary's terrifying first-strike uncertainty. And because first-strike uncertainty is easily established, even risk-averse states can agree to limit their arsenals to a modest size that makes them easier to control.

The most beneficial step, therefore, may be for the larger nuclear powers to work toward arsenals similar in scope and purpose to those the second-ranking powers sought to deploy during the Cold War. This is a goal that is at once strategically sensible, normatively attractive, and politically attainable. Yet it is a goal that will nevertheless be hard to achieve, especially for the United States and Russia, who must be the

[71]The seriousness of these risks varies by country but, as noted above, is not necessarily a reflection of technological or economic backwardness, a point highlighted by the fact that the major works illuminating the problem focused mainly on the United States and U.S.S.R. See Bruce G. Blair, *Strategic Command and Control*; Blair, *The Logic of Accidental Nuclear War*; Scott D. Sagan, *The Limits of Safety*.

leaders of any such effort. The sources of opposition are predictable. Those who reject what I have suggested are the strategic consequences of the nuclear revolution will insist on retaining the option of using nuclear weapons for military missions other than inflicting punishment. Nuclear warfighting contingencies, whether for offensive or defensive purposes, require large arsenals married to intricate targeting plans whose complexity in turn requires either quick execution, before command and control is significantly degraded, or the predelegation of authority to designated subordinates as a hedge against the loss of communications likely to occur soon after nuclear detonations have begun. The need to ensure positive control in such circumstances conflicts with proposals to tighten negative control.

Others, especially those who condemn nuclear weapons as inherently immoral, will reject the attractiveness of smaller, safer nuclear arsenals as a sufficiently worthy goal. For them, the appropriate goal is nuclear abolition, a position that has been recurrently articulated over the decades of the nuclear age—in the immediate post–World War II period by "one-worlders," during the 1950s and 1960s by various "ban the bomb groups," during the 1970s and 1980s in popular books by Jonathan Schell and in advocacy by Dr. Helen Caldicott's Physicians for Social Responsibility and the Catholic Bishop's statement, and in the 1990s by a growing community of former military and civilian Cold Warriors who believe the end of the Manichaean struggle with the communist menace negates the ethical justification for a nuclear capability. For those who view nuclear weapons (or more precisely threats to use them) as inherently immoral, there is no justifiable goal short of abolition.

Still others will resist efforts to achieve even the modest sort of change in deployment patterns suggested here for reasons that are neither strategically sophisticated nor morally uplifting. Narrow bureaucratic, economic, personal, and political interests will predictably lead some to resist the compromises essential for successful negotiations that would yield smaller, safer nuclear deterrents. Leaders who would craft international arms control agreements, however sensible they may seem, must meet the challenge not only of convincing their foreign counterparts, but also of persuading domestic political rivals as well as the organizations who carry out military policy or profit from its implementation to embrace change.

The enduring legacy of the nuclear revolution is the attractiveness of robust and affordable deterrent strategies for states that perceive serious threats to their security in an uncertain world. The experience of China,

Britain, and France during the Cold War suggests that countries of varying capability can rely on relatively modest nuclear arsenals to satisfy an
interest in maintaining the status quo. This provides grounds for tempered optimism about a future in which more states are likely to possess
nuclear weapons. Those who have focused mainly on the superpowers'
experience during Cold War and their quixotic quest to satisfy the demanding criteria of elaborate warfighting plans (in which neither ever
achieved much confidence) and to deploy nearly invulnerable retaliatory
forces (when uncertainty about modest levels of survivability suffice to
frighten prospective aggressors) may exaggerate the dangers, and over-
look the potential advantages, of a world with a slowly growing number
of nuclear-armed states.

Works Cited

Works Cited

The following abbreviations are used in the Works Cited:

CIA   Central Intelligence Agency
CNC   ClariNet Communications Corp.
CWIHP   Cold War International History Project, available online at *http: //cwihp.si.edu/pdf.htm*
FBIS   *Foreign Broadcast Information Service,* China Daily Report
FRUS   *Foreign Relations of the United States*
HRP   Released through the Historical Review Program of the CIA, available at the National Archives at College Park, Md.
LEXIS   LEXIS-NEXIS, Reed Elsevier, Inc.
NIE   National Intelligence Estimate
NNP   *Nuclear Non-Proliferation 1945–1990,* Virginia Foran, ed., Alexandria, Va.: Chadwyck-Healey, 1992.
SNIE   Special National Intelligence Estimate

Achen, Christopher H., and Duncan Snidal. "Rational Deterrence Theory and Comparative Case Studies," *World Politics,* vol. 41, no. 2 (Jan. 1989), pp. 143–69.

Ackerman, Julia A., and Michael Collins Dunn. "Chinese Airpower Revs Up," *Air Force Magazine,* July 1993, from LEXIS.

"Africans Adopt Treaty to Create Nuclear Free Zone," *Reuters,* June 2, 1995, from clari.tw.nuclear, CNC.

Ahmed, Samina. "Pakistan's Nuclear Weapons Program: Turning Points and Nuclear Choices," *International Security,* vol. 23, no. 4 (Spring 1999), pp. 178–204.

Albright, Joseph, and Marcia Kunstel. *Bombshell: The Secret Story of America's Unknown Atomic Spy Conspiracy.* New York: Times Books, 1997.

Allison, Graham T., and Philip Zelikow. *Essence of Decision: Explaining the Cuban Missile Crisis,* 2nd ed. New York: Longman, 1999.

Almond, Peter. "Defense Budget: RAF to Lose Tactical Missile—and Its Nuclear Role," *The Daily Telegraph,* Oct. 16, 1993, from LEXIS.

Art, Robert J. "A Defensible Defense: America's Grand Strategy After the Cold War," *International Security,* vol. 15, no. 4 (Spring 1991), pp. 5–53.

———. "To What Ends Military Power?" *International Security,* vol. 4, no. 3 (Spring 1980), pp. 3–35.

"Asian News: China's Defense Budget to Increase 15 PC," *Japan Economic Newswire*, Mar. 20, 1990, from LEXIS.

Auton, Graeme P. "Nuclear Deterrence and the Medium Power: A Proposal for Doctrinal Change in the British and French Cases," *Orbis*, vol. 20 (Summer 1976).

Bailey, Kathleen. "Why We Have to Keep the Bomb," *Bulletin of the Atomic Scientists*, vol. 51, no. 1 (Jan. 1995), from LEXIS.

Baker, James A., III. "The Politics of Diplomacy," *Newsweek*, Oct. 2, 1995, pp. 52ff, from LEXIS.

Baldwin, David A. *Economic Statecraft*. Princeton: Princeton University Press, 1985.

———. "Power Analysis and World Politics: New Trends Versus Old Tendencies," *World Politics*, vol. 31, no. 2 (Jan. 1979), pp.161–94.

Ball, Desmond. "Can Nuclear War Be Controlled?" *Adelphi Papers*, no. 169 (London: International Institute for Strategic Studies, 1981).

Ball, Desmond, and Jeffrey Richelson, eds. *Strategic Nuclear Targeting*. Ithaca: Cornell University Press, 1986.

Ball, Desmond, and Robert C. Toth. "Revising the SIOP: Taking War-fighting to Dangerous Extremes," *International Security*, vol. 14, no. 3 (Spring 1990), pp. 65–92.

Barnett, A. Doak. *China and the Major Powers in East Asia*. Washington, D.C.: Brookings Institution, 1977.

———. *Uncertain Passage: China's Transition to the Post-Mao Era*. Washington, D.C.: Brookings Institution, 1974.

Barr, Cameron W. "North Korea's Missile Show Tests Japan's Tolerance," *Christian Science Monitor*, Sept. 4, 1998, from clari.world.asia.koreas, CNC.

———. "Weak by Design, Japan Ponders Its Missile Gap," *Christian Science Monitor*, Sept. 2, 1998, from clari.world.asia.koreas, CNC.

Barry, John. "Our Bomb: The Secret Story," TV program by Britain's LWT for Channel Four, Apr. 6, 1986, Part Two.

Bartlett, C. J. *"The Special Relationship": A Political History of Anglo-American Relations Since 1945*. London: Longman, 1992.

Bassett, Edward W. "France to Modernize Nuclear Forces," *Aviation Week and Space Technology*, June 16, 1980, from LEXIS.

Baylis, John. *Ambiguity and Deterrence: British Nuclear Strategy 1945–1964*. Oxford: Clarendon Press, 1995.

———. *Anglo-American Defense Relations, 1939–1984: The Special Relationship*, 2nd ed. New York: St. Martin's, 1984.

———. *British Defense Policy*. New York: St. Martin's, 1989.

Bell, Gavin. "Firestorm of Fury Rages On," *The Herald* (Glasgow), Aug. 2, 1995, from LEXIS.

———. "French Defence Budget to Upgrade Nuclear Forces," *Reuters North European Service*, Nov. 2, 1983, from LEXIS.

Bellamy, Christopher. "Chirac Overhauls Missile Arsenal," *The Independent*, Oct. 13, 1995, p. 13, from LEXIS.

Berkowitz, Bruce D. "Proliferation, Deterrence, and the Likelihood of Nuclear War," *Journal of Conflict Resolution*, vol. 29, no. 1 (Mar. 1985), pp. 112–36.

Betts, Paul. "France Threatens Nuclear Reply to Chemical Attack," *Financial Times*, Apr. 19, 1985, from LEXIS.

———. "French Spending on Nuclear Deterrent Escapes Budget Cuts," *Financial Times*, Sept. 17, 1985, from LEXIS.

Betts, Richard K. *Nuclear Blackmail and Nuclear Balance*. Washington, D.C.: Brookings Institution, 1987.

———. "A Nuclear Golden Age? The Balance Before Parity," *International Security*, vol. 11, no. 3 (Winter 1986/1987), pp. 3–32.

Biddle, Stephen. "Victory Misunderstood: What the Gulf War Tells Us About the Future of Conflict," *International Security*, vol. 21, no. 2 (Fall 1996), pp. 139–79.

Blainey, Geoffrey. *The Causes of War*. New York: Free Press, 1973.

Blair, Bruce G. *The Logic of Accidental Nuclear War*. Washington, D.C.: Brookings Institution, 1993.

———. "Russia's Doomsday Machine," *New York Times*, Oct. 8, 1993, p. A35.

———. *Strategic Command and Control: Redefining the Nuclear Threat*. Washington, D.C.: Brookings Institution, 1985.

Blechman, Barry M., and Robert Powell. "What in the Name of God Is Strategic Superiority?," *Political Science Quarterly*, vol. 97, no. 4 (Winter 1982/1983), pp. 589–602.

Blight, James G. "*Psychology and Deterrence* Book Review," *International Security*, vol. 11, no. 3 (Winter 1986/87), pp. 175–86.

Bloom, Bridget. "Gaullist Sting in Trident's Tail," *Financial Times*, Mar. 12, 1982, from LEXIS.

Bortin, Mary Ellen. "French Defence Budget to Keep Nuclear Strength Despite Cuts," *Reuters North European Service*, Oct. 9, 1984, from LEXIS.

Botti, Timothy J. *The Long Wait: The Forging of the Anglo-American Nuclear Alliance 1945–1958*. New York: Greenwood, 1987.

Boyer, Mark A. *International Cooperation and Public Goods*. Baltimore: Johns Hopkins University Press, 1993.

Bracken, Paul. *The Command and Control of Nuclear Forces*. New Haven: Yale University Press, 1983.

"Britain Angered by Nuclear Test Criticism," *Reuters*, Nov. 10, 1995, from clari.tw.nuclear, CNC.

"Britain Announces New Rapid Deployment Force," *Reuters*, Aug. 1, 1996, from clari.tw.defense, CNC.

"Britain Decommissions Last Polaris Sub," *Reuters*, Aug. 28, 1996, from clari.tw.nuclear, CNC.

"Britain Rolls Out Second Trident Submarine," *The Reuter European Business Report*, Sept. 29, 1993, from LEXIS.

"Britain to End Air Force's Nuclear Punch by 1998," Apr. 4, 1995, from clari.tw.nuclear, CNC.

"Britain to Scrap Airborne Nuclear Missile," *Agence France-Presse*, July 19, 1993, from LEXIS.

Broad, William J. "Nuclear Arms Builders Move from Creators to Custodians," *New York Times*, Jan. 6, 1997, pp. A1, A14.

Brodie, Bernard. "On the Objectives of Arms Control," in Robert J. Art and Kenneth N. Waltz, eds., *The Use of Force*, 3rd ed. Lanham, Md.: University Press of America, 1988.

————. *War and Politics*. New York: Macmillan, 1973.

Brodie, Ian. "CIA Papers Disclose Plot to Use Bomb on China," *Times Newspapers Limited*, Oct. 2, 1993, from LEXIS.

Brooke, James. "Former Cold Warrior Has a New Mission: Nuclear Cuts," *New York Times*, Jan. 8, 1997, p. A12, from LEXIS.

Brown, Colin. "Navy Bears Brunt of Cuts as Four Submarines Are Axed," *The Independent*, July 6, 1993, from LEXIS.

Brown, David A. "British Seeking a Stronger Nuclear Force Capability," *Aviation Week and Space Technology*, June 16, 1980, from LEXIS.

Brown, Kevin, and Bruce Clark. "UK Agrees N-pact with France: Major and Chirac Take Big Step Towards Common Defence Policy at Summit," *Financial Times*, Oct. 31, 1995, p. 1, from LEXIS.

Buchanan, James M. "An Economic Theory of Clubs," in Bruce M. Russett, ed., *Economic Theories of International Politics*. Chicago: Markham, 1968.

Bueno de Mesquita, Bruce. *The War Trap*. New Haven: Yale University Press, 1981.

Bueno de Mesquita, Bruce, and William H. Riker. "An Assessment of the Merits of Selective Nuclear Proliferation," *Journal of Conflict Resolution*, vol. 26, no. 2 (June 1982), pp. 283–306.

Burr, William, ed. *The Kissinger Transcripts: The Top-Secret Talks with Beijing and Moscow*. New York: New Press, 1999.

Buzan, Barry. *People, States, and Fear*, 2nd ed. Boulder, Colo.: Lynne Rienner, 1991.

Cayol, Thierry. "Nuclear Silos Empty at Last," *The Guardian*, Sept. 17, 1996, p. 13, from LEXIS.

Chakravarty, Pratap. "India Counting Days to Become a True Nuclear-Weapons State," *Agence France-Presse*, May 12, 1999, from clari.tw.-nuclear.

————. "Nuclear India, Pakistan Incapable of Atomic War: Experts," *Agence France-Presse*, June 8, 1999, from clari.tw.nuclear, CNC.

Chang, Gordon H. *Friends and Enemies*. Stanford: Stanford University Press, 1990.

Chen Chongbei, Shou Xiaosong, and Liang Xiaoqiu. *Weishe Zhanlüe*. Beijing: Junshi Kexue Chubanshe, 1989.

Chen Jian. *China's Road to the Korean War*. New York: Columbia University Press, 1994.

Chen Si. "Year Ender: Overall Strategic Considerations Should Be Given

Top Priority," *Xinhua General Overseas News Service*, June 20, 1980, from LEXIS.

Cheung, Tai Ming. "Beijing Puts Priority Back on PLA," *Nikkei Weekly*, Aug. 17, 1991, from LEXIS.

"China Aides Gave U.S. Nuclear Warning, Official Says," *Reuters*, Mar. 17, 1996, from clari.tw.nuclear, CNC.

"China as a Nuclear Power (Some Thoughts Prior to the Chinese Test)," Oct. 7, 1964, Department of Defense, Declassified July 1, 1996, available at National Security Archives, Washington, D.C., Gilpatric Committee File.

"China Criticised as Bar to Nuclear Test Ban Treaty," *Reuters*, May 13, 1996, from clari.tw.nuclear, CNC.

"China Drops Call for 'Peaceful' Nuclear Blasts," *Reuters*, June 6, 1996, from clari.tw.nuclear, CNC.

"China Holds Last Nuclear Test Before Moratorium," *Reuters*, July 28, 1996, from clari.tw.nuclear, CNC.

"China Media Say Japan Shrine Boost to Militarism," *Reuters*, Aug. 1, 1996, from clari.world.asia.china, CNC.

"China Nuclear Test Decision Turns Heat Up on India," *Reuters*, June 7, 1996, from clari.tw.nuclear, CNC.

"China Says Its Nuclear Arms Will Deter U.S., Soviet Union," *Reuters North European Service*, June 4, 1985, from LEXIS.

"China Sketches Out Defense Telecom Network," *Reuters*, Nov. 7, 1995, from clari.tw.defense, CNC.

"China Test Fires ICBM Missile, Diplomats Say," *Reuters*, May 31, 1995, from clari.tw.nuclear, CNC.

"China Test Timed to Avert Criticism but Draws Ire," *Reuters*, June 8, 1996, from clari.tw.nuclear, CNC.

"China to Hold Nuclear Test Soon, Envoy Hints," *Reuters*, June 6, 1996, from clari.tw.nuclear, CNC.

"China Won't Conduct Tests Indefinitely," *United Press International*, May 23, 1996, from clari.tw.nuclear, CNC.

"China's Military Expenditure," *The Military Balance 1995–1996*. London: International Institute for Strategic Studies and Oxford University Press, 1995, pp. 270–75.

"The Chinese Communist Atomic Energy Program," NIE 13-2-60, Dec. 13, 1960, NNP (00715), Declassified Sept. 15, 1981.

Chinese Defense Spending, 1965–1979, National Foreign Assessment Center: CIA, SR 80-10091 (July 1980).

"Chinese Defense Spending on the Rise: CIA," *Agence France-Presse*, July 30, 1993, from LEXIS.

"Chinese Representative on Nuclear Ban," *Xinhua General Overseas News Service*, Jan. 21, 1994, from LEXIS.

Christensen, Thomas J. "China, the U.S.-Japan Alliance, and the Security Dilemma in East Asia," *International Security*, vol. 23, no. 4 (Spring 1999), pp. 49–80.

———. "Chinese Realpolitik," *Foreign Affairs*, vol. 75, no. 5 (Sept./Oct. 1996), pp. 37–52.

———. "Domestic Mobilization and International Conflict: Sino-American Relations in the 1950s." Ph.D. diss., Columbia University, 1993.

———. "Threats, Assurances, and the Last Chance for Peace: The Lessons of Mao's Korean War Telegrams," *International Security*, vol. 17, no. 1 (Summer 1992), pp. 122–54.

———. *Useful Adversaries: Grand Strategy, Domestic Mobilization, and Sino-American Conflict, 1947–1958*. Princeton: Princeton University Press, 1996.

Christensen, Thomas J., and Jack Snyder. "Chain Gangs and Passed Bucks: Predicting Alliance Patterns in Multipolarity," *International Organization*, vol. 44, no. 2 (Spring 1990), pp. 137–68.

Chung Ti. "Visit to China's Nuclear Submarine Unit," from *Ta Kung Pao*, May 7 and 8, 1989, *FBIS*, May 12, 1989.

Churchill, Winston S. "Wars Are Not Won by Evacuations," June 4, 1940, House of Commons, in Robert Rhodes James, ed., *Winston S. Churchill, His Complete Speeches, 1897–1963*, vol. VI: *1935–1942*. New York: Chelsea House Publishers in association with R. R. Bowker Company, 1974, pp. 6225–31.

Clayton, Jonathan. "U.S. Works on Nuclear Deal with Russia," *Reuters*, Jan. 23, from clari.tw.nuclear, CNC.

Cochran, Thomas B., et al. *Soviet Nuclear Weapons*. Series: Nuclear Weapons Databook, vol. 4. New York: Harper & Row, Ballinger Division, 1989.

———. *U.S. Nuclear Warhead Facility Profiles*. Series: Nuclear Weapons Databook, vol. 3. Cambridge, Mass.: Ballinger, 1987.

———. *U.S. Nuclear Warhead Production*. Series: Nuclear Weapons Databook, vol. 2. Cambridge, Mass.: Ballinger, 1987.

Cochran, Thomas B., William M. Arkin, and Milton M. Hoenig. *U.S. Nuclear Forces and Capabilities*. Series: Nuclear Weapons Databook, vol. 1. Cambridge, Mass.: Ballinger, 1984.

Cohen, Avner, *Israel and the Bomb*. New York: Columbia University Press, 1998.

Cohen, Avner, and Benjamin Frankel. "Opaque Nuclear Proliferation," *Journal of Strategic Studies*, vol. 13, no. 3 (Sept. 1990), pp. 14–44.

Cohen, Eliot. "A Revolution in Warfare," *Foreign Affairs*, vol. 5, no. 3 (Mar./Apr. 1996), pp. 37–54.

———. "Toward Better Net Assessment: Rethinking the European Conventional Balance," *International Security*, vol. 13, no. 1 (Summer 1988), pp. 128–79.

Cohen, Roger. "France to Rejoin Military Command of NATO Alliance," *New York Times*, Dec. 6, 1995, from LEXIS.

"Comments on Non-Proliferation Background Papers of December 12, 1964," Memorandum from Robert S. Rochlin to Raymond L. Garthoff, Dec. 31, 1964, pp. 3, 4 U.S. Arms Control and Disarmament Agency, Department of State Case 9200777, Declassified Sept. 5, 1996, available at National Security Archives, Washington, D.C., Gilpatric Committee File.

"Communist Courses of Action in Asia Through 1957," NIE (10-7-54), CIA, Nov. 23, 1954, HRP, June 25, 1993.

"Communist Reactions to Certain Possible U.S. Courses of Action with Respect to the Islands off the Coast of China," Special National Intelligence Estimate, SNIE (100-3-55), CIA, Jan. 25, 1955, HRP, July 6, 1993.

"Communist Reactions to Certain U.S. Courses of Action with Respect to Indochina," SNIE (10-4-54), CIA, June 15, 1954, HRP, June 25, 1993.

Connor, Steve, and Andy Thomas. "How Britain Kept Its Independent Deterrent," New Scientist, vol. 105, no. 1439 (Jan. 1985), p. 4.

"Conversation Between Mao Zedong and E. F. Hill, 28 November 1968," Document no. 2, trans. by Chen Jian, CWIHP Bulletin, issue 11 (Winter 1998), available online, http://cwihp. si.edu/pdf.htm.

"Conversation Between Stalin and Mao, Moscow, 16 December 1949," in CWIHP Bulletin, issues 6–7 (Winter 1995/1996).

"CPSU CC Directive to Soviet Ambassadors in Communist Countries, 4 March 1980," CWIHP Bulletin, issues 6–7 (Winter 1995/1996).

Crossette, Barbara. "In Concession, China Is Ready to Ban A-Tests," New York Times, June 7, 1996, pp. A1, A10.

Cue, Eduardo. "Mitterrand Says French Defense Rests on Atomic Bomb," United Press International, Apr. 12, 1992, from LEXIS.

"Current Intelligence Weekly Review," Sept. 27, 1963, Document no. 358, FRUS, 1961–1963, vol. 5: Soviet Union. Washington, D.C.: U.S. Government Printing Office, 1998.

Cushman, John F., Jr. "Senate Endorses Act to Reduce Strategic Arms," New York Times, Oct. 2, 1992, pp. A1, A6.

Daalder, Ivo H. "What Vision for the Nuclear Future?" The Washington Quarterly, vol. 18, no. 2 (Spring 1995), pp. 127–42.

Davidson, Ian. "France Rejoins Its Allies," Financial Times, May 3, 1983, from LEXIS.

———. "French Play Down US 'Secret Nuclear Help,'" Financial Times, May 30, 1989, from LEXIS.

———. "Nuclear Weapons Escape Cuts in French Defence," Financial Times, May 25, 1989, from LEXIS.

Davis, Zachary S., and Benjamin Frankel, eds. The Proliferation Puzzle: Why Nuclear Weapons Spread (and What Results). Special issue of Security Studies, vol. 2, nos. 3/4 (Spring/Summer 1993).

De Briganti, Giovanni. "Britain Ponders Missile Choices: Buy U.S. or Build with France," Defense News, Nov. 12, 1990, from LEXIS.

———. "Chevenement Indicates French Likely to Scrap Land-Based Nuclear Weapons," Defense News, Oct. 29, 1990, from LEXIS.

———. "French Nuclear Triad May Lose Two Legs; MoD Targets Land-Based Missiles, Mirage Bombers," Defense News, Oct. 22, 1990, from LEXIS.

De Selding, Peter B. "France Halts Development of S45 Nuclear Missile," *Defense News*, July 29, 1991, from LEXIS.

Dean, Gordon. "Memorandum for the Secretary of State and the Secretary of Defense from Chairman of the U.S. Atomic Energy Commission, Aug. 28, 1952, Subject: Interchange of Classified Information with the United Kingdom," *NNP*, 1952/08/28 (00110), Declassified Jan. 20, 1978.

"Defense Estimative Brief: Nuclear Weapons Systems in China," Apr. 24, 1984, Defense Intelligence Agency, declassified and released to the National Security Archive, available online at http://www.seas.gwu. edu/nsarchive/news/19990527/index.html.

Deighton, Ann, ed. *Britain and the First Cold War*. New York: St. Martin's, 1990.

"Deng Warns over Japan's Defense Spending," *Japan Economic Newswire*, Jan. 13, 1987, from LEXIS.

"The Deterioration of Sino-Soviet Relations: 1956–1966," Intelligence Handbook, Director of Intelligence, CIA, Apr. 22, 1966.

Deudney, Daniel H. *Pax Atomica*, forthcoming.

Deudney, Daniel, and G. John Ikenberry. "After the Long War," *Foreign Policy*, no. 94 (Spring 1994), pp. 21–35.

Deutsch, Karl W., and J. David Singer. "Multipolar Power Systems and International Stability," in James N. Rosenau, ed., *International Politics and Foreign Policy*, 2nd ed. New York: Free Press, 1969, pp. 315–24.

Dickson, David. "French Bishops Defend Nuclear Deterrence," *Science*, Dec. 2, 1983, from LEXIS.

Dingman, Roger. "Atomic Diplomacy During the Korean War," *International Security*, vol. 13, no. 3 (Winter 1988/1989), pp. 50–91.

Dinmore, Guy. "China's Military Shakes Up for Regional Conflicts," *The Reuter Library Report*, June 13, 1988, from LEXIS.

Dittmer, Lowell. "The Strategic Triangle: An Elementary Game Theoretical Analysis," *World Politics*, vol. 33, no. 4 (July 1981), pp. 484–515.

Dobbs, Michael. "French General Challenges Cornerstone of Nation's Independent Defense Strategy," *Washington Post*, Mar. 19, 1984, from LEXIS.

Dombey, Norman, and Eric Grove. "Britain's Thermonuclear Bluff," *London Review of Books*, Oct. 22, 1992.

Donnet, Pierre-Antoine. "Japanese Strategists Warn of Renewed Nuclear Arms Race," *Agence France-Presse*, May 12, 1998, from clari.tw.nuclear, CNC.

"Don't Forget the Cheap One," *The Economist*, Mar. 29, 1980, from LEXIS.

Downie, Jr., Leonard. "U.S. Bombers in Britain Become Superpower Pawns; Britain Sacrifices Conventional Arms in Nuclear Strategy," *Washington Post*, Nov. 19, 1981, from LEXIS.

Downing, John. "China's Evolving Maritime Strategy, Part I: Restructuring Begins," *Jane's Intelligence Review*, vol. 8, no. 3 (Mar. 1996), pp. 129ff, from LEXIS.

Doyle, Michael W. "Kant, Liberal Legacies, and Foreign Affairs," *Philosophy and Public Affairs*, vol. 12 (Fall 1983), pp. 323–53.

———. "Liberalism and World Politics," *American Political Science Review*, vol. 80, no. 4 (Dec. 1986), pp. 1151–69.

Dreifus, Claudia. "The Real-Life Dynasty of Benazir Bhutto," *New York Times Magazine*, May 15, 1994.

Dunn, Lewis. "What Difference Will It Make?" in Robert J. Art and Kenneth N. Waltz, eds., *The Use of Force*, 3rd ed. Lanham, Md.: University Press of America, 1988.

Dunn, Michael C. "Mitterrand's France Shapes a Nuclear Defense," *Defense and Foreign Affairs*, July 1983, from LEXIS.

Echikson, William. "Defense Maverick France Shifts Military Strategy and Spending," *The Christian Science Monitor*, Nov. 18, 1985, from LEXIS.

Edinger, Bernard. "Australia, France Bury Nuclear Test Hatchet," *Reuters*, Dec. 16, 1997, from clari.tw.nuclear, CNC.

———. "France's Leotard Vows to Protect Defence Industry," *The Reuter European Business Report*, Nov. 10, 1993, from LEXIS.

"Editorial Note," Jan. 11, 1963, Document no. 162, *FRUS, 1961–1963*, vol. 22: *China, Korea, and Japan*. Washington, D.C.: U.S. Government Printing Office.

"Editorial Note," July 15, 1963, Document no. 180, *FRUS, 1961–1963*, vol. 22: *China, Korea, and Japan*. Washington, D.C.: U.S. Government Printing Office.

"Editorial Note," June 23, 1963, Document no. 164, *FRUS, 1961–1963*, vol. 22: *China, Korea, and Japan*. Washington, D.C.: U.S. Government Printing Office.

"The Emerging Disputes Between Beijing and Moscow: Ten Newly Available Chinese Documents, 1956–1958," trans. and annotated by Zhang Shu Guang and Chen Jian, CWIHP *Bulletin*, issues 6–7 (Winter 1995/1996).

"Enclosure: Defence, Outline of Future Policy," Presented by the Minister of Defence to Parliament by Command of Her Majesty, April 1957, *NNP*, 1957/04/00 (00298).

"Energy Department to Keep Open Experimental Reactor," *Reuters*, Jan. 15, 1997, from clari.tw.nuclear, CNC.

"Energy Dept. Plans to Shrink Nuclear Weapons Complex," *Reuters*, Feb. 28, 1996, from clari.tw.nuclear, CNC.

Enthoven, Alain C., and K. Wayne Smith. *How Much Is Enough? Shaping the Defense Program, 1961–1969*. New York: Harper & Row, 1971.

Epstein, Joshua M. "Dynamic Analysis and the Conventional Balance in Europe," *International Security*, vol. 12, no. 4 (Spring 1988), pp. 154–65.

———. "The 3:1 Rule, the Adaptive Dynamic Model, and the Future of Security Studies," *International Security*, vol. 13, no. 4 (Spring 1989), pp. 90–127.

———. *The 1987 Defense Budget*. Washington, D.C.: Brookings Institution, 1986.

———. *The 1988 Defense Budget.* Washington, D.C.: Brookings Institution, 1987.

Farber, Henry S., and Joanne Gowa. "Polities and Peace," *International Security,* vol. 20, no. 2 (Fall 1995), pp. 123–46.

"Farewell WE117: Royal Air Force Jettisons Its Nuclear Capability Ahead of Schedule," May 1, 1998, *International Defense Review,* vol. 31, no. 5, p. 9, from LEXIS.

Fearon, James G. "Rationalist Explanations for War," *International Organization,* vol. 49, no. 3 (Summer 1995), pp. 379–414.

Feaver, Peter D. "Command and Control in Emerging Nuclear Nations," *International Security,* vol. 17, no. 3 (Winter 1992/1993), pp. 160–87.

———. "Neooptimists and the Enduring Problem of Nuclear Proliferation," *Security Studies,* vol. 6, no. 4 (Summer 1997), pp. 93–125.

Feldman, Shai. *Israeli Nuclear Deterrence: A Strategy For The 1980s.* New York: Columbia University Press, 1982.

Fenton, Ben. "British Confusion over Cuban Missile Crisis; Newly-released Papers Show Commanders Could Have Ignored Orders to Deploy Atomic Weapons," *The Daily Telegraph,* Aug. 4, 1998, p. 4, from LEXIS.

Fetter, Steve. "Ballistic Missiles and Weapons of Mass Destruction: What Is the Threat? What Should Be Done?" *International Security,* vol. 16, no. 1 (Summer 1991), pp. 5–42.

———. "Nuclear Deterrence and the 1990 Indo-Pakistani Crisis," *International Security,* vol. 21, no. 4 (Summer 1996), pp. 176–81.

"First Documented Evidence That U.S. Presidents Predelegated Nuclear Weapons Release Authority to the Military," March 19, 1998, available at the National Security Archive website, http://www.seas.gwu.edu/nsarchive/news/19980319.htm.

Fitchett, Joseph. "Paris Drops Hades Short-Range Missile," *International Herald Tribune,* June 13, 1992, from LEXIS.

Foot, Rosemary J. "Nuclear Coercion and the Ending of the Korean Conflict," *International Security,* vol. 13, no. 3 (Winter 1988/1989), pp. 92–112.

Foran, Virginia, ed. *Nuclear Non-Proliferation, 1945–1990.* Alexandria, Va.: Chadwick-Healey, 1992.

Foxwell, David. "France Weighs Up the Global Price," *Jane's Navy International,* July 1, 1998, vol. 103, no. 6, p. 30, from LEXIS.

"France-Britain Deepen Nuclear Cooperation—Major," *Reuters,* Oct. 30, 1995, from clari.tw.nuclear, CNC.

"France: Budget Spending on Nuclear Forces in 1992 to Be Cut by 3%," *Le Monde,* Oct. 30, 1991, *Reuter Textline,* from LEXIS.

"France Confirms U.S. Nuclear Data-Sharing Pact," *Reuters,* June 17, 1996, from clari.tw.nuclear, CNC.

"France: Defence Minister Speaks of Terrestrial Version of New M5 Missile," *Les Echos,* Nov. 14, 1991, *Reuter Textline,* from LEXIS.

"France, Germany Set Crisis, Nuclear Talks-Paper," *Reuters,* Jan. 24, 1997, from clari.tw.nuclear, CNC.

"France Halts Update of Mobile Land-based Missile," *Agence France-Presse*, July 22, 1991, from LEXIS.

"France Likely to Need More Nuclear Tests—Balladur," *Reuters*, May 11, 1995, from clari.tw.nuclear, CNC.

"France May Rely on Nuclear Weapons for Defense," *United Press International*, Dec. 7, 1982, from LEXIS.

"France Mends Fences with EU Nuclear Critics," *Reuters*, May 21, 1996, from clari.tw.nuclear, CNC.

"France Needs Up to 20 More Nuclear Tests—Chirac," *The Reuter Library Report*, Oct. 8, 1993, from LEXIS.

"France Offers Germany Security," *Associated Press*, Sept. 7, 1995, from clari.tw.nuclear, CNC.

"France Qualifies ASMP Nuclear Missile," *Aviation Week and Space Technology*, Mar. 31, 1986, from LEXIS.

"France Reorientates Strategy Against Soviet Threat," *Xinhua General Overseas News Service*, Jan. 12, 1977, from LEXIS.

"France: S4 Strategic Missile Project Could Be Shelved," *Le Monde*, Sept. 17, 1988, *Reuter Textline*, from LEXIS.

"France Says Will Maintain Nuclear Deterrent," *The Reuter European Community Report*, Oct. 6, 1993, from LEXIS.

"France Sees Guarantees for India on N-test Treaty," *Reuters*, Sept. 11, 1996, from clari.tw.nuclear, CNC.

"France Shuts Down Nuclear Missile Base This Month," *Reuters*, Sept. 6, 1996, from clari.tw.nuclear, CNC.

"France Succeeds in Test-firing New Nuclear Missile," *Xinhua*, Feb. 15, 1995, from LEXIS.

"France Tightens Military Ties with NATO," *United Press International*, Jan. 17, 1996, from LEXIS.

"France to Reduce Nuclear Forces," *Reuters*, Feb. 29, 1996, from clari.tw.nuclear, CNC.

"France to Replace Aging N-bombers," *Reuters*, Dec. 28, 1995, from clari.tw.nuclear, CNC.

"France to Scrap Land-Based N-Missiles in September," *Reuters*, Apr. 23, 1996, from clari.tw.nuclear, CNC.

"France Upgrading Nuclear Force Despite East-West Détente," *Reuters*, Sept. 17, 1990, from LEXIS.

"France Will Not Sign Nuclear Ban If It Needs Tests," *The Reuter European Community Report*, Oct. 13, 1993, from LEXIS.

"France's Draft Defence Budget for 1983 Makes the Country's Nuclear Deterrent the Year's Absolute Priority," *Le Monde*, Oct. 8, 1982, *Reuter Textline*, from LEXIS.

"Franco-German Defense Plan Helps NATO, Minister," *Reuters*, Jan. 29, 1997, from clari.tw.defense, CNC.

Freedman, Lawrence. "Britain's Defense Policy," in Edwin H. Fedder, ed., *Defense Politics of the Atlantic Alliance*. New York: Praeger, 1980.

———. "British Nuclear Targeting," in Desmond Ball and Jeffrey Richelson, eds., *Strategic Nuclear Targeting*. Ithaca: Cornell University Press, 1986.

———. *The Evolution of Nuclear Strategy*. New York: St. Martin's, 1981.

Freedman, Lawrence, Martin Navias, and Nicholas Wheeler. "Independence in Concert: The British Rationale for Possessing Strategic Nuclear Weapons," Occasional Paper 5. College Park, Md.: Center for International Studies at Maryland, 1989.

"French Cabinet Backs Cuts in Defence Budget," *Reuters*, May 13, 1996, from clari.tw.nuclear, CNC.

"The French Cabinet Has Approved a Defence Budget Up by 6% in Real Terms for the Five Year Period from 1987 to 1991," *Le Monde*, Nov. 6, 1986, *Reuter Textline*, from LEXIS.

"French Debate Dropping Triad Concept," *Aviation Week and Space Technology*, Sept. 4, 1978, from LEXIS.

"French Defence White Paper Vague on Nuclear Deterrent," *Agence France-Presse*, Feb. 23, 1994, from LEXIS.

"French Defense Minister Calls Nuclear Tests Indispensable," *Xinhua General Overseas News Service*, Nov. 12, 1993, from LEXIS.

"French Expert Calls Nuclear Tests a Success," *Reuters*, Feb. 13, 1996, from clari.tw.nuclear, CNC.

"French General Wants French-British Nuclear Ties," *Reuters*, Mar. 18, 1996, from clari.tw.nuclear, CNC.

"French Halt Study Work on S45 Nuclear Missile," *Aviation Week and Space Technology*, July 29, 1991, from LEXIS.

"French Minister Says Experts Want Nuclear Tests," *Reuters*, June 6, 1995, from clari.tw.nuclear, CNC.

"French Nuclear Command Post Enters Operational Service," *Aviation Week and Space Technology*, Feb. 8, 1988, from LEXIS.

"French Prime Minister on France's Nuclear Policy," *Xinhua General Overseas News Service*, July 4, 1977, from LEXIS.

"French Prime Minister on Strategy of Deterrence," *Xinhua General Overseas News Service*, Sept. 18, 1984, from LEXIS.

"French Public Vigilant Against Soviet 'Détente' Fraud," *Xinhua General Overseas News Service*, Jan. 3, 1978, from LEXIS.

"French Shun Disarmament Trend, Says Poll," *Reuters Ltd.*, Apr. 21, 1987, from LEXIS.

"French to Build Laser to Test Nuclear Weapon," *Associated Press*, Apr. 21, 1995, from clari.tw.nuclear, CNC.

Fukuda, Eiko. "General Says French Defence Doctrine a Recipe for Catastrophe," *Reuters North European Service*, Mar. 16, 1984, from LEXIS.

"Further Thoughts by Marshal Chen Yi on Sino-American Relations," Document no. 12, trans. by Chen Jian, CWIHP *Bulletin*, issue 11 (Winter 1998).

Gaddis, John Lewis. "The Long Peace: Elements of Stability in the Postwar International System," in Sean M. Lynn-Jones, ed., *The Cold War and After*. Cambridge: MIT Press, 1991.

————. *Strategies of Containment: A Critical Appraisal of Postwar American National Security Policy*. New York: Oxford University Press, 1982.

Gallagher, Michael G. "China's Illusory Threat to the South China Sea," *International Security*, vol. 19, no. 1 (Summer 1994), pp. 169–94.

Gallois, Pierre. *The Balance of Terror: Strategy for the Nuclear Age*, trans. by Richard Howard. Boston: Houghton Mifflin, 1961.

————. "French Defense Planning—The Future in the Past," *International Security*, vol. 1, no. 2 (Fall 1976), pp. 15–31.

Ganguly, Sumit. "India's Pathway to Pokhran II: The Prospects and Sources of New Delhi's Nuclear Weapons Program," *International Security*, vol. 23, no. 4 (Spring 1999), pp. 148–77.

Garrett, Banning N., and Bonnie S. Glaser. "Chinese Perspectives on Nuclear Arms Control," *International Security*, vol. 20, no. 3 (Winter 1995/1996), pp. 43–78.

————. *War and Peace: The Views from Moscow and Beijing*. Berkeley: Institute of International Studies, 1984.

Garthoff, Raymond L. *Reflections on the Cuban Missile Crisis*. Washington, D.C.: Brookings Institution, 1987.

Garver, John W. "The Chinese Communist Party and the Collapse of Soviet Communism," *The China Quarterly*, no. 133 (Mar. 1993), pp. 1–26.

Gates, William R., and Katsuaki L. Terasawa. "Commitment, Threat Perceptions, and Expenditures in a Defense Alliance," *International Studies Quarterly*, vol. 36, no. 2 (Mar. 1992), pp. 101–18.

Glaser, Charles L. "Realists as Optimists: Cooperation as Self-Help," *International Security*, vol. 19, no. 3 (Winter 1994/1995), pp. 50–90.

Godwin, Paul H. B. *The Chinese Defense Establishment: Continuity and Change in the 1980s*. Boulder, Colo.: Westview Press, 1983.

————. "The Chinese Defense Establishment in Transition: The Passing of a Revolutionary Army?" in A. Doak Barnett and Ralph N. Clough, eds., *Modernizing China*. Boulder, Colo.: Westview Press, 1986.

————. "Force Projection and China's National Military Strategy," in C. Dennison Lane, Mark Weisenbloom, and Dimon Liu, eds., *Chinese Military Modernization*. New York: Kegan Paul International, 1996.

————. "From Continent to Periphery: PLA Doctrine, Strategy and Capabilities Towards 2000," *The China Quarterly*, no. 146 (June 1996), pp. 464–87.

Goldstein, Avery. "Discounting the Free Ride: Alliances and Security in the Postwar World," *International Organization*, vol. 49, no. 1 (Winter 1995), pp. 39–71.

————. *From Bandwagon to Balance-of-Power Politics: Structural Constraints and Politics in China, 1949–1978*. Stanford: Stanford University Press, 1991.

————. "Great Expectations: Interpreting China's Arrival," *International Security*, vol. 22, no. 3 (Winter 1997/98), pp. 36–73.

————. "Robust and Affordable Security: Some Lessons from the Second-ranking Powers During the Cold War," *Journal of Strategic Studies*, vol. 15, no. 4 (Dec. 1992), pp. 476–527.

———. "Understanding Nuclear Proliferation: Theoretical Explanation and China's National Experience," *Security Studies*, vol. 2, no. 3/4 (Spring/Summer 1993), pp. 213–55.

Goncharov, Sergei N., John W. Lewis, and Xue Litai. *Uncertain Partners: Stalin, Mao, and the Korean War*. Stanford: Stanford University Press, 1993.

Goodman, Anthony. "Ukraine Worried About Potential Nuclear Neighbors," *Reuters*, Sept. 26, 1996, from clari.tw.nuclear, CNC.

Goodpaster, A. J. "Memorandum of Conference with the President, August 3, 1960," Declassified Dec. 18, 1978, *NNP*, 1960/08/08 (00662).

———. "Memorandum of Conference with the President, Mar. 8, 1956, 8:30," *NNP*, 1956/03/08 (00248), Declassified Nov. 16, 1976.

———. "Memorandum of Conference with the President, October 25, 1957," *NNP*, 1957/10/26 (00345), Declassified June 9, 1982.

Gormly, James L. "The Washington Declaration and the 'Poor Relation': Anglo-American Atomic Diplomacy, 1945–46," *Diplomatic History*, Spring 1984, pp. 125–43.

Gottfried, Kurt, and Bruce G. Blair. *Crisis Stability and Nuclear War*. New York: Oxford University Press, 1988.

Gray, Colin. "Nuclear Strategy: A Case for a Theory of Victory," *International Security*, vol. 4, no. 1 (Summer 1979), pp. 54–87.

"Greenpeace to Take 'Soft' Approach to China," *Reuters*, May 20, 1996, from clari.tw.nuclear, CNC.

Gromyko, Andrei. *Memoirs*, trans. by Harold Shulman, forward by Henry A. Kissinger. New York: Doubleday, 1989.

Hagerty, Devin T. "The Author Replies," *International Security*, vol. 21, no. 4 (Summer 1996), pp. 181–85.

———. *The Consequences of Nuclear Proliferation: Lessons from South Asia*. Cambridge: MIT Press, 1998.

———. "Nuclear Deterrence in South Asia: The 1990 Indo-Pakistani Crisis," *International Security*, vol. 20, no. 2 (Winter 1995/1996), pp. 79–114.

Hall, Eric. "Chinese Forces Changing for More Effective Strategic Role," *Reuters North European Service*, Mar. 5, 1984, from LEXIS.

Hamrin, Carol L. "China Reassesses the Superpowers," *Pacific Affairs*, vol. 56, no. 2 (Summer 1983).

Hanami, Andrew. *The Military Might of Modern Japan*. Dubuque, Iowa: Kendall/Hunt, 1995.

Hao Yufan and Zhai Zhihai. "China's Decision to Enter the Korean War: History Revisited," *China Quarterly*, no. 121 (Mar. 1990), pp. 94–115.

Harding, Harry. "The Domestic Politics of China's Global Posture," in Thomas Fingar, ed., *China's Quest for Independence*. Boulder, Colo.: Westview Press, 1980.

Haydon, Simon. "France Boosts Nuclear Force Amid Worries Over Missile Deal," *The Reuter Library Report*, Nov. 26, 1987, from LEXIS.

He Zong. "Changes and Development Trends in the International Situation," *Shijie Zhishi*, June 1, 1983, in *FBIS*, July 21, 1983, pp. A3–A5.

Heinzig, Dieter. "Stalin, Mao, Kim and Korean War Origins, 1950: A Russian Document Discrepancy," CWIHP *Bulletin*, issues 8–9 (Winter 1996/1997).

Heisbourg, François. "The British and French Nuclear Forces," *Survival*, vol. 31, no. 4 (July/Aug. 1989).

Herring, George C., and Richard H. Immerman. "Eisenhower, Dulles, and Dienbienphu: 'The Day We Didn't Go to War' Revisited," *The Journal of American History*, vol. 71, no. 2 (Sept. 1984), pp. 343–63.

Hiatt, Fred. "Russians Are Leaning Toward Nuclear Reliance for Security," *Philadelphia Inquirer*, Nov. 26, 1992, p. A22.

Hibbs, Mark. "Tomorrow, a Eurobomb? Possibility of a European Nuclear Defense," *Bulletin of the Atomic Scientists*, vol. 52, no. 1 (Jan./Feb. 1996), available online at http://www.bullatomsci.org/issues/1996/jf96/jf96Hibbs.html.

"Highlights from Secretary of State Rusk's Policy Planning Meeting," Oct. 15, 1963, Document no. 191, *FRUS, 1961–1963*, vol. 22: *China, Korea, and Japan*. Washington, D.C.: U.S. Government Printing Office, 1996.

Hildebrandt, Gregory G. "Measuring the Burden of Alliance Activities," *Rand Note*, N-3048-PCT.

Holloway, David. *Stalin and the Bomb: The Soviet Union and Atomic Energy, 1939–1956*. New Haven: Yale University Press, 1994.

Holum John. "A Powerful Barrier to Future Nuclear Tests," *Christian Science Monitor*, Sept. 30, 1996, from clari.tw.nuclear, CNC.

Holzman, Franklyn. "Are the Russians Really Outspending the U.S. on Defense?" *International Security*, vol. 4, no. 3 (Spring 1980), pp. 86–104.

———. "Politics and Guesswork: CIA and DIA Estimates of Soviet Military Spending," *International Security*, vol. 14, no. 1 (Fall 1989), pp. 101–31.

———. "Soviet Military Spending: Assessing the Numbers Game," *International Security*, vol. 6, no. 3 (Spring 1982), pp. 78–101.

Hopkins, John C., and Weixing Hu, eds. *Strategic Views from the Second Tier: The Nuclear Weapons Policies of France, Britain, and China*. New Brunswick, N.J.: Transaction Publishers, 1995.

Housego, David. "Economy Squeezes Future Shape of France's Defence," *Financial Times*, Nov. 26, 1982, from LEXIS.

———. "French Army Sounds Alarm on Defence Cuts," *Financial Times*, Dec. 7, 1982, from LEXIS.

Hu Wenlong, Zha Jinlu et al., eds. *Xiandai Junbingzhong Zhanshu*. Hubei: Junshi Kexue Chubanshe, 1991.

Huntington, Samuel P. "The Clash of Civilizations?" *Foreign Affairs*, vol. 72, no. 3 (Summer 1993), pp. 22–49.

———. *The Clash of Civilizations and the Remaking of World Order*. New York: Touchstone, 1997.

———. "The U.S.—Decline or Renewal?" *Foreign Affairs*, vol. 67, no. 2 (Winter 1988/1989), pp. 76–96.

"Implications for the Free World and the Communist Bloc of Growing Nuclear Capabilities," NIE (100-5-59), CIA, Feb. 3, 1959, HRP, July 9, 1993.

"Implications of Growing Nuclear Capabilities for the Communist Bloc and the Free World," NIE (100-4-57), CIA, July 9, 1957, HRP, July 7, 1993.

"Incoming Telegram, Department of State," excised and declassified July 7, 1992, available at National Security Archive, Washington, D.C., NNP, Unpublished Collection, Box 7, file #1898.

"Incoming Telegram, Department of State. Subject: Effect of CCNE on GRC and Implications for US Policy," Oct. 29, 1964, *NNP*, 1964/10/29 (1030).

"Incoming Telegram: From Paris to Secretary of State, no. 6252, June 28, 11PM," June 28, 1958, *NNP*, 1959/06/28 (00441).

"India Analysts Say Nuclear Test Pact Full of Holes," *Reuters*, June 16, 1996, from clari.tw.nuclear, CNC.

"India Keeps Option to Build Nuclear Arms," *Reuters*, June 5, 1996, from clari.tw.nuclear, CNC.

"India's Nuclear Blasts Lose Their Impact," *Agence France-Presse*, May 10, 1999, from clari.tw.nuclear, CNC.

"Indian Air Force Cannot Take on China, Pakistan in War: Report," *Agence France-Presse*, Apr. 30, 1999, from clari.world.asia, CNC.

"Indian Newspapers Hail Government's Nuclear Stand," *Reuters*, June 21, 1996, from clari.tw.nuclear, CNC.

"Indian Parties Bash U.S. over Nuclear Test Report," *Reuters*, Dec. 12, 1995, from clari.tw.nuclear, CNC.

"Information Memorandum from the Acting Deputy Under Secretary of State for Political Affairs (Thompson) to Secretary of State Rusk: China Study," July 15, 1965, Document no. 94, *FRUS, 1964–1968*, vol. 30: *China*. Washington, D.C.: U.S. Government Printing Office, 1998.

"The International Institute for Strategic Studies Has Reported to the Commons Select Committee on Defence Evaluating the Various Options for a British Nuclear Deterrent in the Coming Decades," *Guardian*, July 10, 1980, *Reuter Textline*, from LEXIS.

"Interoffice Memorandum, Joint Committee on Atomic Energy, from Leonard M. Trosten, Staff Counsel to John T. Conway, Executive Director, November 18, 1965, Subject: Transfer of Restricted Data to France," *NNP*, 1965/11/18 (01147).

Intriligator, Michael D., and Dagobert L. Brito. "Nuclear Proliferation and the Probability of Nuclear War," *Public Choice*, vol. 37, no. 2 (1981), pp. 247–60.

James, Robert Rhodes, ed. *Winston S. Churchill, His Complete Speeches, 1897–1963*, vol. VI, *1935–1942*. New York: Chelsea House Publishers in association with R. R. Bowker Company, 1974.

"Japan in 1969 Ensured Nuclear Arms Potential—Daily," *Reuters*, Aug. 1, 1994, from clari.tw.nuclear, CNC.

"Japan Ponders Building Nuclear Weapons," *Associated Press*, May 4, 1995, from clari.tw.nuclear, CNC.

"Japan Says It Can Attack Nkorean Launch Site If Hit by Missile," *Agence France-Presse*, Sept. 4, 1998, from clari.tw.defense, CNC.

Jarry, Emmanuel. "France Denies Changing Nuclear Doctrine," *Reuters*, Jan. 30, 1997, from clari.tw.nuclear, CNC.

———. "France to Signal Change in Defence Priorities—Sources," *The Reuter Library Report*, Feb. 15, 1994, from LEXIS.

———. "French Left Charges Defence Sell-out to U.S., NATO," *Reuters*, Jan. 29, 1997, from clari.tw.defense, CNC.

Jehl, Douglas. "Threats in the Gulf: The Bush Legacy Clinton's Line in the Sand; The President Seeks to Avoid Bush's Error of Not Clearly Warning the Iraqis in 1990," *New York Times*, Oct. 10, 1994, p. A1, from LEXIS.

Jencks, Harlan. "Defending China in 1987," *Current History*, vol. 86 (Sept. 1987), pp. 266–73.

———. "People's War Under Modern Conditions: Wishful Thinking, National Suicide, or Effective Deterrent?" *China Quarterly*, no. 98 (June 1984), pp. 305–19.

Jenkins, Brian M. "Is Nuclear Terrorism Plausible?" in Paul Leventhal and Yonah Alexander, eds., *Nuclear Terrorism: Defining the Threat*. Washington: Pergamon-Brassey's, 1986.

Jervis, Robert. "Cooperation Under the Security Dilemma," *World Politics*, vol. 30, no. 2 (Jan. 1978), pp. 167–214.

———. *The Illogic of American Nuclear Strategy*. Ithaca: Cornell University Press, 1986.

———. *The Meaning of the Nuclear Revolution*. Ithaca: Cornell University Press, 1989.

———. "The Political Effects of Nuclear Weapons: A Comment," in Sean M. Lynn-Jones, ed., *The Cold War and After*. Cambridge: MIT Press, 1991.

———. "Strategic Theory: What's New and What's True," *Journal of Strategic Studies*, vol. 9, no. 4 (Dec. 1986), pp. 135–62.

Jervis, Robert, Richard Ned Lebow, and Janice Gross Stein. *Psychology and Deterrence*. Baltimore: Johns Hopkins University Press, 1985.

Jia Bei. "Gorbachev's Policy Toward the Asian Pacific Region," *Guoji Wenti Yanjiu* (Apr. 1987), *FBIS*, May 14, 1987, pp. C8–C14.

"Jin Shinian Wo Jun Junfei Chengdijian Qushi," *Guofang* (Feb. 1991), p. 45.

Joffe, Ellis. *The Chinese Army After Mao*. Cambridge: Harvard University Press, 1987.

Johnson, Chalmers A. *Peasant Nationalism and Communist Power: The Emergence of Revolutionary China, 1937–1945*. Stanford: Stanford University Press, 1962.

Johnson, Robert H. "Letter," *Newsletter, The Society for Historians of American Foreign Relations*, vol. 26, no. 3 (Sept. 1996).

———. "Memorandum, Subject: 422nd NSC Meeting, Thursday October 29, 1959," *NNP*, 1959/10/29 (00599), Declassified Dec. 8, 1989.

Johnston, Alastair Iain. "China's New 'Old Thinking': The Concept of Limited Deterrence," *International Security*, vol. 20, no. 3 (Winter 1995/96), pp. 5–42.

———. *Cultural Realism: Strategic Culture and Grand Strategy*. Princeton: Princeton University Press, 1995.

———. "Prospects for Chinese Nuclear Force Modernization: Limited Deterrence Versus Multilateral Arms Control," *China Quarterly*, no. 146 (June 1996), pp. 548–76.

Kaplan, Fred. *The Wizards of Armageddon*. New York: Simon and Schuster, 1983.

Karl, David J. "Proliferation Pessimism and Emerging Nuclear Powers," *International Security*, vol. 21, no. 3 (Winter 1996/1997), pp. 87–119.

Kaufmann, William W. *Assessing the Base Force: How Much Is Too Much?* Washington, D.C.: Brookings Institution, 1992.

———. *Glasnost, Perestroika, and U.S. Defense Spending*. Washington, D.C.: Brookings Institution, 1990.

———. *A Reasonable Defense*. Washington, D.C.: Brookings Institution, 1986.

Kaufmann, William W., and Lawrence J. Korb. *The 1990 Defense Budget*. Washington, D.C.: Brookings Institution, 1989.

Kaufmann, William W., and John D. Steinbruner. *Decisions for Defense: Prospects for a New Order*. Washington, D.C.: Brookings Institution, 1991.

Kaysen, Carl. "Is War Obsolete? A Review Essay," in Sean M. Lynn-Jones, ed., *The Cold War and After*. Cambridge: MIT Press, 1991.

Kelleher, Catherine M., and Gale A. Mattox, eds. *Evolving European Defense Policies*. Lexington, Mass.: Lexington, 1987.

Kemp, Geoffrey. "Nuclear Forces for Medium Powers, Part I: Targets and Weapons Systems," *Adelphi Paper* 106. London: International Institute for Strategic Studies, 1974.

———. "Nuclear Forces for Medium Powers, Parts II and III: Strategic Requirements and Options," *Adelphi Paper*, 106. London: International Institute for Strategic Studies, 1974.

Kennedy, Paul. *The Rise and Fall of the Great Powers*. New York: Vintage, 1987.

Kennedy, Robert F. *Thirteen Days: A Memoir of the Cuban Missile Crisis*. New York: Mentor, 1969.

"Kennedy-Macmillan Nassau Meeting, December 19–20, 1962, Background Paper, Current Political Science in the United Kingdom," Dec. 13, 1962, *NNP*, 1962/12/13 (00927), Declassified Oct. 31, 1975.

Khalip, Andrei. "Russia May Use Nuclear Weapons First in Self-defence," *Reuters*, Feb. 11, 1997, from clari.tw.nuclear, CNC.

Khotin, Rostislav. "Ukraine to Keep Making Missiles Despite U.S. Pressure," *Reuters*, May 19, 1997, from clari.tw.defense, CNC.

Kirshner, Jonathan. *Currency and Coercion: The Political Economy of In-*

ternational Monetary Power. Princeton: Princeton University Press, 1995.

Kissinger, Henry. *Diplomacy*. New York: Simon and Schuster, 1994.

Kohl, Wilfred L. *French Nuclear Diplomacy*. Princeton: Princeton University Press, 1971.

Kramer, Mark. "Declassified Materials from CPSU Central Committee Plenums: Sources, Context, Highlights," CWIHP *Bulletin*, issue 10 (Mar. 1998).

——. "Realism, Nuclear Proliferation, and East-Central European Strategies," unpublished ms.

——. "The USSR Foreign Ministry's Appraisal of Sino-Soviet Relations on the Eve of the Split, September 1959," CWIHP *Bulletin*, issues 6–7 (Winter 1995/1996), pp. 170–85.

Krauthammer, Charles. "The Unipolar Moment," *Foreign Affairs*, vol. 70, no. 1 (Winter 1991), pp. 23–33.

Kristof, Nicholas D. "Japanese Look at the Possibility of a Military Role in Asia," *New York Times*, May 28, 1996, p. A8.

——. "Tension with Japan Rises Alongside China's Star," *New York Times*, June 16, 1996, p. E3.

Kupchan, Charles A. *The Vulnerability of Empire*. Ithaca: Cornell University Press, 1994.

Laird, Robin. "France's Strategic Posture," *Defense and Foreign Affairs*, May 1986, from LEXIS.

——. "Mitterrand's New Strategic Vision," *Defense and Foreign Affairs* (Oct./Nov. 1988), from LEXIS.

Landau, Martin. "Redundancy, Rationality, and the Problem of Duplication and Overlap," *Public Administration Review*, vol. 29, no. 4 (July/Aug. 1969), pp. 346–58.

Landau, Martin, and Russell Stout, Jr. "To Manage Is Not to Control: Or the Folly of Type II Errors," *Public Administration Review* vol. 39, no. 2 (Mar.–Apr. 1979), pp. 148–56.

Larkin, Bruce D. *Nuclear Designs: Great Britain, France, and China in the Global Governance of Nuclear Arms*. New Brunswick, N.J.: Transaction, 1996.

Layne, Christopher. "Kant or Cant: The Myth of the Democratic Peace," *International Security*, vol. 19, no. 2 (Fall 1994), pp. 5–49.

——. "The Unipolar Illusion: Why New Great Powers Will Rise," *International Security*, vol. 17, no. 4 (Spring 1993), pp. 5–49.

Lederer, Edith M., and Sergei Shargorodsky. "New Reluctance on Giving Up Their Nuclear Arms," *Philadelphia Inquirer*, June 14, 1992, p. A3.

Lenorovitz, Jeffrey M. "French Boost 1989 Defense Budget for Conventional, Nuclear Upgrades," *Aviation Week and Space Technology*, Sept. 26, 1988, from LEXIS.

——. "French Budget Sets $8 Billion for Equipment," *Aviation Week and Space Technology*, Nov. 14, 1983, from LEXIS.

"Letter from French President Charles De Gaulle to U.S. President Dwight

D. Eisenhower," Oct. 6, 1959, Department of State, Division of Language Services (trans.), *NNP*, 1959/10/06 (00594).

Levy, Jack S. *War in the Great Power System, 1495–1975*. Lexington: University of Kentucky Press, 1983.

Lewis, J. A. C. "All Change for France: How the Big Shake-Out Will Shape-up," *Jane's Defence Weekly*, vol. 25, no. 11 (Mar. 13, 1996), pp. 19ff, from LEXIS.

———. "France Makes $7b Savings on Projects," *Jane's Defence Industry Report*, Sept. 1, 1998, p. 4, from LEXIS.

———. "France to Trim Nuclear Forces, End Conscription," *Jane's Defence Weekly*, vol. 25, no. 9 (Feb. 28, 1996), pp. 4ff, from LEXIS.

Lewis, John W. "China's Military Doctrines and Force Posture," in Thomas Fingar, ed., *China's Quest for Independence*. Boulder, Colo.: Westview Press, 1980.

Lewis, John Wilson, and Hua Di. "China's Ballistic Missile Programs: Technologies, Strategies, Goals," *International Security*, vol. 17, no. 2 (Fall 1992), pp. 5–40.

Lewis, John W., and Litai Xue. *China Builds the Bomb*. Stanford: Stanford University Press, 1988.

———. *China's Strategic Seapower*. Stanford: Stanford University Press, 1994.

Li Dai. "Independence and China's External Relations," *Shijie Zhishi*, no. 19 (Oct. 1, 1981), *FBIS*, Nov. 19, 1981, pp. A1–A5.

Li Yuanchao. "The Politics of Artillery Shelling: A Study of the Taiwan Strait Crisis," *Beijing Review*, vol. 35 (Sept. 7, 1992), pp. 32–38.

Liberman, Peter. "The Spoils of Conquest," *International Security*, vol. 18 no. 2 (Fall 1993), pp. 125–53.

Lim, Benjamin Kang. "China Nuclear Halt May Stem from Deal—Analysts," *Reuters*, Aug. 6, 1996, from clari.tw.nuclear, CNC.

Lin, Chong-Pin. *China's Nuclear Weapons Strategy*. Lexington, Mass.: Lexington, 1988.

———. "The Military Balance in the Taiwan Straits," *The China Quarterly*, no. 146 (June 1996), pp. 577–95.

———. "The Power Projection Capabilities of the People's Liberation Army," in C. Dennison Lane, Mark Weisenbloom, and Dimon Liu, eds., *Chinese Military Modernization*. New York: Kegan Paul International, 1996.

Lindquist, Robert S. "Airgram, from US Embassy, Taipei. Subject: Comments re Effectiveness and Credibility of US Nuclear Deterrent in Far East in Wake of Chinese Communist Nuclear Detonation," Oct. 27, 1964, *NNP*, 1964/10/27 (01025), declassified Feb. 26, 1991.

Liu, Leo Yueh-yun. "The Modernization of the Chinese Military," *Current History*, vol. 79 (Sept. 1980), pp. 9–13.

Lovejoy, Charles D., and Bruce W. Watson, eds. *China's Military Reforms*. Boulder, Colo.: Westview Press, 1986.

Luttwak, Edward N. *Strategy: The Logic of War and Peace.* Cambridge: Harvard University Press, 1987.

Mack, Andrew. "Why Big Nations Lose Small Wars: The Politics of Asymmetric Conflict," *World Politics*, vol. 27, no. 2 (Jan. 1975), pp. 175–200.

MacLeod, Alexander. "Clinton's Stay of Nuclear Tests Irks Britain," *The Christian Science Monitor*, July 7, 1993, from LEXIS.

"Main Trends in Soviet Capabilities and Policies, 1958–1963," NIE 11-4-58, HRP, no date.

Majendie, Paul. "UK's Labour Promises Defence Review but No Cuts," *Reuters*, Apr. 24, 1997, from clari.tw.defense, CNC.

"Major Stresses Need of Britain's Nuclear Shield," *Xinhua General Overseas News Service*, Jan. 14, 1992, from LEXIS.

Malone, Peter. *The British Nuclear Deterrent.* New York: St. Martin's, 1984.

Mandelbaum, Michael. *The Nuclear Revolution.* Cambridge: Cambridge University Press, 1981.

Mann, James. *About Face: A History of America's Curious Relationship with China, from Nixon to Clinton.* New York: Knopf, 1999.

Mansfield, Edward D. *Power, Trade, and War.* Princeton: Princeton University Press, 1994.

———. "Review—Coercive Cooperation: Explaining Multilateral Economic Sanctions," *World Politics*, vol. 47, no. 3 (July 1995), pp. 575–605.

Mansfield, Edward D., and Jack Snyder. "Democratization and the Danger of War," *International Security*, vol. 20, no. 1 (Summer 1995), pp. 5–38.

Mansourov, Alexandre Y. "Stalin, Mao, Kim, and China's Decision to Enter the Korean War, Sept. 16–Oct. 15, 1950: New Evidence from the Russian Archives," CWIHP *Bulletin*, issues 6–7 (Winter 1995/1996).

Mao Zedong. "Diguozhuyi Ruguo Fadong dui Woguo de Qinlüe Zhanzheng Women Jiang Shixian Quanmin Jiebing," Dec. 10, 1958, in *Mao Zedong Junshi Wenji*, vol. 6. Beijing: Junshi Kexue Chubanshe, Zhongyang Wenxian Chubanshe, 1993.

———. "Guanyu Bawo Da Jinmen Shiji Gei Peng Dehuai, Huang Kecheng de Xin," July 27, 1958, in *Jianguo Yilai Mao Zedong Wengao*, vol. 7. Beijing: Zhongyang Wenxian Chubanshe, 1992.

———. "Guanyu Guoji Xingshi de Jianghua Tigang," Dec. 1959, in *Jianguo Yilai Mao Zedong Wengao*, vol. 8. Beijing: Zhongyang Wenxian Chubanshe, 1993.

———. "Guanyu Sulian Qingqiu Zai Zhongguo Jianli Tezheng Changbo Wuxian Diantai Wenti," June 7, 1958, in *Mao Zedong Waijiao Wenxuan*. Beijing: Zhongyang Wenxian Chubanshe, Shijie Zhishi Chubanshe, 1994.

———. "Guanyu Taiwan Jushi Deng Wenti Fu Hu Zhiming de Dianbao," Sept. 10, 1958, in *Jianguo Yilai Mao Zedong Wengao*, vol. 7. Beijing: Zhongyang Wenxian Chubanshe, 1992.

———. "Guanyu Yanjiu Heluxiaofu Gei Aisenhaoer de Xingao de Piyu,"

Sept. 7, 1968, in *Jianguo Yilai Mao Zedong Wengao*, vol. 7. Beijing: Zhongyang Wenxian Chubanshe, 1992.

———. "Heluxiaofu de Rizi Buhao Guo," Jan. 17, 1964, in *Mao Zedong Waijiao Wenxuan*. Beijing: Zhongyang Wenxian Chubanshe, Shijie Zhishi Chubanshe, 1994.

———. "Jingji Jianshe he Guofang Jianshe de Guanxi," Apr. 25, 1956, in *Mao Zedong Junshi Wenji*, vol. 6. Beijing: Junshi Kexue Chubanshe, Zhongyang Wenxian Chubanshe, 1993.

———. *Selected Works of Mao Tse-tung*, vol. 2. Peking: Peking Foreign Languages Press, 1965.

———. "Shijie Renmin Shi Fandui Yong Yuanzidan Sha Ren de," Aug. 22, 1964, in *Mao Zedong Waijiao Wenxuan*. Beijing: Zhongyang Wenxian Chubanshe, Shijie Zhishi Chubanshe, 1994.

———. "Tong Sulian Zhu Hua Dashi Youjin de Tan Hua," July 22, 1958, in *Mao Zedong Waijiao Wenxuan*. Beijing: Zhongyang Wenxian Chubanshe, Shijie Zhishi Chubanshe, 1994.

———. "Yao Gao Yidian Yuanzidan Qidan," June 21, 1958, in *Mao Zedong Junshi Wenji*, vol. 6. Beijing: Junshi Kexue Chubanshe, Zhongyang Wenxian Chubanshe, 1993.

———. "Ying Zhuajin dui Jianduan Wuqi de Yanzhi Gongzuo," June 8, 1962, in *Mao Zedong Junshi Wenji*, vol. 6. Beijing: Junshi Kexue Chubanshe, Zhongyang Wenxian Chubanshe, 1993.

———. "Yiqie Fandongpai dou Shi Zhi Laohu," Nov. 18, 1957, *Mao Zedong Junshi Wenji*, vol. 6. Beijing: Junshi Kexue Chubanshe, Zhongyang Wenxian Chubanshe, 1993.

———. "Zai Di Shiwuci Zuigao Guowu Huiyishang de Jianghua," Sept. 5, 8, 1958, in *Jianguo Yilai Mao Zedong Wengao*, vol. 7. Beijing: Zhongyang Wenxian Chubanshe, 1992.

———. "Zai Guofang Weiyuan Diyici Huiyishang de Jianghua," Oct. 18, 1954, in *Mao Zedong Junshi Wenji*, vol. 6. Beijing: Junshi Kexue Chubanshe, Zhongyang Wenxian Chubanshe, 1993.

———. "Zhengqu Bijiao Chang de Heping Shijian Shi Kenengde," Oct. 18, 1958, in *Mao Zedong Waijiao Wenxuan*. Beijing: Zhongyang Wenxian Chubanshe, Shijie Zhishi Chubanshe, 1994.

———. "Zi Sugong Zhongyang Gei Nangong Zhongyang de Xinshang de Piyu," May 15, 1958, in *Jianguo Yilai Mao Zedong Wengao*, vol. 7. Beijing: Zhongyang Wenxian Chubanshe, 1992.

"Mao Zedong's Speech at the First Plenary Session of the CCP's Ninth Central Committee, 28 Apr. 1969," Document no. 8, trans. by Chen Jian, CWIHP *Bulletin*, issue 11 (Winter 1998).

"Mao Zedong's Talk at a Meeting of the Central Cultural Revolution Group (excerpt), 15 Mar. 1969," Document no. 4, trans. by Chen Jian, CWIHP *Bulletin*, issue 11 (Winter 1998).

"Mao's Cable Explains Drive Into Korea," *New York Times*, Feb. 26, 1992, p. A8.

Marsh, David. "The High Price of Independence," *Financial Times*, Mar. 6, 1985, from LEXIS.

Martin, Lisa L. *Coercive Cooperation: Explaining Multilateral Economic Sanctions*. Princeton: Princeton University Press, 1992.

Massonet, Philippe. "Exercises Point to True Size of China's Military Budget, Say Experts," *Agence France-Presse*, Mar. 21, 1996, from LEXIS.

Mastanduno, Michael. "Preserving the Unipolar Moment: Realist Theories and U.S. Grand Strategy After the Cold War," *International Security*, vol. 21, no. 4 (Spring 1997), pp. 49–88.

McDermott, Rose. *Risk-Taking in International Politics: Prospect Theory in American Foreign Policy*. Ann Arbor: University of Michigan Press, 1998.

McKillop, James. "UK: Rifkind to Cut Trident Power as Treasury Wins Price War," *Glasgow Herald*, Nov. 16, 1993, *Reuter Textline*, from LEXIS.

"McNamara Press Conference," *NNP*, c. 1962/06/20 (00883).

Mearsheimer, John J. "Assessing the Conventional Balance: The 3:1 Rule and Its Critics," *International Security*, vol. 13., no. 4 (Spring 1989), pp. 54–89.

———. "Back to the Future: Instability in Europe After the Cold War," *International Security*, vol. 15, no. 1 (Summer 1990), pp. 5–56.

———. "The Case for a Ukrainian Nuclear Deterrent," *Foreign Affairs*, vol. 72, no. 4 (Summer 1993), pp. 50–66.

———. *Conventional Deterrence*. Ithaca: Cornell University Press, 1983.

———. "The False Promise of International Institutions," *International Security*, vol. 19, no. 3 (Winter 1994/1995), pp. 5–49.

———. "Numbers, Strategy, and the European Balance," *International Security*, vol. 12, no. 4 (Spring 1988), pp. 174–85.

Melissen, Jan. "Prelude to Interdependence: The Anglo-American Relationship and the Limits of Great Britain's Nuclear Policy, 1952–57," *Arms Control*, vol. 11, no. 3 (Dec. 1990), pp. 205–31.

———. "The Restoration of the Nuclear Alliance: Great Britain and Atomic Negotiations with the United States, 1957–58," *Contemporary Record: The Journal of Contemporary British History*, vol. 6, no. 1 (Summer 1992).

———. *The Struggle for Nuclear Partnership: Britain, the United States and the Making of an Ambiguous Alliance, 1952–1959*. Groningen: STYX Publications, 1993.

"Memoir, 'Inside Story of the Decision Making During the Shelling of Jinmen,'" from *Zhuanji Wenxue*, no. 1 (1994), pp. 5–11, reprinted in CWIHP *Bulletin*, issues 6–7 (Winter 1995/1996), pp. 208–15, trans. and annotated by Li Xiaobing, Chen Jian, and David L. Wilson.

"Memorandum by Dean Acheson," Feb. 20, 1963, *NNP*, 1963/02/20 (00942).

"Memorandum for the Joint Chiefs of Staff to Secretary of Defense McNamara, Subject: Possible Responses to the ChiCom Nuclear

Threat," Jan. 16, 1965, document no. 76, *FRUS, 1964–1968,* vol. 30: *China.* Washington, D.C.: U.S. Government Printing Office, 1998.

"Memorandum for the President, Subject: The Diffusion of Nuclear Weapons with and without a Test Ban Agreement," Feb. 12, 1963, in *NNP, 1945–1990,* microfiche, 1963/2/12 (0941), Declassified June 21, 1977, p. 1.

"Memorandum from Director of Central Intelligence McCone to the Executive Director of Central Intelligence (Kirkpatrick)," Feb. 25, 1963, Document no. 298, *FRUS, 1961–1963,* vol. 5: *Soviet Union.* Washington, D.C.: U.S. Government Printing Office, 1998.

"Memorandum from Robert W. Komer of the National Security Council Staff to the President's Special Assistant for National Security Affairs (Bundy)," Nov. 5, 1963, Document no. 193, *FRUS, 1961–1963,* vol. 22: *China, Korea, and Japan.* Washington, D.C.: U.S. Government Printing Office, 1996.

"Memorandum from Robert W. Komer of the National Security Council Staff and the President's Special Assistant for National Security Affairs (Bundy) to President Johnson," Nov. 25, 1964, Document no. 69, *FRUS, 1964–1968,* vol. 30: *China.* Washington, D.C.: U.S. Government Printing Office, 1998.

"Memorandum from Robert W. Komer of the National Security Council Staff to the President's Special Assistant for National Security Affairs (Bundy)," Sept. 18, 1964, Document no. 51, *FRUS, 1964–1968,* vol. 30: *China.* Washington, D.C.: U.S. Government Printing Office, 1998.

"Memorandum from Robert W. Komer of the National Security Council Staff to the President's Special Assistant for National Security Affairs (Bundy)," Feb. 26, 1964, Document no. 14, *FRUS, 1964–1968,* vol. 30: *China.* Washington, D.C.: U.S. Government Printing Office, 1998.

"Memorandum from the Assistant Secretary of Defense for International Security Affairs (Nitze) to Secretary of Defense McNamara," May 11, 1963, Document no. 177, *FRUS, 1961–1963,* vol. 22: *China, Korea, and Japan.* Washington, D.C.: U.S. Government Printing Office, 1996.

"Memorandum from the President's Special Assistant (Rostow) to President Johnson," Apr. 20, 1967, Document no. 252, *FRUS, 1964–1968,* vol. 30: *China.* Washington, D.C.: U.S. Government Printing Office, 1998.

"Memorandum from the Republic of China Country Director (Bennett) to the Deputy Assistant Secretary of State for East Asian and Pacific Affairs (Berger)," July 11, 1967, Document no. 273, *FRUS, 1964–1968,* vol. 30: *China.* Washington, D.C.: U.S. Government Printing Office, 1998.

"Memorandum of Conversation Between the President's Special Assistant for National Security Affairs (Bundy) and the Soviet Ambassador (Dobrynin)," May 17, 1963, Document no. 322, *FRUS, 1961–1963,* vol. 5: *Soviet Union.* Washington, D.C.: U.S. Government Printing Office, 1998.

"Memorandum of Conversation with Ambassador Dobrynin," Sept. 25, 1964, 1–3:30 PM, Document no. 54, *FRUS, 1964–1968,* vol. 30: *China.* Washington, D.C.: U.S. Government Printing Office, 1998.

"Memorandum of Conversation, Subject: Communist China," July 27, 1967, 12:30 PM, Document no. 274, *FRUS, 1964–1968*, vol. 30: *China*. Washington, D.C.: U.S. Government Printing Office, 1998.

"Memorandum of Conversation, Subject: US-Soviet-Chinese Relations," Dec. 21, 1968, 7–10 PM, Document no. 334, *FRUS, 1964–1968*, vol. 30: *China*. Washington, D.C.: U.S. Government Printing Office, 1998.

"Memorandum of Conversation, United States Delegation to the Bermuda Meeting, March 21–22, 1957, Subject: Atomic Energy Items: (1) French Request (2) Test Limitations," Department of State, declassified with deletions Feb. 23, 1996, available at National Security Archive, NNP, Unpublished Collection, Box #7, file 7128.

"Memorandum of Conversation," Jan. 30, 1962, Document no. 150, *FRUS, 1961–1963*, vol. 5: *Soviet Union*. Washington, D.C.: U.S. Government Printing Office, 1998.

"Memorandum of Conversation: Secretary's Visit to Taipei," Apr. 16–17, 1964, Document no. 26, *FRUS, 1964–1968*, vol. 30: *China*. Washington, D.C.: U.S. Government Printing Office, 1998.

"Memorandum on the Substance of Discussion at a Department of State–Joint Chiefs of Staff Meeting," undated, c. Feb. 1963, Document no. 289, *FRUS, 1961–1963*, vol. 5: *Soviet Union*. Washington, D.C.: U.S. Government Printing Office, 1998.

"Memorandum Prepared by the Central Intelligence Agency: The New Phase of Soviet Policy," Aug. 9, 1963, Document no. 347, *FRUS, 1961–1963*, vol. 5: *Soviet Union*. Washington, D.C.: U.S. Government Printing Office, 1998.

Mendl, Wolf. *Deterrence and Persuasion*. New York: Praeger, 1970.

Meng Lin. "Deng Xiaoping Reportedly Comments on Relations with the United States," *Ching Pao*, Sept. 5, 1993, *British Broadcasting Corporation*, from LEXIS.

Mercer, Jonathan. *Reputation and International Politics*. Ithaca, N.Y.: Cornell University Press, 1996.

Miles, James. "Deng Says Nuclear Arms Necessary for Peace," *United Press International*, May 5, 1987, from LEXIS.

Milhollin, Gary, and Jennifer Weeks. "Keeping the Lid on Nuclear Arms; Nuclear Arms Control in Argentina and Brazil," *New Scientist*, vol. 131, no. 1782 (Aug. 17, 1991), pp. 26–30, from LEXIS.

The Military Balance 1987–1988. London: International Institute for Strategic Studies and Oxford University Press, 1987.

The Military Balance 1989–1990. London: International Institute for Strategic Studies and Oxford University Press, 1989.

The Military Balance 1991–1992. London: International Institute for Strategic Studies and Oxford University Press, 1991.

Miller, Charles. "Reduced Trident Will Still Have Muscle," *Press Association Newsfile*, Nov. 16, 1993, from LEXIS.

Miller, Steven E. "The Case Against a Ukrainian Nuclear Deterrent," *Foreign Affairs*, vol. 72, no. 4 (Summer 1993), pp. 67–80.

Miller, Steven E., and Stephen Van Evera, eds. *The Star Wars Controversy*. Princeton: Princeton University Press, 1986.

Milner, Helen V. "The Assumption of Anarchy in International Relations Theory," *The Review of International Studies*, vol. 17, no. 2 (Jan. 1991), pp. 67–85.

Mitchell, Ronald G. "Chinese Defense Spending in Transition," in *China Under the Four Modernizations*, Joint Economic Committee, Congress of the United States, Aug. 13, 1982. Washington, D.C.: U.S. Government Printing Office, 1982.

"Mitterrand: France Has Enough Nuclear Power for Deterrence," *Xinhua General Overseas News Service*, July 14, 1993, from LEXIS.

"Mitterrand Predicts Successors Won't Resume N-tests," *Reuters*, May 5, 1994, from clari.tw.nuclear, CNC.

"Mitterrand Reaffirms Independent Nuclear Deterrent," *Xinhua General Overseas News Service*, Mar. 15, 1988, from LEXIS.

"Mitterrand Shows Military Brass Round Nuclear Control Bunker," *Reuters North European Service*, Feb. 8, 1986, from LEXIS.

Mochizuki, Mike M. "Japan's Search for Strategy," *International Security*, vol. 8, no. 3 (Winter 1983/1984), pp. 152–79.

"More Than 60 Percent Turn Out to Vote in Polynesian Elections," *Agence France-Presse*, May 13, 1996, from LEXIS.

Morgan, Patrick M. *Deterrence: A Conceptual Analysis*. Beverly Hills: Sage, 1977.

Morgenthau, Hans. *Politics Among Nations*, 5th ed. New York: Knopf, 1973.

"Moscow Makes Crucial Decisions on Nuclear Defence," Apr. 30, 1999, *Agence France-Presse*, from clari.tw.nuclear, CNC.

Mueller, John. "The Essential Irrelevance of Nuclear Weapons: Stability in the Postwar World," in Sean M. Lynn-Jones, ed., *The Cold War and After*. Cambridge: MIT Press, 1991.

———. *Retreat from Doomsday: The Obsolescence of Major War*. New York: Basic Books, 1989.

Murdoch, James C., and Todd Sandler. "A Theoretical and Empirical Analysis of NATO," *Journal of Conflict Resolution*, vol. 26, no. 2 (June 1982), pp. 237–63.

Murray, Brian. "Working Paper no. 12: Stalin, the Cold War, and the Division of China: A Multiarchival Mystery," CWIHP (June 1995), available online at http://cwihp.si.edu/pdf/Wp12.pdf.

Murray, Douglas J., and Paul R. Viotti, eds. *The Defense Policies of Nations: A Comparative Study*. Baltimore: Johns Hopkins University Press, 1982.

Murray, R. "Problems of Nuclear Proliferation Outside Europe (Problem 2)," Dec. 7, 1964, Department of Defense, Declassified July 1, 1996, available at National Security Archives, Washington, D.C., Gilpatric Committee File.

Nalebuff, Barry. "Rational Deterrence in an Imperfect World," *World Politics*, vol. 43, no. 3 (Apr. 1991), pp. 313–35.

"National Intelligence Estimate: Authority and Control in the Communist Movement," Aug. 8, 1961, Document no. 49, *FRUS, 1961–1963*, vol. 22: *China, Korea, and Japan*. Washington, D.C.: U.S. Government Printing Office, 1996.

"National Intelligence Estimate: Communist China's Foreign Policy," May 5, 1965, Document no. 85, *FRUS, 1964–1968*, vol. 30: *China*. Washington, D.C.: U.S. Government Printing Office, 1998.

"National Intelligence Estimate: Communist China's Military Establishment," Mar. 10, 1965, Document no. 80, *FRUS, 1964–1968*, vol. 30: *China*. Washington, D.C.: U.S. Government Printing Office, 1998.

"National Intelligence Estimate: The Outlook for Sino-Soviet Relations," Dec. 1, 1966, Document no. 223, *FRUS, 1964–1968*, vol. 30: *China*. Washington, D.C.: U.S. Government Printing Office, 1998.

Naughton, Barry "The Third Front: Defence Industrialization in the Chinese Interior," *China Quarterly*, no. 115 (Sept. 1988), pp. 351–86.

Navias, Martin S. "Nuclear Weapons and British Alliance Commitments, 1955–56," in Ann Deighton, ed., *Britain and the First Cold War*. New York: St. Martin's, 1990.

Nelsen, Harvey W. *Power and Insecurity: Beijing, Moscow, and Washington, 1949–1988*. Boulder, Colo.: Lynn-Rienner, 1989.

Neustadt, Richard. *Alliance Politics*. New York: Columbia University Press, 1970.

"New Policy Group Wants Ban On Nuclear Weapons," *United Press International*, Feb. 19, 1997, from clari.tw.nuclear, CNC.

Ng-Quinn, Michael. "The Analytical Study of Chinese Foreign Policy," *International Studies Quarterly*, vol. 27 (June 1983), pp. 203–24.

———. "Effects of Bipolarity on Chinese Foreign Policy," *Survey*, vol. 26 (Spring 1982), pp. 102–30.

———. "International Systemic Constraints on Chinese Foreign Policy," in Samuel S. Kim, ed., *China and the World*. Boulder, Colo.: Westview Press, 1984.

Nie Rongzhen. "How China Develops Its Nuclear Weapons," *Beijing Review*, Apr. 29, 1985, pp. 15–18.

Nitze, Paul. "Deterring Our Deterrent," *Foreign Policy*, no. 25 (Winter 1976/1977), pp. 195–210.

———. "Is It Time to Junk Our Nuclear Weapons? The New World Disorder Makes Them Obsolete," *Washington Post*, Jan. 16, 1994, p. C1, from LEXIS.

"No Europe Nuclear Force This Century," *Reuters World Service*, Jan. 5, 1995, from LEXIS.

"No Substitute for Nuclear Weapons as Deterrence, Says Thatcher," *Xinhua General Overseas News Service*, Apr. 6, 1986, from LEXIS.

Norris Robert S., and William M. Arkin. "Natural Resources Defense Council Notebook: Chinese Nuclear Forces, 1999," *The Bulletin of the Atomic Scientists*, vol. 55, no. 4 (May/June 1999), p. 79.

———. "U.S. Strategic Nuclear Forces, End of 1994," *Bulletin of the Atomic Scientists*, vol. 51, no. 1 (Jan. 1995), pp. 69ff, from LEXIS.

Norris, Robert S., Andrew S. Burrows, and Richard W. Fieldhouse. *British, French, and Chinese Nuclear Weapons*. Series: Nuclear Weapons Databook, vol. 5. Boulder, Colo.: Westview Press, 1994.

"Nuclear Deterrence Still Priority for France: Chevenement," *Xinhua General Overseas News Service*, Dec. 7, 1988, from LEXIS.

"Nuclear Deterrence Vital, Says Former French Prime Minister," *Xinhua General Overseas News Service*, Dec. 29, 1987, from LEXIS.

"Nuclear Secrets," *The Economist*, June 3, 1989, from LEXIS.

"Nuclear Strategy: Top Physicist Outlines China's Strategy on Nuclear War and Proliferation," BBC Summary of World Broadcasts, The Far East, China, FE/1747/B2, July 22, 1993, from LEXIS.

Nundy, Julian. "Hades Missiles Go Into the Cold," *The Independent*, June 13, 1992, p. 11, from LEXIS.

"Nunn: Russia Eyes Nuclear Arms," *Associated Press*, May 5, 1995, from clari.tw.nuclear, CNC.

Nye, Joseph S. *Bound to Lead*. New York: Basic Books, 1990.

Nye, Joseph S., Jr., and William A. Owens. "America's Information Edge," *Foreign Affairs*, vol. 75, no. 3 (Mar./Apr. 1996), pp. 20–36.

O'Hanlon, Michael. "Can High Technology Bring U.S. Troops Home?" *Foreign Policy* (Winter 1998), no. 113, pp. 72–86.

———. *Defense Planning for the Late 1990s: Beyond the Desert Storm Framework*. Washington, D.C.: Brookings Institution, 1995.

Olson, Mancur. *The Logic of Collective Action*, rev. ed. Cambridge, Mass.: Harvard University Press, 1971.

Olson, Mancur, and Richard Zeckhauser. "An Economic Theory of Alliances," *Review of Economics and Statistics*, vol. 48, no. 3 (Aug. 1966), pp. 266–79.

Oneal, John R. "The Theory of Collective Action and Burden Sharing in NATO," *International Organization*, vol. 44, no. 3 (Summer 1990), pp. 379–402.

Oneal, John R., and Mark A. Elrod. "NATO Burden Sharing and the Forces of Change," *International Studies Quarterly*, vol. 33 (Dec. 1989), pp. 435–56.

Ostermann, Christian F. "New Evidence on the Sino-Soviet Border Dispute, 1969–71," CWIHP *Bulletin*, issues 6–7 (Winter 1995/1996), pp. 186–93.

Owens, John M. "How Liberalism Produces Democratic Peace," *International Security*, vol. 19, no. 2 (Fall 1994).

"Pakistan Setting Up Nuclear Command and Control System," *Agence France-Presse*, May 18, 1999, from clari.tw.nuclear, CNC.

"Pakistan Vows Tit-for-tat Nuclear Reply to India," *Reuters*, Mar. 12, 1996, from clari.tw.nuclear, CNC.

"Pakistanis Pin Blame for South Asian Nuclearisation on India," *Agence France-Presse*, May 21, 1999, from clari.tw.nuclear, CNC.

Pape, Robert A. *Bombing to Win: Air Power and Coercion In War*. Ithaca, NY: Cornell University Press, 1996.

"Paper Prepared in the Policy Planning Council: The Implications of a Chinese Communist Nuclear Capability," Apr. 30, 1964, Document no. 30, *FRUS, 1964–1968*, vol. 30: *China*. Washington, D.C.: U.S. Government Printing Office, 1998.

"Paper Presented in the Policy Planning Council: An Exploration of the Possible Bases for Action Against the Chinese Communist Nuclear Facilities," Apr. 14, 1964, Document no. 25, *FRUS, 1964–1968*, vol. 30: *China*. Washington, D.C.: U.S. Government Printing Office, 1998.

"Paris, US Deny U2 Plane Made Spy Mission," *United Press International*, May 3, 1996, from clari.tw.nuclear, CNC.

Peng Di. "Prospects for World Peace as Viewed from the Present International Strategic Posture," *Jiefangjun Bao*, Jan. 2, 1987, pp. 1, 4, *FBIS*, Feb. 4, 1987, pp. A5–A9.

Peng Guangqian, Wang Guangxu et al., eds. *Junshi Zhanlüe Jianlun*. Beijing: Jiefangjun Chubanshe, 1989.

"*People's Daily* Article: 'Get Rid of Blind Belief in Nuclear Weapons,'" *Xinhua General Overseas News Service*, May 14, 1977, from LEXIS.

"Peres: ME Should Be Nuclear-Free," *Associated Press*, Jan. 5, 1996, from clari.tw.nuclear, CNC.

Perkins, Dwight. "The International Consequences of China's Economic Development," in Richard Solomon, ed., *The China Factor*. Englewood Cliffs, N.J.: Prentice Hall, 1981.

"Perry Criticized on Taiwan," *Associated Press*, Feb. 28, 1996, from clari.world.asia.china, CNC.

Philps, Alan. "France Scales Back on Developing New Strategic Nuclear Missile," *The Reuter Library Report*, Sept. 22, 1988, from LEXIS.

———. "French Parliamentary Panel Backs Mobile Missile," *Reuters Ltd.*, Oct. 17, 1986, from LEXIS.

Pierre, Andrew J. *Nuclear Politics: The British Experience with an Independent Strategic Force*. New York: Oxford University Press, 1972.

"PLA Marching Towards Modernization: Zhang Aiping," *Xinhua General Overseas News Service*, June 23, 1987, from LEXIS.

"Political Developments in the USSR and the Communist World," NIE 1-5-62, Feb. 21, 1962, HRP, Feb. 18, 1994.

Porteus, Holly. "China's View of Strategic Weapons," *Jane's Intelligence Review*, vol. 8, no. 3. (Mar. 1996), pp. 134–37.

Posen, Barry R. *Inadvertent Escalation: Conventional War and Nuclear Risks*. Ithaca: Cornell University Press, 1991.

———. "Is NATO Decisively Outnumbered?" *International Security*, vol. 12, no. 4 (Spring 1988), pp. 186–202.

———. *The Sources of Military Doctrine*. Ithaca: Cornell University Press, 1984.

Posen, Barry R., and Steven Van Evera. "Defense Policy and the Reagan

Administration: Departure from Containment," *International Security*, vol. 8, no. 1 (Summer 1983), pp. 3–45.

"Possible Changes in the Sino-Soviet Relationship," NIE (11/13/6-73), CIA, Oct. 25, 1973, HRP, Jan. 31, 1994.

Postol, Theodore A. "Correspondence: The Author Replies" [re: Stein], vol. 17, no. 1 (Summer 1992), pp. 225–40.

———. "Lessons of the Gulf War Experience with Patriot," *International Security*, vol. 16, no. 2 (Winter 1991/1992), pp. 119–71.

Powell, Robert. "Crisis Bargaining, Escalation, and MAD," *American Political Science Review*, vol. 81, no. 3 (Sept. 1987), pp. 717–35.

———. "Guns, Butter, and Anarchy," *American Political Science Review*, vol. 87, no. 1 (Mar. 1993), pp. 115–32.

———. "Nuclear Brinkmanship with Two-Sided Incomplete Information," *American Political Science Review*, vol. 82, no. 1 (Mar. 1988), p. 155–78.

———. "Nuclear Deterrence and the Strategy of Limited Retaliation," *American Political Science Review*, vol. 83, no. 2 (June 1989), pp. 503–19.

———. *Nuclear Deterrence Theory*. New York: Cambridge University Press, 1990.

———. "The Theoretical Foundations of Strategic Nuclear Deterrence," *Political Science Quarterly*, vol. 100, no. 1 (Spring 1985), pp. 75–96.

Powell, Stewart M. "Britain's Defense Shakeup," *Air Force Magazine*, Apr. 1993, from LEXIS.

"Premier Hua Guofeng Discusses China's Development of Strategic Weaponry," *Xinhua General Overseas News Service*, May 30, 1980, from LEXIS.

"President's Visit to De Gaulle, Paris, May 31–June 2, 1961, Background Paper: Differences in Release of Information to U.K., France and Germany," May 26, 1961, *NNP*, 1961/05/26 (00775), Declassified June 11, 1973.

"Probable Chinese Communist and Soviet Intentions in the Taiwan Strait Area," Special NIE, SNIE (100-11-58), CIA Sept. 16, 1958, HRP, July 13, 1993.

"Probable Communist Reactions to Certain Possible UN/US Military Courses of Action with Respect to the Korean War," Special Estimate (SE-41), CIA, Apr. 8, 1953, HRP, June 24, 1993.

"Probable Effects on the Soviet Bloc of Certain Courses of Action Directed at the Internal and External Commerce of Communist China," Special Estimate (SE-37), CIA, Mar. 9, 1953, HRP, June 24, 1993.

"Probable Sino-Soviet Reactions to US Deployment of Nuclear Weapons Systems," SNIE (100-7-57), CIA, June 11, 1957, HRP, July 7, 1993.

"Professor Roger Fisher's Comments on Selected Portions of Course III," c. Fall 1964, Declassified Feb. 6, 1996, available at National Security Archives, Washington, D.C., Gilpatric Committee File.

"Program to Limit the Spread of Nuclear Weapons," Annex A, U.S. Arms Control and Disarmament Agency, Nov. 3, 1964, Declassified Sept. 5, 1996, available at National Security Archives, Gilpatric Committee File (Garthoff).

"Proposed French Budget Barely Keeps Pace with Inflation," *Defense Daily*, vol. 168, no. 56, Sept. 19, 1990, from LEXIS.

"Proposed US-UK Agreement for a Substitute Weapon Incident to Skybolt Cancellation," Dec. 17, 1962, *NNP*, 1962/12/17 (00930), Declassified Oct. 26, 1977.

Putnam, Robert D. "Diplomacy and Domestic Politics: The Logic of Two-level Games," *International Organization*, vol. 42, no. 3 (Summer 1988), pp. 427–60.

Qiang Zhai. "Beijing and the Vietnam Conflict, 1964–1965: New Chinese Evidence," CWIHP *Bulletin*, issues 6–7 (Winter 1995/1996).

Quester, George H. *Deterrence Before Hiroshima: The Airpower Background of Modern Strategy*. New York: Wiley, 1966.

———. "The Future of Nuclear Deterrence," *Survival*, vol. 34, no. 1 (Spring 1992), pp. 74–88.

———. "Nuclear Proliferation and Stability," in Dagobert L. Brito, Michael D. Intriligator, and Adele E. Wick, eds. *Strategies for Managing Nuclear Proliferation*. Lexington, Mass.: Lexington, 1983.

Quinlan, Michael. "British Nuclear Weapons Policy: Past, Present, and Future," in John C. Hopkins and Weixing Hu, eds., *Strategic Views from the Second Tier*. New Brunswick, N.J.: Transaction Publishers, 1995.

Raitberger, François. "Australia, France Patch Up Nuclear Dispute," *Reuters*, Sept. 16, 1996, from clari.tw.nuclear, CNC.

Rathjens, G. W. "Destruction of Chinese Nuclear Weapons Capabilities," U.S. ACDA, Dec. 14, 1964, Declassified Sept. 5, 1996, National Security Archives, Washington, D.C., Gilpatric Committee File.

"The Rational Deterrence Debate: A Symposium," *World Politics*, vol. 41, no. 2 (Jan. 1989).

Ray, James Lee. "The Abolition of Slavery and the End of International War," *International Organization*, vol. 43, no. 3 (Summer 1989), pp. 405–39.

"Record of Meeting Between President Kennedy and Prince Bernhard and Ambassador von Roijen, the Netherlands Embassy," *NNP*, 1961/04/25 (00765).

"Relations Between the Chinese Communist Regime and the USSR: Their Present Character and Probable Future Courses," NIE (58), CIA, Sept. 10, 1952, HRP, June 24, 1993.

Ren, Yue. "National Image-Conflicts and the Pursuit of Nuclear Independence: Nuclear Policies of China Under Mao Zedong and France Under Charles de Gaulle." Ph.D. diss., Columbia University, 1994.

"Report by Four Chinese Marshals—Chen Yi, Ye Jianying, Nie Rongzhen, and Xu Xiangqian—to the CCP Central Committee, 'Our Views About the Current Situation' (excerpt) 17 September 1969," Document no. 11, trans. by Chen Jian and Li Di, CWIHP *Bulletin*, issue 11 (Winter 1998).

"Report by Four Chinese Marshals—Chen Yi, Ye Jianying, Xu Xiangqian, and Nie Rongzhen,—to the Central Committee, 'A Preliminary Evaluation of the War Situation' (excerpt), 11 July 1969," Document no. 9, trans. by Chen Jian and Li Di, CWIHP *Bulletin*, issue 11 (Winter 1998).

"Report Raps China Military," *Associated Press*, Feb. 8, 1996, available from clari.world.asia.china, CNC.

Rhodes, Edward. *Power and MADness: The Logic of Nuclear Coercion*. New York: Columbia University Press, 1989.

Rhodes, Richard. *Dark Sun: The Making of the Hydrogen Bomb*. New York: Simon & Schuster, 1995.

Richardson, Michael. "China's Secretive Arms Buildup Is Making Asian Neighbors Jittery," *International Herald Tribune*, Apr. 1, 1993, from LEXIS.

Riding, Alan. "France Concedes Its Faults in War," *New York Times*, May 8, 1991, p. A17.

———. "France Drops Plans to Build New Nuclear Missile System," *New York Times*, July 23, 1991, from LEXIS.

"Rifkind Maintains Right to Use Nuclear Weapons First," *Xinhua General Overseas News Service*, Nov. 23, 1993, from LEXIS.

Ripsman, Norrin M. "The Impact of Decision-Making Autonomy Upon Democratic Peace-Making Policies." Ph.D. diss., University of Pennsylvania, 1997.

Rochlin, Gene I. "The Economic Burden of a Nuclear Force: No Data in Search of a Theory," in Dagobert L. Brito, Michael D. Intriligator, and Adele E. Wick, eds., *Strategies for Managing Nuclear Proliferation*. Lexington, Mass.: Lexington, 1983.

Rodin, Ivan. "Russian Legislators Back New Arms Cuts, Oppose START," *Reuters*, Jan. 23, 1997, from clari.tw.defense, CNC.

Rogov, Sergei. "Several Questions to the Treaty," *Moscow News*, Mar. 17, 1993, from LEXIS.

Ropelewski, Robert R. "French Emphasizing Nuclear Weapons," *Aviation Week and Space Technology*, Aug. 2, 1976, from LEXIS.

———. "French Push Updated Conventional Forces," *Aviation Week and Space Technology*, June 14, 1976, from LEXIS.

Rosecrance, Richard N. "Bipolarity, Multipolarity, and the Future," in James N. Rosenau, ed., *International Politics and Foreign Policy*, 2nd ed. New York: Free Press, 1969, pp. 325–35.

———. *Defense of the Realm: British Strategy in the Nuclear Epoch*. New York: Columbia University Press, 1968.

———. *The Rise of the Trading State: Commerce and Conquest in the Modern World*. New York: Basic Books, 1985.

Ross, Robert S. "From Lin Biao to Deng Xiaoping: Elite Instability and China's U.S. Policy," *China Quarterly*, no. 118 (June 1989), pp. 265–99.

———. "The Geography of the Peace: East Asia in the Twenty-first Century," vol. 23, no. 4 (Spring 1999), pp. 81–118.

———. *Negotiating Cooperation: The United States and China, 1969–1989*. Stanford: Stanford University Press, 1995.

Rostow, W. W. "Memorandum for the President, Subject: The Growing Shadow of a European Nuclear Force," Dec. 6, 1965, NNP, 1965/12/06 (01148), Declassified July 8, 1991.

Roy, Denny. "Hegemon on the Horizon? China's Threat to East Asian Security," International Security, vol. 19, no. 1 (Summer 1994), pp. 149–68.

Russett, Bruce. Grasping the Democratic Peace. Princeton: Princeton University Press, 1993.

——. What Price Vigilance? New Haven: Yale University Press, 1970.

"Russia Adopts 'Top Secret' Nuclear Document," Apr. 29, 1999, Agence France-Presse, from clari.tw.nuclear, CNC.

"Russia Must Drop 'No-first-strike'—Moscow Official," Reuters, Feb. 11, 1997, from clari.tw.nuclear, CNC.

"Russians Call for Nuclear Testing," Associated Press, Nov. 3, 1994, from clari.tw.nuclear, CNC.

Sagan, Scott D. The Limits of Safety: Organizations, Accidents, and Nuclear Weapons. Princeton: Princeton University Press, 1993.

——. "More Will Be Worse," in Scott D. Sagan and Kenneth N. Waltz, eds., The Spread of Nuclear Weapons: A Debate. New York: W. W. Norton, 1995, pp. 47–91.

——. "The Perils of Proliferation: Organization Theory, Deterrence Theory, and the Spread of Nuclear Weapons," International Security, vol. 18, no. 3 (Spring 1994), pp. 66–107.

——. "SIOP-62: The Nuclear War Plan Briefing to President Kennedy," International Security, vol. 12, no. 4 (Summer 1987), pp. 22–51.

——. "Why Do States Build Nuclear Weapons? Three Models in Search of a Bomb," International Security, vol. 21, no. 3 (Winter 1996/1997), pp. 54–86.

Sagan, Scott D., and Kenneth N. Waltz, eds., The Spread of Nuclear Weapons: A Debate. New York: W. W. Norton, 1995.

Salisbury, Harrison E. The New Emperors. Boston: Little, Brown, 1992.

Sandler, Todd. "Impurity of Defense: An Application to the Economics of Alliances," Kyklos, vol. 30 (1977), pp. 443–60.

Sandler, Todd, and Jon Cauley. "On the Economic Theory of Alliances," Journal of Conflict Resolution, vol. 19, no. 2 (June 1975), pp. 330–48.

Sandler, Todd, and John F. Forbes. "Burden Sharing, Strategy, and the Design of NATO," Economic Inquiry, vol. 18 (July 1980), pp. 425–44.

Sanger, David E. "Poll Finds Japanese Less Sure of Future," New York Times, Dec. 30, 1994, p. A8.

Scheinman, Lawrence. Atomic Energy Policy in France Under the Fourth Republic. Princeton: Princeton University Press, 1965.

Schelling, Thomas C. Arms and Influence. New Haven: Yale University Press, 1966.

——. The Strategy of Conflict. London: Oxford University Press, 1960.

——. "Thinking About Nuclear Terrorism," International Security, vol. 6, no. 4 (Spring 1982), pp. 61–77.

Schelling, Thomas C., and Morton H. Halperin, with the assistance of Donald G. Brennan. *Strategy and Arms Control*. New York: Twentieth Century Fund, 1961.

Schurmann, Franz. *Ideology and Organization in Communist China*, 2nd ed., enlarged. Berkeley: University of California Press, 1968.

Schwartz, Benjamin I. *Chinese Communism and the Rise of Mao*. Cambridge, Mass.: Harvard University Press, 1979.

Schweller, Randall L. "Bandwagoning for Profit: Bringing the Revisionist State Back In," *International Security*, vol. 19, no. 1 (Summer 1994), pp. 72–107.

Scott, William B. "Admission of 1979 Nuclear Test Finally Validates Vela Data," *Aviation Week and Space Technology*, vol. 147, no. 3, p. 33, July 21, 1997, from LEXIS.

"Secret Papers from '60s Reveal British Nuclear Strategy," *United Press International*, Jan. 1, 1994, from LEXIS.

"Security Guarantees and Non-Proliferation of Nuclear Weapons," Dec. 28, 1964, U.S. Arms Control and Disarmament Agency, Declassified Sept. 5, 1996, available at National Security Archives, Washington, D.C., Gilpatric Committee File.

Segal, Gerald. "China Takes on Pacific Asia," *Jane's Defence '96 The World in Conflict*, pp. 62–70.

———. "China's Strategic Posture and the Great-Power Triangle," *Pacific Affairs*, vol. 53, no. 4 (Winter 1980/1981), pp. 682–97.

———. "East Asia and the 'Constrainment' of China," *International Security*, vol. 20, no. 4 (Spring 1996), pp. 107–35.

Seng, Jordan. "Less Is More: Command and Control Advantages of Minor Nuclear States," *Security Studies*, vol. 6, no. 4 (Summer 1997), pp. 50–92.

———. "Optimism in the Balance: A Response to Peter Feaver," *Security Studies*, vol. 6, no. 4 (Summer 1997), pp. 126–36.

Sharpe, Gene. *Making Europe Unconquerable*. Cambridge, Mass.: Ballinger, 1985.

Shaw, David. "Trident Cut 'Won't Harm Our Defences,'" *Evening Standard*, Nov. 16, 1993, from LEXIS.

Shen Dingli. "The Current Status of Chinese Nuclear Forces and Nuclear Policies," Princeton University, Center for Energy and Environmental Studies, Report no. 247, Feb. 1990.

Shen Zhihua. "The Discrepancy Between the Russian and Chinese Versions of Mao's 2 October 1950 Message to Stalin on Chinese Entry in the Korean War: A Chinese Scholar's Reply," trans. by Chen Jian, CWIHP *Bulletin*, issues 8–9 (Winter 1996/1997).

Sherman, Jill, and Michael Evans. "Major Faces Battle over Defence Cuts," *The Times*, Oct. 16, 1993, from LEXIS.

Shifrin, Carole A. "U.K.'s New Defense Strategy Stresses Role in Preserving International Stability," *Aviation Week and Space Technology*, July 13, 1992, from LEXIS.

Shimshoni, Jonathan. *Israel and Conventional Deterrence: Border Warfare from 1953 to 1970*. Ithaca: Cornell University Press, 1988.

"The Short Version of the Negotiation Between CPSU and CCP Delegations (September 1960)," CWIHP *Bulletin*, issue 10 (Mar. 1998).

Simpson, John. *The Independent Nuclear State*. New York: St. Martin's, 1983.

Singer, J. David, and Melvin Small. "National Material Capabilities Data, 1816–1985" [computer file]. Ann Arbor, Mich.: J. David Singer, University of Michigan; and Detroit, Mich.: Melvin Small, Wayne State University [producers], 1990. Ann Arbor, Mich.: Inter-university Consortium for Political and Social Research [distributor], 1993.

"Sino-Soviet and Free World Reactions to US Use of Nuclear Weapons in Limited Wars in the Far East," SNIE (100-7-58), CIA, July 22, 1958, HRP, July 12, 1993.

"Sino-Soviet Relations," NIE 110-3-60, Aug. 9, 1960, HRP, Feb. 24, 1994.

"Sino-Soviet Relations in the Early 1980s," National Intelligence Estimate," NIE (11/13-80), CIA, June 5, 1980, HRP, Jan. 7, 1994.

SIPRI Yearbook, World Armaments and Disarmament. New York: Oxford University Press, 1986.

Slevin, Peter. "China Could Not Easily Overwhelm Taiwan, Analysts Agree," *The Philadelphia Inquirer*, Feb. 16, 1996, p. A4.

Smith, Michael. "Atom Bomb Pilots Faced One-way Trip," *The Daily Telegraph*, Feb. 1, 1993, from LEXIS.

Smith, R. Jeffrey. "An Ex-Warrior's About-Face on U.S. Nuclear Policy," *International Herald Tribune*, Dec. 5, 1996, from LEXIS.

Snyder, Glenn H. *Deterrence and Defense*. Princeton: Princeton University Press, 1961.

———. "Deterrence and Defense," in Robert J. Art and Kenneth N. Waltz, eds., *The Use of Force*, 3rd ed. Lanham, Md.: University Press of America, 1988.

———. "The Security Dilemma in Alliance Politics," *World Politics*, vol. 36, no. 4 (July 1984), pp. 461–95.

Soutou, Georges-Henri. "The French Military Program for Nuclear Energy, 1945–1981," Nuclear History Program (University of Maryland: Center for International Security Studies, 1989), Occasional Paper no. 3.

"Soviet Goals and Expectations in the Global Power Arena," NIE 11-4-78, HRP, Oct. 6, 1993.

"Soviet Policy in Asia," NIE (11-9-71), CIA, Apr. 15, 1971, HRP, Jan. 31, 1994.

"Special National Intelligence Estimate: Communist China in 1971," Sept. 28, 1961, Document no. 62, *FRUS, 1961–1963*, vol. 22: *China, Korea, and Japan*. Washington, D.C.: U.S. Government Printing Office, 1996.

Spiro, David E. "The Insignificance of the Liberal Peace," *International Security*, vol. 19, no. 2 (Fall 1994), pp. 50–86.

"Spokesman on China's Nuclear Testing," *Xinhua General Overseas News Service*, Oct. 7, 1993, from LEXIS.

Starr, John Bryan. "From the 10th Party Congress to the Premiership of Hua Kuo-feng: The Significance of the Color of the Cat," *China Quarterly*, no. 67 (Sept. 1976), pp. 457–88.

Stein, Janice Gross. "Deterrence and Compellence in the Gulf, 1990–91: A Failed or Impossible Task?" *International Security*, vol. 17, no. 2 (Fall 1992), pp. 147–79.

Stein, Robert M. "Patriot Experience in the Gulf War" [re: Postol], *International Security*, vol. 17, no. 1 (Summer 1992), pp. 199–225.

"Stenogram: Meeting of the Delegations of the Communist Party of the Soviet Union and the Chinese Communist Party, Moscow, 5–20 July 1963," CWIHP *Bulletin*, issue 11 (Winter 1998).

Stott, Michael. "Mitterrand Says French Nuclear Weapons Only for Massive Strike," *The Reuter Library Report*, Oct. 22, 1987, from LEXIS.

Sun Mingming and Cai Xiaohong. *Dongdangzhong de Guojia Anquan*. Beijing: Jiefangjun Chubanshe, 1988.

"Swiss Kept Atomic Bomb Option, Magazine Says," *Reuters*, May 23, 1996, from clari.tw.nuclear, CNC.

"A Symbol of Trust," *Defense News*, June 6, 1994, p. 26, from LEXIS.

"Telegram from the Consulate General at Hong Kong to the Department of State," Feb. 19, 1966, Document no. 125, *FRUS, 1964–1968*, vol. 30: *China*. Washington, D.C.: U.S. Government Printing Office, 1998.

"Telegram from the Embassy in the Soviet Union to the Department of State, Moscow July 18, 1963, 5 PM," Document no. 331, *FRUS, 1961–1963*, vol. 7: *Arms Control and Disarmament*. Washington, D.C.: U.S. Government Printing Office, 1995.

Thies, Wallace J. "Alliances and Collective Goods," *Journal of Conflict Resolution*, vol. 31, no. 2 (June 1987), pp. 298–322.

———. *When Governments Collide: Coercion and Diplomacy in the Vietnam Conflict, 1964–1968*. Berkeley: University of California Press, 1980.

Thompson, James D., and Arthur Tuden. "Strategies, Structures, and Processes of Organizational Decision," in James D. Thompson et al., eds., *Comparative Studies in Administration*. Pittsburgh: University of Pittsburgh Press, 1959.

Trachtenberg, Marc. "The Influence of Nuclear Weapons in the Cuban Missile Crisis," *International Security*, vol. 10, no. 1 (Summer 1985), pp. 136–63.

———. "'A Wasting Asset': American Strategy and the Shifting Nuclear Balance, 1949–1954," *International Security*, vol. 13, no. 3 (Winter 1988/1989), pp. 5–49.

Travis, Alan. "UK: Defence Spending Could Be Halved Under Liberal Democrats," *Guardian*, Aug. 31, 1990, *Reuter Textline*, from LEXIS.

"Trident Nuclear Power Being Scaled Down—Rifkind," *Agence France-Presse*, Nov. 16, 1993, from LEXIS.

"Trident's Future," *The Times*, Aug. 20, 1993, from LEXIS.

Twining, N. F. "Memorandum for the Secretary of Defense, Subject: French

Proposal for a Tripartite World-Wide Organization," Oct. 30, 1958, *NNP*, 1958/10/30 (00488), Declassified Aug. 9, 1979.

Tyler, Patrick E. "As China Threatens Taiwan, It Makes Sure U.S. Listens," *New York Times*, Jan. 24, 1996, p. A3.

———. "China Warns Against 'Star Wars' Shield for U.S. Forces in Asia," *New York Times*, Feb. 18, 1995, p. A4.

———. "Shadow Over Asia: A Special Report; China's Military Stumbles Even as Its Power Grows," *New York Times*, Dec. 3, 1996, p. A1.

Uhlig, Robert. "Swiss Kept Nuclear Arms Secret for 43 Years," *The Daily Telegraph*, May 23, 1996, p. 10, from LEXIS.

"U.K. Labor Party Votes to Keep Nuclear Deterrent," *Armed Forces Newswire Service*, Oct. 6, 1995, from LEXIS.

"Ukrainian Deputies Criticize Security Assurances," *Reuters*, Dec. 6, 1994, from clari.tw.nuclear, CNC.

Ullman, Richard H. "The Covert French Connection," *Foreign Policy*, no. 75 (Summer 1989), pp. 3–33.

"U.N. Council Gives Assurances to Non-nuclear States," *Reuters*, Apr. 11, 1995, from clari.tw.nuclear, CNC.

The United States, China, and the Bomb, National Security Archive Electronic Briefing Book, no. 1, http: //www.seas.gwu.edu/nsarchive/NSAEBB/NSAEBB1/nsaebb1.htm.

"The United States House of Representatives Select Committee on U.S. National Security and Military/Commercial Concerns with the People's Republic of China," from http://www.house.gov/coxreport/cont/gncont.html.

"U.S. and China Make Deal on Side at Nuclear Talks," *Reuters*, Aug. 9, 1996, from clari.tw.nuclear, CNC.

U.S. Arms Control and Disarmament Agency, *World Military Expenditures and Arms Transfers*. Washington, D.C.: U.S. Government Printing Office, 1987.

"U.S. Kept Veto on Polaris: 1964," *The Guardian*, Jan. 2, 1995, from LEXIS.

"USA and Russia Agree to 'Detarget' Missiles," *Jane's Defence Weekly*, vol. 21, no. 3, Jan. 22, 1994, p. 5, from LEXIS.

Van Evera, Steven. "Why Europe Matters, Why the Third World Doesn't: American Grand Strategy After the Cold War," *Journal of Strategic Studies*, vol. 13, no. 2 (June 1990), pp. 1–51.

Verma, Sonali. "China Nuclear Test Could Harden India Treaty Stand," *Reuters*, July 30, 1996, from clari.tw.nuclear, CNC.

Walt, Stephen M. "Building Up New Bogeymen," *Foreign Policy*, no. 106 (Spring 1997), pp. 176–89.

———. "The Case for Finite Containment," *International Security*, vol. 14, no. 1 (Summer 1989), pp. 5–49.

———. *The Origins of Alliances*. Ithaca: Cornell University Press, 1988.

Waltz, Kenneth N. "The Emerging Structure of International Politics," *International Security*, vol. 18, no. 2 (Fall 1993), pp. 44–79.

———. "International Structure, National Force, and the Balance of World Power," in James N. Rosenau, ed., *International Politics and Foreign Policy*, 2nd ed. New York: Free Press, 1969, pp. 304–14.

———. "More May Be Better," in Scott D. Sagan and Kenneth N. Waltz, eds., *The Spread of Nuclear Weapons: A Debate*. New York: W. W. Norton, 1995, pp. 1–46.

———. "Nuclear Myths and Political Realities," *American Political Science Review*, vol. 84, no. 3 (Sept. 1990), pp. 731–44.

———. "The Spread of Nuclear Weapons: More May Be Better," *Adelphi Paper*, no. 171 (London: International Institute of Strategic Studies, Autumn 1981).

———. "A Strategy for the Rapid Deployment Force," in Robert Art and Kenneth N. Waltz, eds., *The Use of Force*. Lanham, Md.: University Press of America, 1988.

———. *Theory of International Politics*. Menlo Park, Calif.: Addison-Wesley, 1979.

———. "Toward Nuclear Peace," in Robert Art and Kenneth N. Waltz, eds., *The Use of Force*. Lanham, Md.: University Press of America, 1988.

Wang, Robert S. "China's Evolving Strategic Doctrine," *Asian Survey*, vol. 24, no. 10 (Oct. 1984), pp. 1040–55.

Wang, Shaoguang. "Estimating China's Defence Expenditure: Some Evidence from Chinese Sources," *China Quarterly*, no. 147 (Sept. 1996), pp. 889–911.

Webb, Ben. "No Clear Deterrent; United Kingdom's Nuclear Weapons," *New Statesman and Society*, vol. 6, no. 264, Aug. 6, 1993, from LEXIS.

Webster, Paul. "France Nods to Germany and Scraps Hades Missile," *Guardian*, June 13, 1992, from LEXIS.

"Weekly Intelligence Summary," Defense Intelligence Agency, July 16, 1982, *NNP*, 1982/07/16 (01969).

Wei Shiyan. "Eluomihe Guanyu Taiwan Jushi tong Mao Zedong Zhuxi Tanhua de Huiyi yu Shishi Bufu," in *Xin Zhongguo Waijiao Fengyun*. Beijing: Shijie Zhishi Chubanshe, 1990.

Wheeler, Nicholas. "The Atlee Government's Nuclear Strategy, 1945–51," in Ann Deighton, ed., *Britain and the First Cold War*. New York: St. Martin's, 1990, pp. 130–45.

White, David. "Paris Gives Priority to Nuclear Arms Spending," *Financial Times*, Oct. 8, 1982, from LEXIS.

White, Michael, and David Fairhall. "Rifkind Set to Cut Trident Firepower," *Guardian*, Nov. 16, 1993, from LEXIS.

Whiting, Allen S. *China Crosses the Yalu, the Decision to Enter the Korean War*. Stanford: Stanford University Press, 1968.

———. *The Chinese Calculus of Deterrence: India and Indochina*. Ann Arbor: University of Michigan Press, 1975.

Whitney, Craig R. "After NATO Overtures, France Is Ready to Resume Military Role," *New York Times*, June 9, 1996, p. 8.

———. "Delay Seen in Restoring NATO Role for France," *New York Times,* Feb. 23, 1997, p. 4.

———. "France and Germany to Discuss Joint Nuclear Deterrent," *New York Times,* Jan. 25, 1997, p. 3.

———. "France Ending Nuclear Tests that Caused Broad Protests," *New York Times,* Jan. 30, 1996, pp. A1, A4.

"Why France Spends More on Its Nuclear Arsenal," *Financial Times,* Mar. 12, 1982, from LEXIS.

Wich, Richard. *Sino-Soviet Crisis Politics.* Cambridge, Mass.: Harvard University Press, 1980.

Wilkie, Tom. "First H-bomb Built Amid Safety Fears," *The Independent,* June 25, 1993, from LEXIS.

Williams, Brian. "Japan Sees China as Growing Military Challenge," *Reuters,* July 19, 1996, from clari.world.asia.china, CNC.

Wittner, Lawrence S. *The Struggle Against the Bomb,* vol. 1: *One World or None: A History of the World Nuclear Disarmament Movement Through 1953.* Stanford: Stanford University Press, 1993.

———. *The Struggle Against the Bomb,* vol. 2: *Resisting the Bomb: A History of the World Nuclear Disarmament Movement, 1954–1970.* Stanford: Stanford University Press, 1997.

Wohlforth, William Curti. *The Elusive Balance.* Ithaca: Cornell University Press, 1993.

———. "The Perception of Power: Russia in the Pre-19194 Balance," *World Politics,* vol. 39, no. 3 (Apr. 1987), pp. 353–81.

———. "The Stability of a Unipolar World," *International Security,* vol. 24, no. 1 (Summer 1999), pp. 5–41.

Wood, David. "Navy Subs Give Washington Control over Nuclear Missiles," *Star Tribune,* Jan. 8, 1995, p. 6A, from LEXIS.

World Military Expenditures and Arms Transfers, 1987. U.S. Arms Control and Disarmament Agency. U. S. Government Printing Office: Washington, D.C., 1988.

Wortzell, Larry M., ed. *China's Military Modernization.* New York: Greenwood, 1988.

Wren, Christopher S. "Making It Easier to Uncover Nuclear Arms," *New York Times,* June 16, 1995, p. A6.

WuDunn, Sheryl. "After the War: War Astonishes Chinese and Stuns Their Military," *New York Times,* Mar. 20, 1991, from LEXIS.

Xie Wenqing. "US-Soviet Military Contention in the Asia-Pacific Region," *Shijie Zhishi* (Mar. 16, 1987), in *FBIS,* Mar. 31, 1987, p. A2.

Xing Shuguang, Li Yunhua, and Liu Yingna. "Soviet-US Balance of Power and Its Impact on the World Situation in the 1980s," *Guoji Wenti Yanjiu* (Jan. 1983), in *FBIS,* Apr. 21, 1983, pp. A3–A5.

Ya Qi and Zhou Jirong. "Does the Soviet Union Have a Global Strategy," *Renmin Ribao* (May 20, 1981), in *FBIS,* China Daily Report, May 21, 1981, p. C4.

Yang Xuhua and Cai Renzhao. *Weishe Lun*. Beijing: Guofang Daxue Chubanshe, 1990.

Yang, Dali L. *Calamity and Reform in China: State, Rural Society, and Institutional Change Since the Great Leap Famine*. Stanford: Stanford
University Press, 1996.

Yarynich, Valery. "The Doomsday Machine's Safety Catch," *New York
Times*, Feb. 1, 1994, p. A17, tr. Melanie Allen.

Yost, David S. *France and Conventional Defense in Central Europe*. Boulder, Colo.: Westview Press, 1985.

————. "France's Deterrent Posture and Security in Europe. Part I: Capabilities and Doctrine," *Adelphi Paper* 194. London: International Institute for Strategic Studies, 1984/1985.

————. "France's Deterrent Posture and Security in Europe, Part II: Capabilities and Doctrine," *Adelphi Paper* 95. London: International Institute
for Strategic Studies, 1984/1985.

————. "French Defense Budgeting: Executive Dominance and Resource
Constraints," *Orbis*, vol. 23 (Fall 1979), pp. 579–608.

————. "French Nuclear Targeting," in Desmond Ball and Jeffrey Richelson, eds., *Strategic Nuclear Targeting*. Ithaca: Cornell University Press,
1986.

————. "Nuclear Weapons Issues in France," in John C. Hopkins and Weixing Hu, eds., *Strategic Views from the Second Tier*. New Brunswick,
N.J.: Transaction Publishers, 1995.

————. "Radical Change in French Defense Policy," *Survival*, vol. 28, no. 1
(Jan.–Feb. 1986), pp. 53–68.

Ypserle de Strihou, Jacques. "Comment," in Roland N. McKean, ed., *Issues
in Defence Economics*. New York: Columbia University Press, 1967, pp.
58–63.

————. "Sharing the Defense Burden Among Western Allies," *Review of
Economics and Statistics*, vol. 49, no. 4 (Nov. 1967), pp. 527–36.

Zagare, Frank. "Rationality and Deterrence," *World Politics*, vol. 42, no. 2
(Jan. 1990), pp. 238–60.

Zagoria, Donald. *The Sino-Soviet Conflict, 1956–1961*. Princeton: Princeton University Press, 1962.

"Zhang Aiping on National Defense Modernization," *Xinhua General
Overseas News Service*, Mar. 3, 1983, from LEXIS.

Zhang Jianzhi. "Views on Medium-Sized Nuclear Powers' Nuclear Strategy," *Jiefangjun Bao*, Mar. 20, 1987, p. 3, *FBIS*, Apr. 1, 1987, pp. K29–K33.

Zhang, Shu Guang. *Mao's Military Romanticism: China and the Korean
War, 1950–1953*. Lawrence: University Press of Kansas, 1995.

Zhang, Shuguang. *Deterrence and Strategic Culture: Chinese-American
Confrontations, 1949–1958*. Ithaca: Cornell University Press, 1992.

Zhao, Suisheng. "Deng Xiaoping's Southern Tour: Elite Politics in Post-
Tiananmen China," *Asian Survey*, vol. 33, no. 8 (Aug. 1993), pp. 739–56.

Zhongguo Renmin Jiefangjun, shang. Beijing: Dangdai Zhongguo Chubanshe, 1994.

Zhou Enlai. *Zhou Enlai Nianpu*, vols. 2, 3. Beijing: Zhongyang Wenxian Chubanshe, 1997.

Zubok, Vladislav. "Atomic Espionage and Its Soviet 'Witnesses,'" CWIHP *Bulletin*, issue 4 (Fall 1994).

———. "Khrushchev's 1960 Troop Cut: New Russian Evidence," CWIHP *Bulletin*, issues 8–9 (Winter 1996/1997).

———. "Khrushchev's Nuclear Promise to Beijing During the 1958 Crisis," CWIHP *Bulletin*, issues 6–7 (Winter 1995/1996).

Index

In this index an "f" after a number indicates a separate reference on the next page, and an "ff" indicates separate references on the next two pages. A continuous discussion over two or more pages is indicated by a span of page numbers, e.g., "57–59." *Passim* is used for a cluster of references in close but not consecutive sequence.